# The ACT Advantage

XAMonline, Inc., Melrose, MA 02176
© 2017 by Sharon A. Wynne.
Contributing authors:
Steve Reiss, The Math Magician
Sreela Datta
June Saunders
Rick Colella

Illustrations created by Paige Larkin.
Cover Photos © Stephen Coburn I Dreamstime.com; © Can Stock Photo Inc. / monkeybusiness; © Can Stock Photo Inc. / devon

Published 2017
Printed in the United States
1 2 3 4 5 6 7 13 12 11 10 09 08

To obtain permission(s) to use the material from this work for any purpose, including workshops or seminars, please submit a written request to:

XAMonline, Inc.
21 Orient Avenue
Melrose, MA 02176
Toll Free 1-800-301-4647
Fax: 1-617-583-5552
Email: info@xamonline.com
Web: www.xamonline.com


Text and Illustrations:  Sharon A. Wynne


*Library of Congress Catalog Card Number:* (pending)


Wynne, Sharon S..
     The ACT advantage:  beat your best score!

     360 pp., ill.
     1.  Title 2. Achievement Tests - Study Guides 3. ACT assessment - Study Guides.


     LB2353.48 W966 2012     378.1 1662  W99 2012
     ISBN:  978-1-60787-498-0

# Table of Contents

## About the ACT Exam

The ACT (American College Testing) exam, created and administered by ACT, Inc., is a standardized test for college admissions that is accepted by all 4-year colleges and universities in the United States. The exam is meant to assess high school students' general educational achievement and to measure their potential to succeed in the entry-level college courses generally taken by first-year college students.

The ACT exam is offered in two formats: the standard ACT Assessment and the optional ACT Assessment Plus Writing. The ACT Assessment covers English, Mathematics, Reading, and Science Reasoning. The ACT Assessment Plus Writing includes the four core subject areas as well as an essay writing section.

Each of the main subject areas is worth 36 points. The final score is a composite score that reflects the average of the four subject area scores. This average is then scaled to yield a final score. The scaling is done to account for the fact that different test takers are taking different versions of the exam with different questions.

For English, Reading, and Mathematics, the test taker will also receive a scaled score for the subcategories (out of 18), but these subcategory scores and the overall score for the category have no mathematical relation.

The optional Writing section is worth 12 points and is scored separately. If an individual takes the ACT Assessment Plus Writing, they will receive a composite score (out of 36) for the four subject areas in addition to a separate English/Writing score (out of 36) and a sub-score for the Writing section (out of 12).

The ACT exam is offered 4-6 times a year, depending on the state in which it is taken (September, October, December, February, April, and June) and is always given on a Saturday, unless a student requires an exemption due to religious affiliation.

Many colleges use ACT exam scores as only one of several factors in determining admissions eligibility. It is highly recommended that students contact colleges and universities directly to learn their own ACT admissions requirements.

# ACT Assessment Exam

|  | ENGLISH | MATHEMATICS | READING | SCIENCE REASONING |
|---|---|---|---|---|
| **Points** | 36 points | 36 points | 36 points | 36 points |
| **Time** | 45 minutes | 60 minutes | 35 minutes | 35 minutes |
| **Questions** | 75 questions | 60 questions | 40 questions | 40 questions |
| **Format** | Multiple choice, 4 answer choices | Multiple choice, 5 answer choices | Multiple choice, 4 answer choices | Multiple choice, 4 answer choices |
| **Passages** | 5 passages | None | 4 passages (1 prose fiction, 1 humanities, 1 social studies, 1 natural sciences) | 7 passages (3 data representation, 3 research summary, 1 conflicting viewpoints) |
| **Question Type 1** | Sentence structure, grammar, usage, punctuation (40) | Pre-algebra (14) and elementary algebra (10) | Extract detail, draw conclusions, and determine main points | Analyze charts and graphs |
| **Question Type 2** | Style, strategy, revision, organization (35) | Intermediate algebra (9) and coordinate geometry (9) | Determine tone and/or point of view | Compare data from multiple experiments |
| **Question Type 3** |  | Plane geometry (14) and trigonometry (4) | Define vocabulary in context | Scrutinize conflicting viewpoints |

NOTE:
In the English, Reading, and Science Reasoning sections, odd numbered questions have answer choices A, B, C, and D and even numbered questions have answer choices F, G, H, and J. In the Mathematics sections, odd numbered questions have answer choices A, B, C, D, and E and even numbered questions have answer choices F, G, H, J, and K.

# ACT ASSESSMENT

# PRACTICE TEST ONE

# ENGLISH PRACTICE TEST 1

45 Minutes - 75 Questions

Directions: Read the provided passage. You will notice that words or phrases are underlined and numbered. Pay particular attention to these underlined words and phrases. Most questions on the test will offer you four alternatives to the underlined words or phrases, including the option of No change. Select the answer that best expresses the idea, style, or intention of the passage; is free of grammatical and punctuation errors, reflects standard usage in English, and works best within the context of the passage. Some questions may refer to parts of the passage or the whole passage rather than the underlined parts.

**The following passage is the basis for Questions 1-2:**

## Mark Twain and the Mississippi

**(1)** For humorous and profound insights into human nature, one could do <u>worser</u> than to pick up a book
1

by Mark Twain. The adventures of Twain's characters offer both humor and pathos and <u>provide for avid</u>
2

<u>reading</u>.

1. **Which of the following changes, if any, should be applied to underlined section 1?**

   A. No change
   B. better
   C. much worse
   D. worse

2. **In underlined section 2, it is the essay author's intention to:**

   F. dissuade people from reading Mark Twain's books
   G. note that Mark Twain's books are engaging
   H. encourage people to put Mark Twain's books on the bestseller list
   J. discount Mark Twain as a serious American author

**The following passage is the basis for Questions 3-6:**

**(2)** Mark Twain was the *nom de plume* of Samuel Clemens. The term "Mark Twain" was a depth of water
3

measured during the great Mississippi steamboat era. The <u>apparitions</u> of the great white ships with their
4

large paddle wheels, layers of decks, bells and whistles, were always <u>an occasion</u> for celebration and
5

wonder in the small town of Hannibal, Missouri, where Samuel Clemens grew up. Clearly<u>, the</u>
6

<u>steamboat's allure had a marked effect on him</u>.

3. **Which of the following changes, if any, should be applied to underlined section 3?**

   A. No change
   B. aliases
   C. nomenclature
   D. pencil name

4. **Which of the following changes, if any, should be applied to underlined section 4?**

   F. No change
   G. apartheids
   H. appearances
   J. apertures

5. **Which of the following changes, if any, should be applied to underlined section 5?**

   A. No change
   B. occasions
   C. occasional
   D. occasionally

6. **What is the purpose of underlined section 6?**

   F. To tie the together the topic sentence and the idea of the Mississippi River's influence on Twain
   G. To belabor a point already made about Clemens
   H. To introduce a new idea in the midst of argumentation in order to gain leverage for rebuttal later; it is a strategy that is followed in arguments in parliamentary debates
   J. To serve as a transition point between paragraphs, reflecting the transition of Mark Twain from steamboat captain to author

---

**The following passage is the basis for Questions 7-10:**

(3) The Mississippi River is an identifying feature of <u>Hannibal, and it figures</u> largely in Twain's books. In
                                                              7
*The Adventures of Tom Sawyer*, adventurous boys play in ancient caves near the river; they hide out in

small "islands" in the river when they decide to go "pirating" for a few <u>days, swimming</u> and fishing in the
                                                                              8
river are major activities. <u>When hooky-playing boys are thought to be dead</u>, they shoot cannonballs over
                                                    9
the river <u>to hopefully raise</u> the bodies to the surface—common practice in a river town where drowning
              10
was probably one of the leading causes of death among children as it is nationwide today.

---

7. **Which of the following changes, if any, should be applied to underlined section 7?**

   A. No change
   B. Hannibal: it figures
   C. Hannibal. it Figures
   D. Hannibal. Its figures

8. **Which of the following changes, if any, should be applied to underlined section 8?**

   F.  No change
   G.  days; swimming
   H.  days. Swim
   J.  days: swimming

9. **Which of the following changes, if any, should be applied to underlined section 9?**

   A.  No change
   B.  When hooky-playing boys are thinking to be dead,
   C.  When hooky-playing boys are dead to be thought of,
   D.  When the townspeople fear hooky-playing boys are dead,

10. **Which of the following changes, if any, should be applied to underlined section 10?**

    F.  No change
    G.  in hopes of raising
    H.  hope fitfully raising
    J.  profitably raising

---

**The following passage is the basis for Questions 11-14:**

(4) Yet the Mississippi River is more than a physical reality in Twain's books. It is <u>a symbol of deliverance</u>
11
and transcendence. In *The Adventures of Tom Sawyer*, the first thing Tom sees <u>when he escapes, from</u>
12
<u>being trapped, in a cave</u> is the broad Mississippi rolling by. In *The Adventures of Huckleberry Finn*, the

river is a route to human freedom. <u>Rivers are like highways, transporting goods.</u> Huck is escaping from an
13
abusive father, and Jim is escaping from slavery. For this unlikely pair, the river is almost like a theater

with their raft serving as a stage. <u>Upon the raft</u>, they enact profound human dramas regarding
14
conscience, equality, justice, and friendship.

---

11. **Which of the following changes, if any, should be applied to underlined section 11?**

    A.  No change
    B.  cymbal of deliverance
    C.  cymbal of delivery
    D.  symbol of deliverancy

12. **Which of the following changes, if any, should be applied to underlined section 12?**

    F.  No change
    G.  when he, escapes from being, trapped in a cave
    H.  when he escapes from being trapped in a cave
    J.  when he escapes from, being trapped, in a cave

**13. Which of the following changes, if any, should be applied to underlined section 13?**

    A. No change
    B. rivers are like highways transporting goods.
    C. underlined section 13 should be removed
    D. rivers are the byways transporting goods.

**14. In an essay for a modern journal, which of the following changes, if any, should be applied to underlined section 14?**

    F. No change
    G. Before the raft
    H. On the raft
    J. Behind the raft

---

**The following passage is the basis for Question 15:**

## Mark Twain and the Mississippi

**(1)** For humorous and profound insights into human nature, one could do worser than to pick up a book by Mark Twain. The adventures of Twain's characters offer both humor and pathos and provide for avid reading.

**(2)** Mark Twain was the *nom de plume* of Samuel Clemens. The term "Mark Twain" was a depth of water measured during the great Mississippi steamboat era. The apparitions of the great white ships with their large paddle wheels, layers of decks, bells and whistles, were always an occasion for celebration and wonder in the small town of Hannibal, Missouri, where Samuel Clemens grew up. Clearly, the steamboat's allure had a marked effect on him.

**(3)** The Mississippi River is an identifying feature of Hannibal, and it figures largely in Twain's books. In *The Adventures of Tom Sawyer*, adventurous boys play in ancient caves near the river; they hide out in small "islands" in the river when they decide to go "pirating" for a few days, swimming and fishing in the river are major activities. When hooky-playing boys are thought to be dead, they shoot cannonballs over the river to hopefully raise the bodies to the surface—common practice in a river town where drowning was probably one of the leading causes of death among children as it is nationwide today.

**(4)** Yet the Mississippi River is more than a physical reality in Twain's books. It is a symbol of deliverance and transcendence. In *The Adventures of Tom Sawyer*, the first thing Tom sees when he escapes, from being trapped, in a cave is the broad Mississippi rolling by. In *The Adventures of Huckleberry Finn*, the river is a route to human freedom. Rivers are like highways, transporting goods. Huck is escaping from an abusive father, and Jim is escaping from slavery. For this unlikely pair, the river is almost like a theater with their raft serving as a stage. Upon the raft, they enact profound human dramas regarding conscience, equality, justice, and friendship.

---

**15. Which of the following statements most effectively summarizes the essay?**

    A. Mark Twain was from Hannibal, Missouri on the Mississippi River.
    B. The Mississippi River was dangerous physically and morally to children growing up in Hannibal, Missouri.
    C. Because it was a dominating feature of his home town, the Mississippi River figured prominently in Twain's imagination and writings.
    D. Mark Twain drew his name and his characters from people he had known on the Mississippi River of his boyhood.

The following passage is the basis for Questions 16-21:

## Decision Point

(1) Loretta <u>was given and has</u> two choices in her life. The first is to attend university at a liberal arts
16

college. <u>Universities select.</u> The second is to do a one year course in medical assisting<u>, that is her</u>
17                                       18

<u>preference,</u> at a training school. Loretta and her parents have been <u>at odds</u> over this choice for several
19

months. <u>They are</u> concerned about Loretta's future, Loretta's parents want her to make the best decision.
20

Loretta thinks she knows what she wants <u>to certainly do.</u>
21

16. **Which of the following changes, if any, should be applied to underlined section 16?**

    F. No change
    G. has (delete "was given and")
    H. have (delete "was given and")
    J. has been given and has

17. **In revising underlined section 17, what would be a justification for editing it out completely?**

    A. it is irrelevant to the paragraph
    B. since universities are selective, Loretta's decision-making process would be over at this point in the essay
    C. it is too short a sentence
    D. it is not a sentence

18. **Which of the following changes, if any, should be applied to underlined section 18?**

    F. No change
    G. ,that she prefers.
    H. ,that which is her preference,
    J. (that is her preference)

19. **Why is the term "at odds" a useful word choice in underlined section 19?**

    A. it implies they see things differently, but it matches in tone the language about her parents' concern for Loretta
    B. it shows how angry they are at one another and implies many toe-to-toe confrontations
    C. it shows how odd Loretta thinks her parents are and how hard it is to reconcile her thinking with theirs
    D. it's a subtle way of saying this is a continuation of a lifetime of disagreements between parents and child

20. **Which of the following changes, if any, should be applied to underlined section 20?**

    F. No change
    G. Because they are
    H. If they are
    J. Once they are

**21. Which of the following changes, if any, should be applied to underlined section 21?**

    A. No change
    B. to do certainly
    C. certainly to do
    D. to do for certain

---

**The following passage is the basis for Questions 22-28:**

(2) <u>Although she realizes that it is more traditional to go to a four year college, Loretta wants to take a</u>
22

<u>different route, as she believes</u> that the best preparation for a career in medicine is practical experience in

a hospital or clinic. <u>Which is why she rejects the four year college.</u> Her plan is to do one year of <u>study, she</u>
23                                        24

<u>likes</u> things to be targeted. Then she wants to begin working in the field as a medical assistant. As she

works, <u>she intend</u> to take night classes in nursing <u>and work toward her</u> LPN. Once she achieves that and
25                                    26

uses her hospital or clinic experience to land a job as an LPN, <u>is why</u> she aims to go on to get her RN.
27

Over time she hopes to complete a Bachelor's degree in Nursing. Although it is a long range plan, Loretta

eventually hopes to be a Nurse Anesthetist. Not only is this a high-paying job, Loretta has always hated to

see people in pain. <u>Being a good nurse involves caring about people, to be considerate, and that you</u>
28

<u>know how to do your job in real time.</u> Loretta believes hands-on experience from the get-go will make her

into a better nurse.

---

**22. What would you say is the overall impression of Loretta's character in underlined section 22?**

    F. Defiant and disobedient
    G. A person who thinks for herself
    H. Someone who does not believe in careful planning
    J. Someone who has not bothered to gather information about or map out a career path

**23. Why does underlined section 23 need to be revised?**

    A. it needs no revision
    B. it is part of a run-on sentence
    C. it is a sentence fragment
    D. it is too short

**24. Which of the following changes, if any, should be applied to underlined section 24?**

    F. No change
    G. study. she likes
    H. study: she likes
    J. study; she likes

**25. Which of the following changes, if any, should be applied to underlined section 25?**

    A. No change
    B. she intended
    C. her intentions
    D. she intends

**26. Which of the following changes, if any, should be applied to underlined section 26?**

    F. No change
    G. and work to her
    H. and work through her
    J. and work untoward her

**27. Which of the following changes, if any, should be applied to underlined section 27?**

    A. No change
    B. that is why
    C. delete "is why"
    D. which is why

**28. Which of the following changes, if any, create parallel construction in underlined section 28?**

    F. None
    G. Being a good nurse involves caring about people, being considerate, and knowing how to do your job in real time.
    H. Being a good nurse is involved in caring about people, to be considerate, and to know how to do your job in real time.
    J. Being a good nurse is involved; you must care about people, to be considerate, and that you know how to do your job in real time.

---

**The following passage is the basis for Questions 29-30:**

## Decision Time

**(1)** Loretta was given and has two choices in her life. The first is to attend university at a liberal arts college. Universities select. The second is to do a one year course in medical assisting, that is her preference, at a training school. Loretta and her parents have been at odds over this choice for several months. They are concerned about Loretta's future, Loretta's parents want her to make the best decision. Loretta thinks she knows what she wants to certainly do.

**(2)** Although she realizes that it is more traditional to go to a four year college, Loretta wants to take a different route, as she believes that the best preparation for a career in medicine is practical experience in a hospital or clinic. Which is why she rejects the four year college. Her plan is to do one year of study, she likes things to be targeted. Then she wants to begin working in the field as a medical assistant. As she works, she intend to take night classes in nursing and work toward her LPN. Once she achieves that and uses her hospital or clinic experience to land a job as an LPN, is why she aims to go on to get her RN. Over time she hopes to complete a Bachelor's degree in Nursing. Although it is a long range plan, Loretta eventually hopes to be a Nurse Anesthetist. Not only is this a high-paying job, Loretta has always hated to see people in pain. Being a good nurse involves caring about people, to be considerate, and that you know how to do your job in real time. Loretta believes hands-on experience from the get-go will make her into a better nurse.

**29. If the writer of this essay was assigned to present two complete sides of an argument, would this essay fulfill that assignment?**

    A. No, because the essay presents Loretta' point of view, not her parents'.
    B. No, because the essay presents her parent's argument in the first paragraph.
    C. Yes, because the essay presents Loretta's parents' emotions.
    D. Yes, because it is a one-sided argument.

**30. If you were revising passage (2) and decided to break it into two paragraphs, where would you start the new paragraph?**

    F. as she believes
    G. Her plan
    H. Not only
    J. Loretta believes

---

**The following passage is the basis for Questions 31-35:**

## The Internet

**(1)** The advance of the Internet changed the world in three major ways. Human life will never be the same because of these far-reaching changes, and <u>we are the better for them.</u>
                                     31

**(2)** First, the Internet <u>have revolutionized</u> the way the world does business, saving time and money.
                               32
Record-keeping became computerized and easy to transmit from place to <u>place; research</u> could be found
                                                  33
while sitting at one's desk rather than going through dusty volumes in a library; through email, businesses could communicate with one another much more quickly than in the past. <u>Further more</u>, businesses
                                                              34
around the world could collaborate on projects, introducing the ideas of <u>virtual cyber offices</u> and virtual
                                                                     35
stores.

---

**31. Underlined section 31 may be characterized as what kind of a statement?**

    A. a derisive statement
    B. an editorial statement
    C. a factual statement
    D. a deductive statement

**32. Which of the following changes, if any, should be applied to underlined section 32?**

    F. No change
    G. will have revolutionized
    H. has revolutionized
    J. did revolutionize

**33. Which of the following changes, if any, should be applied to underlined section 33?**

A. No change
B. place. Research
C. place, research
D. place: research

**34. Which of the following changes, if any, should be applied to underlined section 34?**

F. No change
G. And further more
H. Furthermost
J. Furthermore

**35. Which of the following changes, if any, should be applied to underlined section 35?**

A. No change
B. virtual, cyber offices
C. virtual; cyber offices
D. virtual: cyber offices

---

**The following passage is the basis for Questions 36-39:**

(3) Second, the unprecedented flow of information meant that <u>people knew about things more quickly all</u>
                                                                                                    36
<u>over the globe and therefore had the power of knowledge</u>. For example, political news now travels <u>very</u>
                                                                                                            37
<u>fast and an individual or country's actions</u> can "go viral" at any moment. <u>The Internet has given "people</u>
                                                                                                               38
<u>power" to consumers as well, in one case, a guitar player made a video criticizing an airline that had</u>

<u>damaged his guitar through careless baggage handling.</u> The video went viral on YouTube. The video had

such impact that the <u>airlines</u> stock took a large hit. When the airline realized that this lone guitar player
                        39
was costing them a great deal of money, the airline begged him to accept compensation and also if they

could use his film to train personnel in better customer service.

---

**36. In underlined section 36, the author's perspective may be expressed best by what famous saying?**

F. absolute power corrupts absolutely
G. power to the people
H. knowledge is power
J. to know all is to forgive all

**37. Which of the following changes, if any, should be applied to underlined section 37?**

A. No change
B. very fast, and an individual or country's actions
C. very fast; and an individual or country's actions
D. very fast: and an individual or country's actions

**38. What revision would improve underlined section 38?**

    F.  No change
    G.  delete "in one case,"
    H.  Begin the sentence with "Through careless baggage handling" and end it with a period after the word "guitar"
    J.  Place a period after "as well" and begin a new sentence with "In one case"

**39. Which of the following changes, if any, should be applied to underlined section 39?**

    A.  No change
    B.  airline's
    C.  airlines'
    D.  airline

---

**The following passage is the basis for Question 40:**

(4) The third way the Internet has changed the world is through social networking. People can now communicate with one another cheaply and easily. They can upload <u>photos and videos, that bridge the gaps of distance</u>. The Internet thus made the world smaller, contributing to awareness that we live in a global village.

                                          40

---

**40. What revision would improve underlined section 40?**

    F.  No change
    G.  photos and videos that bridge the gaps of distance
    H.  photos and videos, that bridges the gaps of distance
    J.  photos and videos, that's the bridge over the gaps of distance

---

**The following passage is the basis for Questions 41-42:**

(5) The modern world includes cyber reality and this has transformed and benefited the world in a number of ways. There are a few caveats, however. Virtual reality is sometimes easier to cope with than reality. <u>It may be easier to interact with people behind the protection of a computer screen than to deal with them in face-to-face interactions.</u> A micro-expression might reveal more than a person intends and result in conflict. However, if people approach the virtual world as a convenience of communication but continue to attend assiduously to their relationships in real life, they may find the two worlds co-exist quite companionably.

                                          41

**41. What revision would improve underlined section 41?**

    A.  No change
    B.  They may be easier to interact with people behind the protection of a computer screen than to deal with them in face-to-face interactions.
    C.  It may be easier to interact with people behind the protection of a computer screen than to deal with them in face-off interactions.
    D.  It may be easier to interact behind the protection of a computer screen with people than to deal with them in face-to-face interactions.

**42. This concluding paragraph may be characterized as:**

    F.  a summary that brings in a new point as food for thought
    G.  a wrap-up of the essay's arguments against extensive use of the Internet
    H.  a point of complete departure from the essay's theme
    J.  a point-by-point repetition of the contents of the essay

---

**The following passage is the basis for Questions 43-45:**

# The Internet

**(1)** The advance of the Internet changed the world in three major ways. Human life will never be the same because of these far-reaching changes, and we are the better for them.

**(2)** First, the Internet have revolutionized the way the world does business, saving time and money. Record-keeping became computerized and easy to transmit from place to place; research could be found while sitting at one's desk rather than going through dusty volumes in a library; through email, businesses could communicate with one another much more quickly than in the past. Further more, businesses around the world could collaborate on projects, introducing the ideas of virtual cyber offices and virtual stores.

**(3)** Second, the unprecedented flow of information meant that people knew about things more quickly all over the globe and therefore had the power of knowledge. For example, political news now travels very fast and an individual or country's actions can "go viral" at any moment. The Internet has given "people power" to consumers as well, in one case, a guitar player made a video criticizing an airline that had damaged his guitar through careless baggage handling. The video went viral on YouTube. The video had such impact that the airlines stock took a large hit. When the airline realized that this lone guitar player was costing them a great deal of money, the airline begged him to accept compensation and also if they could use his film to train personnel in better customer service.

**(4)** The third way the Internet has changed the world is through social networking. People can now communicate with one another cheaply and easily. They can upload photos and videos, that bridge the gaps of distance. The Internet thus made the world smaller, contributing to awareness that we live in a global village.

**(5)** The modern world includes cyber reality and this has transformed and benefited the world in a number of ways. There are a few caveats, however. Virtual reality is sometimes easier to cope with than reality. It may be easier to interact with people behind the protection of a computer screen than to deal with them in face-to-face interactions. A micro-expression might reveal more than a person intends and result in conflict. However, if people approach the virtual world as a convenience of communication but continue to attend assiduously to their relationships in real life, they may find the two worlds co-exist quite companionably.

**43. The tone of the essay "The Internet" may be characterized as:**

    A. critical of the Internet
    B. neutral toward the Internet
    C. puzzled by the Internet
    D. positive toward the Internet

**44. If this essay were to include a paragraph addressing social networking more explicitly, where should that paragraph be placed?**

    F. after paragraph 1
    G. after paragraph 2
    H. after paragraph 3
    J. after paragraph 4

**45. If this essay were to include a few observations about other technologies that have changed the world, where should that material be placed?**

    A. in paragraph 1
    B. in paragraph 2
    C. in paragraph 5
    D. between paragraph 3 and 4

---

**The following passage is the basis for Questions 46-48:**

## Smith-Corona: Heavy Metal

**(1)** The first time I set my fingers on the slick keys of my <u>first typewriter, it was</u> a watershed moment. My
                                                         46

father had given me his old Smith-Corona manual typewriter. <u>There, it gleamed, inviting me</u> to compose
                                                          47

the Great American novel. It was black, made out of heavy metal; its silver-ringed black keys with white

script letters triggered engraved silver spokes to strike an inked ribbon and imprint the letter on the paper.

<u>Adding machines were cumbersome in those days too.</u>
                48

---

**46. Which of the following changes, if any, should be applied to underlined section 46?**

    F. No change
    G. first typewriter, a first it was
    H. first, typewriter, it was
    J. first typewriter; it was

**47. Which of the following changes, if any, should be applied to underlined section 47?**

    A. No change
    B. There it gleamed, inviting me
    C. There, it gleamed inviting me
    D. There it invited me by gleaming

**48. What would be a justification for eliminating underlined section 48?**

    F.  it should not be eliminated
    G.  it is irrelevant to the topic
    H.  it is not the topic sentence
    J.  it fits better in the next paragraph

---

**The following passage is the basis for Questions 49-52:**

(2) It was a noisome thing. <u>I had to pound</u> the keys to make the spokes strike the page hard enough to
                                49

make an imprint. The ribbon rose to the paper through a clinking metal mechanism; the ribbon spools

jiggled and spun. The paper snapped each time a spoke struck it. The typewriter <u>clanked and clattered</u>
                                                                               50

<u>and thumped</u>. I think the racket was music to <u>my parents ears</u>, though. They were thrilled that I was
                                                         51

following <u>what was seen by them </u>as a natural proclivity toward the written word.
                    52

---

**49. In keeping with the style of the essay, underlined section 49 should read:**

    A.  No change
    B.  He had to pound
    C.  She had to pound
    D.  You had to pound

**50. Which of the following changes, if any, should be applied to underlined section 50?**

    F.  No change
    G.  clanked clattered and thumped
    H.  clanked, clattered, thumped
    J.  clanked, clattered, and thumped

**51. Which of the following changes, if any, should be applied to underlined section 51?**

    A.  No change
    B.  my parent's ears
    C.  my parents' ears
    D.  my parents's ears

**52. Why would it be a good idea to revise underlined section 52?**

    F.  it should not be revised
    G.  it is in the passive voice; good writing uses the active voice as much as possible
    H.  it is irrelevant
    J.  "was seen" is an improper verb

**The following passage is the basis for Questions 53-56:**

**(3)** Good luck to the person who made a mistake in those days before the "Delete" button. A hand eraser and a brush to whisk away the pink eraser crumbs <u>was essential tools</u>. There was always the danger of
53
erasing too <u>zealous, though,</u> tearing the paper. When a merciful person invented white-out liquid, <u>typists
54                                                                                                                        55
all over the world heaved a sigh of relief.</u> White-out liquid looked and smelled like white nail polish. It

blotted out all errors. However, when it was held up to the light, a page with white-out on it showed

fluorescent blotches. In business circles, <u>a maximum of two blotches per page were acceptable</u>. There
56
was also a white tape a person could apply to the paper and then retype the error. The tape contained

white powder that filled and covered the mistaken ink imprint. This was the most subtle approach to

mistake correction.

**53. Which of the following changes, if any, should be applied to underlined section 53?**

- A. No change
- B. was essentially tools
- C. were essential tools
- D. was essential as tools

**54. Which of the following changes, if any, should be applied to underlined section 54?**

- F. No change
- G. zealously, though,
- H. zealous though
- J. zealous, thorough,

**55. The style of underlined section 55 may be said to be:**

- A. factual
- B. advocating
- C. hyperbolic
- D. global

**56. Which of the following changes, if any, should be applied to underlined section 56?**

- F. No change
- G. a maximum of two blotches per page was acceptable
- H. a maximum per page of two blotches were acceptable
- J. a maximum were acceptable of two blotches per page

**The following passage is the basis for Questions 57-58:**

**(4)** I saw an old Smith-Corona, just like the one I learned to write on, in an antique shop a year or so ago. It was very reasonably priced, yet I did not buy it. Nostalgia could not overcome memories of the inconvenience coupled with my unabashed love for my laptop. Gazing upon the ancient thing, caused me
57
to remember the sounds, smells, and strenuousness of using one, all I could think was: "How on earth did
58
Jane Austen ever write Pride and Prejudice with a quill pen?"

**57. Which of the following changes, if any, should be applied to underlined section 57?**

- A. No change
- B. Gazing, upon the ancient thing caused me
- C. Gazing, upon the ancient thing, caused me
- D. Gazing upon the ancient thing caused me

**58. As this is the concluding paragraph of the essay, is underlined section 58 an appropriate last line?**

- F. no, because the author shouldn't be introducing a new idea like this at the end
- G. no, because the essay was about typewriters, not quill pens; therefore it is irrelevant
- H. yes, because it leaves the reader with a memorable punch line related to the topic of the essay
- J. yes, because the essay is about technological innovations

**The following passage is the basis for Questions 59-60:**

## The Smith-Corona: Heavy Metal

**(1)** The first time I set my fingers on the slick keys of my first typewriter, it was a watershed moment. My father had given me his old Smith-Corona manual typewriter. There, it gleamed, inviting me to compose the Great American novel. It was black, made out of heavy metal; its silver-ringed black keys with white script letters triggered engraved silver spokes to strike an inked ribbon and imprint the letter on the paper. Adding machines were cumbersome in those days too.

**(2)** It was a noisome thing. I had to pound the keys to make the spokes strike the page hard enough to make an imprint. The ribbon rose to the paper through a clinking metal mechanism; the ribbon spools jiggled and spun. The paper snapped each time a spoke struck it. The typewriter clanked and clattered and thumped. I think the racket was music to my parents ears, though. They were thrilled that I was following what was seen by them as a natural proclivity toward the written word.

**(3)** Good luck to the person who made a mistake in those days before the "Delete" button. A hand eraser and a brush to whisk away the pink eraser crumbs was essential tools. There was always the danger of erasing too zealous, though, tearing the paper. When a merciful person invented white-out liquid, typists all over the world heaved a sigh of relief. White-out liquid looked and smelled like white nail polish. It blotted out all errors. However, when it was held up to the light, a page with white-out on it showed fluorescent blotches. In business circles, a maximum of two blotches per page were acceptable. There was also a white tape a person could apply to the paper and then retype the error. The tape contained white powder that filled and covered the mistaken ink imprint. This was the most subtle approach to mistake correction.

**(4)** I saw an old Smith-Corona, just like the one I learned to write on, in an antique shop a year or so ago. It was very reasonably priced, yet I did not buy it. Nostalgia could not overcome memories of the inconvenience coupled with my unabashed love for my laptop. Gazing upon the ancient thing, caused me to remember the sounds, smells, and strenuousness of using one, all I could think was: "How on earth did Jane Austen ever write *Pride and Prejudice* with a quill pen?"

**59. Which of the following statements most effectively summarizes the essay?**

    A.  the old ways are the best ways
    B.  people who live to see technological advances are amused by the old ways and wonder how they and others managed before the advances
    C.  technological advances are a mixed bag of benefits and drawbacks and nostalgia for simpler, easier times is understandable
    D.  a frustrated writer blames the lack of technology in her formative years for her inability to write the Great American novel

**60. Suppose the writer wished to add the following sentence to the essay:** *Ingenious and mechanical, the Smith-Corona was a perfect representation of the Industrial Revolution.* **This new sentence would most logically be placed in paragraph:**

    F.  1
    G.  2
    H.  3
    J.  4

**The following passage is the basis for Questions 61-64:**

## Confessions of a Plant Murderer

**(1)** "Oh, no!" my co-worker cried as she came to her desk the morning of her birthday. "Somebody gave

me a potted plant! No! Don't they know I am a plant killer from way back? <u>This plant is doomed</u>"!
                                                                                     61

**(2)** <u>I could relate.</u> Whatever the opposite of a green thumb is, I've got it. While I'm not a planticidal
        62

maniac, many the green, young thing has expired <u>on my watch.</u> Thank goodness there is no Anti-Cruelty
                                                  63

Society for plants. I would be in their bad books for sure. <u>They would not like me.</u>
                                                                64

**61. Which of the following changes, if any, should be applied to underlined section 61?**

    A.  No change
    B.  transpose the closing quotation mark and the exclamation point
    C.  take away the exclamation point as it adds too much emphasis
    D.  remove the quotation mark

                                     

**62. Which of the following changes, if any, should be applied to underlined section 62?**

    F.  No change
    G.  add the prepositional phrase "to her feelings"
    H.  add the adverb "well"
    J.  add the adverb "good"

**63. What does the author mean by the phrase "on my watch" in underlined section 63?**

    A.  she was timing something relating to plant needs
    B.  plants have died literally on her Rolex
    C.  plants have died under her care
    D.  plants have died quickly under her care

**64. What is underlined section 64?**

    F.  a concluding sentence to a paragraph
    G.  a redundancy
    H.  a metaphor
    J.  a dangling participle

---

**The following passage is the basis for Question 65:**

(3) <u>Its</u> not that I mean to be cruel. I just don't have much faith in photosynthesis. Somehow, I find it
    65
incredible that plants need water and sunlight, as well as the nutrients in the soil, to make their own food.

---

**65. Which of the following changes, if any, should be applied to underlined section 65?**

    A.  No change
    B.  Its'
    C.  'Tis
    D.  It's

---

**The following passage is the basis for Questions 66-69:**

(4) <u>Once upon a time</u>, a friend gave me a set of three flowering plants (foolish girl). They looked lovely on
      66
the bedroom dresser. Then my friend told me they needed sun. I duly put them outside. In a day or so,

<u>they were "dead as doornails",</u> to use Charles Dickens's unforgettable phrase.
        67

(5) "Didn't you water them?" my friend asked in an accusatory tone.

(6) "Once or twice," I hedged.

(7) "They need to be watered in the morning and at night. Didn't you notice them drying up?"

---

          

---

**(8)** Her contempt for me left me as withered as the <u>deceased and desiccated</u> plants. I nodded <u>mute</u> as
68                        69

she vowed she would never entrust me with another living thing.

---

### 66. Why might the author use the expression in underlined section 66?

    F.  No reason
    G.  to refer to the past in a classic and comical way
    H.  because the story has elements of a fairy tale
    J.  because the author does not want the reader to know the exact time frame of the story in order to make it more universal

### 67. What is the author doing in underlined section 67?

    A.  nothing unusual
    B.  plagiarizing Charles Dickens
    C.  not writing in an original way
    D.  quoting a famous work by a famous author

### 68. Underlined section 68 is an example of:

    F.  alliteration
    G.  rhyme
    H.  allegory
    J.  simile

### 69. Which of the following changes, if any, should be applied to underlined section 69?

    A.  No change
    B.  mutedly
    C.  mutely
    D.  mutually

---

**The following passage is the basis for Questions 70-73:**

**(9)** <u>Fortunately, no longer.</u> Now I live in an <u>apartment building that employs a gardener.</u> <u>Flowers and
70                       71                  72
foliage are mine to enjoy without trauma.</u> I greet friends with a clear conscience, knowing I am no longer

responsible for any plant's <u>untimely</u> death.
73

---

### 70. Why should underlined section 70 be revised?

    F.  it should not be revised
    G.  never start a sentence with the word "Fortunately"
    H.  it is not a complete sentence
    J.  there is no need for a comma

**71. A literal reading of underlined section 71 implies:**

    A. that the building itself employs a gardener
    B. that no apartment building should be without a gardener
    C. the author is now free to kill plants with impunity
    D. gardeners are important to apartment complexes

**72. Which of the following changes, if any, should be applied to underlined section 72?**

    F. No change
    G. Flowers and foliage are mine to enjoy without traumatic
    H. Without trauma, I may now enjoy my flowers and foliage
    J. Flowers and triage are mine to enjoy without trauma

**73. What would be an alternative term to use in underlined section 73?**

    A. timeliness
    B. premature
    C. preternatural
    D. timeless

---

**The following passage is the basis for Questions 74-75:**

## Confessions of a Plant Murderer

**(1)** "Oh, no!" my co-worker cried as she came to her desk the morning of her birthday. "Somebody gave me a potted plant! No! Don't they know I am a plant killer from way back? This plant is doomed"!

**(2)** I could relate. Whatever the opposite of a green thumb is, I've got it. While I'm not a planticidal maniac, many the green, young thing has expired on my watch. Thank goodness there is no Anti-Cruelty Society for plants. I would be in their bad books for sure. They would not like me.

**(3)** Its not that I mean to be cruel. I just don't have much faith in photosynthesis. Somehow, I find it incredible that plants need water and sunlight, as well as the nutrients in the soil, to make their own food.

**(4)** Once upon a time, a friend gave me a set of three flowering plants (foolish girl). They looked lovely on the bedroom dresser. Then my friend told me they needed sun. I duly put them outside. In a day or so, they were "dead as doornails", to use Charles Dickens's unforgettable phrase.

**(5)** "Didn't you water them?" my friend asked in an accusatory tone.

**(6)** "Once or twice," I hedged.

**(7)** "They need to be watered in the morning and at night. Didn't you notice them drying up?"

**(8)** Her contempt for me left me as withered as the deceased and desiccated plants. I nodded mute as she vowed she would never entrust me with another living thing.

**(9)** Fortunately, no longer. Now I live in an apartment building that employs a gardener. Flowers and foliage are mine to enjoy without trauma. I greet friends with a clear conscience, knowing I am no longer responsible for any plant's untimely death.

**74. If you were to add another example of a time when the author killed a plant, where would it logically go?**

    F.   After paragraph 1
    G.  After paragraph 3
    H.  After paragraph 5
    J.   After paragraph 8

**75. A good alternative title reflecting the contents of this essay would be:**

    A.  Green Thumb Grief
    B.  Horticulture and Home
    C.  Garden Care
    D.  Friendship

# ENGLISH PRACTICE TEST 1 ANSWER KEY

| | |
|---|---|
| 1. D | 39. B |
| 2. G | 40. G |
| 3. A | 41. A |
| 4. H | 42. F |
| 5. B | 43. D |
| 6. F | 44. J |
| 7. A | 45. A |
| 8. G | 46. F |
| 9. D | 47. B |
| 10. G | 48. G |
| 11. A | 49. A |
| 12. H | 50. J |
| 13. C | 51. C |
| 14. H | 52. G |
| 15. C | 53. C |
| 16. G | 54. G |
| 17. A | 55. C |
| 18. J | 56. G |
| 19. A | 57. D |
| 20. G | 58. H |
| 21. D | 59. B |
| 22. G | 60. F |
| 23. C | 61. B |
| 24. J | 62. F |
| 25. D | 63. C |
| 26. F | 64. G |
| 27. C | 65. D |
| 28. G | 66. G |
| 29. A | 67. D |
| 30. G | 68. F |
| 31. B | 69. C |
| 32. H | 70. H |
| 33. B | 71. A |
| 34. J | 72. F |
| 35. B | 73. B |
| 36. H | 74. J |
| 37. B | 75. A |
| 38. J | |

# ENGLISH PRACTICE TEST 1 RATIONALES

**1. Answer: D. worse**
Most descriptive words have three forms: the positive, the comparative, and the superlative, as in bad (positive), worse (comparative), worst (superlative). "Worse" is the comparative form of "bad". Two actions are being compared—picking up a book by Mark Twain and picking up a book by someone else—thus the comparative form "worse" is the best choice. "Worser" is never correct.

**2. Answer: G. note that Mark Twain's books are engaging**
The word "avid" means enthusiastic; by using this word, the author is saying that the reader will be enthusiastic about reading Twain's books.

**3. Answer: A. No change**
Stylistically, use of well-known foreign phrases adds variety and interest. Sometimes a foreign phrase sums up a thought more elegantly and completely than can be done in English. *Nom de plume* is the familiar French term for "pen name" or "name of the pen" and is correct as it is.

**4. Answer: H. appearances**
The ships were real, so "apparitions" which means supernatural appearances, is incorrect and must be changed. Among the other choices, "apertures" means openings, and "apartheids" means separations, so neither of them is correct. "Appearances" makes sense in the context of the sentence.

**5. Answer: B. occasions**
The "appearances" of the ships were the "occasions" for celebrations, and since "appearances" is in the plural, "occasions" must also be in the plural to match it.

**6. Answer: F. To tie the together the topic sentence and the idea of the Mississippi River's influence on Twain**
Each sentence in a paragraph must relate to the topic sentence. The topic sentence is usually the first sentence, as it is here, giving Samuel Clemens's pen name of Mark Twain. Underlined section 6, the last sentence of the paragraph, relates the thoughts in the paragraph about steamboats to the topic sentence, because the pen name was taken from steamboat terminology. It also serves as a summary of the paragraph.

**7. Answer: A. No change**
The first sentence of paragraph 3 contains two complete sentences. These are called "independent clauses" because each one of them could stand alone as a complete sentence. There are several correct ways to deal with such a sentence, but one correct way is to put a comma after the first independent clause and then join the two independent clauses with a coordinating conjunction such as "and". This is the way it is done in underlined section 7, and it is correct.

**8. Answer: G. days; swimming**
Underlined section 8 incorrectly joins two independent clauses (or two complete sentences) with a comma. This is called a "comma splice" and is incorrect. A comma splice between two independent clauses may be corrected by changing the comma into a semi-colon, which is a stronger pause and indicates the presence of two complete sentences.

**9. Answer: D. When the townspeople fear hooky-playing boys are dead,**
The phrase "when hooky-playing boys are thought to be dead" is in the passive voice; someone is being acted upon rather than taking action. It is better to name a subject in the sentence—"the townspeople"— and then use the active voice by showing what action the subject took. The active voice is the preferred style in standard English as it makes for stronger and clearer sentences.

**10. Answer: G. in hopes of raising**
An infinitive is the verb form "to" plus a verb. In this case, the infinitive is "to raise". It is incorrect to "split" an infinitive by inserting another word between "to" and the verb, such as "to hopefully raise". The split infinitive cannot be corrected in this case by changing the word order: "hopefully to raise" or "to raise hopefully" do not make sense in the sentence. It is better to rephrase it to read "in hopes of raising".

**11. Answer: A. No change**
The sentence is correct as it is.

**12. Answer: H. when he escapes from being trapped in a cave**
The words "from" and "in" are prepositions; they mark the beginning of prepositional phrases. Prepositional phrases serve as adjectives and adverbs, and they are not separated from the words they describe by commas.

**13. Answer: C. underlined section 13 should be removed**
The sentence is irrelevant to the topic of the paragraph. The topic of the paragraph is the way the Mississippi River figures specifically in Mark Twain's books; it is not about rivers in general or the characteristics and functions of rivers. Out of place, it should be removed.

**14. Answer: H. On the raft**
"Upon" is an old-fashioned preposition. "On" is a more modern preposition. Since the question asks about an essay in a "modern" journal, the more modern preposition should be used.

**15. Answer: C. Because it was a dominating feature of his home town, the Mississippi River figured prominently in Twain's imagination and writings.**
The essay covers the derivation of Twain's pen name, showing how the lore of the river captured Twain's imagination. The essay also shows how the Mississippi River figures in *The Adventures of Tom Sawyer* and *The Adventures of Huckleberry Finn*, Twain's most famous writings. Answer C mentions both Twain's imagination and writings and is the best summary of the essay's main points.

**16. Answer: G. has (delete "was given and")**
"Was given" and "has" mean the same thing in this context and are repetitive, therefore, one of the phrases should be deleted. The phrase "was given" is passive in that the action is happening to Loretta rather than being taken by her, so "has" is the best choice to stay in the sentence.

**17. Answer: A. it is irrelevant to the paragraph**
In the context, underlined section 17 is irrelevant as the fact that universities select does not specifically pertain to Loretta's choices.

**18. Answer: J. (that is her preference)**
Parentheses enclose material that is supplemental, digresses slightly, or is an "aside" or afterthought. Loretta's preference is supplemental information and needs enclosure by parentheses. Commas are too weak to properly enclose this supplemental information.

**19. Answer: A. it implies they see things differently, but it matches in tone the language about her parents' concern for Loretta**
Stylistically, "at odds" is in tone with the fact that Loretta's parents want the best for her; it is a soft way of saying they disagreed.

**20. Answer: G. Because they are**
The phrase at the beginning of the sentence is a dependent clause, meaning the words do not make sense alone and must be tied to the rest of the sentence. The phrase needs a word that is called a "dependent marker" that will tie it to the rest of the sentence. "Because" is an appropriate dependent marker in the context of the sentence.

### 21. Answer: D. to do for certain
An infinitive is the verb form "to" plus a verb. In this case, the infinitive is "to do". It is incorrect to "split" an infinitive by inserting another word between "to" and the verb, such as "to certainly do". "To do for certain" corrects the split infinitive and expresses the thought firmly and clearly.

### 22. Answer: G. A person who thinks for herself
The use of the word "traditional" in the sentence shows that Loretta is aware of the way things are usually done; however, she has thought this through and drawn a reasonable conclusion on her own, showing she is a person who thinks for herself.

### 23. Answer: C. it is a sentence fragment
Underlined section 23 is not a complete sentence; it does not have a subject or a verb. As it is written, it is a dependent clause or sentence fragment needing more words in order to stand alone.

### 24. Answer: J. study; she likes
Independent clauses are complete sentences in themselves. There are several correct ways to punctuate and structure two independent clauses. Linking two independent clauses with a semi-colon is one correct way to punctuate and structure two independent clauses in one sentence.

### 25. Answer: D. she intends
Subjects and verbs must "agree"—that is, the form of the verb must match the amount of the subject. "She" is a singular pronoun, indicating only one person. The verb form is "intends". "She intend to go to the store" is incorrect; "She intends to go to the store" is correct.

### 26. Answer: F. No change
The phrase is correct as it is. "And work toward" is part of what Loretta intends to do.

### 27. Answer: C. delete "is why"
A mixed construction is when a sentence contains parts that do not fit together within the grammatical structures of English. That phrase "is why" in underlined section 27 is an unnecessary outlier and takes the sentence in a wrong direction. Deleting "is why" corrects this mixed construction.

### 28. Answer: G. Being a good nurse involves caring about people, being considerate, and knowing how to do your job in real time.
Parallel construction means that the grammatical forms in a sentence match. Using the gerund or "ing" forms of the verbs in this sentence, rather than a mixture of forms, makes them match and creates parallel construction, making for a much smoother read.

### 29. Answer: A. No, because the essay presents Loretta' point of view, not her parents'.
Although her parents' point of view is noted, the essay elaborates on Loretta's point of view almost exclusively. Loretta's side of the argument dominates the essay. The other point of view or side of the argument (her parents) is given very little space.

### 30. Answer: G. Her plan
The sentences after the words "Her plan" delineate exactly, step by step, what Loretta plans to do. Therefore, "Her plan" is an appropriate place to begin a new paragraph depicting Loretta's plan of action.

### 31. Answer: B. an editorial statement
The statement expresses an opinion and is therefore an editorial statement.

### 32. Answer: H. has revolutionized
Since "The Internet" is the subject of the sentence, the singular verb form "has revolutionized" is needed for subject-verb agreement.

## 33. Answer: B. place. Research
Underlined section 33 is part of a run-on sentence. A run-on sentence is a sentence that is overly long. A run-on sentence often consists of poorly connected independent clauses, which could stand alone as complete sentences. Breaking up the independent clauses into sentences with correct punctuation and capitalization helps correct the problem.

## 34. Answer: J. Furthermore
"Furthermore" is one word, so Answer D. is the correct answer. Adding "And" as in Answer B, or changing the word to the superlative form "Furthermost" as in Answer C would be incorrect.

## 35. Answer: B. virtual, cyber offices
"Virtual" and "cyber" are both adjectives describing the noun "offices". They are equal in importance and their order could be reversed in the sentence. Such adjectives are called "coordinate" adjectives, and it is proper to put a comma between coordinate adjectives.

## 36. Answer: H. knowledge is power
The sentence uses the words "the power of knowledge" and has a positive tone about the greater flow of information in the world, thus the saying "knowledge is power" most accurately expresses the author's perspective.

## 37. Answer: B. very fast, and an individual or country's actions
Two independent clauses or complete sentences within one sentence need to be properly linked with a conjunction such as "and". The first independent clause or complete sentence is marked by a comma before the "and".

## 38. Answer: J. Place a period after "as well" and begin a new sentence with "In one case"
Underlined section 38 is part of a run-on sentence. A run-on sentence is a sentence that is overly long. A run-on sentence often consists of poorly connected independent clauses, which could stand alone as complete sentences. Breaking up the independent clauses into sentences with correct punctuation and capitalization helps correct the problem.

## 39. Answer: B. airline's
The sentence is referring to a single airline's stock. The singular possessive form of a noun requires an apostrophe after the noun and an "s".

## 40. Answer: G. photos and videos that bridge the gaps of distance
"That bridge the gaps of distance" is an adjective phrase that directly modifies the nouns "photos and videos". Adjectives are not separated from the nouns they modify by commas.

## 41. Answer: A. No change
The sentence is correct as it is.

## 42. Answer: F. a summary that brings in a new point as food for thought
The concluding paragraph of an essay both summarizes what has gone before and also may suggest a new line of thought.

## 43. Answer: D. positive toward the Internet
The essay states in the first paragraph that "we are the better" for the changes the Internet has brought about. Paragraph 2 mentions that businesses save time and money through use of the Internet. Paragraph 3 affirms that the Internet empowers people with knowledge. Paragraph 4 maintains that people are more aware of a shared world because of the Internet, and paragraph 5 says that the Internet has "benefited the world in a number of ways." The general tone of the essay, shown in these specific statements, is positive toward the Internet.

**44. Answer: J. after paragraph 4**
Paragraph 4 introduces the topic of social networking and expands on it for a few sentences. A logical place for further elaboration on the topic of social networking is after paragraph 4.

**45. Answer: A. in paragraph 1**
The introductory paragraph, paragraph 1, could provide examples of other world-changing technologies in order to bring the essay from the general (world-changing technologies) to the specific (the Internet). Many essays begin with general statements and then address more specific points.

**46. Answer: F. No change**
The long introductory phrase requires the use of a comma for the appropriate pause.

**47. Answer: B. There it gleamed, inviting me**
"There" is a placeholder and needs no comma after it. However, it is also an introductory phrase and should be separated from the gerund phrase starting with "inviting" by a comma.

**48. Answer: G. it is irrelevant to the topic**
The paragraph (and essay) is specifically about the author's Smith-Corona; it has nothing to do with adding machines.

**49. Answer: A. No change**
The essay is written in the first person, therefore it is correct as it is.

**50. Answer: J. clanked, clattered, and thumped**
For a series (three or more items listed) only one "and" is required. Commas are placed between the items in the series.

**51. Answer: C. my parents' ears**
Since "parents" is plural, the plural possessive form is used, requiring the apostrophe to come after the "s".

**52. Answer: G. it is in the passive voice; good writing uses the active voice as much as possible**
The sentence would be stronger and clearer if the passive verb "was seen" (something being acted upon) is replaced by an active verb, such as "they saw" (someone taking action). In general, writers, editors, and readers prefer the active voice.

**53. Answer: C. were essential tools**
The subject of the sentence is a compound one consisting of two elements: the hand eraser and a brush. This makes the subject plural and it requires a plural form of the verb "were" rather than the singular verb form "was".

**54. Answer: G. zealously, though,**
"Erasing" is a verb form, and verbs are modified by adverbs. Many adverbs are formed by adding "ly" to adjectives. "Zealously" is the adverb form of the adjective "zealous" and should be used in this case.

**55. Answer: C. hyperbolic**
Clearly, it is an exaggeration to say what typists all over the world did; the author is using a hyperbolic, or exaggerated style to invoke humor.

**56. Answer: G. a maximum of two blotches per page was acceptable**
The verb "was" is referring to "maximum", not "blotches", and, as a singular noun, it requires a singular verb.

**57. Answer: D. Gazing upon the ancient thing caused me**
The gerund ("ing") phrase "Gazing upon the ancient thing" is serving as the subject of the sentence, and subjects are not separated from their verbs by commas.

**58. Answer: H. yes, because it leaves the reader with a memorable punch line related to the topic of the essay**
It is desirable to end an essay strongly, and introducing a new "take" on the subject that is related to the theme and topic leaves the reader with food for thought.

**59. Answer: B. people who live to see technological advances are amused by the old ways and wonder how they and others managed before the advances**
The essay takes an amused look back at the limitations of a manual typewriter: "it was a noisome thing" and erasing errors is described as particularly difficult. "Nostalgia" over her old machine "could not overcome memories of the inconvenience"; nor could it overcome her "unabashed love for my laptop." Remembering the manual typewriter's clumsy technology, the author wonders how great authors of the past managed with even less advanced technology; thus, Answer B is the best summary of the essay.

**60. Answer: F. 1**
This physical description of the Smith-Corona belongs in the first paragraph where the machine is first being described.

**61. Answer: B. transpose the closing quotation mark and the exclamation point**
In a direct quote, the closing quotation mark is always outside the punctuation that ends the sentence.

**62. Answer: F. No change**
Having a subject and a verb, the sentence is complete as it is.

**63. Answer: C. plants have died under her care**
The idiom "on my watch" means while one was responsible, under one's jurisdiction or care; therefore, the author means that plants have died under her care.

**64. Answer: G. a redundancy**
The sentence repeats the exact same idea as the sentence before it, making it a redundancy.

**65. Answer: D. It's**
In the sentence "Its" is meant to be the contraction form of "It is". "It's", Answer D., is the proper form of the contraction of "It is".

**66. Answer: G. to refer to the past in a classic and comical way**
The author is using this classic fairy tale opening for the sake of humor and to indicate that her friends have long since understood that they should not give her plants.

**67. Answer: D. quoting a famous work by a famous author**
This quote from the beginning of Charles Dickens's *A Christmas Carol* is fairly well-known and quite descriptive.

**68. Answer: F. alliteration**
Using words beginning with the same consonant within close proximity of one another is alliteration, a well-known literary device.

**69. Answer: C. mutely**
This is the correct form of "mute" as it is an adverb modifying the verb "nodded"."Mutely" is the adverb form of the adjective "mute". Many adverbs are formed by adding "ly" to adjectives. Since the author is describing how she nodded, an adverb is needed. Adverbs answer such questions as "How?" When?" "Where?" "Why?" and they modify verbs such as "nodded".

**70. Answer: H. it is not a complete sentence**
Lacking a subject and a verb, this is a sentence fragment and needs to be revised.

**71. Answer: A. that the building itself employs a gardener**
It needs to made clear that people—"building managers" perhaps, or a collective such as "building management"—employ or employs a gardener. As it is written, the sentence implies that the building itself employs a gardener, which is an impossibility.

**72. Answer: F. No change**
The sentence is correct as it is.

**73. Answer: B. premature**
In relation to death, "untimely" usually does indicate "premature" or "unexpected".

**74. Answer: J. After paragraph 8**
Inserting another example of a time the author killed a plant would be appropriate here, after the first example but before the concluding paragraph.

**75. Answer: A. Green Thumb Grief**
This title would be in keeping with the essay's humorous tone and subject matter.

# MATHEMATICS PRACTICE TEST 1

60 Minutes - 60 Questions

Directions: Each question has five answer choices. Choose the best answer for each question.

1.  **If $4x - 3 = 13$, then $5x + 7 = ?$**

    A.  15
    B.  22
    C.  27
    D.  31
    E.  34

2.  **Simplify the following expression: $(-3x^2 y)^2 (2xy)^3$**

    F.  $12x^4 y^5$

    G.  $18 x^7 y^5$

    H.  $48 x^8 y^6$

    J.  $54 x^5 y^8$

    K.  $72 x^7 y^5$

3.  **Let f(x) = $\dfrac{-2x^2}{x+3}$. What is the value of f(-1)?**

    A.  -2
    B.  -1
    C.  0
    D.  1
    E.  2

4.  **What is the slope of a line perpendicular to $5x + 8y = 17$?**

    F.  $\dfrac{8}{5}$

    G.  $\dfrac{5}{8}$

    H.  The slope is undefined.

    J.  $-\dfrac{5}{8}$

    K.  $-\dfrac{8}{5}$

5. The following graph represents the number of children living in the Gutierrez family. In what year did the Gutierrez family have twins?

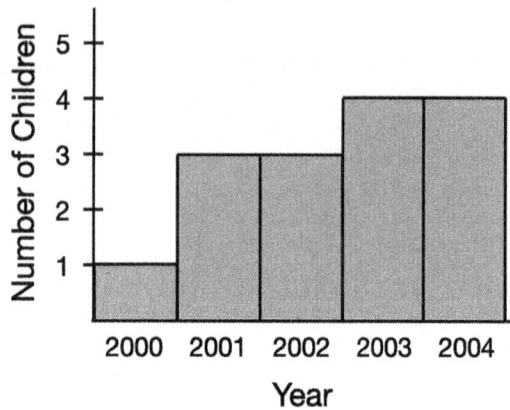

A. 2000
B. 2001
C. 2002
D. 2003
E. The family did not have twins in any year.

6. What is $14.058 + 261.12 + 0.006$ rounded to the nearest hundredth?

F. 300.00
G. 275.19
H. 275.184
J. 275.18
K. 275

7. If 17 tomato plants produce 127 tomatoes, then how many tomatoes will be produced by 9 plants (round your answer to nearest whole number)?

A. 64
B. 65
C. 66
D. 67
E. 68

8. For what value(s) of x is the equation |2x − 3| = 12 true?

F. x = 7.5 only
G. x = -4.5 only
H. x = 7.5 and x = -4.5
J. x = -7.5 and x = 4.5
K. All real numbers make this equation true.

**9. What type of triangle is pictured below?**

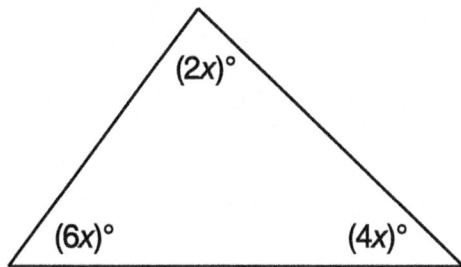

    A. Obtuse scalene
    B. Equilateral
    C. Acute isosceles
    D. 45-45-90
    E. 30-60-90

**10. If a, b, and c are positive integers such that ab = 12 and bc = 48 and c = 16, what is the value of a?**

    F. 4
    G. 6
    H. 12
    J. 16
    K. 24

**11. Jamie needs to earn an 80% average to receive a 'B' grade for a certain class. If all three of her tests are equally weighted and she scored 75% and 65% respectively on the first two tests, what must Jamie score on her final test to earn an 80% for the class?**

    A. 85
    B. 90
    C. 95
    D. 100
    E. 110

**12. What is the area of the unshaded portion of the circle?**

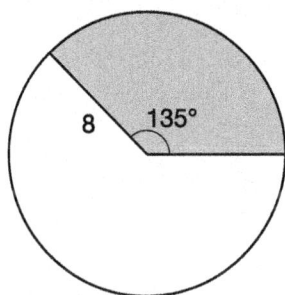

    F. $8\pi$
    G. $16\pi$
    H. $24\pi$
    J. $36\pi$
    K. $40\pi$

**13. Which expression is equivalent to $\dfrac{x^3-1}{x^2-1}$?**

A. $x$

B. $x-1$

C. $\dfrac{x+1}{x-1}$

D. $\dfrac{x-1}{x^2-x+1}$

E. $\dfrac{x^2+x+1}{x+1}$

**14. What are the x-intercepts of the circle with the equation $x^2+y^2=169$?**

F. (26,0), (-13,0)
G. (0,13), (-13,0)
H. (13,0), (0,-13)
J. (26,0), (0,-26)
K. (13,0), (-13,0)

**15. The cost of a suit is increased by 20% in week 1 and then has its cost reduced by 10% in week 2. What percent of the original price is the cost of the shirt in week 2?**

A. 8%
B. 80%
C. 96%
D. 108%
E. 180%

**16. $\angle A$ and $\angle B$ form a linear pair. If the measure of $\angle A$ is (x + 10)° and the measure of $\angle B$ is (3x – 50)°, what is the measure of the larger angle?**

F. 125°
G. 115°
H. 55°
J. 55°
K. 47.5°

**17. If $9^{3x+6}=27^{x-4}$, what is the value of x?**

A. -12
B. -8
C. 2
D. 8
E. 12

**18. Let x and y vary inversely. If x = 3 when y = 12, then what is the value of y when x = 8?**

    F.  4.5
    G.  6
    H.  8
    J.  12
    K.  18

**19. Which value for *s* makes the following expression a trinomial square?**

$$x^2 + 7x + s$$

    A.  7

    B.  14

    C.  $\dfrac{49}{4}$

    D.  21

    E.  $\dfrac{49}{2}$

**20. Jean receives an allowance of $8.00 per week as well as $3.50 for each chore she does around her home. If *e* represents her weekly earnings and *c* represents the number of weekly chores she does, which equation represents her weekly income?**

    F.  $8 = 3.5e + c$
    G.  $c = 3.5e + 8$
    H.  $e = 8c + 3.5$
    J.  $e = 4.5c$
    K.  $e = 3.5c + 8$

**21. What is the measure of x?**

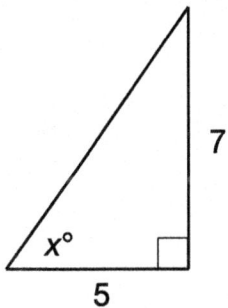

    A.  58.1°
    B.  56.2°
    C.  54.5°
    D.  48.2°
    E.  47.4°

**22. What is the equation, in standard form, of the line pictured in the graph?**

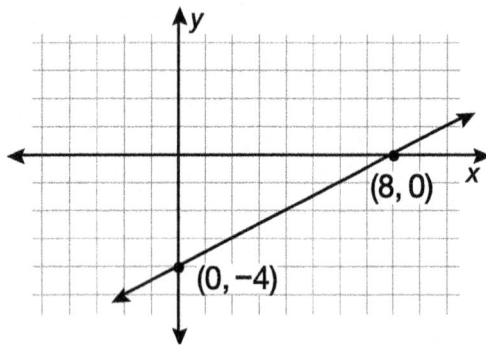

F. $2x - y = 8$

G. $x - 2y = 8$

H. $2x + y = 8$

J. $x + 2y = 8$

K. $y = \dfrac{1}{2}x - 4$

**23. Which of the following statements about prime numbers is false?**

A. The only even prime number is 2.

B. The product of two prime numbers is never a prime number.

C. 1 is not a prime number.

D. The sum of two prime numbers can never be a prime number.

E. If $a$ and $b$ are prime numbers and $a > b$, then $\dfrac{a}{b} > 1$

**24. If $2x - 5y = 17$ and $3x + 4y = -9$, what is the value of $4x - 7y$?**

F. 51

G. 27

H. 25

J. 17

K. -11

**25. A bag contains 7 white marbles, 6 red marbles, and 4 green marbles. If marbles are drawn from the bag without replacement, what is the probability of drawing a green marble and then a white marble?**

A. $\dfrac{231}{272}$

B. $\dfrac{13}{17}$

C. $\dfrac{11}{17}$

D. $\dfrac{11}{68}$

E. $\dfrac{7}{68}$

**26. A rectangle has a width measuring 5 inches and a diagonal measuring 13 inches. In square inches, what is the area of the rectangle?**

F. 17
G. 28
H. 34
J. 60
K. 65

**27. What is the lowest common denominator of the fractions $\dfrac{5}{8}, \dfrac{1}{6}$, and $\dfrac{7}{10}$?**

A. 120
B. 100
C. 80
D. 60
E. 24

**28. Express 72% as a fraction in lowest terms.**

F. $\dfrac{18}{25}$

G. $\dfrac{72}{100}$

H. $\dfrac{36}{50}$

J. $\dfrac{16}{50}$

K. $\dfrac{3}{4}$

**29. If sin A = $\dfrac{9}{10}$, what is the value of $\dfrac{\sin A}{\csc A}$?**

A. 0.81
B. 0.76
C. 0.66
D. 0.48
E. 0.36

**30. What is the midpoint of the segment with endpoints having coordinates (7,6) and (-4,5)?**

    F.  (7,4.5)
    G.  (-28,30)
    H.  (1.5,5.5)
    J.  (-0.5,2.5)
    K.  (-3.5,6)

**31. For large banquets, a restaurant charges an 18% gratuity. If a meal costs $220.00, what is the cost of the meal including the gratuity?**

    A.  $262.20
    B.  $259.60
    C.  $238.00
    D.  $39.60
    E.  $26.90

**32. Which of the following is a factor of $(r + 2)(2r - 5) = 0$?**

    F.  5
    G.  3
    H.  $\dfrac{5}{2}$
    J.  2
    K.  $\dfrac{-5}{2}$

**33. Which expression will give the slope of the line containing (6,-2) and (-3,7) in a standard coordinate (x,y) plane?**

    A.  $\dfrac{6-(-3)}{-2-7}$

    B.  $\dfrac{6-(-2)}{-3-7}$

    C.  $\dfrac{7-(-2)}{-3-6}$

    D.  $\dfrac{6-7}{-2-(-3)}$

    E.  $\dfrac{-3-6}{7-(-2)}$

**34.** $-|-7| \times |7| = ?$

    F.  49
    G.  14
    H.  0
    J.  -14
    K.  -49

**35. What is the value of** $\log_3 81$ **?**

    A.  4
    B.  9
    C.  27
    D.  84
    E.  243

**36. The x or y coordinate of a point in a standard coordinate plane is negative. In which quadrant(s) could the point lie?**

    F.  II or IV
    G.  II only
    H.  III only
    J.  I or II
    K.  IV only

**37. What is the slope of a line that is parallel to** $y = -\dfrac{x}{2} + 7$ **?**

    A.  $\dfrac{13}{2}$
    B.  2
    C.  $\dfrac{1}{2}$
    D.  0
    E.  $-\dfrac{1}{2}$

**38. What is the equation of the circle graphed below?**

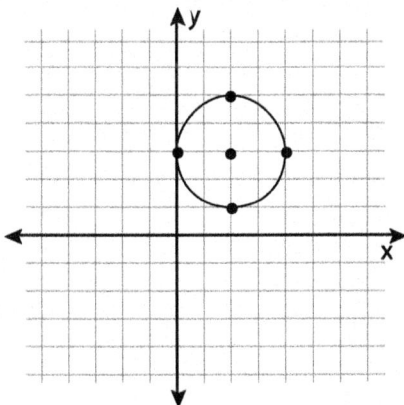

F. $(x+2)^2 + (y+3)^2 = 4$

G. $(x-2)^2 + (y-3)^2 = 4$

H. $(x-2)^2 - (y-3)^2 = 4$

J. $(x-2)^2 + (y+3)^2 = 4$

K. $x^2 + y^2 = 8$

**39. What is the surface area of a cube with a surface area measuring 216 cubic inches?**

A. 216 square inches
B. 144 square inches
C. 27 square inches
D. 36 square inches
E. 6 square inches

**40. In the standard (x, y) coordinate plane, how many times does the graph of**
$y = (x-9)(2x+3)(x+2)(2x-3)$ intersect the x-axis?

F. 8
G. 7
H. 6
J. 5
K. 4

**41. In parallelogram ABCD, if m $\angle DAB = (2x+10)°$, and m $\angle ABC = (4x+20)°$, what is the value of x?**

A. 120
B. 80
C. 60
D. 45
E. 25

**42. What is the new price of a shirt that was priced at $18.00 if it is being sold at a 25% discount?**

F. $13.50
G. $13.25
H. $12.00
J. $10.00
K. $8.00

**43. What is the area of a square with a diagonal measuring 6 inches?**

A. 24 square inches
B. 18 square inches
C. $6\sqrt{2}$ square inches
D. $3\sqrt{3}$ square inches
E. $3\sqrt{2}$ square inches

**44.** If $\sqrt[3]{x-1} - 3 = 2$, what is the value of x?

    F.  26
    G.  82
    H.  126
    J.  170
    K.  217

**45. The product of a prime number and a composite number is:**

    A.  Always prime.
    B.  Composite, except when the prime number is 2.
    C.  Prime, except when the prime number is 2.
    D.  Always composite.
    E.  Neither prime nor composite.

**46. A square photograph is mounted in a square frame. If the photograph is 8 inches on a side and the frame is 2 inches wide, what is the area of the frame?**

    F.  36 square inches
    G.  48 square inches
    H.  60 square inches
    J.  80 square inches
    K.  108 square inches

**47. What is the value of m in the triangle below?**

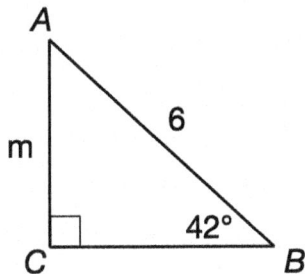

    A.  4.01
    B.  4.84
    C.  6.22
    D.  6.89
    E.  7.08

**48.** $\sqrt{179}$ **lies between what two whole numbers?**

    F.  9 and 10
    G.  10 and 11
    H.  11 and 12
    J.  12 and 13
    K.  13 and 14

49. What is the circumference of a circle with an area equal to $\dfrac{49}{4}\pi$ ?

    A.   $70\,\pi$

    B.   $28\,\pi$

    C.   $14\,\pi$

    D.   $7\,\pi$

    E.   $\dfrac{7}{2}\pi$

50. Which of the following must be added to $4x^2 + 2x - 7$ to get a sum of $2x^2 - 5x + 3$?

    F.   $2x^2 + 7x - 10$

    G.   $-2x^2 - 7x + 10$

    H.   $6x^4 + 3x^2 + 10$

    J.   $6x^2 + 3x + 10$

    K.   $8x^4 - 10x + 21$

51. Which of the following is a factor of $2x^2 + 2x - 112$?

    A.   2x²

    B.   (x + 8)

    C.   (x + 7)

    D.   (x − 8)

    E.   (x − 14)

52. A man whose height measures 6 feet casts a shadow 8 feet long. How tall is an adjacent building that casts an 18 foot shadow?

    F.   13.5 feet

    G.   16.25 feet

    H.   18 feet

    J.   27 feet

    K.   32.25 feet

53. If the scale on a map is 1 inch = 17 miles, what is the actual distance between two cities that are 6 inches apart on the map?

    A.   17

    B.   34

    C.   68

    D.   85

    E.   102

54. What regular polygon has an exterior angle that measures 45°?

    F.   Decagon

    G.   Octagon

    H.   Heptagon

    J.   Hexagon

    K.   Pentagon

**55.** If x = -3 and y = 2, what is the value of $2x^2 y - 3x^3 y^2$ ?

    A.  -288
    B.  -144
    C.  288
    D.  360
    E.  1080

**56.** Which of the following graphs is the solution set of 2x – 6 > 2?

    F.

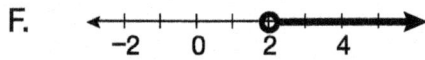

    G.

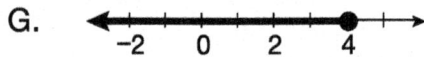

    H.

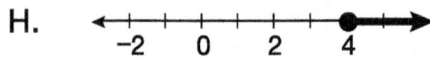

    J.

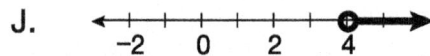

    K.

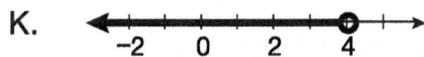

**57.** What does csc $\theta$ (tan $\theta$ ) =?

    A.  1
    B.  sin $\theta$
    C.  cot $\theta$
    D.  cos $\theta$
    E.  sec $\theta$

**58.** If the slope of a line containing the points (7,4) and (x,11) is $-\dfrac{1}{2}$ , what is the value of x?

    F.  -7
    G.  -3
    H.  0
    J.  3
    K.  7

**59.** If the base of a parallelogram is (x – 4) units and the height is (2x + 3) units, what is the area of the parallelogram?

    A.  2
    B.  2x
    C.  3x – 7
    D.  $2x^2 - 5x - 12$
    E.  $\dfrac{1}{2}(2x^2 - 5x - 12)$

**60. What is the distance on a standard coordinate plane (x,y) between the points** (-6,4) and (-1,9)?

    F.  50
    G.  25
    H.  $5\sqrt{2}$
    J.  5
    K.  $2\sqrt{5}$

# MATHEMATICS PRACTICE TEST 1 ANSWER KEY

| | |
|---|---|
| 1. C | 31. B |
| 2. K | 32. H |
| 3. B | 33. C |
| 4. F | 34. K |
| 5. B | 35. A |
| 6. J | 36. F |
| 7. D | 37. E |
| 8. H | 38. G |
| 9. E | 39. A |
| 10. F | 40. K |
| 11. D | 41. E |
| 12. K | 42. F |
| 13. E | 43. B |
| 14. K | 44. H |
| 15. D | 45. D |
| 16. G | 46. J |
| 17. B | 47. A |
| 18. F | 48. K |
| 19. C | 49. D |
| 20. K | 50. G |
| 21. C | 51. B |
| 22. G | 52. F |
| 23. D | 53. E |
| 24. H | 54. G |
| 25. E | 55. D |
| 26. J | 56. J |
| 27. A | 57. E |
| 28. F | 58. F |
| 29. A | 59. D |
| 30. H | 60. H |

# MATHEMATICS PRACTICE TEST 1 RATIONALES

### 1. Answer: C. 27
Solve for x in the first equation, then substitute that value in the subsequent expression:

$4x - 3 = 13$

$4x = 16$

$x = 4$

$5(4) + 7 = 27$

### 2. Answer: K. $72x^7y^5$
Simplify each parentheses separately. When raising one power to another, remember to multiply the exponents. For example, $(x^2)^3 = x^{2\times3} = x^6$.

$(-3x^2y)^2 = 9x^4y^2$

$(2xy)^3 = 8x^3y^3$

When multiplying like terms, add the exponents. For example, $x^2 \times x^3 = x^{2+3} = x^5$.

$(9x^4y^2)(8x^3y^3) = 72x^7y^5$

### 3. Answer: B. -1
The *f(x)* means "the function of x". To find the f(-1), the "function of -1", substitute -1 for each x in the function:

$$\frac{-2(-1)^2}{-1+3} = \frac{-2}{2} = -1$$

### 4. Answer: F. $\frac{8}{5}$
The equation $5x + 8y = 17$ is in the standard form of a line. Lines that are perpendicular have slopes that are the opposite reciprocals of one another. To identify the slope of $5x + 8y = 17$, transform the line from standard form to slope-intercept form (y = mx + b).

$5x + 8y = 17$

$8y = -5x + 17$

$y = -\frac{5}{8}x + \frac{17}{8}$

Thus, if the slope of the first line is $-\frac{5}{8}$, then the slope of a line perpendicular to that line is $\frac{8}{5}$.

**5. Answer: B. 2001**
In 2000, the family had one child in the family. In 2001, there were three children. Thus, the Gutierrez family added two more children, twins, in 2001.

**6. Answer: J. 275.18**
$$14.058 + 261.12 + 0.006 = 275.184$$

The number in the hundredth's place is 8. If the number to its immediate right is 5 or larger, the number is rounded to the next larger number. However, since the number to its right is 4, the 8 does not increase, leaving 275.18.

**7. Answer: D. 67**
A comparison of the number of plants to tomatoes is called a ratio. When two ratios are equivalent, the resulting equation is called a proportion. Use a proportion in the form of:

$$\frac{plants}{tomatoes} = \frac{plants}{tomatoes}:$$

$$\frac{17}{127} = \frac{9}{x}$$

Cross-multiply and solve for x:

$$17x = 1,143$$
$$x = 67.24$$

Rounded to the nearest whole number, 9 plants will produce 67 tomatoes.

**8. Answer: H. x = 7.5 and x = -4.5**
The symbol "| |" means the absolute value. The absolute value of a number is its distance from zero. For example |6| = 6 and |-6| = 6.

|2x – 3| = 12 means $2x - 3 = 12$ and $2x - 3 = -12$.

| | |
|---|---|
| $2x - 3 = 12$ | $2x - 3 = -12$ |
| $2x = 15$ | $2x = -9$ |
| $x = 7.5$ | $x = -4.5$ |

**9. Answer: E. 30-60-90**
Since the sum of the angles in a triangle equals 180°, add the angles and set their sum equal to 180°.

$$6x + 4x + 2x = 180$$
$$12x = 180$$
$$x = 15$$

Substitute 15 for x in each angle:

$6 \times 15 = 90$

$4 \times 15 = 60$

$2 \times 15 = 30$

The triangle is a special right triangle called a 30-60-90 triangle.

**10. Answer: F. 4**
Substitute 16 for c:

$16b = 48$

$b = 3$

Substitute 3 for b:

$3a = 12$

$a = 4$

**11. Answer: D. 100**
To find the average of the three tests, let x equal the final test score:

$\dfrac{75 + 65 + x}{3} = 80$

$\dfrac{140 + x}{3} = 80$

$140 + x = 240$

$x = 100$

**12. Answer: K. 40 $\pi$**
Use the formula Area = $\pi r^2$ to find the area of the entire circle:

Area = $\pi(8)^2 = 64\pi$

Since the shaded area represents 135º, then the unshaded area represents 225º of the circle because 360 – 135 = 225 (The number of degrees in a circle is 360).

To find the area of the unshaded portion of the circle, multiply the circle's area by $\dfrac{225}{360}$ :

$64\pi(\dfrac{225}{360}) = 40\pi$

**13. Answer: E.** $\dfrac{x^2 + x + 1}{x + 1}$

The quantity in the numerator is called the difference of cubes. It factors using the model $a^3 - b^3 = (a - b)(a^2 + ab + b^2)$. The quantity in the numerator is called the difference of squares. It factors using the model $a^2 - b^2 = (a + b)(a - b)$.

Factor the numerator and denominator and divide common factors:

$$\frac{x^3 - 1}{x^2 - 1} =$$

$$\frac{(x - 1)(x^2 + x + 1)}{(x + 1)(x - 1)} =$$

$$\frac{x^2 + x + 1}{x + 1}$$

**14. Answer: K. (13,0), (-13,0)**
To find the x-intercepts of a graph, let y = 0. To find the y-intercepts of a graph, let x = 0.

Let y = 0 to find the x-intercepts:

$$x^2 + (0)^2 = 169$$

$$x^2 = 169$$

$$x = \pm 13$$

The x-intercepts are (13,0) and (-13,0).

**15. Answer: D. 108%**
Suppose the suit cost $100. The 20% price increase in the cost of the suit elevates the price to $120 because:

100 + (0.20)(100) = 120

After the 10% price decrease in week 2, the new cost of the suit is $108 because:

120 − (0.1)(120) = 108.

108 is 108% of 100

**16. Answer: G. 115°**
A linear pair is a pair of adjacent supplementary angles. The sum of two supplementary angles is 180°. Since the sum of the measures of the angles is 180°, add both measures and set them equal to 180:

$$(x+10)+(3x-50)=180$$

$$4x-40=180$$

$$4x=220$$

$$x=55$$

The measure of $\angle B$, the larger angle, is (3)(55) – 50 = 115°. The measure of $\angle A$ is 180 – 115 = 65°

**17. Answer: B. -8**
If $7^x=7^4$, we know x = 4 because the bases, 7, are the same. In the problem $9^{3x+6}=27^{x-4}$, we cannot set the exponents equal to one another because the bases, 9 and 27, are not equivalent. Thus, we need to convert each expression to base 3:

$$9^{3x+6}=27^{x-4}$$

$$(3^2)^{3x+6}=(3^3)^{x-4}$$

$$3^{6x+12}=3^{3x-12}$$

$$6x+12=3x-12$$

$$3x=-24$$

$$x=-8$$

**18. Answer: F. 4.5**
Numbers vary inversely when their product equals some constant, *k*. Use the model xy = k for inverse variation.

(3)(12) = k
k = 36
8y = 36
y = 4.5

**19. Answer: C. $\dfrac{49}{4}$**

A trinomial is an expression with three unlike terms. A trinomial is a square when it is in the form of $(a+b)^2 = a^2+2ab+b^2$. To make $x^2+7x+s$ a trinomial square, it is necessary to complete the square. Multiply the *b* term, 7, by $\dfrac{1}{2}$ and square the product:

$$x^2+7x+(7\times\frac{1}{2})^2$$

$$x^2+7x+\frac{49}{4}$$

**20. Answer: K.** $e = 3.5c + 8$
Jean's weekly earnings include the weekly allowance of $8.00 and $3.50 for each chore she does. Thus the equation $e = 3.5c + 8$ represents her total earnings in any week.

**21. Answer: C. 54.5°**
Given that the sides opposite and adjacent of x are known, use the tangent to calculate the measure of x.

$$\tan^{-1}(\frac{7}{5}) = 54.5°$$

In most calculators, $\tan^{-1}$ can be found by hitting the second (or inverse) button and then the tangent (tan) button. Make sure your calculator is set to the **degree** mode.

**22. Answer: G.** $x - 2y = 8$
Find the equation of the line in slope-intercept form, $y = mx + b$, and then transform the equation into standard form, $Ax + By = C$ (remember A, B, and C must be integers and A > 0).

Find the slope using the formula $\dfrac{y_2 - y_1}{x_2 - x_1}$:

$$\frac{0 - (-4)}{8 - 0} = \frac{1}{2}$$

Inspecting the graph, we see the y-intercept is (0,-4), so we replace $b$ with -4:

$$y = \frac{1}{2}x - 4$$

Transform the equation into standard form:

$$y = \frac{1}{2}x - 4$$

$$-\frac{1}{2}x + y = -4$$

$$-2(-\frac{1}{2}x + y = -4)$$

$$x - 2y = 8$$

**23. Answer: D. The sum of two prime numbers can never be a prime number.**
A prime number has only two factors, 1 and itself. 5, 7, and 11 are examples of prime numbers. The sums of most prime numbers, such as 7 + 11 = 18, equal composite numbers (i.e., numbers that are not prime). However, there are some examples, such as 2 + 3 = 5, in which the sum of two prime numbers does equal another prime number.

**24. Answer: H. 25**
Solve for x and y using the elimination method:

$$2x - 5y = 17$$
$$3x + 4y = -9$$

Multiply the top equation by 4 and the bottom equation 5:

$$8x - 20y = 68$$
$$15x + 20y = -45$$

Add the two equations to arrive at:

$$23x = 23$$
$$x = 1$$

Substitute 1 for x in either equation:

$$2(1) - 5y = 17$$
$$-5y = 15$$
$$y = -3$$

Substitute x = 1 and y = -3 in the expression 4x – 7y:

$$4(1) - 7(-3) = 25$$

**25. Answer: E.** $\dfrac{7}{68}$

To find the probability of an event occurring, use the formula $\dfrac{favored\ outcomes}{all\ outcomes}$. Since there are 17 marbles, 4 of which are green, there is a $\dfrac{4}{17}$ probability of drawing a green marble on the first draw. With one marble removed, there are now 16 marbles left. There now is a $\dfrac{7}{16}$ probability of drawing a white marble on the second draw. To find the probability of both events occurring, multiply the probabilities of each:

$$\frac{4}{17} \times \frac{7}{16} = \frac{7}{68}$$

**26. Answer: J. 60**

The diagonal creates two right triangles in the rectangle. Use the Pythagorean Theorem, $a^2 + b^2 = c^2$, to calculate the base:

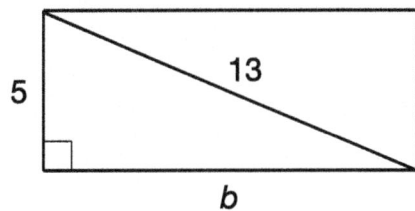

$$5^2 + b^2 = 13^2$$
$$25 + b^2 = 169$$
$$b^2 = 144$$
$$b = 12$$

Use the formula Area = length x width to find the area of the rectangle:

5 x 12 = 60

**27. Answer: A. 120**

Find the prime factorization of 8, 6, and 10:

$$8 = 2^3$$
$$6 = 2 \times 3$$
$$10 : 2 \times 5$$

Find the product of the largest power of each factor:

$$2^3 \times 3 \times 5 = 120$$

**28. Answer: F. $\dfrac{18}{25}$**

72% means $\dfrac{72}{100}$. Simplify $\dfrac{72}{100}$:

$$\frac{72}{100} \div \frac{4}{4} = \frac{18}{25}$$

**29. Answer: A. 0.81**

The cosecant and sin are reciprocal functions such that $cosecant\ (\text{csc})\theta = \dfrac{1}{\sin\theta}$. Thus the cosecant A

$= 1 \div \dfrac{9}{10} = \dfrac{10}{9}$.

$\dfrac{\sin A}{\csc A} = \dfrac{9}{10} \div \dfrac{10}{9} = \dfrac{9}{10} \times \dfrac{9}{10} = \dfrac{81}{100} = 0.81$

**30. Answer: H. (1.5, 5.5)**

Use the midpoint formula, $\dfrac{x_1 + x_2}{2}, \dfrac{y_1 + y_2}{2}$ to calculate the midpoint:

$\dfrac{7 + -4}{2}, \dfrac{6+5}{2} = (1.5, 5.5)$

**31. Answer: B. $259.60**

Express 18% as a decimal to facilitate calculation: 18% = 0.18

Find 18% of $220.00 and add it to $220.00:

$220 + (0.18)(220) = $220 + 39.60 = $259.60

**32. Answer: H. $\dfrac{5}{2}$**

Given that (r + 2)(2r – 5) = 0, then r + 2 = 0 or 2r – 5 = 0. Solving for r we find:

r = -2 or r = $\dfrac{5}{2}$. Selection H suggests that r = $\dfrac{5}{2}$.

**33. Answer: C. $\dfrac{7-(-2)}{-3-6}$**

The slope of a line connecting two known points is found by using the formula $\dfrac{y_2 - y_1}{x_2 - x_1}$. Although either

point can be deemed $(x_1, y_1)$, let (6,-2) be the first point and (-3, 7) be the second point.

Therefore, $\dfrac{y_2 - y_1}{x_2 - x_1} = \dfrac{7-(-2)}{-3-6}$

**34. Answer: K. -49**

The "| |" symbol means the "absolute value" of a quantity. The absolute value of a quantity represents the distance, expressed as a positive number, from 0.

$|-7| = 7$ and $-|-7| = -7$

$-|-7| \times |-7| = -7 \times 7 = -49$

**35. Answer: A. 4**

The expression $\log_3 81$, referred to as "log 3 of 81" means 3 to what power equals 81. Simplifying logarithms is easier when the logarithmic expression is rewritten in exponential form.

$\log_3 81 =$

$3^x = 81$

$3^x = 3^4$

$x = 4$

**36. Answer: F. II or IV**

The signs of the coordinate plane are listed below:

Plot two points, such as (3,-1) and (-3,1) and note that they lie in quadrants II and IV.

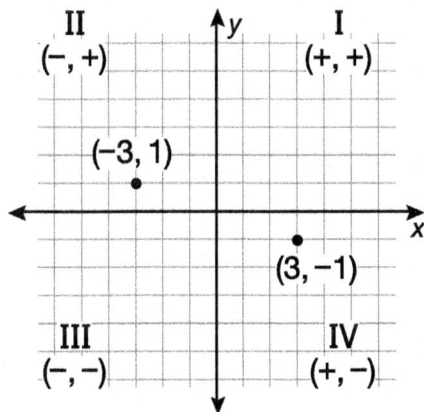

**37. Answer: E. $-\dfrac{1}{2}$**

Parallel lines have identical slopes. The slope of the line $y = -\dfrac{x}{2} + 7$ is $-\dfrac{1}{2}$. Therefore, the slope of a parallel line will also be $-\dfrac{1}{2}$.

**38. Answer: G.** $(x-2)^2 + (y-3)^2 = 4$

The equation of a circle in general form is $(x-h)^2 + (y-k)^2 = r^2$, where (h, k) is the center and r is the radius. The center of the circle is (2, 3) and the radius is 2. Therefore, the equation for the circle is $(x-2)^2 + (y-3)^2 = 4$.

**39. Answer: A. 216 square inches**
The volume of a cube is found by using the formula volume = s³, where s is a side, or edge, of the cube.

216 = s³

Take the cube root of both sides to find the length of one side:

$\sqrt[3]{216} = \sqrt[3]{s^3}$

$6 = s$

Find the area of one square face by using the formula area = s²:
Area = 6² = 36

A cube has six square faces, all with identical areas. Multiply the area of one square face by 6:
$36 \times 6 = 216$ square inches

**40. Answer: K. 4**
To find where a graph intersects the x-axis, find the x-intercept(s) of a graph by letting y = 0:

$0 = (x-9)(2x+3)(x+2)(2x-3)$

Solve for x by setting each quantity equal to 0:

| | |
|---|---|
| x – 9 = 0 | x-intercept is (9,0) |
| 2x + 3 = 0 | x-intercept is ($\frac{-3}{2}$,0) |
| x + 9 = 0 | x-intercept is (-9,0) |
| 2x – 3 = 0 | x-intercept is ($\frac{3}{2}$,0) |

There are four x-intercepts for the graph of $y = (x-9)(2x+3)(x+2)(2x-3)$.

**41. Answer: E. 25**

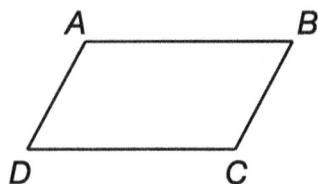

Consecutive angles in a parallelogram are supplementary which means their sum is 180º.

Add the measures of the angles and set that sum equal to 180:

$$4x + 20 + 2x + 10 = 180$$
$$6x + 30 = 180$$
$$6x = 150$$
$$x = 25$$

## 42. Answer: F. $13.50
Subtract 25% of $18.00 from $18.00 to find the sale price. Expressing 25% as a decimal, 0.25, facilitates calculation:

$18.00 – (18.00) (0.25) =
$18.00 – 4.50 = $13.50

## 43. Answer: B. 18 square inches
The area of a square is found by squaring the length of a side:

Area = s $^2$

Since the diagonal of a square creates two, congruent right triangles, use the Pythagorean Theorem, a$^2$ + b$^2$ = c$^2$, to find the length of a side:

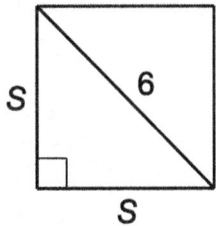

s$^2$ + s$^2$ = 6$^2$
2s$^2$ = 36
s$^2$ = 18

Note: The calculation to solve this problem can stop at this point. The area of a square is given by the formula A = s$^2$. Since s$^2$ = 18, the area of the square is 18.

## 44. Answer: H. 126
Solve for x by isolating the cube root:

$$\sqrt[3]{x-1} - 3 = 2$$
$$\sqrt[3]{x-1} = 5$$

Raise each side of the equation to the third power to eliminate the cube root:

$$\left(\sqrt[3]{x-1}\right)^3 = 5^3$$
$$x - 1 = 125$$
$$x = 126$$

### 45. Answer: D. Always composite.

A composite number has factors in addition to 1 and itself. The number 9 is composite, for example, because its factors are 1, 3, and 9. When a composite number is multiplied by a prime number, the product has more factors than the composite number.

Example: $9 \times 7 = 63$
The factors of 63 are 1, 3, 7, 9, 21, and 63.

### 46. Answer: J. 80 square inches

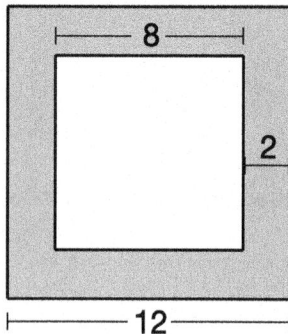

Find the area of the frame by subtracting the area of the smaller square from the area of the larger square. Remember to add the two-inch border to both sides of the smaller square.

2 + 8 + 2 = 12, so 12 is the length of the frame. 8 is the length of the photograph.

12² – 8² = 144 – 64 = 80 square inches

### 47. Answer: A. 4.01

Use trigonometric ratios to solve the problem. The expression **sohcahtoa** is a useful mnemonic to remember the three basic trigonometric ratios:

$$\sin = \frac{opposite\ side}{hypotenuse}$$

$$\cos ine = \frac{adjacent\ side}{hypotenuse}$$

$$tangent = \frac{opposite\ side}{adjacent\ side}$$

Since the angle opposite $m$ and the hypotenuse are known, use the sin function to find $m$:

$$\sin 42° = \frac{m}{6}$$

$$6\sin 42 = m$$

$$6(0.6691) = m$$

$$4.01 = m$$

Make sure your calculator is in the **degree** mode when calculating sin 42°.

## 48. Answer: K. 13 and 14

The "$\sqrt{\phantom{x}}$" symbol means the square root of a number. For any numbers $a$ and $b$, if $a^2 = b$, then $a$ is a square root of $b$.

$$\sqrt{169} = 13 \quad \sqrt{196} = 14$$

$$\sqrt{169} < \sqrt{179} < \sqrt{196}$$
$$13 < \sqrt{179} < 14$$

$\sqrt{179}$ lies between the whole numbers 13 and 14.

## 49. Answer: D. $7\pi$

The formula for the area of a circle is $A = \pi r^2$ where $r$ is the circle's radius.

Insert $\frac{49}{4}\pi$ for the area of the circle and solve for $r$.

$$\frac{49}{4}\pi = \pi r^2$$

$$r^2 = \frac{49}{4}$$

$$r = \frac{7}{2}$$

The circumference of a circle is found by using the formula $C = 2\pi r$:

$$C = 2(\frac{7}{2})\pi = 7\pi$$

## 50. Answer: G. $-2x^2 - 7x + 10$

Subtract $4x^2 + 2x - 7$ from $2x^2 - 5x + 3$ to find the missing addend:

$$(2x^2 - 5x + 3) - (4x^2 + 2x - 7) = -2x^2 - 7x + 10$$

**51. Answer: B. (x + 8)**

Factor $2x^2 + 2x - 112$ completely by first extracting the greatest common factor (GCF):

$$2x^2 + 2x - 112 = 2(x^2 + x - 56)$$

Next, factor the expression $x^2 + x - 56$. Think of factors of -56 with a sum of 1, the coefficient of x:

$$8 \times (-7) = -56$$
$$8 + (-7) = 1$$

Thus, $2x^2 + 2x - 112$, factored completely, is 2(x + 8)(x – 7).

Choice B offers x + 8.

**52. Answer: F. 13.5 feet**

In the diagram shown below, the man and his shadow and the building and its shadow create similar triangles.

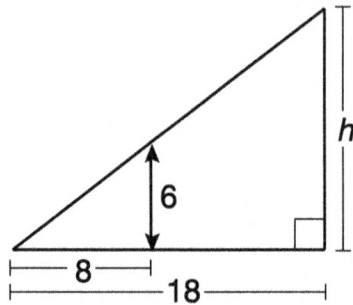

Similar triangles have congruent angles and corresponding lengths are proportional.

Find the height of the building using the proportion:

$$\frac{height}{shadow} = \frac{height}{shadow}:$$

$$\frac{6}{8} = \frac{x}{18}$$
$$8x = 108$$
$$x = 13.5$$

**53. Answer: E. 102**

Use the proportion $\dfrac{map\ distance}{actual\ distance} = \dfrac{map\ distance}{actual\ distance}$.

$$\frac{1}{17} = \frac{6}{x}$$
$$x = 102$$

**54. Answer: G. Octagon**

A regular polygon is a figure with corresponding sides that are proportional and angles that are congruent. Regardless of the number of sides in a regular polygon, the sum of the exterior angles is always 360º. To find the number of sides in a regular polygon with an exterior angle that measures 45º, divide 360 by 45:

$$360 \div 45 = 8$$

An eight-sided regular polygon is called an octagon.

**55. Answer: D. 360**

Substitute -3 and 2 for x and y respectively, then simplify:

$$2(-3)^2(2) - 3(-3)^3(2)^2$$
$$36 - (-324) = 360$$

**56. Answer: J.**

Solve the inequality and graph.

$$2x - 6 > 2$$
$$2x > 8$$
$$x > 4$$

When dividing or multiplying an inequality by a negative number, remember to reverse the direction of the inequality sign. Since the inequality was divided by 4, the inequality maintains its original direction.

The inequality x >4 means that any number greater than 4, but not equal to 4, is part of the solution set. The open circle at 4 demonstrates that 4 is not part of the solution set. The darkened number line to the right of 4 indicates that numbers greater than 4 *are* part of the solution set.

**57. Answer: E. sec $\theta$**

In addition to the sine (sin), cosine (cos), and tangent (tan) functions, there are reciprocal functions called the cotangent (cot), secant (sec), and cosecant (csc) functions. Although the tangent of an angle in a right triangle is the ratio of the opposite side to the adjacent side, it can also be thought of as the ratio of the sine to the cosine of that angle.

The reciprocal functions are as follow:

$$cot = \frac{1}{tan}$$

$$sec = \frac{1}{cos}$$

$$csc = \frac{1}{sin}$$

$$csc\,\theta\,(tan\,\theta) = \frac{1}{sin\,\theta}(\frac{sin\,\theta}{cos\,\theta}) = \frac{1}{cos\,\theta} = sec\,\theta$$

## 58. Answer: F. -7

The slope of a line connecting two points is found by using the formula $m = \frac{y_2 - y_1}{x_2 - x_1}$, where m represents the slope. Input the known data:

$y_2 = 4$

$y_1 = 11$

$x_2 = 7$

$x_1 = x$

$$\frac{4-11}{7-x} = -\frac{1}{2}$$

$$-\frac{7}{7-x} = -\frac{1}{2}$$

Cross-multiply the proportion and solve for x:

-1(7 – x) = -7(2)

-7 + x = -14

x = -7

## 59. Answer: D. $2x^2 - 5x - 12$

The area of a parallelogram is found by using the formula Area = base x height (A = bh). Multiply the base, (x – 4), by the height, (2x + 3).

$(x-4)(2x+3) =$

$2x^2 + 3x - 8x - 12 =$

$2x^2 - 5x - 12$

**60. Answer: H.** $5\sqrt{2}$

Use the distance formula to calculate the distance between two points in a coordinate plane.

$$\text{distance} = \sqrt{(x_1 - x_2)^2 + (y_1 - y_2)^2}$$

Input the known data and simplify.

$$\sqrt{(-6 - (-1)^2 + (4 - 9)^2}$$
$$\sqrt{25 + 25} =$$
$$\sqrt{50}$$

Simplify $\sqrt{50}$ by dividing out its largest square.

$$\sqrt{50} = \sqrt{25} \times \sqrt{2} = 5\sqrt{2}$$

# READING PRACTICE TEST 1

35 Minutes - 40 Questions

Directions: Each of the four reading passages in this section is followed by ten reading questions. Choose the best answer for each question.

## The House of Seven Gables

Excerpt from *The House of the Seven Gables* by Nathaniel Hawthorne, first published in 1851

Halfway down a by-street of one of our New England towns stands a rusty wooden house, with seven acutely peaked gables, facing towards various points of the compass, and a huge, clustered chimney in the midst. The street is Pyncheon Street; the house is the old Pyncheon House; and an elm-tree, of wide circumference, rooted before the door, is familiar to every town-born child by the
5    title of the Pyncheon Elm. On my occasional visits to the town aforesaid, I seldom failed to turn down Pyncheon Street, for the sake of passing through the shadow of these two antiquities,—the great elm-tree and the weather-beaten edifice.

The aspect of the venerable mansion has always affected me like a human <u>countenance</u>, bearing
10    the traces not merely of outward storm and sunshine, but expressive also, of the long lapse of mortal life, and accompanying vicissitudes that have passed within. Were these to be worthily recounted, they would form a narrative of no small interest and instruction, and possessing, moreover, a certain remarkable unity, which might almost seem the result of artistic arrangement. But the story would include a chain of events extending over the better part of two centuries, and,
15    written out with reasonable amplitude, would fill a bigger folio volume, or a longer series of duodecimos, than could prudently be appropriated to the annals of all New England during a similar period. It consequently becomes imperative to make short work with most of the traditionary lore of which the old Pyncheon House, otherwise known as the House of the Seven Gables, has been the theme. With a brief sketch, therefore, of the circumstances amid which the foundation of the house
20    was laid, and a rapid glimpse at its quaint exterior, as it grew black in the prevalent east wind,— pointing, too, here and there, at some spot of more verdant mossiness on its roof and wall,—we shall commence the real action of our tale at an epoch not very remote from the present day. Still, there will be a connection with the long past—a reference to forgotten events and personages, and to manners, feelings, and opinions, almost or wholly obsolete—which, if adequately translated to
25    the reader, would serve to illustrate how much of the old material goes to make up the freshest novelty of human life. Hence, too, might be drawn a weighty lesson from the little-regarded truth, that the act of the passing generation is the germ which may and must produce good or evil fruit in a far-distant time; that, together with the seed of the merely temporary crop, which mortals term expediency, they inevitably sow the acorns of a more enduring growth, which may darkly
30    overshadow their posterity.

The House of the Seven Gables, antique as it now looks, was not the first habitation erected by civilized man on precisely the same spot of ground. Pyncheon Street formerly bore the humbler appellation of Maule's Lane, from the name of the original occupant of the soil, before whose
35    cottage-door it was a cow-path. A natural spring of soft and pleasant water—a rare treasure on the sea-girt peninsula where the Puritan settlement was made—had early induced Matthew Maule to build a hut, shaggy with thatch, at this point, although somewhat too remote from what was then the centre of the village. In the growth of the town, however, after some thirty or forty years, the site covered by this rude hovel had become exceedingly desirable in the eyes of a prominent and
40    powerful personage, who asserted plausible claims to the proprietorship of this and a large adjacent tract of land, on the strength of a grant from the legislature. Colonel Pyncheon, the claimant, as we gather from whatever traits of him are preserved, was characterized by an iron energy of purpose. Matthew Maule, on the other hand, though an obscure man, was stubborn in the defence of what he considered his right; and, for several years, he succeeded in protecting the

45    acre or two of earth which, with his own toil, he had hewn out of the primeval forest, to be his garden ground and homestead. No written record of this dispute is known to be in existence. Our acquaintance with the whole subject is derived chiefly from tradition. It would be bold, therefore, and possibly unjust, to venture a decisive opinion as to its merits; although it appears to have been at least a matter of doubt, whether Colonel Pyncheon's claim were not unduly stretched, in order to
50    make it cover the small metes and bounds of Matthew Maule. What greatly strengthens such a suspicion is the fact that this controversy between two ill-matched antagonists—at a period, moreover, laud it as we may, when personal influence had far more weight than now—remained for years undecided, and came to a close only with the death of the party occupying the disputed soil. The mode of his death, too, affects the mind differently, in our day, from what it did a century and a
55    half ago. It was a death that blasted with strange horror the humble name of the dweller in the cottage, and made it seem almost a religious act to drive the plough over the little area of his habitation, and obliterate his place and memory from among men.

Old Matthew Maule, in a word, was executed for the crime of witchcraft.

1. **From this passage the reader can infer that the narrator of the story is:**

   A.  A long-time resident of the town.
   B.  A onetime resident of the town who often returns to visit.
   C.  A person who has never resided in the town but lives in close proximity.
   D.  An individual who has never been to the town but has heard many stories about it.

2. **When the narrator describes the house and likens it to a human *countenance* (line 9), this is likely to mean:**

   F.  The house is built like a human face with windows resembling eyes and gables resembling ears and a nose.
   G.  The house has a weathered exterior that reflects not only the storms of nature but the battles of those who have lived in it.
   H.  The seven gables on the house, from which the story was named, can each be counted on to tell a separate tale from when it was built.
   J.  The house looks like it is haunted with the ghosts of past residents.

3. **According to the passage, the narrator is likely basing his retelling of the story on which of the following sources?**

   A.  Early and public court transcripts from the Salem witch trials.
   B.  Legal records from the land dispute between Matthew Maule and Colonel Pyncheon.
   C.  Stories passed down among the townspeople through the generations.
   D.  The biography of Matthew Maule, written by a descendant to clear his family name.

4. **Summarizing the description of the Pyncheon House, the narrator generalizes that:**

   F.  The house is from a bygone era and is not particularly unique in its construction or countenance.
   G.  Despite the interesting countenance of the Pyncheon House, the elm tree in front is the most significant part of the property.
   H.  The house and its circumstances are of great interest and unique among houses in New England.
   J.  The character of the house evokes stories from the time of its construction to the present day.

**5. As a literary tool, author Nathaniel Hawthorne uses the narrator's long description of the Pyncheon house as:**

    A. A simple way to discuss the setting where the story takes place.
    B. A way to get the reader to think about how each house has its own story to tell.
    C. A method of introducing the narrator to the reader.
    D. A way of creating an interesting and unifying character in the story that is also the tale's setting for its human characters.

**6. Which trait of the original Maule property likely made it so desirable to Colonel Pyncheon?**

    F. The unique and exquisite seven gables that adorned the exterior of the house.
    G. Its quiet location outside of the village center.
    H. The large and bountiful garden that covered the acreage.
    J. The natural spring that was within the natural borders of the property.

**7. The history of the Pyncheon House begins with:**

    A. A dispute between a military officer and a farmer over property rights.
    B. A farmer who has found a source of fresh water on a wooded hill.
    C. Matthew Maule being accused of witchcraft.
    D. The Puritans arriving in New England and taking over the coastal land.

**8. As the narrator confides to the reader, the character of Colonel Pyncheon:**

    F. Was a man who was granted the land that included Matthew Maule's claim.
    G. Was a heroic man who felt it best that the land not belong to witches.
    H. Was a greedy man who saw good land and was going to have it by any possible means.
    J. Was in the right place at the right time and the fortune of Matthew Maule's death allowed Pyncheon to finally purchase Maule's land.

**9. By reading this passage it may be inferred that, considering the charge of witchcraft:**

    A. Matthew Maule was not a witch and he was falsely accused in order for another to confiscate his land.
    B. Matthew Maule was such a strange character that others in the village could not help but to think him a witch.
    C. Witches were not uncommon in the area and the Puritans routinely persecuted them.
    D. The House of the Seven Gables had a history of magical residents, beginning with the witch, Matthew Maule.

**10. The time period between the actual events of the passage and the retelling of the story is best described by which of the following?**

    F. The events of the story occurred within the narrator's lifetime.
    G. The events of the story occurred at least 150 years before the narrator's retelling.
    H. The events of the story occurred 30-40 years before the passage was written.
    J. The events of the story occurred during the American Revolution.

## Improvisational Theatre

"O.k., for this scene our actors will use a trigger word! If they're off stage when they hear the trigger word, they need to come on stage. If they're on stage, no matter what is happening, they need to leave." The improvisational comedy troupe, "Plan B" is playing a local venue and setting the scene for the next skit, called *Entrances & Exits*. The audience contributes the trigger words of *wow*,
5 *shiny*, and *celery* to the three participating actors. An audience member also gives the situation: raking leaves. The first actor begins to pantomime the annual autumn chore, speaking her thoughts out loud, building the tension until, weaving it into her monologue, she casually mentions the word *celery*. Suddenly another actor enters, jumping spread eagle onto the imaginary pile of leaves! The audience roars! What will happen during the next five minutes is anyone's guess, but it is certain to
10 be spontaneous, attention-grabbing, and hilarious!

When most people think about a comedy performance, they envision traditional stand-up: an audience sitting passively before a comedian who stands on the stage alone, microphone in hand, delivering jokes and extended monologues. On the surface, what may seem like a free-flowing and
15 spontaneous comedic performance is, in fact, carefully planned and pre-scripted. There is a tremendous amount of pressure on comedians to provide their audiences with an entertaining and humorous experience, not only for their own reputations but also for the sake of the venue in which they appear. Developing written routines in advance provides an opportunity to refine and perfect material, and increase chances for a successful performance in front of a live audience.
20

Yet, a lot of what makes a person laugh comes from the unexpected. A joke or situation is funny because it is unique and has never been experienced before. Hearing a joke more than once, no matter how amusing, lessens the surprise and the objective of the joke: laughter. For this reason one might have to wait several months to a year for a favorite stand-up comedian to come up with
25 material for a new show. However, one can go night after night to an improvisational performance and never see the same thing twice! Spontaneous and completely unpredictable, improvisational performances require a degree of comedic skill, instinct, and confidence that not all stand-up comedians feel comfortable with.

30 Improvisational comedy relies on the stimuli given off by random situations (often supplied by audience members one has never worked with before) and spontaneous action (at times, also provided by unfamiliar participants). Improvisational performers first learn and then perfect their craft by joining an *improv* group and practicing the techniques of successful improvisation as a member of a comedic team. Truly successful improv requires each performer to be attuned to their
35 fellow performers as they spontaneously co-create the characters, dialogue, plot, and action of the performance. The performers respond to each other's comedic prompts, following basic improvisational rules, but without any pre-scripted elements to the performance and no knowledge beforehand of exactly what their fellow performers are going to say. The performers literally don't know what will happen next, or how the performance will unfold until the action begins. This type of
40 creative flexibility and risk-taking is part of the thrill of watching an improvisational performance take place.

The audience is crucial to a successful improv performance. Suggestions from onlookers to start or guide the general content or theme of the performance allow for an interactive, rather than passive,
45 relationship with the audience and also 'proves' to the viewer that the performance is being created in a completely spontaneous manner. For example, the audience could supply the general setting for the scene by suggesting that it takes place at a shopping mall or a car dealership, or by suggesting that the performers are all complete strangers to each other. These imaginary constraints placed on the performance guide the improv performers as they develop their
50 characters and dialogue.

There are very few rules to improv, but the ones that do exist are critical for keeping the performance going. Perhaps the most important concept in improvisational theatre is the idea of making and accepting offers. Every word that is spoken and every action that is taken by a

55  performer is called an *offer*: an invitation to another performer for an appropriate, yet spontaneous, response. The offer also endows the other character with a given trait or creates a situational reality for them. In order to keep the action of the scene developing, performers are expected to accept each offer, no matter how ridiculous the offer may seem. What this means is that when one performer defines some aspect of the performance or of the other person's character, the other

60  performers have to accept and respond to that newly defined reality. For example, one character may say to another, "Why did you paint your car banana yellow?" The other performer has to respond directly to the new reality of owning a car that they recently painted bright yellow. In making their response, they are expected to create a new 'offer' that builds specifically on the earlier one; in this way the scene continues to move ahead, sometimes with uproarious results! For

65  example, the response might be, "Because, my dear, when it was broccoli green it clashed with your apple red hair!" This process of offer and accept forms the backbone of improvisational technique; each new piece of information added by the performers helps to refine the characters and the scene and move the performance ahead in a spontaneous, unscripted way.

70  It can take years of practice for performers to become skilled at and comfortable with improvisational performance. Two of the best known improv groups are *The Second City* and *The Groundlings*. Both of these groups have produced some of the best comedians of our time, including many of the original cast members of the hit comedy show *Saturday Night Live*. To witness a professional, comedic improv group perform can be an amazingly entertaining

75  experience and when it is done well, one really gets the sense of the skill, talent, and comedic courage involved in performing spontaneously before an audience. From Charlie Chaplin to Buster Keaton to the comedic performers of our own time, the evidence suggests there will always be a place for improvisational performance. While carefully scripted and planned performances do have their place and powerful impact, there will always be both performers and audiences who enjoy,

80  and even prefer, the sheer thrill of spontaneous creation!

**11. The tone of the passage can best be described as:**

    A. A solemn attempt to educate the reader about an art form that does not get much attention in the entertainment world.

    B. A scholarly description, with step-by-step instructions, of the methods of creating improvisational comedy.

    C. An enthusiastic attempt by the author to pass on to the reader an appreciation for the art of improvisational comedy.

    D. A resentful display of the author's preference for stand-up comedy and a methodical cataloging of the faults of improvisational comedy.

**12. The opening paragraph can best be described as:**

    F. Step-by-step instructions on how improvisational theater works.

    G. An explanation of the role of the audience in improvisational theater.

    H. A review of the comedy troupe "Plan B" in their recent performance *Entrances and Exits*.

    J. An example of improvisational performance in order to immediately grab the reader's attention.

**13. In comparing the stand-up comedian to the improv group, the author demonstrates:**

    A. That an improv group would stumble on stage without some degree of pre-scripted and pre-planned material.

    B. That the stand-up comedian relies mostly on spontaneous interaction with the audience for program ideas.

    C. That the stand-up comedian adheres to a carefully prepared routine that the improv group avoids.

    D. That the stand-up comedian and the improv group both rely on spontaneous interaction with their audiences in order to be successful.

**14. By paragraph 3, the author has expressed a clear opinion of stand-up comedians. This opinion is that:**

F.  Few stand-up comedians could become successful members of an improv comedy troupe.
G.  Any stand-up comedian could have success within an improvisational comedy troupe.
H.  Few improv comedy troupe players could make it as stand-up comedians.
J.  The venue where the performance is held is the most crucial part of the stand-up comedian's act.

**15. The passage notes that the techniques of improvisational comedy are best learned as a member of an improv group. The reason for this is that:**

A.  While the art of stand-up comedy can be learned in isolation, improvisational comedy can only be learned in a group environment.
B.  A skill-set as difficult and risk-taking as improvisational performance can only be learned by apprenticing with an established improv group.
C.  Some of the best comedians of our time have been trained in professional improv troupes such as *The Second City* and *The Groundlings*.
D.  The spontaneous nature of improvisational comedy requires performers to be keenly attuned to each other; this responsiveness can only be learned by doing.

**16. According to the passage, why do most traditional stand-up comedians write their material in advance?**

F.  Audiences often have to wait months, and sometimes up to a year, to see their favorite comedians and when they do so, they expect freshly written material.
G.  Developing pre-scripted routines allows them to perfect their material before performing it; this increases their chances for a successful performance.
H.  The audiences who attend traditional stand-up performances want perfected and refined material, not spontaneous performance.
J.  In order for jokes and dramatic monologues to be considered funny, they have to be carefully crafted in advance.

**17. In improv performances, the role of the audience is best described by which of the following?**

A.  The audience has only one job to do: sit back and enjoy the show!
B.  The audience members write parts of the routine before it is performed; in this way, the performance is collaboration between the audience and the performers.
C.  The audience often provides the structure and constraints within which the actors work.
D.  The audience is an active member of the performance, spontaneously adding dialog during natural pauses in the performance.

**18. The *'offer'* is one of the most critical concepts in improv comedy because:**

F.  The offer provides each character with traits that can be expounded upon in order to move the performance forward.
G.  The offer lets each performer know when it is their turn to contribute a line to the unfolding dialog.
H.  The offer allows each performer to select which character trait they want to endow their character with; they either accept or decline each offer made to them.
J.  Offers create boundaries for the actors and provide easy cues for actors to enter and leave the stage.

**19. Which of the following is an example of an 'offer' and an 'accept'?**

   A.  Performer 1: Why were you late to the horserace yesterday? Performer 2: What are you talking about? I've never been to a horserace in my life!
   B.  Performer 1: Why were you late to the horserace yesterday? Performer 2: I wasn't late! I came an hour early to switch the numbers on the horses.
   C.  Performer 1: Why were you late to the horserace yesterday? Performer 2: Because the cheap watch you gave me broke!
   D.  Performer 1: Why were you late to the horserace yesterday? Performer 2: Why are you always picking on me?

**20. According to the passage, the author feels the future of improv comedy is:**

   F.  Threatened by the popularity of traditional stand-up comedy, for which television has a special affinity.
   G.  Bright because there will always be people who are interested in creating and experiencing spontaneous art.
   H.  In danger due to the great length of time it takes to train professional-level improvisational comedians.
   J.  Bright, because improvisational performances result in higher-quality entertainment that traditional stand-up routines.

## The East Asian Shadow

China has been a <u>germinal</u> influence in East Asia culturally, economically, and politically. Korea, Japan, and Southeast Asia all can trace Confucianism, Buddhism, government and military structure, calligraphy, pottery, and even diet to the Middle Kingdom. Through trade, religious missions, invasion, and migration, East Asia has incurred the whims and missions of the Chinese
5   down through the centuries. In ancient times, China's massive influence upon her neighbors was in accordance with her geographic size but is China's regional influence still as powerful today? Do nations like Vietnam and South Korea still <u>kowtow</u> to the Dragon?

The Han emperor, Wudi, invaded Korea and set up a military colony in 108 B.C.E. This was the
10  first time Koreans came into contact with Confucian tradition and the ideas of Chinese government. Buddhist missionaries spread their teachings several hundred years later leading to Chinese words and written language permeating the Korean peninsula. From Korea, Japan encountered Chinese architecture, the idea of an all-powerful emperor, philosophy, and literacy. In the 700s, Japanese students studied in Tang dynasty China and brought back, along with ideas and plans for the
15  Japanese capital of Nara, Chinese language, fashion, and an elaborate tea ceremony. Chinese music and dance also spread throughout the Japanese court. Southeast Asia was manipulated by China through the spice trade as China controlled the vital Malacca and Sunda straits that commanded all sea routes to India. China also periodically invaded from the north into Annam (modern day Vietnam) and Thailand to take advantage of the plentiful rice paddies to feed its
20  armies and gargantuan labor force.

China's catastrophic encounter with western imperialism during the 19<sup>th</sup> century diverted its regional influence until after the Second World War when Communist forces, led by Mao Zedong, took over China in 1949. Except for the areas where European and American nations had strong
25  military bases (Japan and South Korea), nations like North Korea and Northern Vietnam also adopted Communist forms of government and, much to the chagrin of the West, stubbornly survived the Cold War of the mid-twentieth century with Chinese military and economic aid. After the death of Mao Zedong, the focus of the Chinese government was on raising personal income as well as personal consumption and, to this end, the farm collectives were broken up and the
30  peasant farmer was finally allowed to sell surplus production; in other words, to make a profit. Western corporations were allowed to invest in China as well. With the construction of many hydroelectric dams and expanded coal mining, the new infrastructure began to smooth the way for the Chinese agricultural and industrial sectors. The Chinese economy began to grow by an average of over 9% each year in the 1990s and with it, trade with its neighbors, among them South
35  Korea, Japan, and Vietnam.

Chinese students, who had been recently allowed to study overseas in Western universities, began to bring back new ideas and expertise to their homeland. Chinese technology and business practice became more competitive. Chinese SOEs (state owned enterprises) were allowed to be
40  sold and privatized. Many soon became profitable. By 2003, the Communist-style government of China passed legislation to protect private property rights. This prohibition against random government confiscation increased business incentive even further and, early in the first decade of the 21<sup>st</sup> century, China's economy boomed at an annual 10% growth rate. China's workforce was, during its recent economic rise, under-educated and very low-paid. Many foreign companies made
45  outlandish profits at the expense of the Chinese people. However, as the economy grew, China's government began to pass legislation to increase access to education, medical care, and old age benefits. China's middle class has been rapidly expanding and, with this new affluence, consumption of both Chinese and foreign products has soared.

50  China's colossal population and economy have sizeable needs. Its elephantine presence as a trade partner in East Asia creates endless opportunity for its neighbors. Japan and South Korea are in the top five of any category relating to trade with China; the Southeast Asian nations of Singapore, Taiwan, Malaysia, and Thailand are in the top ten. Vietnam is also a major trading partner and low-priced Chinese technology and cellphone products are in high demand and

                                                    

55  fulfilling a crucial need in the poorer countries of Indonesia and the Philippines. The amount of South Korean, Japanese, and Vietnamese students who are now studying in China has grown largely due to an <u>innate</u> interest in Chinese language and writing. However, regardless of any underlying reasons, the regional economic web has made Chinese music, movies, fashion, herbal medicine, automobiles, and household products ubiquitous in Asia.

60

Yet, because of China's gargantuan economic shadow there is also a global wariness of Chinese intentions. In order to manufacture the products to trade with its neighbors, China must procure petroleum resources from wherever it can around the planet and has established partnerships with governments that are not on good terms with western nations, such as Sudan and Iran. Also, in
65  order to trade freely with its neighbors, China has grown protective of its coastal waters in the East and South China Sea and, especially, the Strait of Taiwan. Politically, China still considers Taiwan, where many people are descendants of refugees from the 1949 Civil War, a rogue province and has publically acknowledged that military means will not be ruled out to someday bring Taiwan back into the mainland fold. Equally discomforting for the region is China's close relationship with
70  an unpredictable regime in North Korea that has flexed its muscles by sinking South Korean ships, firing missiles across the Japanese archipelago, and exporting nuclear technology to rogue nations.

China sees itself *not* as an ideologically driven nation, such as the democracy of the United States,
75  but as a nation with thousands of years of cultural power and solidity. China seeks to create the best opportunities for its people in the old Confucian perspective of the enlightened and educated ruler. For millennia, China has had to worry about border incursions by foreign powers. Today, China uses its economic, cultural, and military influences to create a symbiotic relationship with its neighbors and is crucially involved in the regional power-games of East Asia. The great Asian
80  civilizations of the ancient and medieval worlds could not escape the immigration and invasion of Chinese people and products. Today, China has made itself indispensable in its sphere of influence because China has what other countries want, both culturally and economically if not politically. It is now possible to say that the human path of the twenty-first century will wind through the belly of the Dragon: the People's Republic of China.

**21. As it is used in <u>line 1</u>, the word *germinal* means:**

A.  Using subtle means as in quietly spreading germs.
B.  To displace other ideas in favor of Chinese ideas.
C.  Having provided the seeds of development.
D.  Having a lethal effect as in a marauding force.

**22. When the author asks if other Asian countries still *kowtow* to the Dragon (<u>line 7</u>), the author really means:**

F.  East Asian heads of state must perform the ancient ritual of bowing to Chinese government officials in a display of submission.
G.  Heads of state from Vietnam and Korea are in extremely powerful positions that the Chinese government must respect.
H.  East Asian nations still must submit politically and militarily to China because of China's enormous power and influence.
J.  East Asian people still believe that there are large reptiles in China that they must respect and worship.

**23. The main point of this passage is:**

A. That the East Asian world of the 21st century has little in common with the dynamics of ancient East Asia.
B. That China is a threat to the global power structure and should be contained.
C. That the dramatic rise of China's economy cannot be rationalized and has little historical precedent.
D. That there is continuity to China's influence in East Asia.

**24. The main point made in paragraph 2 is:**

F. China has historically made cultural impacts on Japan and Korea, but Southeast Asia largely escaped China's shadow.
G. China has historically made powerful cultural impacts on Korea, Japan, and Southeast Asia that include Confucianism, Buddhism, and aspects of government.
H. The Han emperor Wudi invaded Korea in 108 B.C.E.
J. The impact of Buddhism was the most historically significant cultural impact made by China upon East Asia.

**25. From the information given, in it can reasonably be inferred that:**

A. After World War II, the West had little interest in seeing China succeed in influencing her East Asian neighbors.
B. North Korea and North Vietnam were trouble spots for the Communist Chinese government and needed to be reckoned with.
C. The West wished to help North Korea and North Vietnam but China was able to come to their rescue first.
D. The West and China were cooperating in building strong military bases in East Asia.

**26. The statement that the Chinese government passed legislation prohibiting random government confiscation of private property means that:**

F. Business owners in China need to worry about the government taking their property without warning.
G. The Chinese government decreed that property and businesses are owned collectively, as is consistent with Communist ideals.
H. Business owners in China do not need to worry that the government will take their business away once the business becomes efficient and profitable.
J. Business owners in China will be exempt from private property laws passed by the Chinese government.

**27. According to the passage, China's largest regional trading partners are:**

A. Japan and Taiwan
B. South Korea and Japan
C. Singapore, Taiwan, Malaysia, and Thailand
D. Vietnam and Thailand

**28. From the context of paragraph 5 and the passage as a whole it can be inferred that the word *innate* (line 57) means:**

F. Existing in one from birth.
G. Joined together in a peaceful union.
H. Having bounds or limits.
J. Associated by close personal relation.

**29. One of the main points made in paragraph 5 is that:**

    A. Chinese culture is no longer relevant in the 21st century.
    B. A large portion of East Asia's people are suspicious of the influence of Chinese culture in their homelands.
    C. The Chinese economy is taking over and subtly replacing the most common things in everyday East Asian life.
    D. The Chinese economy is so large that East Asian businesses see it as an opportunity to profit by trading with China.

**30. When discussing China's geopolitical motives in paragraphs 6 and 7 the author is implying that:**

    F. China is becoming a major aggressor in the East Asian region and its recent international policies are evidence of this.
    G. China has been making poor decisions in its international relationships.
    H. China creates its national policy based on its material needs.
    J. China has little control or influence over its neighbors and is especially helpless in its relationship with North Korea.

## The Endangered California Condor

The following passage is adapted from the United States Forest Service Research and Development publication titled "Status of the California Condor (Gymnogyps californianus) and efforts to achieve its recovery." Walters, Jeffrey R.; Derrickson, Scott R.; Fry, D. Michael; Haig, Susam M.; Marzluff, John M.; Wunderle Jr., Joseph. 2010. The Auk. 127(4):969-1001.

The California Condor has long been symbolic of avian conservation in the United States. Its large size, inquisitiveness, and association with remote places make it highly charismatic, and its decline to the brink of extinction aroused a continuing public interest in its plight. By 1982, only 22 individuals remained of this species whose range once encompassed much of North America. The

5    last wild bird was trapped and brought into captivity in 1987, which rendered the species extinct in the wild. In the 1980s, some questioned whether viable populations could ever again exist in the natural environment, and whether limited conservation funds should be expended on what they viewed as a hopeless cause. Nevertheless, since that low point, a captive-breeding and release program has increased the total population by an <u>order of magnitude</u>, and condors fly free again in

10   California, Arizona, Utah, and Baja California, Mexico. As of summer 2009, more than 350 condors exist, 180 of which are in the wild. The free-living birds face severe challenges, however, and receive constant human assistance. The intensive management applied to the free-living populations, as well as the ongoing monitoring and captive-breeding programs, are tremendously expensive and become more so as the population grows. Thus, the program has reached a

15   crossroads, caught between the financial and logistical pressures required to maintain an increasing number of condors in the wild and the environmental problems that preclude establishment of naturally sustainable, free-ranging populations.

### Condor Biology

20   The condor is by far the largest soaring bird in North America, with a wingspan of 2.8 m and body weight of 8.5 kg. The species had a wide distribution in North America before the late Pleistocene megafaunal extinctions (*extinction of large mammals, birds, and reptiles), but by the late 19th century it was largely restricted to the West Coast, from British Columbia to Baja California. By the middle of the 20th century, the species was confined to southern California. In modern times,

25   condors inhabited a variety of western landscapes from coasts to deserts to high mountain ranges that included beaches, shrublands, and forests. Modern records of nest sites of wild condors are all from California and include rugged cliffs and ancient trees.

Condors feed exclusively on carrion, primarily medium-to-large-sized mammal carcasses.

30   Prehistoric condors evidently fed on carcasses of (now extinct) megafaunal species and marine mammals, and the diet of modern condors includes domestic livestock as well as native terrestrial and marine species. Condors use their exceptional soaring abilities to cover large distances in search of food. Meretsky and Snyder (1992) reported nesting birds traveling up to 180 km from the nest in a single trip in search of food, and foraging ranges of nonbreeding birds of 7,000 km².

35   Condors are highly <u>gregarious</u> in feeding and most other activities, with the exception of nesting, which occurs in caves in cliffs or natural cavities on nesting territories defended by pairs. Theirs is a textbook example of a long-lived life history, characterized by high survival rates and exceedingly low reproductive rates, with breeding pairs producing, if all goes well, two fledglings in a 3-year period.

40

The biological challenges of establishing viable populations of a large, wide-ranging species with a low population growth rate are daunting, and there are serious obstacles to achieving that objective for condors. Below, we evaluate the major biological issues, the solutions to which lie in existing science and in research yet to be conducted.

45

### Lead Exposure

Any discussion of the biological challenges confronting the condor program must begin with the issue of lead. A basic tenet of conservation biology is that reintroductions will inevitably fail if the factors that caused the species to decline in the first place have not been addressed.

50    Reintroduction of condors may illustrate this principle, lead exposure being the recurring factor. Habitat loss and direct persecution through shooting and poisoning of carcasses were certainly involved in the decline of the condor through the 19th and into the 20th century, but there is compelling evidence that elevated mortality attributable to lead poisoning was a major cause of continuing decline at the time the birds were brought into captivity. Although the significance and
55    source of lead exposure in reintroduced condors were debated just a few years ago, there is now widespread consensus and considerable evidence that poisoning from ingestion of lead ammunition fragments in carcasses currently precludes the establishment of viable populations in the wild.

60    The condor is a long-lived species with a low reproductive rate, such that adult mortality rates certainly must be <10%, and likely <5%, for population to be self-sustaining. We conclude that condors are exposed to lead through ingestion of ammunition fragments frequently enough that, were the birds not treated, mortality rates would rise above those required for sustainability. There is a risk of lead exposure from virtually every type of carcass on which condors feed: big game,
65    small mammals, coyotes, domestic livestock, feral hogs, even (albeit rarely) marine mammals—all are sometimes shot with lead ammunition. Alternative views about the threat posed by lead and sources of lead exposure, which were plausible only a few years ago, are no longer credible.

      Reintroductions that have limited success because of failure to remove limiting factors can still be
70    informative. Such is the case for condors. Although there has been some awareness that predatory and scavenging birds could be poisoned by lead in their food, the plight of the condors has brought attention to the lead issue, resulting in much better understanding of the dynamics of lead exposure, the pervasiveness of the problem, and the actions required to solve it. The lead ammunition issue goes well beyond condors, affecting other terrestrial scavengers and potentially
75    even human health. Thus, condors have functioned as <u>sentinels</u> of an environmental problem that has yet to be adequately addressed in the western ecosystems they inhabit.

**31. Through the context of paragraph 1, the reader can infer that the phrase *order of magnitude* (line 9) implies that:**

   A.  The Condor population has risen very little; however if we magnify the numbers we can see that the population has risen somewhat.
   B.  The Condor population has risen due to an order by the people.
   C.  The Condor population has risen dramatically.
   D.  The Condor population is important in today's world but it has risen quite slowly.

**32. The passage relates that some people have questioned whether it is viable to save the California Condor from extinction for the reason that:**

   F.  Government programs to build the populations of endangered species are generally lost causes.
   G.  Expensive captive breeding programs prove that the Condor cannot survive long-term in the wild.
   H.  The California Condor is again prevalent in the Southwest United States and needs to be taken off of the Endangered Species list.
   J.  The Condor population cannot presently survive without intensive human intervention.

**33. According to paragraph 2, the condor's distribution:**

   A.  Has decreased since ancient times due to the decline of large animals in its ecosystems.
   B.  Has experienced a relatively recent decline since the 1800s.
   C.  Has historically been restricted to the western coasts of North America.
   D.  Occurs throughout North America's deserts, shrublands, and forests.

**34. Paragraph 3 implies that the California Condors' place in its eco-system is as a:**

F.  Herbivore
G.  Scavenger
H.  Bird of prey
J.  Omnivore

**35. In describing the range of California Condors, paragraph 3 reports that:**

A.  Nesting pairs travel further to find food than nonbreeding Condors.
B.  Meretsky and Snyder report that nonbreeding birds are more gregarious in their search for food.
C.  Condors use their exceptional soaring abilities to prey upon marine species.
D.  Nonbreeding condors travel the furthest in search of food.

**36. As used in <u>line 35</u>, the word *gregarious* means that the California Condor is:**

F.  Able to tolerate other condors while feeding at the same site.
G.  Unable to tolerate other condors while feeding at the same site.
H.  Highly competitive and territorial when a feeding site has been found.
J.  Swallows incredibly large chunks of food while feeding.

**37. According to the passage, the biggest reason for the modern decline in the population of the California Condor has been:**

A.  The failure of Condors upon release from captive breeding programs to find mates in the wild.
B.  Exposure to lead through severe environmental pollution brought about by nearby factories.
C.  The biological introduction of lead through firearm ammunition.
D.  The fact that breeding pairs only produce two fledglings in a three year period.

**38. The authors believe that the present California Condor population will be sustainable if:**

F.  Less than 5 birds per every hundred die each year.
G.  Less than 10 birds die each year.
H.  At least 10 birds in the population die each year.
J.  More than 15 birds per every hundred are born each year.

**39. As used in <u>line 75</u>, the word *sentinels* means that:**

A.  Condors are the victims of environmental problems that have long plagued western ecosystems.
B.  Condors are alerting humans to a problem that may affect other species in western ecosystems.
C.  Condors will fight this environmental problem with or without human assistance.
D.  The pervasiveness of this environmental problem is such that condors are the only functional defense in western ecosystems.

**40. The final conclusion of this passage about the plight of the California Condor is that:**

F.  The environmental problems facing the condor are insurmountable.
G.  Humans and condors have little in common except for the threat of exposure to lead ammunition.
H.  Even environmental programs of limited success can provide information for future endeavors.
J.  Condors are making a huge comeback and conservationists are finally able to claim success.

# READING PRACTICE TEST 1 ANSWER KEY

| | |
|---|---|
| 1. B | 21. C |
| 2. G | 22. H |
| 3. C | 23. D |
| 4. H | 24. G |
| 5. D | 25. A |
| 6. J | 26. H |
| 7. B | 27. B |
| 8. H | 28. F |
| 9. A | 29. D |
| 10. G | 30. G |
| 11. C | 31. C |
| 12. J | 32. J |
| 13. C | 33. A |
| 14. F | 34. G |
| 15. D | 35. D |
| 16. G | 36. F |
| 17. C | 37. C |
| 18. F | 38. F |
| 19. C | 39. B |
| 20. G | 40. H |

# READING PRACTICE TEST 1 RATIONALES

**1. Answer: B. A onetime resident of the town who often returns to visit.**
The narrator mentions that he has "occasional visits to the town," (line 5) so one could infer he does not live currently there (eliminating answer A) and because of these occasional visits, answer choice D cannot be correct either. He could very well be a person who has never resided in the town but lives in close proximity (answer C), however, it would be unlikely that someone who has never lived in the town could be so intimately connected to it as to seldom fail "to turn down Pyncheon Street, for the sake of passing through the shadow of these two antiquities,—the great elm-tree and the weather-beaten edifice." (lines 5-7)

The passage suggests the narrator is extremely knowledgeable about the town's history, more so than one who has just happened upon the house in his travels. The narrator mentions that the old elm is "familiar to every town-born child by the title of the Pyncheon Elm." (lines 4-5) This statement implies that he has intimate knowledge of the culture of the town from more than just a visitor's viewpoint and likely lived there or grew up there. Answer B is the best choice when considering all the evidence presented in the passage.

**2. Answer: G. The house has a weathered exterior that reflects not only the storms of nature but the battles of those who have lived in it.**
Although houses of this period could have windows and doors arranged in a way that evokes facial characteristics, this is not mentioned specifically in the passage and is a much too *literal* interpretation of the narrator's meaning. Answer B is the best choice because the narrator implies that the house itself bears traces of the emotional turmoil that was experienced by those associated with it (lines 9-11). By speaking of the house as having a human countenance, the author is using a writing technique called personification, whereby an inanimate object is described as having human qualities or traits.

**3. Answer: C. Stories passed down among the townspeople through the generations.**
From lines 46-47, we learn that that there is no written record of the dispute between Maule and Pyncheon and that everything that is known about the matter comes "chiefly from tradition". This implies that the narrator is retelling the story based on the stories that the townspeople themselves have passed down through the generations, referred to by the narrator as the "traditionary lore of which the old Pyncheon House...has been the theme" (lines 17-19).

**4. Answer: H. The house and its circumstances are of great interest and unique among houses in New England.**
The Pyncheon House, with its seven gables, presents a unique countenance to the casual passerby (negating answer A). While the elm-tree is of great interest to the young of the town, this passage does not describe its importance, only its immediate appearance (eliminating answer B). The stories relating to the house begin with its preconstruction history, but this is a specific recounting and not a summarizing or a generalization (ruling out answer D).

In paragraph 2, the narrator speaks of the history of the house and its stories by saying "the story would include a chain of events extending over the better part of two centuries, and, written out with reasonable amplitude, would fill a bigger folio volume, or a longer series of duodecimos, than could prudently be appropriated to the annals of all New England during a similar period." (lines 14-17) This would imply that the Pyncheon home is no ordinary house and that the events surrounding it are of great interest. Answer C would be the best choice.

**5. Answer: D. A way of creating an interesting and unifying character in the story that is also the tale's setting for its human characters.**
Having the narrator speak of the house in detail is the method that Hawthorne uses to draw his characters into the story. The setting is discussed at the beginning in order to provide a context for the characters and their interactions. However, in describing the house in detail and speaking of its humanlike

countenance, the narrator implies that the house is more than just a passive background to the story and is a character in the story itself.

**6. Answer: J. The natural spring that was within the natural borders of the property.**
The Maule property was not a seven-gabled house but a small cottage that the narrator describes as a "hut, shaggy with thatch" (line 37). Although the Maule hut was distant from the center of the village and did contain a garden, the passage makes it clear that the most desirable characteristic of the property was its fresh water natural spring. As stated in lines 35-36, the property had a natural spring of "soft and pleasant water—a rare treasure on the sea-girt peninsula". In describing the spring as a rare treasure, the narrator is conveying how truly important the spring was—not only to Maule, but to others as well.

**7. Answer: B. A farmer who has found a source of fresh water on a wooded hill.**
Matthew Maule was accused of witchcraft (answer C) by the end of the passage, but that is not the beginning of the story. The Puritans arriving (answer D) would normally be the beginning of the history of the Pyncheon House, but the narrator himself begins the story with Matthew Maule, mentioning the Puritans as an aside. While a dispute over property rights does enter the story when Colonel Pyncheon desires the land that Matthew Maule's thatch hut is settled on (answer A), the history begins as the narrator relates how Maule found a spring in a remote area of the Puritan settlement and then cleared the land for his hut there. Answer B is best choice.

**8. Answer: H. Was a greedy man who saw good land and was going to have it by any possible means.**
While the narrator claims to relinquish judgment concerning the whole ordeal (lines 47-48), he does sneak in a few editorial comments that reveal what he thinks of Pyncheon. He calls the dispute "this controversy between two ill-matched antagonists" (line 51) suggesting that Matthew Maule was up against a powerful foe and at a clear disadvantage. The narrator also implies that Pyncheon was untruthful in claiming Maule's land as his own when he says "although it appears to have been at least a matter of doubt, whether Colonel Pyncheon's claims were not unduly stretched, in order to make it cover the small metes and bounds of Matthew Maule." (lines 48-50)

While Pyncheon was granted the tract of land adjacent to Maule's, it was in clear dispute whether or not the grant actually included Maule's land (answer A). The narrator paints Pyncheon as a "powerful personage...characterized by an iron energy of purpose;" (lines 40-43) but nowhere does the narrator mention that Pyncheon was a hero in a defense against witches (answer B). Pyncheon also seemed to benefit greatly from Maule's death, which implies it wasn't just through luck that Pyncheon prevailed in the dispute (answer D). In total, the narrator paints Pyncheon as a greedy man by nature who may have been willing to go to great lengths to get the land he wanted. Answer C is the best choice.

**9. Answer: A. Matthew Maule was not a witch and he was falsely accused in order for another to confiscate his land.**
The passage does not say that Matthew Maule was a witch, only that he was executed for the crime of witchcraft (line 59). The narrator states that "It was a death that blasted with strange horror the humble name of the dweller in the cottage, and made it seem almost a religious act to drive the plough over the little area of his habitation, and obliterate his place and memory from among men." (lines 55-57) From the passage, it seems that Colonel Pyncheon, in all probability, used the paranoia of the era to place an undue accusation upon Matthew Maule in order to confiscate Maule's land that was adjacent to his own. Answer A is the best choice.

**10. Answer: G. The events of the story occurred at least 150 years before the narrator's retelling.**
There is much evidence in the passage to indicate that the events of the story occurred a long time in the past, relative to the retelling of the story. In line 14, the narrator states that "the story would include a chain of events extending over the better part of two centuries" and later refers to the story having "a connection with the long past—a reference to forgotten events and personages" (line 23). The most concrete evidence comes from lines 54-55, however, when the narrator discusses the execution of Matthew Maule: "the mode of his death, too, affects the mind differently, in our day, from what it did a

century and a half ago". This makes it clear that the story is being retold at least 150 years after the events took place.

## 11. Answer: C. An enthusiastic attempt by the author to pass on to the reader an appreciation for the art of improvisational comedy.
The author uses an exclamation point at the end of paragraph 1 to say that an improvisational performance "is certain to be spontaneous, attention-grabbing, and hilarious!" In paragraph 3, the author gives the opinion that stand-up comedy jokes can't be as fresh each night as the spontaneity of improvisational comedy. In the final paragraph, the author states that there will always be people who "prefer the sheer thrill of spontaneous creation!" From these statements, we can deduce that the author is enthusiastic about improv comedy and that they would like to pass on this enthusiasm to the reader.

## 12. Answer: J. An example of improvisational performance in order to immediately grab the reader's attention.
The passage begins with an improv performance in progress and the author explains the action in a way that catches the nuances of a basic improv experience. Opening the passage this way immediately grabs the reader's attention, draws them into the essay, and sets the tone for the information that is to follow.

## 13. Answer: C. That the stand-up comedian adheres to a carefully prepared routine that the improv group avoids.
In lines 14-15, the author writes about stand-up comedians that "On the surface, what may seem like a free-flowing and spontaneous comedic performance is, in fact, carefully planned and pre-scripted." Also, at the end of paragraph 2, the author writes: "Developing written routines in advance provides an opportunity to refine and perfect material" (lines 18-19). This pre-planning by the stand-up comedian is in clear contrast to the spontaneous nature of improvisational performance described by the author throughout the passage.

## 14. Answer: F. Few stand-up comedians could become successful members of an improv comedy troupe.
In lines 26-28, the author states that "Spontaneous and completely unpredictable, improvisational performances require a degree of comedic skill, instinct, and confidence that not all stand-up comedians feel comfortable with." Answer A is the best choice.

## 15. Answer: D. The spontaneous nature of improvisational comedy requires performers to be keenly attuned to each other; this responsiveness can only be learned by doing.
While there is truth to be found in each of the other answer choices, the best answer choice is D. Paragraph 4 explains that the process of spontaneous co-creation requires that performers be highly attuned to each other. This level of responsiveness can't be learned in isolation; the very nature of co-creation is that it involves other performers. Lines 34-36 state that "truly successful improv requires each performer to be attuned to their fellow performers as they spontaneously co-create the characters, dialogue, plot, and action of the performance." It makes sense that the best way to learn improv is by practicing with other improvisational performers and to learn by doing.

## 16. Answer: G. Developing pre-scripted routines allows them to perfect their material before performing it; this increases their chances for a successful performance.
The author spends the beginning part of the passage contrasting traditional stand-up comedy with improvisational theater. In lines 15-18 the author explains that there is a lot of pressure on stand-up comedians to provide their audiences with an entertaining experience. One way to achieve this is to craft their material in advance and refine it before performing it. In contrast, improvisational performances are completely spontaneous performances that do not rely on pre-written material.

## 17. Answer: C. The audience often provides the structure and constraints within which the actors work.
We know right from the first paragraph that the audience can suggest trigger words or situations for the actors to work within. Paragraph 5 further elaborates on the role of the audience. In lines 43-44, the author writes that suggestions from the audience can "start or guide the general content or theme of the

performance" and create an interactive relationship between the audience and the performance. For example, the author states that the audience contribution could be to suggest a setting for the scene or to define the relationships between the performers. In this way, the audience sets basic constraints and structure within which the performance must develop.

**18. Answer: F. The offer provides each character with traits that can be expounded upon in order to move the performance forward.**
The offer is defined in paragraph 6 as any word or action taken by the performers (lines 54-55). With every word spoken and every action taken, new realities are introduced into the scene and onto the characters. It is expected that each offer is accepted, which means that each character accepts the new reality defined by the offer and reacts to it specifically. In this way, each offer acts as "an invitation to another performer for an appropriate, yet spontaneous, response" (lines 55-56) and drives the scene forward. Without the concept of an offer and the rule that all offers must be accepted, the spontaneous performance could come to a dead-end, with nothing to move the performance forward.

**19. Answer: C. Performer 1: Why were you late to the horserace yesterday? Performer 2: Because the cheap watch you gave me broke!**
According to lines 54-56, an offer is any word or action that invites a spontaneous response from another performer. One rule of improvisation is that every offer has to be accepted, which means that whatever new reality is created by the offer has to be accepted by fellow performers (lines 56-58). In this example, the correct response is the one where Performer 2 accepts the new reality that they were, in fact, late to the horserace yesterday. Only answer choice C does that.

**20. Answer: G. Bright because there will always be people who are interested in creating and experiencing spontaneous art.**
At the end of the passage (lines 79-80), the author offers his opinion that "there will always be both performers and audiences who enjoy, and even prefer, the sheer thrill of spontaneous creation!" This indicates that the author believes the future of improvisational comedy is a bright one.

**21. Answer: C. Having provided the seeds of development.**
Germinal has the same root as the word 'germinate', which means to sprout or to begin life. The process of germination is when a plant root or stem bursts from a seed. In line 1 and in the first paragraph, the author implies that China planted the cultural, economic, and political seeds of the most powerful nations in East Asia.

**22. Answer: H. East Asian nations still must submit politically and militarily to China because of China's enormous power and influence.**
Although many Asian people still bow to each other before and after engaging in the western ritual of shaking hands, this is a sign of mutual respect, not submission. As dragons are ancient symbols of Chinese power, the author is using the reference to a dragon as a metaphor for China itself. The passage underscores the idea that East Asian nations cannot ignore the power and influence of China and are by necessity obligated to submit to it. In this way, C is the correct answer.

**23. Answer: D. That there is continuity to China's influence in East Asia.**
Line 1 introduces the passage by stating that "China has been a germinal influence in East Asia culturally, economically, and politically". Paragraph 2 describes the early spread of Chinese Confucianism, written language, architecture, art, philosophy, and music through both military engagements and trade, which establishes China's ancient influence on its neighbors. The passage builds to and ends with a description of China's current manufacturing, economic, and military might, establishing China's modern day influence. The entire passage is devoted to showing how throughout the ages, China has been a major influence in the region of East Asia.

**24. Answer: G. China has historically made powerful cultural impacts on Korea, Japan, and Southeast Asia that include Confucianism, Buddhism, and aspects of government.**
While paragraph 2 does state that the Han emperor Wudi invaded Korea in 108 B.C.E. (answer C), this fact is not the main point of the paragraph; it is stated in order to explain how the Korean people first

came into contact with important Chinese cultural ideas and traditions. The main point of the paragraph is that all parts of East Asia have had some important contact with China over the millennia, including Korea, Japan, and Southeast Asia. The most important cultural diffusions were the spread of Confucianism and its emphasis on a rigid structure of personal interactions and Buddhism. In this way, B is the correct answer.

### 25. Answer: A. After World War II, the West had little interest in seeing China succeed in influencing her East Asian neighbors.

According to paragraph 3, those East Asian countries where Western nations had a strong military presence after World War II did not fall under the influence of Communism. This fact implies that the West retained a military presence explicitly in order to undermine China's influence on its East Asian neighbors and to prevent the spread of Chinese communism. If the West was interested in expanding China's influence, the writer would not have described the survival of communist North Korea and Northern Vietnam as having happened "much to the chagrin" of the West.

### 26. Answer: H. Business owners in China do not need to worry that the government will take their business away once the business becomes efficient and profitable.

As stated in lines 40-43, the Chinese government passed legislation to protect private property rights, which increased incentives for business owners and contributed directly to China's economic boom. The implication is that, without the worry that a government will take away your business if it becomes profitable, entrepreneurs can make the reasonable assumption that their hard work will bring them profit and opportunities for expansion. The entrepreneur has an incentive to invest in further endeavors, hiring and training local workers and bringing prosperity to the region. This makes answer C the correct choice.

### 27. Answer: B. South Korea and Japan

While the Southeast Asian nations of Singapore, Taiwan, Malaysia, and Thailand are stated to be in the top 10 list of regional trading partners (lines 52-53), lines 51-52 state that Japan and South Korea are among the top 5 of "any category relating to trade with China".

### 28. Answer: F. Existing in one from birth.

The philosophical ideals of Confucianism (formal relationship structures and great respect towards one's elders and authority) and Buddhism (calm acceptance and emotional control) are pan-Asian characteristics that come from thousands of years of Chinese influence (paragraphs 1 and 2). As well, some East Asian writing systems began, or were influenced by, Chinese calligraphy—through which many Chinese words have come into other Asian languages (lines 11-12). In this way, it could be said that much current East Asian interest in China comes from an innate interest that arises from thousands of years of cross-cultural influence.

### 29. Answer: D. The Chinese economy is so large that East Asian businesses see it as an opportunity to profit by trading with China.

One of the chief characteristics of the Chinese economy is its immensity. With a fifth of the world's population within its borders, China has a large population and equally large needs for goods and services (line 50). Businesses around East Asia see an infinite market to be tapped. The word 'elephantine' in line 50 and the statement that China provides 'endless opportunity for its neighbors' makes answer D the correct choice.

### 30. Answer: G. China creates its national policy based on its material needs.

The author states that China's material needs are large, using the word 'gargantuan' in line 61 to describe its economy. The author also explains that the Chinese nation must provide power for itself even if that means it must trade with states shunned by more ideologically driven nations. In lines 74-75, the author explains that China is not as ideologically motivated as other nations in the world, thus implying that it is motivated by its large material needs.

**31. Answer: C. The Condor population has risen dramatically.**

As the passage explains in paragraph 1, by 1982 only 22 condors remained from a population that had once ranged over the entire North American continent. However, by 2009, due to intervention by the U.S. Department of the Interior, over 350 birds existed with over half living in the wild. This evidence supports the implication that 'an order of magnitude' is a dramatic rise in the condor population of 94% (answer C).

**32. Answer: J. The Condor population cannot presently survive without intensive human intervention.**

In the first paragraph of the passage the authors state that the challenges faced by the free-living California Condors are such that they "receive constant human assistance" (line 12); some of the assistance includes the captive-breeding and monitoring programs. Paragraph 4 explains that there are "serious obstacles" and biological challenges that are further explained in the section on Lead Exposure.

While government programs to rebuild endangered populations are expensive and, by no means, guarantee success, they are not (answer A) lost causes. While there is plenty of human effort towards working for the condor's survival, it has yet to be proven that the bird cannot survive long-term (answer B). Lastly, while the condor has made a dramatic comeback, it is far from being out of the woods as there are currently less than 400 living birds (answer C). Thus, answer D is the best answer choice.

**33. Answer: A. Has decreased since ancient times due to the decline of large animals in its ecosystems.**

According to paragraph 2, the condor has experienced decline since the Pleistocene megafaunal extinctions, a dying off of large mammals, birds, and reptiles (lines 21-22). The implication is that the ancient Condor population was sustained by the abundant supply of carcasses of dead mammoths, mastodons, and others. Once these animals were extinct, the condor's distribution was limited to places where relatively large animals still thrived: the North American west.

**34. Answer: G. Scavenger**

As an eater of carrion (line 29), or the carcasses of dead animals, the California Condor would be classified as a scavenger within its ecosystem. Scavengers are, by their nature, carnivores, or meat eaters. Herbivores (answer A) are plant eaters; omnivores (answer D) eat both plants and animals; and birds of prey (answer C) are carnivores that hunt live animals, or prey.

**35. Answer: D. Nonbreeding condors travel the furthest in search of food.**

Lines 32-34 address the feeding range of the condor; all condors travel extraordinarily large distances to track food. While nesting birds can range "up to 180 km from the nest in a single trip in search of food," birds that are not involved in a breeding pair can travel up to 7,000 square kilometers for food—a much larger distance than that covered by breeding pairs.

**36. Answer: F. Able to tolerate other condors while feeding at the same site.**

The condor is able to share, with other condors, a found meal of carrion. This is because of the condor's gregarious or sociable nature with members of its own species (answer A). This meaning can be deduced by contrasting their gregarious feeding behavior with their more private, nesting behavior which is explained as happening in caves and defended against the intrusion of other condors (lines 35-36).

**37. Answer: C. The biological introduction of lead through firearm ammunition.**

Beginning with line 47, the passage begins to explain that exposure to lead fragments in food has contributed to the modern decline of the condor population. Answers A and D may also be factors, however, to a great extent the carcasses that condors feed upon are animals that have been shot by humans with lead ammunition. These animals may be "big game, small mammals, coyotes, domestic livestock, feral hogs, even (albeit rarely) marine mammals" (lines 64-65).

**38. Answer: F. Less than 5 birds per every hundred die each year.**
In <u>lines 60-61</u>, the passage reads, "adult mortality rates certainly must be <10%, and likely <5%, for population to be self-sustaining." The most likely parameter for sustaining the population (<5%) means 'less than five percent', or literally: less than five out of every one hundred. This would mean that answer A would be the best choice.

**39. Answer: B. Condors are alerting humans to a problem that may affect other species in western ecosystems.**
In the last paragraph, the authors of the passage relate that the "plight of the condors" has shed light on the pervasive problem of lead exposure in western ecosystems. The authors also say that the issue of lead contamination "goes well beyond condors" and can affect other scavengers and potentially humans as well. Condors are labeled in the paragraph as "sentinels of an environmental problem". From the context, it can be inferred that a sentinel acts as a warning, as the issues challenging the condors point to a more general environmental threat.

**40. Answer: H. Even environmental programs of limited success can provide information for future endeavors.**
The sections 'Condor Biology' and 'Lead Exposure' bring forth evidence of both the discoveries made by and the limitations of the condor program. In <u>lines 48-49</u>, the authors explain that, "a basic tenet of conservation biology is that reintroductions will inevitably fail if the factors that caused the species to decline in the first place have not been addressed." However, in the last paragraph of the passage, the authors conclude in <u>lines 69-70</u>, that "reintroductions that have limited success because of failure to remove limiting factors can still be informative." The authors clearly believe that what is learned in any program, even those that are less than successful, can still be applied to future undertakings.

# SCIENCE REASONING PRACTICE TEST 1

35 Minutes - 40 Questions

Directions: Following are seven passages and questions that refer to each passage. Choose the best answer for each question.

## Heart Disease in America

Heart disease is the leading cause of death in America. Risk factors for heart disease include high blood pressure, obesity, sedentary lifestyle, and family history of heart disease. A major risk factor is high cholesterol. The main carriers of cholesterol in the blood are LDL (low-density lipoprotein) molecules that are commonly referred to as "bad cholesterol". Studies have shown that high levels of LDL and low levels of HDL (high-density lipoprotein) or "good cholesterol" are strongly linked to cardiovascular disease including heart attacks and strokes.

Statins are the most popular class of cholesterol lowering drugs currently in use. These act by inhibiting the enzyme HMG-CoA reductase which facilitates the production of cholesterol in the liver. Currently, statins are recommended for those who already have cardiovascular disease and LDL levels greater than 70mg/dL or for those without any history of cardiovascular disease but elevated levels of LDL cholesterol above 130mg/dL.

A recent study of 18,000 people, however, shows that statins are highly effective in reducing heart disease risk even for people who have normal levels of LDL cholesterol below 130 mg/dL. All study participants had elevated levels of C-reactive protein, an indicator of inflammation. Based on these findings, many experts recommend that the guidelines be changed to prescribe statins to people with normal LDL levels. Other experts disagree. New proposed guidelines to recommend statin use for men over 55 and women over 65 with normal LDL cholesterol but at least one risk factor for heart disease are currently under review.

### Expert 1
About one-third of patients who develop cardiovascular disease have normal levels of LDL cholesterol. Changed guidelines to prescribe statins for healthy patients may help save the lives of many patients in this category. The study demonstrated a 44% reduction in heart disease due to the use of statins. The results were so significant that the study was halted earlier than scheduled so that the control group, initially on placebos, could be given the drug. Given the strength of the study results, there should be no hesitation in adopting the proposed guidelines despite the potential side effects. In fact, it would be beneficial to start statin treatment for everyone at the age of thirty so that their LDL levels never rise beyond 30 mg/dL. Research has shown that those who have low cholesterol all their lives have significantly fewer heart attacks than those who lower their cholesterol levels when they are older.

### Expert 2
Although the study participants were apparently healthy and had normal LDL cholesterol levels, a quarter of them were obese while 16 percent were smokers. Statins have potentially serious side effects such as liver damage and muscle problems which in severe cases can lead to rhabdomyolysis or breakdown of muscle cells. Some studies have shown that statins can increase the risk of developing diabetes by 9%. Even for people who showed no side effects in this study, the long-term effects of statin use are unknown. Also, the typical rate of heart disease in the population under study is very small to begin with. So, even a significant change in percentage does not represent a large number of people. Considering all of these factors, there is no justification for adopting the proposed guidelines.

1. **According to current guidelines, LDL levels are considered higher than normal if they are above:**

   A. 130 mg/dL
   B. 70 mg/dL
   C. 150 mg/dL
   D. 30 mg/dL

2. **According to the passage, which of the following is not true?**

   F. Statins act by reducing the action of the enzyme HMG-CoA reductase.
   G. The enzyme HMG-CoA reductase prevents cholesterol production.
   H. Obesity is a risk factor for heart disease.
   J. High-density lipoprotein is "good cholesterol".

3. **Expert 2 thinks that statins should not be prescribed for people with normal levels of LDL cholesterol because:**

   A. The risks outweigh the benefits.
   B. A large percentage of the study participants were not healthy.
   C. The study did not continue long enough to support this finding.
   D. All of the above.

4. **A third expert contends that the U.S. population overall is not very healthy due to high rates of obesity. Only one-third of the population can be said to be in excellent health. This information supports the position of:**

   F. Expert 1
   G. Expert 2
   H. Both Expert 1 and Expert 2
   J. Neither Expert 1, nor Expert 2

5. **Experts 1 and 2 agree that:**

   A. Statins have been shown to be effective in reducing heart disease risk for healthy people.
   B. Statins have been shown to be effective in reducing heart disease risk for people with normal LDL levels.
   C. The side effects do not justify the use of statins in those with normal LDL levels.
   D. The new proposed guidelines should be adopted.

6. **Mary is a 60 year old woman with high blood pressure and LDL of 120 mg/dL. She would be a candidate for statin use according to:**

   F. The new proposed guidelines
   G. Expert 2
   H. Expert 1
   J. None of the above

7. **Which of the following studies would be most helpful in clarifying some of the points of disagreement between Expert 1 and Expert 2?**

   A. Repeat the study with participants who have LDL cholesterol above 130 mg/dL.
   B. Repeat the study with participants who only have LDL cholesterol below 70 mg/dL.
   C. Repeat the study with participants who do not have obvious health issues such as obesity or smoking.
   D. Analyze the data for the obese people and the smokers separately.

## Ocean Acidification

Although many people know about problems associated with increasing carbon dioxide concentration in the atmosphere, not many are aware of ocean acidification, the "other $CO_2$ problem". About a third of the carbon dioxide released into the atmosphere is absorbed by the oceans. This seems like a good thing until we realize that this increased concentration of carbon dioxide in the oceans can actually affect marine life adversely. As shown in the box below, the carbon dioxide absorbed by the ocean reacts with water to form carbonic acid which dissociates into hydrogen ions and bicarbonate ions. This increased concentration of hydrogen ions leads to increased acidity (lower pH) of the ocean water. In the last 250 years, average ocean pH has decreased by about 0.12 units to a pH level of 8.1. This actually represents a 30% increase in acidity since the pH scale is logarithmic. There was no such rapid change in the ocean environment in the millions of years prior to this.

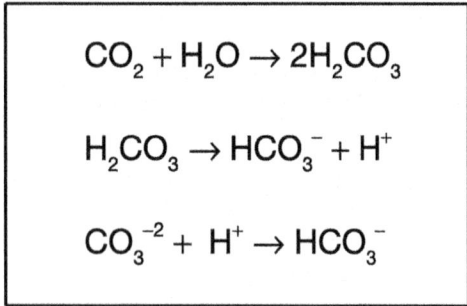

$$CO_2 + H_2O \rightarrow 2H_2CO_3$$

$$H_2CO_3 \rightarrow HCO_3^- + H^+$$

$$CO_3^{-2} + H^+ \rightarrow HCO_3^-$$

Some of the hydrogen ions combine with carbonate ions in the water to form bicarbonate ions. Thus, dropping pH leads to a lower ratio of carbonate to bicarbonate ions. Since calcium carbonate minerals are used to build the shells and skeletons of many marine animals, increased acidity will end up weakening their shells. The decrease in pH also disrupts bodily processes such as growth and reproduction. If we continue adding carbon dioxide into the atmosphere at the current rate, the pH of ocean water will continue to drop to levels that could destroy many marine species. The graph below shows the projected change in pH from pre-industrial times at different depths from the ocean surface.

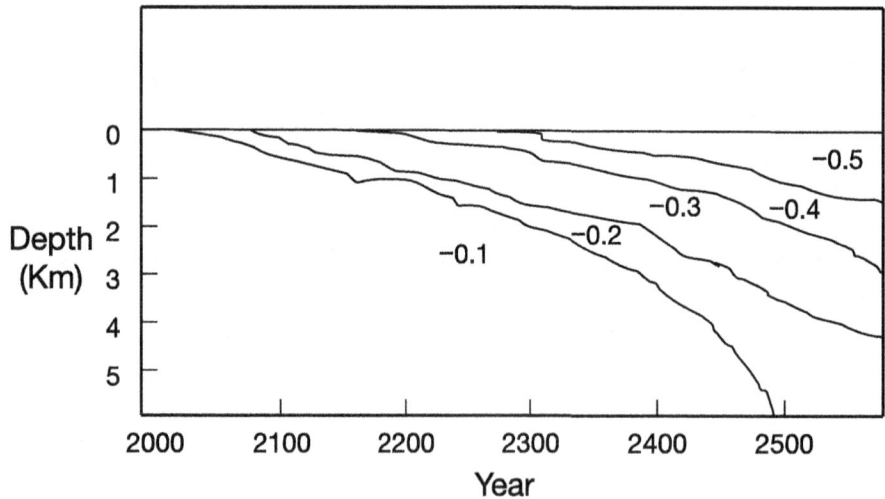

8.  The chemical formula for a bicarbonate ion is:

    F.  $H_2CO_3$
    G.  $HCO_3^-$
    H.  $CO_3^{-2}$
    J.  $CO_2$

9.  Scientists have estimated that ocean pH could drop from 8.1 to 7.8 by the year 2100 if the current rate of greenhouse gas emission continues. This represents:

    A.  An increase in acidity of about 150%.
    B.  An increase in acidity of about 4%.
    C.  A decrease in acidity of about 4%.
    D.  An increase in acidity of about 20%.

10. If the pH of the ocean water was 8.2 in pre-industrial times, what is the pH predicted to be 2.5 Km below the surface in the year 2400?

    F.  -0.2
    G.  8.4
    H.  8.0
    J.  7.8

11. According to the passage, which of the following statements is true?

    A.  Some of the atmospheric carbon dioxide being absorbed by the ocean is good for the environment.
    B.  A higher concentration of hydrogen ions implies lower acidity.
    C.  Lower pH disrupts the bodily processes of marine animals.
    D.  Ocean pH has been falling for the last 7 or 8 centuries.

12. Based on the projected pH graph, by how much will ocean pH at a depth of 4 Km change between the years 2400 and 2500?

    F.  It will increase by 0.1
    G.  It will decrease by 0.1
    H.  It will decrease by 0.2
    J.  It will decrease by 0.3

## The Power of Gravity

Gravity keeps many things on the earth—rocks, people, cars, and even the atmosphere. Without gravity, no planet could have an atmosphere since all the gas molecules in the air would escape into space. Because of the existence of gravity, any object—rocket or molecule—must move with a minimum velocity known as the escape velocity ($V_e$) in order to go beyond the pull of a planet. The escape velocity of a planet depends on its acceleration due to gravity (g) and radius (R), specifically the product of the two (gR). The escape velocities for the moon and several planets are listed in the table below.

| Planet | g = Acceleration due to gravity (m/s$^2$) | R = Radius (Km) | $V_e$ = Escape velocity (Km/s) |
|---|---|---|---|
| Earth | 9.8 | 6,370 | 11.2 |
| Moon | 1.6 | 1,740 | 2.3 |
| Venus | 8.9 | 6,050 | 10.3 |
| Saturn | 11.2 | 58,100 | 36 |
| Uranus | 9.7 | 24,500 | 22 |
| Neptune | 11.3 | 24,600 | 24 |

For a gas molecule, just having the right velocity is not enough for it to leave the atmosphere of a planet. It must also be far enough away from the surface so that the density of the gas is low and the probability of colliding with another molecule is low. The distance at which the probability of collision between two molecules is practically zero is called the escape level. For earth, the escape level is about 500 Km above the surface.

The speed of a molecule of gas depends on its mass and temperature. This does not imply that for a gas at a particular temperature all the molecules will be moving with the same speed. Instead, the speeds of the molecules are distributed over a range of values that are concentrated around the most probable value. The most probable speed ($V_0$) for a molecule of gas with a given mass (m) at a specified temperature (T) is $v_0 = \sqrt{\dfrac{2kT}{m}}$ where $k$ is a constant known as the Boltzmann constant. Hydrogen has a most probable speed of 2.24 Km/s at 300K, 3.16 Km/s at 600K, and 3.87 Km/s at 900K. Oxygen has a most probable speed of 0.56 Km/s at 300K, 0.79 Km/s at 600K, and 0.97 Km/s at 900K.

Since the molecular speeds are distributed over a range, even when the most probable speed is less than the escape speed, a certain fraction of the molecules move with speeds greater than the escape speed. The graph below shows this fraction as a function of the ratio of the escape speed to the most probable speed.

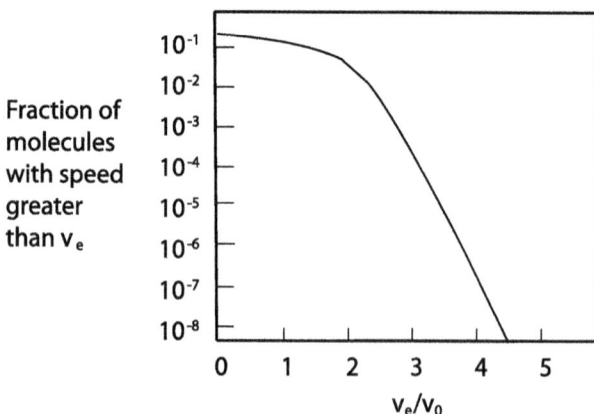

13. **The first table in the passage gives the acceleration due to gravity (g) and the radius (R) of several planets along with the escape velocity ($v_E$) for each planet. Based on the data, which of the following seems to be a plausible formula for escape velocity in terms of g and R?**

   A. $v_E = 2gR$

   B. $v_E = \sqrt{2gR}$

   C. $v_E = 2/gR$

   D. $v_E = 2/\sqrt{gR}$

14. **An explosion releases a gas 50 Km above the surface of the earth. If the most probable speed of the gas molecules is 15 Km/s, which of the following is true?**

   F. Most of the gas will escape the atmosphere since the most probable speed exceeds the escape velocity.
   G. About half of the gas will escape since half the molecules will be headed towards the earth.
   H. Most of the gas will not escape since the molecules will collide with each other.
   J. Most of the gas will not escape because the surrounding air temperature will cool it and slow it down.

15. **A new planet is discovered that has an acceleration due to gravity of 4.5 m/s$^2$ and a radius of 12,000 Km. The escape velocity for this planet will be approximately:**

   A. 5 Km/s
   B. 10 Km/s
   C. 20 Km/s
   D. 40 Km/s

16. **The temperature of the escape level on earth is about 600K. What fraction of hydrogen atoms at this altitude will have speeds greater than the escape speed?**

   F. $1.6 \times 10^{-5}$
   G. $2.5 \times 10^{-6}$
   H. $1.2 \times 10^{-7}$
   J. $3.2 \times 10^{-8}$

17. **The information given in the passage can be used to explain:**

   A. Why some planets are more massive than others.
   B. Why certain gases exist in a planet's atmosphere.
   C. The range of sizes for planet radii.
   D. The distribution of molecular speeds.

## Hooke's Law

According to Hooke's law, when a spring is stretched or compressed by a distance x from its equilibrium position, the restoring force F on the spring is given by the relation: $F = -kx$ where k is the spring constant which has a fixed value for a particular spring. This relation is valid for a certain range of x. If the spring is stretched beyond the elastic limit, it will be deformed and Hooke's law will no longer hold true.

### Experiment 1

An experiment is set up to find the spring constant k by measuring x for different values of F. A spring is attached to a glider on an air track. When the spring is un-stretched, its length is $L_0$. A force is applied to the spring via a mass m attached to a pulley. The amount x by which it stretches the spring is measured. Since the mass is at rest, the force of gravity on it is balanced by the restoring force of the spring (kx). Hence $mg = kx$ where g is the acceleration due to gravity. This is the measure of the extending force exerted on the spring.

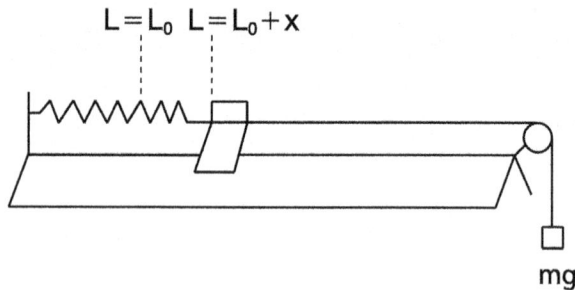

$$L = L_0 \quad L = L_0 + x$$

mg

The table below shows the data obtained for different values of m.

| Mass m (Kg) | Extension x (cm) |
|---|---|
| 0 | 0 |
| 1 | 1.9 |
| 2 | 4.1 |
| 2.5 | 5.1 |
| 3.5 | 6.9 |
| 5 | 10.2 |

The data for Experiment 1 is graphed below:

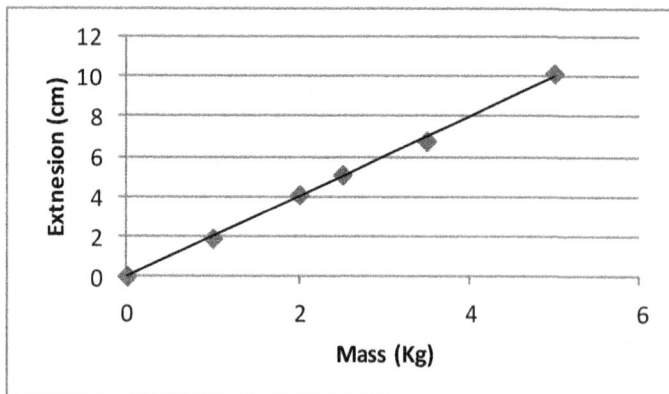

## Experiment 2

The same spring that was used in Experiment 1 is hung vertically and a mass is suspended at the end. The extension of the spring from its rest length $L_0$ (found in Experiment 1) is measured for different values of the mass m. The results are shown in the table below.

| Mass m (Kg) | Extension x (cm) |
|---|---|
| 0 | 0.5 |
| 1 | 2.5 |
| 2 | 4.6 |
| 2.5 | 5.6 |
| 3.5 | 7.5 |
| 5 | 10.6 |
| 8 | 13.0 |

18. Given the relation kx = mg, x = (g/k) m. Therefore, the slope of the line plotted with x on the y-axis and m on the x-axis is equal to g/k. If the acceleration due to gravity g = 9.8 m/s$^2$, the spring constant k calculated from the data of Experiment 1 is:

   F. 490 Kg/s$^2$
   G. 4.9 Kg/s$^2$
   H. 50 Kg/s$^2$
   J. 0.5 Kg/s$^2$

19. If the first six data points from Experiment 2 are plotted on a graph, the points will lie on:

   A. A line with the same slope as the line from Experiment 1 and a non-zero x-intercept.
   B. A line with the same slope as the line from Experiment 1 and a non-zero y-intercept.
   C. A line with a different slope than Experiment 1.
   D. A line identical to the one from Experiment 1 passing through the origin.

20. In Experiment 2, the extension has a non-zero value even for zero mass because:

   F. An error was made in the measurement.
   G. Hooke's law has a different form when the spring is vertical.
   H. There is an additional force on the spring, the force of gravity.
   J. None of the above.

21. In Experiment 2, if a mass of 3 Kg was hung at the end of the string, the extension measured would be approximately:

   A. 6.0 cm
   B. 6.5 cm
   C. 7.0 cm
   D. 7.5 cm

22. If a new experiment was performed with the air track in Experiment 1 tilted at an angle so that the right end was lower than the left end, the extension of the spring for a mass of 2 Kg would be:

   F. 4.1 cm
   G. 4.6 cm
   H. Less than 4.1 cm
   J. Between 4.1 and 4.6 cm

**23. Based on the data from Experiment 2, the elastic limit for the spring is:**

    A.  Less than 2 Kg
    B.  Between 3 Kg and 5 Kg
    C.  Between 5 Kg and 10 Kg
    D.  Cannot be determined

## Activation Energy

In order for a chemical reaction to occur, the reactants have to reach a minimum energy level known as the activation energy. Reactants at this higher energy level are said to be in the transition state. It is a temporary state in which the reactants rapidly convert to the products. If the activation energy for a particular reaction is too high, the reaction may not occur at all or it may occur at a very slow rate. The job of a catalyst is to speed up a reaction by effectively lowering the activation energy while remaining unchanged itself. An exothermic reaction releases energy and the products of the reaction are at a lower energy level than the reactants. An endothermic reaction absorbs energy so that the products of the reaction end up at a higher energy level than the reactants.

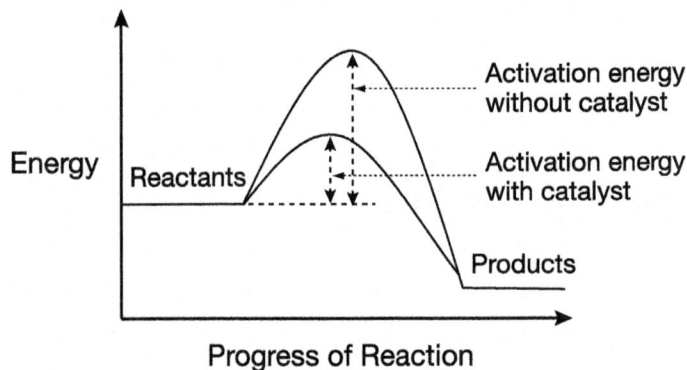

### Experiment 1

An experiment is performed with chemicals A and B which react to produce X.

A + B → X (The energy transitions for the reaction are shown below.)

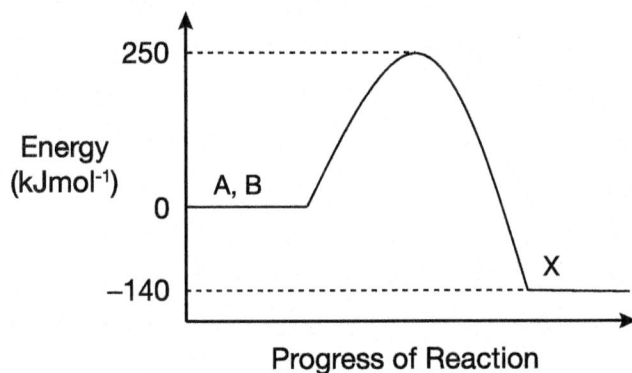

**Experiment 2**
The experiment is repeated, but this time with a catalyst.
A + B + catalyst → X (The energy transitions for the reaction are shown below.)

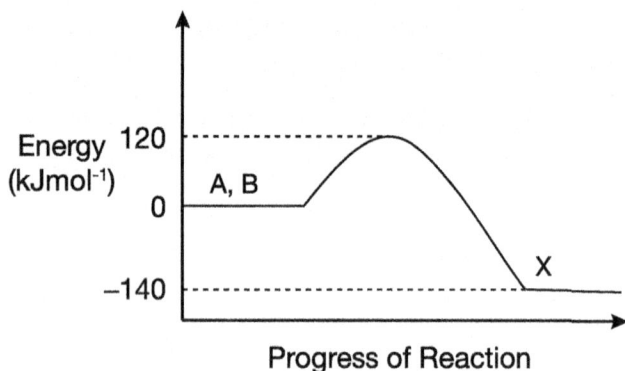

24. **The activation energy for the reaction in Experiment 1 is:**

    F.   140 kJmol$^{-1}$
    G.   250 kJmol$^{-1}$
    H.   390 kJmol$^{-1}$
    J.   110 kJmol$^{-1}$

25. **The difference between Experiments 1 and 2 is that:**

    A.   The reactants are at different energy levels initially.
    B.   The products are at different energy levels.
    C.   The reactions have different products.
    D.   One is performed with a catalyst, the other without.

26. **Based on the initial and final energy levels one can conclude that:**

    F.   Experiments 1 and 2 are both exothermic.
    G.   Experiments 1 and 2 are both endothermic.
    H.   Experiment 1 is exothermic, Experiment 2 is endothermic.
    J.   Experiment 2 is exothermic, Experiment 1 is endothermic.

27. **In comparison with Experiment 1, the catalyst in Experiment 2 reduces the effective activation energy by:**

    A.   130 kJmol$^{-1}$
    B.   120 kJmol$^{-1}$
    C.   20 kJmol$^{-1}$
    D.   260 kJmol$^{-1}$

28. **The total amount of energy released in the reaction A + B → X is**

    F.   250 kJmol$^{-1}$
    G.   390 kJmol$^{-1}$
    H.   260 kJmol$^{-1}$
    J.   140 kJmol$^{-1}$

29. **In a third experiment, a different catalyst is used to catalyze the reaction between A and B to get product X. The activation energy for this reaction is 170 kJmol$^{-1}$. The reaction in this third experiment will be:**

   A.  Slower than the reaction in Experiment 1.
   B.  Faster than the reaction in Experiment 2.
   C.  Slower than the reaction in Experiment 2.
   D.  At a rate that cannot be determined.

## Elevation Relative to Sea Level

A hypsometric curve or graph shows elevations for part or whole of the earth's surface. The vertical axis displays elevations above and below sea level (0 Km). The horizontal axis shows what percent of the earth's surface is above a certain elevation. The percentage plotted on the horizontal axis is thus cumulative.

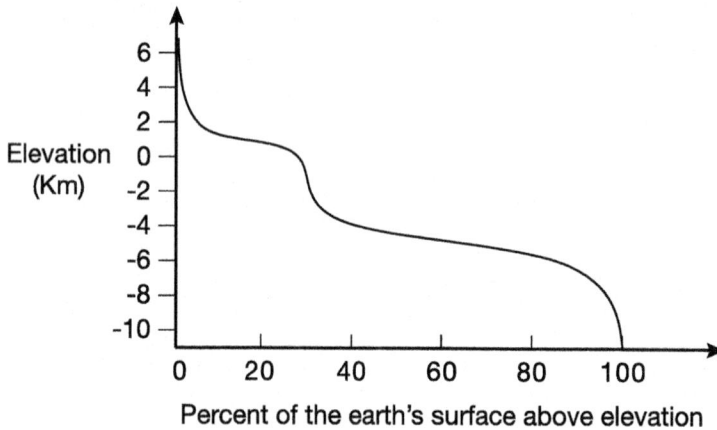

The information shown in the above graph can also be displayed in a histogram. The histogram shows the percent of the earth's surface that is within a certain range.

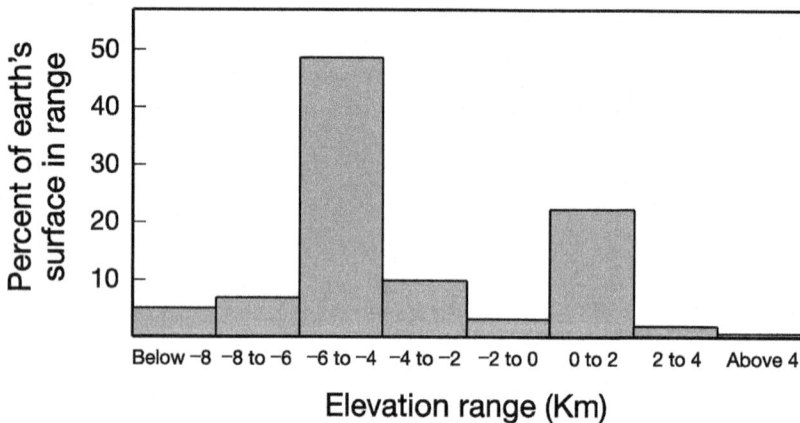

The histogram reveals that most of the earth's surface is within two ranges; 4 to 6 Km below sea level and 0 to 2 Km above sea level. It provides evidence for the two kinds of crust on the earth—the continental crust and the oceanic crust.

**30. About 50% of the earth's surface is:**

- F.  Above sea level
- G.  2000 m above sea level
- H.  500 m below sea level
- J.  4000 m below sea level

**31. The highest point in the Rocky Mountains is approximately 4 Km above sea level. What fraction of the earth's surface is above this elevation?**

    A.  1
    B.  0.5
    C.  0.1
    D.  0.01

**32. A rare ocean plant is found only at elevations lower than 6000 m below sea level. In what percentage of the earth's surface could this plant be found?**

    F.  12%
    G.  20%
    H.  35%
    J.  40%

**33. What percentage of the earth's surface is at elevations between 5.1Km and 5.2 Km?**

    A.  5%
    B.  2%
    C.  1%
    D.  Cannot be determined from given data.

**34. A student says that the histogram is wrong. The column height for range -6 Km to -4 Km should be 60%. The column height for range 0 Km to 2 Km should be 30%. All the other column heights should remain unchanged.**

    F.  The student is correct.
    G.  The student is wrong because no column height in the histogram can be greater than 50%.
    H.  The student is wrong because the column heights on the histogram must add up to 100%.
    J.  It is not possible to determine whether the student is wrong or right.

## Inherited Characteristics

Inherited characteristics in organisms are controlled by the combined effect of genes from both parents. This can happen in many different ways. One scenario is a trait that is controlled by a gene that has two alleles, i.e., two different types. For such a trait, a child inherits two genes that may be identical or one of each type. In the second case, if one of the alleles is dominant, the phenotype or physical appearance of the child is identical to that of the parent contributing the dominant gene. The non-dominant or recessive allele is unexpressed in that generation but can come back in another generation when combined in an offspring with another gene of the same type.

The scientist Mendel experimented with traits of this type in the late 19th century. The height of the pea plant he worked with was controlled by a gene with two alleles, tall (T) and short (t). He crossbred pure-breeding tall plants (TT) with pure-breeding short plants (tt). In the next generation, all the plants had alleles Tt (one from each parent) and all of them were tall since the T allele was dominant. The recessive allele for shortness (t), however, stayed hidden within the genetic makeup of the plants and was expressed in the next generation when Tt plants were crossbred with other Tt plants. Their offspring had the following combinations: TT, Tt and tt in the ratio 1:2:1. The tt plants turned out to be short while the rest were tall. This scenario is known as complete dominance.

When there is incomplete dominance, the phenotype of the child is a blend of that of the parents. Snapdragons show incomplete dominance with regard to color. When red (RR) and white (WW) snapdragons are crossbred, the offspring (RW) turn out to be pink. However, this does not mean that the red and white characteristics are lost. The next generation produces offspring with red (RR) and white (WW) flowers in addition to pink (RW) ones. The red, pink, and white flowers are in the ratio 1:2:1 as expected. This scenario is different from co-dominance where both phenotypes are expressed at once when an offspring carries different alleles for a trait. If the snapdragon color trait showed co-dominance instead of incomplete dominance, the flowers with genotype RW would have red and white splotches on them instead of being a uniform pink color.

### Experiment 1
A scientist breeds pink snapdragons with other pink snapdragons. The number of offspring for each color is given in the table below.

| Red | Pink | White |
| --- | --- | --- |
| 105 | 197 | 98 |

### Experiment 2
In another experiment, pink snapdragons are bred with red snapdragons. The number of offspring for each color is given in the table below.

| Red | Pink | White |
| --- | --- | --- |
| 192 | 208 | 0 |

### Experiment 3
In the third experiment, pink snapdragons are bred with white snapdragons. The number of offspring for each color is given in the table below.

| Red | Pink | White |
| --- | --- | --- |
| 0 | 199 | 201 |

**35. In all of the above experiments, the pink snapdragons have:**

    A. Genotype RR
    B. Genotype WW
    C. Genotype RW
    D. Different genotypes

**36. No white offspring were found in Experiment 2 because:**

    F. Neither of the parents had an allele for white color.
    G. White color requires two white alleles in an offspring.
    H. Only two white parents can produce a white offspring.
    J. For reasons that cannot be explained.

**37. According to genetic theory, two parents with pink flowers will produce red, pink, and white offspring in the ratio 1:2:1. Experiment 1:**

    A. Validates this theory.
    B. Disproves this theory.
    C. Is inconclusive.
    D. Is not connected to this theory.

**38. The ratio of pink to white snapdragons in Experiment 3 is 1:1 because:**

    F. Half the offspring inherit genes from the pink parent and half from the white one.
    G. Half the offspring get one white and one red allele from the parents, half of them get white alleles from both parents.
    H. The plants with pink flowers are bred only with other plants with pink flowers.
    J. Half the offspring get pink alleles from both parents and half get white alleles from both parents.

**39. If 100 red offspring from Experiment 2 are bred with 100 pink offspring from Experiment 3, the number of red offspring is expected to be approximately:**

    A. 100
    B. 0
    C. 50
    D. 25

**40. Which of the following is correct?**

    F. Experiment 3 is more accurate than Experiment 2 since the numbers more closely approximate the expected ratio 1:1.
    G. All three experiments together provide support for the theory of incomplete dominance of genetic characteristics.
    H. Experiments 2 and 3 do not add any new weight to the theory of incomplete dominance; Experiment 1 would have been sufficient.
    J. Experiments 2 and 3 contradict Experiment 1 since the color ratios are different.

# SCIENCE REASONING PRACTICE TEST 1 ANSWER KEY

| | |
|---|---|
| 1. A | 21. B |
| 2. G | 22. J |
| 3. D | 23. C |
| 4. F | 24. G |
| 5. B | 25. D |
| 6. H | 26. F |
| 7. C | 27. A |
| 8. G | 28. J |
| 9. A | 29. C |
| 10. H | 30. J |
| 11. C | 31. D |
| 12. G | 32. F |
| 13. B | 33. D |
| 14. H | 34. H |
| 15. B | 35. C |
| 16. F | 36. G |
| 17. B | 37. A |
| 18. F | 38. G |
| 19. B | 39. C |
| 20. H | 40. G |

# SCIENCE REASONING PRACTICE TEST 1 RATIONALES

## 1. Answer: A. 130 mg/dL
The passage clearly states that statins have been shown to be effective for people with normal levels of LDL cholesterol below 130 mg/dL. The figures 70 mg/dL and 30 mg/dL are mentioned in the passage, but a careful reading will show that they refer to current and proposed statin use guidelines, not to normal levels of LDL.

## 2. Answer: G. The enzyme HMG-CoA reductase prevents cholesterol production.
The passage states that the enzyme HMG-CoA reductase facilitates the production of cholesterol in the liver, which is the opposite of what is stated in answer choice B. All the other choices are asserted in the passage as true statements.

## 3. Answer: D. All of the above.
Expert 2 mentions all the points made in choices A, B and C in the argument against prescribing statins for people with a normal level of LDL cholesterol.

## 4. Answer: F. Expert 1
The third expert's opinion supports the position of Expert 1 by ruling out one of Expert 2's criticisms of the study. One of Expert 2's arguments against changing the statin use guidelines is that a large percentage of the study participants were not healthy as claimed, which skewed the results. Expert 3 refutes this argument by pointing out that even if the participants were not totally healthy they accurately reflect the health status of typical people in the U.S. population.

## 5. Answer: B. Statins have been shown to be effective in reducing heart disease risk for people with normal LDL levels.
Both Experts 1 and 2 agree on the accuracy of the study results regarding the effectiveness of statins in reducing heart disease risk for people with normal LDL levels. Their disagreement is about whether the guidelines for statin use should be changed based on the study. Choice A is incorrect because Expert 2 does not think that the study participants can be described as healthy. Choice C is something that only Expert 2 believes, while choice D is clearly the opinion of Expert 1 only.

## 6. Answer: H. Expert 1
Expert 1 believes that everyone 30 years old and above should be given statins to keep their LDL levels below 30mg/dL. Choice A is incorrect, even though Mary has a risk factor in the form of high blood pressure, because the proposed guidelines only recommend statins for women over 65. Choice B is incorrect because Expert 2 does not believe that anyone with normal LDL cholesterol below 130 mg/dL should be given statins.

## 7. Answer: C. Repeat the study with participants who do not have obvious health issues such as obesity or smoking.
Choice C is the correct answer because conducting the study with healthy participants only would remove one of the objections that Expert 2 has against the way the study was conducted. This would not totally resolve the disagreement but is the best choice since the other choices don't do anything to address the disagreements between Expert 1 and Expert 2. Choices A and B are incorrect since the two experts do not disagree about the cholesterol levels of the study participants. Choice D is incorrect because the disagreement between the experts has nothing to do with the difference between smokers and obese people.

## 8. Answer: G. $HCO_3^-$
Choices A and D can be eliminated since they are not ions as they do not carry a positive or negative charge. The passage states that carbon dioxide combines with water to produce carbonic acid. Comparing this statement with the first equation in the box, it is clear that the formula for carbonic acid is $H_2CO_3$. The passage also states that the carbonic acid dissociates into hydrogen ions and bicarbonate

ions. This is represented by the second equation in the box which represents a bicarbonate ion as $HCO_3^-$. Hence B is the correct choice.

### 9. Answer: A. An increase in acidity of about 150%.
A drop in pH represents increased acidity, so choice C is incorrect. Although the number 7.8 is about 4% smaller than 8.1, the pH scale is not linear, so choice B cannot be correct. The passage states that a pH drop of 0.12 units to 8.1 represents a 30% increase in acidity, therefore a pH drop of 0.3 units from 8.1 to 7.8 must represent an increase in acidity greater than 30%. Hence A is the correct choice.

### 10. Answer: H. 8.0
According to the graph shown, the point 2.5 Km below the ocean surface in the year 2400 is in the region labeled "-0.2". This represents the projected change in pH compared to pre-industrial times, meaning that the pH will fall from 8.2 to 8.0.

### 11. Answer: C. Lower pH disrupts the bodily processes of marine animals.
Only choice C is true as stated in the passage. Choice A is incorrect since carbon dioxide hurts the ocean ecosystem. Choice B is incorrect since higher concentration of hydrogen ions implies lower pH but higher acidity. Choice D is incorrect because ocean pH has fallen drastically only in the last two to three hundred years since the start of the industrial revolution.

### 12. Answer: G. It will decrease by 0.1
As shown in the graph, in the year 2400, ocean pH 4 Km below the ocean surface will be 0.1 less than that in pre-industrial times. In the year 2500, ocean pH 4 Km below the ocean surface will be 0.2 less than that in pre-industrial times. Therefore, between 2400 and 2500 ocean pH will decrease by 0.1 as stated in choice B.

### 13. Answer: B. $v_E = \sqrt{2gR}$
Choices C and D are incorrect since the data shows that when the product of g and R increases, the escape velocity also increases; this tells us that gR cannot be in the denominator of the formula. If choice A was correct then the value of escape speed would be directly proportional to gR and would change in the same proportion as gR. By comparing the values given for Uranus and earth, we see this is not the case. Uranus has a radius R that is about 4 times that of earth and acceleration due to gravity g that is about the same as that of earth. This gives Uranus a gR value that is about 4 times the value of gR for earth, however, the escape velocity for Uranus is just twice that of the earth. Hence A cannot be correct. Since 2 is the square root of 4, the data for Uranus and earth are consistent with the formula given in choice B.

### 14. Answer: H. Most of the gas will not escape since the molecules will collide with each other.
The escape velocity of the earth is given in the table as 11.2 Km/s. The most probable speed of the gas exceeds the escape velocity of the earth; however, the escape level for earth is stated in the passage as 500 Km, which is far above the altitude at which the explosion occurred. Below this altitude the gas molecules will collide with other molecules and will not be able to escape.

### 15. Answer: B. 10 Km/s
The escape velocity for a planet depends on its acceleration due to gravity g and radius R, specifically the product of the two: gR. Note that for the new planet, g is close to half that of Venus, while R is close to double that of Venus, therefore the product gR for the new planet is close to the same as it is for Venus. Given this information, the escape velocity is expected to be about the same as Venus, i.e., close to 10 Km/s.

### 16. Answer: F. $1.6 \times 10^{-5}$
According to information given in the passage, the most probable speed ($V_0$) for a hydrogen atom at 600K is about 3.16 Km/s. Since the escape speed ($V_e$) of the earth is 11.2 Km/s, the ratio $v_e/v_0 = 3.5$. The graph shows that for this value of the ratio, the fraction of atoms with speeds greater than escape speed is about $10^{-5}$.

Science Reasoning Practice Test 1 Rationales

**17. Answer: B. Why certain gases exist in a planet's atmosphere.**
By calculating the most probable speeds of different molecules and comparing them with the escape velocities of different planets, we can explain why some gases tend to stay in the atmosphere of a particular planet. For instance, earth's atmosphere has oxygen but almost no hydrogen since the hydrogen escapes from the gravitational pull of the earth. Jupiter, on the other hand, is massive enough to hold on to hydrogen. Hence choice B is correct. The other choices list factors that influence escape velocity but are not things that can be explained by using the information in the passage.

**18. Answer: F. 490 Kg/s$^2$**
An accurate value of the slope can be obtained only by finding the slope of the fitted line; however, we can calculate an approximate value by using any two sets of data points (say 2.5 and 5). Slope = (0.102 – 0.051)/(5 – 2.5) = 0.051/2.5 = 0.02 = g/k. (Make sure to convert the centimeters to meters so that 10.2 cm = 0.102 m and 5.1 cm = 0.051 m). The spring constant k = g/0.02 = 9.8/0.02 = 490 Kg/s$^2$.

**19. Answer: B. A line with the same slope as the line from Experiment 1 and a non-zero y-intercept.**
Studying the data carefully, you will note that for the same mass, the extension values in Experiment 2 are about 0.5 cm higher than the ones in Experiment 1. Placing those points on the given graph, you will notice that they form a line with the same slope as the one for Experiment 1. Also, for mass equal to zero, the extension has a non-zero value in Experiment 2; therefore, the plotted line will have a non-zero y-intercept. The same slope value for both experiments is to be expected since it represents the spring constant and the same spring is used in both experiments.

**20. Answer: H. There is an additional force on the spring, the force of gravity.**
The data shows that for each value of the mass, the extension in Experiment 2 is about 0.5 cm more than the extension in Experiment 1. This is due to the fact that in the vertical position, the weight of the spring acts on it, in addition to the mass hung on the end of the spring. Choice A is incorrect because it would be very unusual for the same error of 0.5 cm to be made consistently for all the measurements. Choice B is incorrect since Hooke's law does not refer to the orientation of the spring and is valid up to the elastic limit irrespective of whether the spring is horizontal or vertical.

**21. Answer: B. 6.5 cm**
Since the relation between mass and extension is linear, the extension of the spring with a mass of 3 Kg would be exactly between the extensions for 2.5 Kg and 3.5 Kg. Since these two values are 5.6 cm and 7.5 cm, the extension for a 3 Kg mass would be 6.55 cm.

**22. Answer: J. Between 4.1 and 4.6 cm**
If the air track was tilted, a component of gravity, smaller than the total force of gravity, would act on the spring. Hence the value of the spring extension would be somewhere between the extensions observed in Experiments 1 and 2, i.e., between 4.1 cm and 4.6 cm.

**23. Answer: C. Between 5 Kg and 10 Kg**
Based on Hooke's law, the relationship between m and x is linear. However, for forces larger than the elastic limit, Hooke's law fails. All the data points in Experiment 2 fall on a straight line (the extension increases approximately by 2 cm for every Kg of mass added) except for the last one, where the extension increases only by 2.4 cm for a 3 Kg increase in mass. This means that the elastic limit is exceeded when a mass of 8 Kg is added to the spring; therefore, the elastic limit must be somewhere between 5 and 8 Kg.

**24. Answer: G. 250 kJmol$^{-1}$**
The activation energy of the reaction is the energy needed to raise the reactants to the higher energy level needed for the reaction to proceed. For Experiment 1, reactants starting at energy 0 kJmol$^{-1}$ have to be raised to the transition state which has an energy level of 250 kJmol$^{-1}$, as shown in the diagram.

**25. Answer: D. One is performed with a catalyst, the other without.**
The only difference between the two experiments is that a catalyst has been added to Experiment 2 and hence the effective activation energy has been lowered. The other choices are incorrect since both reactions have exactly the same reactants and products which start out at the same energy level and end at the same energy level.

**26. Answer: F. Experiments 1 and 2 are both exothermic.**
For both experiments, the energy of the product is less than the initial energy of the reactants; therefore, both reactions release energy and are exothermic.

**27. Answer: A. 130 kJmol$^{-1}$**
Note that the question asks what the reduction in activation energy is in Experiment 2 compared to Experiment 1; this is the difference in activation energy for both experiments. Since Experiment 1 has an activation energy of 250 kJmol$^{-1}$ and Experiment 2 has an activation energy of 120 kJmol$^{-1}$, the reduction in activation energy = 250 − 120 = 130 kJmol$^{-1}$.

**28. Answer: J. 140 kJmol$^{-1}$**
The net energy released in the reaction is the difference between the initial and final energy levels. Since the reactants start out at 0 kJmol$^{-1}$ and the product is at -140 kJmol$^{-1}$, the total energy released = 0 − (-140) = 140 kJmol$^{-1}$.

**29. Answer: C. Slower than the reaction in Experiment 2.**
When a catalyst lowers the activation energy of a reaction, the reaction occurs at a faster rate. Since the activation energy in Experiment 3 is between the activation energies in the other two experiments, the reaction will be faster than the one in Experiment 1 and slower than the one in Experiment 2.

**30. Answer: J. 4000 m below sea level**
4000 m below sea level is −4 Km on the hypsometric graph. A horizontal line drawn on the hypsometric graph at the −4 Km level crosses the graph at close to 50%. The other choices are incorrect because the percentage of the earth's surface above all those elevations is less than 50%.

**31. Answer: D. 0.01**
Note that the question asks for the fraction and not the percentage. From the histogram it is clear that the percentage of the earth's surface higher than 4 Km above sea level is much smaller than 10%. The first three choices in terms of percentage are 100%, 50% and 10%, and therefore too large to be the correct number.

**32. Answer: F. 12%**
The range 6000 m below sea level or lower corresponds to the first two bins in the histogram. The sum of the heights of those two columns is clearly less than 20%, making A the only correct answer choice.

**33. Answer: D. Cannot be determined from given data.**
Both the hypsometric graph and the histogram provide information in relatively broad bins. The range 5.1 Km to 5.2 Km is too narrow for the answer to be gleaned from either of these sources.

**34. Answer: H. The student is wrong because the column heights on the histogram must add up to 100%.**
Since the histogram refers to percentages, when the entire surface of the earth is considered, the heights of the columns must add up to 100%. If the histogram is changed according to the student's statement, the column heights will add up to more than 100%.

**35. Answer: C. Genotype RW**
The pink snapdragons inherit one R gene and one W gene from each parent and therefore, they have the genotype RW. Due to incomplete dominance, neither the red nor the white characteristic is fully expressed and the flowers are colored something in between.

**36. Answer: G. White color requires two white alleles in an offspring.**
Due to incomplete dominance, an offspring is white only if it inherits white alleles from both parents. This was not possible in Experiment 2 since the parent with red flowers had genotype RR with only red alleles. Choice A is incorrect since the parent with pink flowers has genotype RW which does include one white allele. Choice C is incorrect because two parents with pink flowers (RW) can produce a white offspring by both contributing a white allele to the offspring.

**37. Answer: A. Validates this theory.**
Looking at the data we see that the offspring for Experiment 1 are approximately in the predicted ratio 1:2:1. Since this is a statistical prediction, i.e., the genotype of any particular offspring cannot be predicted, it is not expected that the numbers will be exact. Hence the data does validate the prediction as stated in Choice A.

**38. Answer: G. Half the offspring get one white and one red allele from the parents, half of them get white alleles from both parents.**
The parent plants with pink flowers have genotype RW and the parent plants with white flowers have genotype WW. The first parent contributes the R allele to half the offspring and the W allele to half the offspring. The second parent contributes only W alleles to all the offspring. So half the offspring have genotype RW and half have genotype WW, making answer choice B correct. Choice A is incorrect because offspring inherit genes from both parents, not just one. Choice C is incorrect because in Experiment 3 pink plants were bred with white plants and not other pink plants. Also, even if pink plants had been bred with other pink plants, the offspring would have included plants with red, pink, and white flowers in the ratio 1:2:1, as in Experiment 1. Choice D is incorrect because there is no such thing as a pink allele.

**39. Answer: C. 50**
This will essentially be a repeat of Experiment 2 since all plants with red flowers have genotype RR and all plants with pink flowers have genotype RW; the expected ratio of red to pink flowers is 1:1. Therefore, half the number of offspring (50), are expected to be red.

**40. Answer: G. All three experiments together provide support for the theory of incomplete dominance of genetic characteristics.**
All three experiments separately verify different predictions made by the theory of incomplete dominance. Choice A is incorrect since these predictions are statistical and are not expected to be exact. Choices C and D are incorrect since the predictions for Experiments 1, 2, and 3 are for different scenarios and need to be verified separately.

# ACT ASSESSMENT

# PRACTICE TEST TWO

# ENGLISH PRACTICE TEST 2

45 Minutes - 75 Questions

Directions: Read the provided passage. You will notice that words or phrases are underlined and numbered. Pay particular attention to these underlined words and phrases. Most questions on the test will offer you four alternatives to the underlined words or phrases, including the option of No change. Select the answer that best expresses the idea, style, or intention of the passage; is free of grammatical and punctuation errors, reflects standard usage in English, and works best within the context of the passage. Some questions may refer to parts of the passage or the whole passage rather than the underlined parts.

---

**The following passage is the basis for Questions 1-2:**

## Six Billion Dollar Baby

**(1)** An old joke goes like this: "If you break down the chemicals comprising a human body into their component parts, you'll find that the materials are worth about ninety-seven cents. So if anyone asks you to sell out for a buck, you should consider the offer." The information about the biochemical worthlessness of the human body was a staple of high school biology textbooks (and high school biology teacher's jokes). Yet there is a lot more to the story of human biochemical value than that.
    1                                                  2

---

1. **Which of the following changes, if any, should be applied to underlined section 1?**

   A. No change
   B. teachers
   C. teachers's
   D. teachers'

2. **What function does underlined section 2 perform in the paragraph?**

   F. No function
   G. contradictory interest-inducing function
   H. introduces the next paragraph and the theme of essay
   J. topical sentence function

---

**The following passage is the basis for Questions 3-6:**

**(2)** Just getting a human being started is difficult on the biochemical level. Each fertilized human egg, whether it is comprised of XX chromosomes, making it female, or XY chromosomes, making it male, have a certain amount of sheer "scarcity" or "rarity" value.
                                                                    3

**(3)** One would not necessarily think so. The World Health Organization is a branch of the United Nations.
                                       4                                            5
WHO estimates that the typical ejaculation of a human male contains forty million sperm. Only one out of those forty million is needed to fertilize the egg in the woman's fallopian tube to produce a human baby.

---

That seems like <u>more than enough, and only about two hundred</u> sperm survive all the way to the fallopian
6
tube. Only one hardy little sperm makes it all the way to fertilization.

3. **Which of the following changes, if any, should be applied to underlined section 3?**

   A. No change
   B. have certain amounts
   C. has a certain amount
   D. have a certain amounts

4. **Which of the following changes, if any, should be applied to underlined section 4?**

   F. No change
   G. eliminate the sentence as it is irrelevant
   H. You would not necessarily think so.
   J. He would not necessarily think so.

5. **Which of the following changes, if any, should be applied to underlined section 5?**

   A. No change
   B. the first sentence should be eliminated as it is irrelevant
   C. The World Health Organization is a branch of the United Nations who estimates
   D. The World Health Organization, a branch of the United Nations, estimates

6. **Which of the following changes, if any, should be applied to underlined section 6?**

   F. No change
   G. more than enough, but only about two hundred
   H. more than enough and only about two hundred
   J. more than enough, yet otherwise only about two hundred

---

**The following passage is the basis for Questions 7-9:**

(4) That means the sperm that gave each person half of <u>their DNA</u> was one special action hero. <u>By
7                  8
beating out millions of also-rans and if he made it that far</u>, that sperm is a conquering hero. That's worth

something.

(5) The journey to the cervix is fraught with peril. There are adverse conditions for a sperm in the cervix,

uterus, and oviducts. Due to acidic and other conditions, millions die or are rendered infertile, and millions

simply fall by the wayside. It's a long, long journey. Only one <u>insipid</u> little sperm fertilizes the egg.
9

---

7. **Which of the following changes, if any, should be applied to underlined section 7?**

   A. No change
   B. its DNA
   C. RNA/DNA
   D. his or her DNA

8. **Which of the following changes, if any, should be applied to underlined section 8?**

   F. No change
   G. By beating out millions of also-rans and making it that far,
   H. By beating out millions of alsos and rans, and if he made it that far,
   J. Beating out millions of also-rans, and if he made it that far,

9. **Which of the following changes, if any, should be applied to underlined section 9?**

   A. No change
   B. intrepid
   C. investigative
   D. invalid

---

**The following passage is the basis for Questions 10-12:**

(6) [1] One scientist was intrigued by the idea that the human body could sell for less than a dollar. [2] Yale University molecular biologist Dr. Harold J. Morowitz decided to do a more detailed study of the monetary value of the human body. [3] He thought that was a little cheap. [4] It turned out the synthesized chemicals would cost a total of about six million dollars, or $6,000,015.44. [5] After procuring a synthetic chemical catalogue from a biochemical company, he added up the cost of all the chemicals comprising the human body.

(7) The synthesized chemicals offered in the catalogue were made from animal <u>sources, and if someone</u>
11
<u>tried</u> to synthesize the body's chemicals from natural, raw materials, the cost would be even more. Dr. Horowitz estimated the cost <u>would then escalate</u> to six billion dollars. That's why every person is a six
12
billion dollar baby.

---

10. **Which of the following would be the best order of sentences 1 through 5 in paragraph 6?**

    F. No change
    G. 2, 5, 3, 1, 4
    H. 5, 3, 1, 4, 2
    J. 1, 3, 2, 5, 4

**11. Which of the following changes, if any, should be applied to underlined section 11?**

    A.  No change
    B.  sources; therefore, if someone tried
    C.  sources and if someone tried
    D.  sources, and if someone might have tried

**12. Which of the following changes, if any, should be applied to underlined section 12?**

    F.  No change
    G.  then would escalate
    H.  would escalate them
    J.  it would then

---

**The following passage is the basis for Questions 13-15:**

## Six Billion Dollar Baby

**(1)** An old joke goes like this: "If you break down the chemicals comprising a human body into their component parts, you'll find that the materials are worth about ninety-seven cents. So if anyone asks you to sell out for a buck, you should consider the offer." The information about the biochemical worthlessness of the human body was a staple of high school biology textbooks (and high school biology teacher's jokes). Yet there is a lot more to the story of human biochemical value than that.

**(2)** Just getting a human being started is difficult on the biochemical level. Each fertilized human egg, whether it is comprised of XX chromosomes, making it female, or XY chromosomes, making it male, have a certain amount of sheer "scarcity" or "rarity" value.

**(3)** One would not necessarily think so. The World Health Organization is a branch of the United Nations. WHO estimates that the typical ejaculation of a human male contains forty million sperm. Only one out of those forty million is needed to fertilize the egg in the woman's fallopian tube to produce a human baby. That seems like more than enough, and only about two hundred sperm survive all the way to the fallopian tube. Only one hardy little sperm makes it all the way to fertilization.

**(4)** That means the sperm that gave each person half of their DNA was one special action hero. By beating out millions of also-rans and if he made it that far, that sperm is a conquering hero. That's worth something.

**(5)** The journey to the cervix is fraught with peril. There are adverse conditions for a sperm in the cervix, uterus, and oviducts. Due to acidic and other conditions, millions die or are rendered infertile, and millions simply fall by the wayside. It's a long, long journey. Only one insipid little sperm fertilizes the egg.

**(6)** One scientist was intrigued by the idea that the human body could sell for less than a dollar. Yale University molecular biologist Dr. Harold J. Morowitz decided to do a more detailed study of the monetary value of the human body. He thought that was a little cheap. It turned out the synthesized chemicals would cost a total of about six million dollars, or $6,000,015.44. After procuring a synthetic chemical catalogue from a biochemical company, he added up the cost of all the chemicals comprising the human body.

**(7)** The synthesized chemicals offered in the catalogue were made from animal sources, and if someone tried to synthesize the body's chemicals from natural, raw materials, the cost would be even more. Dr. Horowitz estimated the cost would then escalate to six billion dollars. That's why every person is a six billion dollar baby.

**13. Where is the best placement for the following sentence?**

**Biochemically, human beings are invaluable.**

A. paragraph 1
B. paragraph 2
C. paragraph 4
D. paragraph 7

**14. Where is the best placement for the following paragraph?**

**Once this sperm has arrived at fertilization, the egg's surface goes through changes that prevent other sperm from penetrating it. Those that arrive even a nanosecond too late are rejected and fall away. One out of forty million sperm is fast and hardy enough to fertilize the egg.**

F. after paragraph 2
G. after paragraph 4
H. after paragraph 5
J. after paragraph 7

**15. Which of the following sentences provides the best conclusion?**

A. No change
B. Baby, it's cold outside.
C. Baby, you're worth it all.
D. Adults are also included in this value estimation.

---

**The following passage is the basis for Questions 16-18:**

## First Aid

(1) First Aid means the first help anyone gives to another person who has been injured or who has experienced a negative health event. First Aid may include administering Cardio-Pulmonary Resuscitation, performing the Heimlich Maneuver, or applying a tourniquet. It is important to be trained before trying to perform any of the tasks listed above, <u>which are means of restoring</u> a person's breathing
                                                                                      16
or heart rate, liberating a person from choking, <u>and tying off severed arteries that are causing blood loss</u>
                                                                                      17
<u>respectfully.</u> For a first aid giver, the responsibility of giving emergency aid to another person is a challenging, daunting task; however, for the <u>recipients, it's survival.</u>
                                                                                      18

---

**16. Which of the following changes, if any, should be applied to underlined section 16?**

F. No change
G. which are meanings to restore
H. which are meant in total to restore
J. which are means by which a person may restore

**17. Which of the following changes, if any, should be applied to underlined section 17?**

A. No change
B. and tying off several arteries that are causing blood loss respectfully.
C. and tying off severed arteries that are causing blood loss, respectfully.
D. and tying off severed arteries that are causing blood loss, respectively.

**18. Which of the following changes, if any, should be applied to underlined section 18?**

F. No change
G. recipients, its survival
H. recipients, its' survival
J. recipient, it's survival

---

**The following passage is the basis for Questions 19-21:**

(2) The first rule of any medical assistance is "Do No Harm." A person who has not been trained in First

Aid could do more harm than good <u>if they attempt to help without proper understanding</u>. Training is often
                                                                    19
available for free through the Red Cross or local health agencies. Yet, even without training, <u>there are</u>
                                                                                                        20
<u>generally rules</u> of First Aid that every person does well to memorize. <u>By learning these general principles,</u>
                                                                                                        21
<u>an untrained person can be of great help in an emergency situation.</u>

---

**19. Which of the following changes, if any, should be applied to underlined section 19?**

A. No change
B. if trying to attempt to help without proper understanding.
C. if he or she attempts to help without proper understanding.
D. if those people attempt to help without proper understanding.

**20. Which of the following changes, if any, should be applied to underlined section 20?**

F. No change
G. there are general rules
H. there are rules generally applying
J. there are General rules

**21. What is the purpose of underlined section 21?**

A. to encourage people to learn First Aid
B. to assure untrained people that they cannot be of much help
C. to warn people not to intervene in emergency situations unless they are trained
D. to encourage lay people that they can help in emergency situations

**The following passage is the basis for Questions 22-27:**

(3) 911 is, of course, a very handy number to reach in any emergency situation. Cell phones have made it
    22
easier to reach emergency services. In the past, a person had to search for a public phone. The sooner

professional medical help comes, the better. If you have a cell phone, use it quickly and look for cross

street signs so as to be able to give the location. Aren't you glad cell phones were invented? If you do not
                                                                 23
have a cell phone and there is no phone nearby, shout and wave to attract help.

(4) Don't move the injured person unless you absolutely must. If the person is in danger of being burned,

electrocuted, run over by a vehicle, or is in the way of falling concrete, bricks, or rocks, he or she should
                                                                                              24
be moved gently. You should move yourself out of danger as well. If there is no imminent danger, keeping
                                                                                                      26
the person immobilized and cover him or her with a blanket or jacket to ward off shock. Do not give the

person food or drink; there may be internal injuries that will result in choking or asphyxiation if the person

swallows. Try to stay out of contact with the person's saliva and blood. Reassure the person. Speak in a
                                                                                                  27
calm and encouraging voice. Hold the person's hand. When trained personnel do arrive, get out of their

way and let them do their jobs. Stay nearby, though, so you can provide all the details you know to help

them understand the situation better. Everyone can be a helper in an emergency situation. By following a

few easy-to-remember guidelines, you can be the difference between life and death for a suffering fellow

human being.

**22. Stylistically, what would be a good revision of underlined section 22?**

    F.   No revision
    G.  Nine-one-one is, of course,
    H.  911 is of course
    J.   A very handy number to reach in any emergency situation is, of course, 911.

**23. What kind of a sentence is underlined section 23?**

    A.  a dependent sentence
    B.  an imperative
    C.  an interrogative sentence
    D.  a declarative sentence

**24. What would be a good revision of underlined section 24?**

    F.  No revision
    G.  he or she should be moved gentler.
    H.  gently move him or her.
    J.  he or she should be moved.

**25. Note a good place to insert the following sentence: In this age of HIV/AIDS, it is important to be careful when handling an unknown person's bodily fluids.**

    A.  after the sentence that reads: "Do not give the person food or drink; there may be internal injuries that will result in choking or asphyxiation if the person swallows."
    B.  after the sentence that reads: "If there is no imminent danger, keep the person immobilized and cover him or her with a blanket or jacket to ward off shock."
    C.  before the sentence that reads: "Hold the person's hand."
    D.  before the sentence that reads: "You should move yourself out of danger as well."

**26. Which of the following changes, if any, should be applied to underlined section 26?**

    F.  No change
    G.  keeping the person immobilized, covering him or her with a blanket or jacket
    H.  keeping the person immobilized and covering him or her with a blanket or jacket
    J.  keep the person immobilized and cover him or her with a blanket or jacket

**27. What kind of a sentence is underlined section 27?**

    A.  constructive sentence
    B.  compound sentence
    C.  imperative sentence
    D.  interrogative sentence

---

**The following passage is the basis for Questions 28-30:**

## First Aid

**(1)** First Aid means the first help anyone gives to another person who has been injured or who has experienced a negative health event. First Aid may include administering Cardio-Pulmonary Resuscitation, performing the Heimlich Maneuver, or applying a tourniquet. It is important to be trained before trying to perform any of the tasks listed above, which are means of restoring a person's breathing or heart rate, liberating a person from choking, and tying off severed arteries that are causing blood loss respectfully. For a first aid giver, the responsibility of giving emergency aid to another person is a challenging, daunting task; however, for the recipients, it's survival.

**(2)** The first rule of any medical assistance is "Do No Harm." A person who has not been trained in First Aid could do more harm than good if they attempt to help without proper understanding. Training is often available for free through the Red Cross or local health agencies. Yet, even without training, there are generally rules of First Aid that every person does well to memorize. By learning these general principles, an untrained person can be of great help in an emergency situation.

**(3)** 911 is, of course, a very handy number to reach in any emergency situation. Cell phones have made it easier to reach emergency services. In the past, a person had to search for a public phone. The sooner professional medical help comes, the better. If you have a cell phone, use it quickly and look for cross street signs so as to be able to give the location. Aren't you glad cell phones were invented? If you do not have a cell phone and there is no phone nearby, shout and wave to attract help.

**(4)** Don't move the injured person unless you absolutely must. If the person is in danger of being burned, electrocuted, run over by a vehicle, or is in the way of falling concrete, bricks, or rocks, he or she should be moved gently. You should move yourself out of danger as well. If there is no imminent danger, keeping the person immobilized and cover him or her with a blanket or jacket to ward off shock. Do not give the person food or drink; there may be internal injuries that will result in choking or asphyxiation if the person swallows. Try to stay out of contact with the person's saliva and blood. Reassure the person. Speak in a calm and encouraging voice. Hold the person's hand. When trained personnel do arrive, get out of their way and let them do their jobs. Stay nearby, though, so you can provide all the details you know to help them understand the situation better. Everyone can be a helper in an emergency situation. By following a few easy-to-remember guidelines, you can be the difference between life and death for a suffering fellow human being.

**28.** **The assignment for the writer of the above essay was to provide information that would allow any person to be helpful in an emergency situation. Did the writer fulfill the assignment?**

    F.  no, there was too much technical First Aid advice given
    G.  no, there was not enough information for a person to be truly helpful in such a situation
    H.  yes, the writer gave some good general tips and the reasons for them
    J.  yes, the reader will feel a strong urge to become trained in First Aid

**29.** **How could the conclusion of the essay be strengthened?**

    A.  write a new concluding paragraph
    B.  make a new paragraph beginning with the sentence "Everyone can be a helper in an emergency situation" and let that be the concluding paragraph
    C.  the conclusion is strong enough as it is
    D.  include statistics about roadside deaths

**30.** **What would be a good alternative title to the essay?**

    F.  First Aid: First Things First in First Aid
    G.  A CPR Primer
    H.  Everyone a First Responder
    J.  Tips and Tourniquets: Trying Your Hand at First Aid

**The following passage is the basis for Questions 31-35:**

## The Great Debate

**(1)** In recent times televised debates between candidates for political office have become very popular.

Candidates participate in many debates over the courses of <u>their campaigns, and they</u> must display the
                                                              31

ability to think on their feet, get their points across succinctly, respond well to questions, and keep their

emotions under control when challenges are presented. It is a grueling test under the <u>bright hot lights</u> of
                                                                                 32

television, with the understanding that many voters are watching.

---

**(2)** Putting political candidates through their paces by holding public debates is not new. <u>The famous</u>
33
<u>Lincoln-Douglas Debates changed the course of the nation's history.</u>

**(3)** Contrary to common misconceptions, the Lincoln-Douglas Debates did not take place during Abraham Lincoln's successful run for the presidency. They took place during his unsuccessful run for a Senate seat in 1858, two years before the presidential election. Lincoln was challenging the incumbent Senator from Illinois, Stephen Douglas, for his Senate seat. The candidates held seven debates in seven different cities in Illinois. Great crowds turned out to see them. <u>Many people attended the debates.</u>
34

**(4)** <u>The excellent turn-out may be attributed to the era being a television-less one, but</u> today's televised
35
debates are watched by millions of people, indicating that political debates draw great crowds, whether they are televised or take place in person. People of all eras seem to care about the issues and the candidates' positions on them.

---

**31. Which of the following changes, if any, should be applied to underlined section 31?**

    A. No change
    B. their campaigns: and they
    C. their campaigns and they
    D. their campaigns. They

**32. Which of the following changes, if any, should be applied to underlined section 32?**

    F. No change
    G. bright, hot lights
    H. bright-hot lights
    J. red hot lights

**33. Which of the following changes, if any, should be applied to underlined section 33?**

    A. No change
    B. The famous Lincoln-Douglas Debates changed the course outline of the nation's history.
    C. The famous Lincoln-Douglas Debates changed courses in the nation's history.
    D. The famous Lincoln-Douglas Debates change the course of the nation's history.

**34. The sentence "Many people attended the debates" in underlined section 34 should be edited out during a revision on what basis?**

    F. it should not be edited out
    G. it's redundant
    H. it's grammatically incorrect
    J. it's a false historical statement

**35. What might be a good revision of underlined section 35?**

   A. No change
   B. There was no television during the era, so the excellent turn-out may be attributed to that; however,
   C. This is not a television era we are talking about, so the excellent turn-out may be attributed to that, but
   D. The television era had not dawned, so the excellent turned-out maybe attributed to that, but

---

**The following passage is the basis for Questions 36-42:**

**(5)** The seven Lincoln-Douglas debates revolved around slavery, which was a divisive issue in the United States at the time. Abraham Lincoln spoke against the expansion of slavery, expressed hope for its extinction through quarantine, and maintained that the Declaration of Independence promised equality for all people. Douglas authored legislation allowing slavery to expand and multiply into new states <u>and</u>
                                                                                                                36
<u>maintaining that</u> the Declaration of Independence and its promises of equality applied only to whites. Eventually, the debates devolved down to the issue of right and wrong. Abraham Lincoln maintained that it was not right to institutionalize moral evil, even if was legal: "If slavery is not wrong, nothing is wrong," he told the audiences.

**(6)** Lincoln lost the election to the Senate, but the Lincoln-Douglas Debates brought <u>Lincoln the self-</u>
                                                                                                                37
<u>educated frontiersman</u> to national prominence. The debate transcripts were distributed all over the nation. Lincoln would win the presidency two years later, in part on the strength of his debate performances. Lincoln was reasonable, folksy, <u>knowledgeable, sincere; he had a good sense of humor</u>. He had the
                                                                      38
moral high ground of opposing the expansion of slavery. This was a position with which many people in the North heartily agreed.

**(7)** Modern Lincoln-Douglas debates are often called "values debates" because they revolve around issues of right and wrong, as the original Lincoln-Douglas Debates did. For policy-type debates, parliamentary debate is used. The two types of debates have in common that both consider a motion. One debate team argues that the <u>motion is correct, the other argues</u> the motion is incorrect or else <u>offer</u>
                                                          39                                                                    40
<u>and support</u> an alternative.

**(8)** The format of the original Lincoln-Douglas Debates was that the first speaker spoke for a full hour; the second speaker spoke for ninety minutes; then the first speaker was allowed a final half hour. In

parliamentary debate and modern Lincoln-Douglas debates, speakers speak only for minutes at a time. <u>People are less patient these days.</u>
       41

**(9)** Parliamentary debate is a respectful and orderly way of presenting arguments by turns, usually through two debaters on a side, moderated by a Speaker or Judge. Speakers have from four to eight minutes to make their points, taking turns to construct their own arguments and to refute one another's arguments.

**(10)** Whatever format it follows, debate remains a popular way for people to examine positions on moral and other issues. <u>By hearing both sides, the nation is informed to be able to make intelligent decisions.</u>
            42
Debates also give audiences chances to see candidates in action and observe their manners, characters, and abilities to defend their positions in courteous yet cogent ways.

**36. Which of the following changes, if any, should be applied to underlined section 36?**

    F.  No change
    G.  and was for maintaining that
    H.  and he held the maintenance that
    J.  and maintained that

**37. Which of the following changes, if any, should be applied to underlined section 37?**

    A.  No change
    B.  Lincoln, the self-educated frontiersman,
    C.  Lincoln, who had educated himself while battling the western frontier,
    D.  Lincoln; the self-educated frontiersman,

**38. Which of the following changes, if any, should be applied to underlined section 38?**

    F.  No change
    G.  knowledgeable, sincere, but he had a good sense of humor.
    H.  knowledgeable, and sincere: he had a good sense of humor.
    J.  knowledgeable, sincere, and he had a good sense of humor.

**39. Which of the following changes, if any, should be applied to underlined section 39?**

    A.  No change
    B.  motion is correct. the other argues
    C.  motion is correct; the other argues
    D.  motion is correct, while the other argue

**40. Which of the following changes, if any, should be applied to underlined section 40?**

    F.  No change
    G.  they do offer and support
    H.  offered and supported
    J.  offers and supports

**41. What kind of a statement is underlined section 41?**

    A.  a factual statement
    B.  an editorial statement
    C.  an obligatory statement
    D.  an obituary statement

**42. Because it enlarges upon the experience of one group of people (those who watch the debates) to the experience of a larger group of people (the nation) underlined section 42 may be said to be called an:**

    F.  adherence
    G.  advocate
    H.  inference
    J.  invective

---

**The following passage is the basis for Questions 43-45:**

## The Great Debate

**(1)** In recent times televised debates between candidates for political office have become very popular. Candidates participate in many debates over the courses of their campaigns, and they must display the ability to think on their feet, get their points across succinctly, respond well to questions, and keep their emotions under control when challenges are presented. It is a grueling test under the bright hot lights of television, with the understanding that many voters are watching.

**(2)** Putting political candidates through their paces by holding public debates is not new. The famous Lincoln-Douglas Debates changed the course of the nation's history.

**(3)** Contrary to common misconceptions, the Lincoln-Douglas Debates did not take place during Abraham Lincoln's successful run for the presidency. They took place during his unsuccessful run for a Senate seat in 1858, two years before the presidential election. Lincoln was challenging the incumbent Senator from Illinois, Stephen Douglas, for his Senate seat. The candidates held seven debates in seven different cities in Illinois. Great crowds turned out to see them. Many people attended the debates.

**(4)** The excellent turn-out may be attributed to the era being a television-less one, but today's televised debates are watched by millions of people, indicating that political debates draw great crowds, whether they are televised or take place in person. People of all eras seem to care about the issues and the candidates' positions on them.

**(5)** The seven Lincoln-Douglas debates revolved around slavery, which was a divisive issue in the United States at the time. Abraham Lincoln spoke against the expansion of slavery, expressed hope for its extinction through quarantine, and maintained that the Declaration of Independence promised equality for all people. Douglas authored legislation allowing slavery to expand and multiply into new states and maintaining that_the Declaration of Independence and its promises of equality applied only to whites. Eventually, the debates devolved down to the issue of right and wrong. Abraham Lincoln maintained that it was not right to institutionalize moral evil, even if was legal: "If slavery is not wrong, nothing is wrong," he told the audiences.

**(6)** Lincoln lost the election to the Senate, but the Lincoln-Douglas Debates brought Lincoln the self-educated frontiersman to national prominence. The debate transcripts were distributed all over the nation. Lincoln would win the presidency two years later, in part on the strength of his debate performances. Lincoln was reasonable, folksy, knowledgeable, sincere; he had a good sense of humor. He had the moral high ground of opposing the expansion of slavery. This was a position with which many people in the North heartily agreed.

**(7)** Modern Lincoln-Douglas debates are often called "values debates" because they revolve around issues of right and wrong, as the original Lincoln-Douglas Debates did. For policy-type debates, parliamentary debate is used. The two types of debates have in common that both consider a motion. One debate team argues that the motion is correct, the other argues the motion is incorrect or else offer and support an alternative.

**(8)** The format of the original Lincoln-Douglas Debates was that the first speaker spoke for a full hour; the second speaker spoke for ninety minutes; then the first speaker was allowed a final half hour. In parliamentary debate and modern Lincoln-Douglas debates, speakers speak only for minutes at a time. People are less patient these days.

**(9)** Parliamentary debate is a respectful and orderly way of presenting arguments by turns, usually through two debaters on a side, moderated by a Speaker or Judge. Speakers have from four to eight minutes to make their points, taking turns to construct their own arguments and to refute one another's arguments.

**(10)** Whatever format it follows, debate remains a popular way for people to examine positions on moral and other issues. By hearing both sides, the nation is informed to be able to make intelligent decisions. Debates also give audiences chances to see candidates in action and observe their manners, characters, and abilities to defend their positions in courteous yet cogent ways.

**43. If the essay writer was assigned the task to write an essay comparing and contrasting Lincoln-Douglas and parliamentary debates, would you say he or she succeeded?**

    A. no, because the essay is more about the Lincoln-Douglas Debates than it is about parliamentary debates

    B. no, because the essay contrasts the original Lincoln-Douglas Debates with modern Lincoln-Douglas debates

    C. yes, because most of the essay compares and contrasts the finer points of parliamentary debate with Lincoln-Douglas debates

    D. yes, because parliamentary debate takes most of its format from the Lincoln-Douglas Debates

**44. Choose a logical place to insert the following sentence: "Lincoln felt that the containment and decline of slavery was the vision of the Founding Fathers."**

    F. between the sentence beginning "Abraham Lincoln spoke against the expansion of slavery" and the sentence beginning "Douglas authored legislation allowing slavery to expand and multiply"

    G. between the sentence beginning "Lincoln lost the election to the Senate" and the sentence beginning "The debate transcripts"

    H. after the sentence beginning "Abraham Lincoln maintained that it was not right to institutionalize moral evil" as an end to paragraph 5

    J. there is no place in the essay where this sentence properly fits

**45. What would be an appropriate concluding sentence to the essay?**

A. There is no need for a concluding sentence.
B. Modern candidates are right to call for a revival of Lincoln-Douglas style debates.
C. There are too many debates in modern presidential campaigns.
D. Perhaps a modern-day Abraham Lincoln will reveal himself through the debate process.

---

**The following passage is the basis for Questions 46-50:**

## Into the Sea

**(1)** Hunter Scott was only twelve years old when he watched the movie *Jaws*. Full of horrifying attacks by a great white shark, the movie had audiences gasping and fearing to go swimming in the ocean. Yet the shark attacks weren't the part of the movie that most intrigued Hunter Scott. He was interested in the scene where <u>Quint, captain of a fishing boat,</u> gives <u>an account for being</u> shipwrecked during World War II
                         46                       47
and surrounded by sharks in the open ocean. Quint mentions in the movie that the name of the ship was *The U.S.S. Indianapolis.*

**(2)** A little research showed Scott that there was <u>indeed</u> a ship named *The U.S.S. Indianapolis* which
                                        48
sank near the Philippines after being torpedoed by the Japanese. <u>On a secretive mission to deliver</u>
                                       49
<u>nuclear bomb components,</u> the ship was not rescued right away, and <u>many of them</u> were killed and eaten
                                       50
by sharks. Scott asked his history teacher if he could do a research project on *The U.S.S. Indianapolis* for credit, and he was given permission to do so.

---

**46. Which of the following changes, if any, should be applied to underlined section 46?**

F. No change
G. Quint, captain of a fishing boat
H. Quint captain of a fishing boat,
J. Captain Quint of a fishing boat

**47. Which of the following changes, if any, should be applied to underlined section 47?**

A. No change
B. an account with being
C. an account to being
D. an account of being

**48. In underlined section 48, for what purpose did the writer of the essay choose to place the word "indeed" in the sentence?**

    F.  it has no purpose
    G.  for emphasis
    H.  to sound old-fashioned like the story itself
    J.  to make sure the reader understands the deeds that were done

**49. How could underlined section 49 be revised to convey more clearly the meaning that the reason for the delayed rescue was the ship's secretive mission?**

    A.  No change
    B.  Because it was on a secretive mission to deliver nuclear bomb components,
    C.  Being it was on a secretive mission to deliver nuclear bomb components,
    D.  Being as how it was on a secretive mission to deliver nuclear bomb components,

**50. Which of the following changes, if any, should be applied to underlined section 50?**

    F.  No change
    G.  many of these
    H.  many, many, many
    J.  many of the men

---

**The following passage is the basis for Questions 51-55:**

**(3)** Fortunately for Scott, some of the original crew members were still alive and had formed a survivors' group so they could easily put him in touch with the other survivors. What was more, their proud
                51
descendants had formed a support group called The Second Watch to remember the sacrifice and bravery of their ancestors. There was plenty of material for a history project.

**(4)** Scott found out that of the over one thousand crew members of *The U.S.S. Indianapolis*, only a third of them lived to tell the tale of being stranded in the ocean for four or five days. These three hundred or
                                52
so men they had plenty of memories to share with Scott. They remembered watching comrades grow delirious from sun exposure or drinking seawater and they swam off only to be swallowed by the deep.
                                    53
They remembered beating the water and screaming when they saw sharks circling their numbers and prowling on the attack. They remembered watching unfortunate comrades bitten and eaten by sharks. They watched other comrades slowly succumb to the wounds they have received during the torpedo
                                    54
attack.

**(5)** Yet this group had a camaraderie and unity that inspired Scott. Over half of the survivors had been in Ensign Harlan Twible's group, and Ensign Twible had heroically enjoined them to help one another. They

---

              

> tied themselves together with ropes so that no one could drift off or drown if his face slipped into the water during sleep. They shared lifejackets and helped one another into ones they took off the dead. They exhorted one another not to give up hope and to keep fighting for survival. It was their group that hallooed and waved to a low-flying plane and caught the attention of the pilot, who then arranged for their rescue. Twible was later awarded Navy and Marine Corps medals for his heroism in keeping the group together and enhancing their chances for survival.

**51. What would be a good revision, if any, to apply to underlined section 51?**

    A.  No change
    B.  edit it out as unnecessary
    C.  move it to the end of the essay
    D.  edit it out as redundant

**52. Which of the following changes, if any, should be applied to underlined section 52?**

    F.  No change
    G.  These three hundred or so men had
    H.  These three hundred or so men have
    J.  These three hundred or so men would have had

**53. Which of the following changes, if any, should be applied to underlined section 53?**

    A.  No change
    B.  and they swum off
    C.  and swammed off
    D.  and swim off

**54. Which of the following changes, if any, should be applied to underlined section 54?**

    F.  No change
    G.  they having received
    H.  they had received
    J.  having been received

**55. What is the tone of paragraph 5 in relation to paragraph 4?**

    A.  No difference in tone
    B.  the tone goes from one of horror and suffering to one of hope and unity
    C.  the tone goes from one of hope for rescue to one of resignation to fate
    D.  the tone goes from the sailors being realistic about their situation to being irrationally hopeful

The following passage is the basis for Questions 56-57:

(6) <u>Surprising, Scott found</u> that the survivors were not as haunted by their horrific days in the water as
       56
they were by the knowledge that their captain had suffered charges over the incident. He was accused of

not properly zig-zagging the ship in order to avoid torpedo fire. The men who had gone into the water did

not think their captain was to blame, and they wanted to clear his name.

(7) With Scott's help and encouragement, they supported one another as they had during <u>the most awful</u>
                                57

<u>incident of their lifes.</u> They won that battle as they won the battle for survival in the frightening, powerful,

and shark-ridden sea—by sticking together and supporting one another. They began a campaign, and in

the year 2000 these intrepid survivors appeared as a group before Congress to ask for the exoneration of

their captain.

56. Which of the following changes, if any, should be applied to underlined section 56?

    F.  No change
    G.  Surprise,
    H.  Surprisingly,
    J.  With a surprise like a birthday present,

57. Which of the following changes, if any, should be applied to underlined section 57?

    A.  No change
    B.  the most awful incident of their lives.
    C.  the most awful incident of their life styles
    D.  the most awful incident of their saved lifes

The following passage is the basis for Questions 58-60:

## Into the Sea

(1) Hunter Scott was only twelve years old when he watched the movie *Jaws*. Full of horrifying attacks by a great white shark, the movie had audiences gasping and fearing to go swimming in the ocean. Yet the shark attacks weren't the part of the movie that most intrigued Hunter Scott. He was interested in the scene where Quint, captain of a fishing boat, gives an account for being shipwrecked during World War II and surrounded by sharks in the open ocean. Quint mentions in the movie that the name of the ship was *The U.S.S. Indianapolis*.

(2) A little research showed Scott that there was indeed a ship named *The U.S.S. Indianapolis* which sank near the Philippines after being torpedoed by the Japanese. On a secretive mission to deliver nuclear bomb components, the ship was not rescued right away, and many of them were killed and eaten by sharks. Scott asked his history teacher if he could do a research project on *The U.S.S. Indianapolis* for credit, and he was given permission to do so.

**(3)** Fortunately for Scott, some of the original crew members were still alive and had formed a survivors' group so they could easily put him in touch with the other survivors. What was more, their proud descendants had formed a support group called The Second Watch to remember the sacrifice and bravery of their ancestors. There was plenty of material for a history project.

**(4)** Scott found out that of the over one thousand crew members of *The U.S.S. Indianapolis*, only a third of them lived to tell the tale of being stranded in the ocean for four or five days. These three hundred or so men they had plenty of memories to share with Scott. They remembered watching comrades grow delirious from sun exposure or drinking seawater and they swam off only to be swallowed by the deep. They remembered beating the water and screaming when they saw sharks circling their numbers and prowling on the attack. They remembered watching unfortunate comrades bitten and eaten by sharks. They watched other comrades slowly succumb to the wounds they have received during the torpedo attack.

**(5)** Yet this group had a camaraderie and unity that inspired Scott. Over half of the survivors had been in Ensign Harlan Twible's group, and Ensign Twible had heroically enjoined them to help one another. They tied themselves together with ropes so that no one could drift off or drown if his face slipped into the water during sleep. They shared lifejackets and helped one another into ones they took off the dead. They exhorted one another not to give up hope and to keep fighting for survival. It was their group that hallooed and waved to a low-flying plane and caught the attention of the pilot, who then arranged for their rescue. Twible was later awarded Navy and Marine Corps medals for his heroism in keeping the group together and enhancing their chances for survival.

**(6)** Surprising, Scott found that the survivors were not as haunted by their horrific days in the water as they were by the knowledge that their captain had suffered charges over the incident. He was accused of not properly zig-zagging the ship in order to avoid torpedo fire. The men who had gone into the water did not think their captain was to blame, and they wanted to clear his name.

**(7)** With Scott's help and encouragement, they supported one another as they had during the most awful incident of their lifes. They won that battle as they won the battle for survival in the frightening, powerful, and shark-ridden sea—by sticking together and supporting one another. They began a campaign, and in the year 2000 these intrepid survivors appeared as a group before Congress to ask for the exoneration of their captain.

**58. What would be a good alternative title to the essay?**

    F.  Shark Attack!
    G.  Adversity, Unity, and Victory
    H.  Futility on the Sea
    J.  Men Against Nature and One Another

**59. What rearrangement of the sentence order in paragraph 7 might make for a more powerful conclusion?**

    A.  No change
    B.  switch the first and second sentences
    C.  start the paragraph with the last sentence and end it with the first sentence
    D.  move the second sentence, starting with "They won that battle" to the end of the paragraph as the concluding sentence

**60. What was the writer's purpose in writing this essay?**

    F.  to report on an unfortunate maritime incident

    G.  to show that even in the midst of a horrible situation, people can help one another and salvage some good out of it

    H.  to show that nuclear arms were the cause of a horrific incident at sea

    J.  to expose the heinous nature of war

---

**The following passage is the basis for Questions 61-65:**

# Twelve Steps to Freedom

**(1)** Sometimes when people have an addiction problem, they don't know where to turn. After all,

addictions—whether they are to alcohol, heroin, cocaine, food or other <u>palliatives</u>—are expensive. Often,
<br>61

addicts and their family members <u>have already suffered</u> multiple losses, including financial ones, due to
<br>62

the addiction. They cannot afford therapy. They are <u>at the end of their ropes</u>. Where should they turn?
<br>63


**(2)** There is one easily accessible, low-cost place where not only addicts but those who love and care

about them can turn: the venerable institution of Alcoholics Anonymous and its companion program Al-

Anon. Alcoholics Anonymous addresses the problems of addicts. <u>Al-Anon, addresses</u> the problems of
<br>64

families and friends of addicts.


**(3)** Alcoholics Anonymous began on <u>June 10 1935</u> when a man named Bill W. and his friend Dr. Bob
<br>65

(their last names are rarely spelled out in keeping with the association being anonymous) addressed their

drinking problems. Bill W. had ruined a successful business life and almost destroyed a happy marriage

through his compulsive need to drink.

---

**61. From the context of the sentence, what does underlined section 61 mean?**

    A.  things that abate or relieve discomfort temporarily

    B.  items that are highly desirable

    C.  ingested chemical substances

    D.  things that are palatable

**62. Which of the following changes, if any, should be applied to underlined section 62?**

    F.  No change

    G.  have all ready suffered

    H.  have suffered already

    J.  already have suffered

**63. What stylistic reason is there for revising underlined section 63?**

   A.  No reason
   B.  it is a cliché
   C.  it is a metaphor
   D.  it is a simile

**64. Which of the following changes, if any, should be applied to underlined section 64?**

   F.  No change
   G.  Al-Anon addresses
   H.  Al-Anon address
   J.  Al-Anon, address

**65. Which of the following changes, if any, should be applied to underlined section 65?**

   A.  No change
   B.  June 10th, 1935
   C.  6/10/35
   D.  June 10, 1935

---

**The following passage is the basis for Questions 66-68:**

(4) Bill had been working with "The Oxford Group" to apply principles of living to learn to live alcohol-free. Bill worked toward sobriety with The Oxford Group, but he realized the principles the program was based upon could use some expansion and broadening. The principles of The Oxford Group needed extension
                                                                                                                                                        66
and widening.

(5) Bill W. and Dr. Bob developed Twelve Steps for fighting addiction to alcohol. These Twelve Steps worked to establish order and harmony in alcoholics' chaotic lives, especially when coupled with the support of a group of fellow alcoholics. They introduced also the idea of an "anonymous fellowship" from
                                                                                                               67
which Alcoholics Anonymous derived its name. Hence, to this day both founders are usually referred to in
                                                                                          68
ways that obscure their real names.

(6) About ten years later, the pair developed the Twelve Traditions, which are designed to keep AA non-hierarchical and non-judgmental. The Twelve Traditions limit AA's purpose to helping alcoholics get and become sober. AA membership is open to anyone who has a problem with alcoholism or other addictions regardless of his or her other affiliations or beliefs.

**66. Which of the following changes, if any, should be applied to underlined section 66?**

    F.  No change
    G.  eliminate the sentence as it is repetitive
    H.  move the sentence into the position of the second sentence in the paragraph
    J.  begin the paragraph with the sentence

**67. Which of the following changes, if any, should be applied to underlined section 67?**

    A.  No change
    B.  The Twelve Steps introduced also
    C.  The two men introduced also
    D.  They also introduced

**68. What would be a modern way to express the thought in underlined section 68?**

    F.  This is why even in these days
    G.  Thus, to this day
    H.  This being the reason why, years later,
    J.  Therefore, up to this very day in time

---

**The following passage is the basis for Questions 69-72:**

**(7)** In 1951 Bill's wife Lois realized that her own behavior in relation to his addiction needed amending. This was the beginning of Al-Anon, where friends and family members of people with addictions work on their own lives, strive to achieve serenity, and scrutinize their own contributions to the problem.

**(8)** Friends and family members often find they have been "enabling" the addiction by paying fines, bailing the person out of jail, making excuses to employers for missed work days, and <u>in general covering up, protected, and shielding the addict</u> from consequences. This allows the addiction to go on longer.
69

Through Al-Anon, people who love addicts realize that a lot of their own behavior is <u>neither helpful or loving.</u>
70

**(9)** Many well-known experts and therapists recommend AA and Al-Anon <u>to those effected by addictions</u>. Although the Twelve Steps are not magic, they often bring about profound changes. They are simple, low-cost, readily available and effective programs. They have helped countless people and those who love them cope with and overcome the <u>agonies of addiction.</u>
71
72

    

**69. Which of the following changes, if any, should be applied to underlined section 69?**

    A. No change
    B. in general covering up, protective, and shielding the addict
    C. in general covering up, protecting, and shielding the addict
    D. in general covered up, protected, and shielded the addict

**70. Which of the following changes, if any, should be applied to underlined section 70?**

    F. No change
    G. neither is helpful or loving.
    H. neither helpful or is loving.
    J. neither helpful nor loving.

**71. Which of the following changes, if any, should be applied to underlined section 71?**

    A. No change
    B. affected
    C. effective
    D. affectedly

**72. The writer of the essay has used alliteration—beginning two words that are close together with the same letter or sound—in underlined section 72. Why would the writer do this in this particular section?**

    F. No reason
    G. because it rhymes
    H. to lend poetic expression and lyricism so as not to end on a dull note
    J. to lend emphasis and emotion to the concluding sentence

---

**The following passage is the basis for Questions 73-75:**

## Twelve Steps to Freedom

**(1)** Sometimes when people have an addiction problem, they don't know where to turn. After all, addictions—whether they are to alcohol, heroin, cocaine, food or other palliatives—are expensive. Often, addicts and their family members have already suffered multiple losses, including financial ones, due to the addiction. They cannot afford therapy. They are at the end of their ropes. Where should they turn?

**(2)** There is one easily accessible, low-cost place where not only addicts but those who love and care about them can turn: the venerable institution of Alcoholics Anonymous and its companion program Al-Anon. Alcoholics Anonymous addresses the problems of addicts. Al-Anon, addresses the problems of families and friends of addicts.

**(3)** Alcoholics Anonymous began on June 10 1935 when a man named Bill W. and his friend Dr. Bob (their last names are rarely spelled out in keeping with the association being anonymous) addressed their drinking problems. Bill W. had ruined a successful business life and almost destroyed a happy marriage through his compulsive need to drink.

**(4)** Bill had been working with "The Oxford Group" to apply principles of living to learn to live alcohol-free. Bill worked toward sobriety with The Oxford Group, but he realized the principles the program was based upon could use some expansion and broadening. The principles of The Oxford Group needed extension and widening.

**(5)** Bill W. and Dr. Bob developed Twelve Steps for fighting addiction to alcohol. These Twelve Steps worked to establish order and harmony in alcoholics' chaotic lives, especially when coupled with the support of a group of fellow alcoholics. They introduced also the idea of an "anonymous fellowship" from which Alcoholics Anonymous derived its name. Hence, to this day both founders are usually referred to in ways that obscure their real names.

**(6)** About ten years later, the pair developed the Twelve Traditions, which are designed to keep AA non-hierarchical and non-judgmental. The Twelve Traditions limit AA's purpose to helping alcoholics get and become sober. AA membership is open to anyone who has a problem with alcoholism or other addictions regardless of his or her other affiliations or beliefs.

**(7)** In 1951 Bill's wife Lois realized that her own behavior in relation to his addiction needed amending. This was the beginning of Al-Anon, where friends and family members of people with addictions work on their own lives, strive to achieve serenity, and scrutinize their own contributions to the problem.

**(8)** Friends and family members often find they have been "enabling" the addiction by paying fines, bailing the person out of jail, making excuses to employers for missed work days, and in general covering up, protected, and shielding the addict from consequences. This allows the addiction to go on longer. Through Al-Anon, people who love addicts realize that a lot of their own behavior is neither helpful or loving.

**(9)** Many well-known experts and therapists recommend AA and Al-Anon to those effected by addictions. Although the Twelve Steps are not magic, they often bring about profound changes. They are simple, low-cost, readily available and effective programs. They have helped countless people and those who love them cope with and overcome the agonies of addiction.

73. **The author wants to insert the following sentence into the essay: "Sometimes friends and family members realize they have deep vested interests in keeping the addict dependent upon them." The new sentence would fit most logically into which paragraph?**

   A. paragraph 1
   B. paragraph 4
   C. paragraph 7
   D. paragraph 9

74. **The author was assigned to write an essay about the origins and purpose of Alcoholics Anonymous and Al-Anon. Did the author succeed in this assignment?**

   F. no, because there is not enough about the origins
   G. no, because the purpose is never mentioned
   H. yes, because both the origins and purpose are covered
   J. yes, because the information about Lois W. was particularly interesting

75. **Where would a list and brief description of reputable but expensive treatment centers most logically fit in the essay?**

   A. after paragraph 1
   B. after paragraph 3
   C. after paragraph 6
   D. after paragraph 9

# ENGLISH PRACTICE TEST 2 ANSWER KEY

| | | | |
|---|---|---|---|
| 1. D | | 39. C | |
| 2. H | | 40. J | |
| 3. C | | 41. B | |
| 4. F | | 42. H | |
| 5. D | | 43. A | |
| 6. G | | 44. F | |
| 7. D | | 45. D | |
| 8. G | | 46. F | |
| 9. B | | 47. D | |
| 10. J | | 48. G | |
| 11. B | | 49. B | |
| 12. G | | 50. J | |
| 13. D | | 51. A | |
| 14. H | | 52. G | |
| 15. A | | 53. D | |
| 16. F | | 54. H | |
| 17. D | | 55. B | |
| 18. J | | 56. H | |
| 19. C | | 57. B | |
| 20. G | | 58. G | |
| 21. D | | 59. D | |
| 22. J | | 60. G | |
| 23. C | | 61. A | |
| 24. H | | 62. J | |
| 25. A | | 63. B | |
| 26. J | | 64. G | |
| 27. C | | 65. D | |
| 28. H | | 66. G | |
| 29. B | | 67. C | |
| 30. H | | 68. G | |
| 31. D | | 69. C | |
| 32. G | | 70. J | |
| 33. A | | 71. B | |
| 34. G | | 72. J | |
| 35. B | | 73. C | |
| 36. J | | 74. H | |
| 37. B | | 75. A | |
| 38. J | | | |

# ENGLISH PRACTICE TEST 2 RATIONALES

**1. Answer: D. teachers'**
"Teachers" is a plural noun, and the plural possessive form of nouns is an apostrophe after the "s".

**2. Answer: H. introduces the next paragraph and the theme of essay**
The sentence provides a lead-in to the next paragraph. The rest of the essay is about the value of a human being, so the sentence also serves to introduce the theme of the essay.

**3. Answer: C. has a certain amount**
"Egg" is the subject of the sentence, and as a singular noun it requires the singular verb "has" rather than the plural verb "have" in order for there to be subject-verb agreement.

**4. Answer: F. No change**
The sentence is correct as it is.

**5. Answer: D. The World Health Organization, a branch of the United Nations, estimates**
Standing alone, the sentence "The World Health Organization is a branch of the United Nations" almost appears to be irrelevant. "WHO estimates" is also confusing because the acronym WHO could easily be mistaken for the word "Who". For smoothness and clarity, it is better to incorporate the description of the World Health Organization as a dependent clause within the sentence rather than as a sentence standing alone and to eliminate the acronym WHO.

**6. Answer: G. more than enough, but only about two hundred**
In the context of the sentence and paragraph, the coordinating conjunction "but" is more accurate in meaning than "and". The word "but" changes the direction of the sentence, serving as a transitional word. The transitional word "however" also could have been used.

**7. Answer: D. his or her DNA**
Pronouns are substitute words for nouns. In this sentence, a pronoun is meant to substitute for the noun "person". The noun that comes before the pronoun (in this case "person") is the pronoun's antecedent. A pronoun must agree in number with its antecedent. Yet the sentence uses "their" as the pronoun. "Their" is a plural pronoun. Since the sentence is referring to one person ("each person") the noun is singular and needs a singular pronoun such as "his" or "her".

**8. Answer: G. By beating out millions of also-rans and making it that far,**
As it stands, the sentence is a mixed construction. A mixed construction is when a sentence contains parts that do not fit together within the grammatical structures of English. Changing "and if he made it that far" to "and making it that far" makes it match "beating out millions of also-rans" by using the gerund form "ing" twice.

**9. Answer: B. intrepid**
"Insipid" means weak and does not make sense in the context of the sentence or paragraph. "Intrepid" means enduring, persevering, and strong—a good description.

**10. Answer: J. 1, 3, 2, 5, 4**
The flow and meaning of the paragraph is best in this sentence order. Sentence 3 is closely related to sentence 1 and should come between Sentence 1 and Sentence 2. When it comes to sequence of events, sentence 5 should come before Sentence 4.

**11. Answer: B. sources; therefore, if someone tried**
One way to link two independent clauses (clauses that can stand alone as sentences) is to use a semi-colon. In this case, "therefore" is an independent marker word, indicating the beginning of the second independent clause in the sentence. A semi-colon is needed before the independent marker word to end the first independent clause.

## 12. Answer: G. then would escalate

"Would" is a modal verb showing possibility. It can also be classified as a helping verb. The base verb form is "escalate". If possible, it is better not to separate the modal verb or helping verb from its base verb form.

## 13. Answer: D. paragraph 7

The last paragraph is where the biochemical value of the human body is shown to be astronomical, so the sentence would fit best in that paragraph.

## 14. Answer: H. after paragraph 5

The sequence of events described through paragraph 5, depicting the difficulties of fertilization, makes this a logical place to insert a paragraph about the final challenges. Paragraph 6 introduces the work of a scientist, so after paragraph 5 and before paragraph 6 is the best placement for this paragraph.

## 15. Answer: A. No change

The existing concluding sentence (That's why every person is a six billion dollar baby.) refers back to the title and sums up the theme and point of the essay. None of the other answers do this or do it as well.

## 16. Answer: F. No change

The sentence is fine as it is.

## 17. Answer: D. and tying off severed arteries that are causing blood loss, respectively.

Respectfully means "full of respect". Respectively means in the order given and refers to something that came earlier. Underlined section 17 is the last in a series that refers back to CPR, the Heimlich Maneuver, and applying a tourniquet. A less complicated example of proper use of "respectively" would be "John and Jane want to be a politician and a community organizer, respectively." There is always a comma before "respectively".

## 18. Answer: J. recipient, it's survival

The sentence is referring to one first responder aiding one victim, therefore "recipient" is singular. "It's" is the proper contraction for "it is".

## 19. Answer: C. if he or she attempts to help without proper understanding.

Pronouns are substitute words for nouns. In this sentence, a pronoun is meant to substitute for the noun "person". A pronoun must agree in number with its antecedent ("person"). Yet the sentence uses "they" as the pronoun. "They" is a plural pronoun. The noun ("a person") is singular and needs a singular pronoun such as "he" or "she".

## 20. Answer: G. there are general rules

"Generally" is an adverb. "ly" is the usual way to indicate the adverb form. Adverbs modify verbs. In this sentence, "rules" is being modified, and "rules" is a noun, not an adverb. Adjectives are used to modify nouns. "General" in its usage here is an adjective. Therefore, "there are general rules" is correct.

## 21. Answer: D. to encourage lay people that they can help in emergency situations

The sentence is meant to encourage "lay" people (that is, untrained people) that they can still be of help in emergency situations if they learn and adhere to a few general rules.

## 22. Answer: J. A very handy number to reach in any emergency situation is, of course, 911.

It is not stylistically sound to begin a sentence with a number, so it is best to revise the sentence so that "911" is not at the beginning.

## 23. Answer: C. an interrogative sentence

Because the sentence asks a question, it is an interrogative sentence.

**24. Answer: H. gently move him or her.**
In general it is considered the best style to write in the active voice. The active voice means that a subject is taking action rather than an object being acted upon. In this case, the unspoken but understood subject is "you". Commands are being given to "you" (the reader) to take certain action: "gently move him or her."

**25. Answer: A. after the sentence that reads: "Do not give the person food or drink; there may be internal injuries that will result in choking or asphyxiation if the person swallows."**
The next sentence after this one instructs the reader not to touch the injured person's blood or saliva, so the sentence about HIV/AIDS properly belongs before it.

**26. Answer: J. keep the person immobilized and cover him or her with a blanket or jacket**
This answer corrects a mixed construction. A mixed construction means that the structure of the sentence does not make sense in English. "Cover" and "keep" match in verb form (they are both base verb forms) whereas "keeping" is a different verb form (the gerund or "ing" verb form). Mixing the two different verb forms creates an awkward sentence that does not make sense.

**27. Answer: C. imperative sentence**
Since the writer is giving a "command" or instructions, this is by definition an imperative sentence.

**28. Answer: H. yes, the writer gave some good general tips and the reasons for them**
The writer fulfilled the assignment of providing good general information on how to be helpful in an emergency situation, including such general tips as contacting trained personnel, not moving the injured person unless absolutely necessary, warding off shock by applying a blanket or coat, being reassuring, and staying available when trained personnel arrive.

**29. Answer: B. make a new paragraph beginning with the sentence "Everyone can be a helper in an emergency situation" and let that be the concluding paragraph**
The essay does have a good concluding paragraph that summarizes the essay if these final few sentences are separated into a paragraph that stands alone for emphasis.

**30. Answer: H. Everyone a First Responder**
This alternative title reflects the contents of the essay most succinctly and accurately as the essay is about general rules the average person can follow in order to be helpful in an emergency before trained help arrives.

**31. Answer: D. their campaigns. They**
The sentence is a run-on sentence which not only contains two independent clauses but also contains a lengthy series later in the sentence: "to think on their feet, get their points across succinctly, respond well to questions, and keep their emotions under control". Breaking it into two sentences helps to keep the ideas clear.

**32. Answer: G. bright, hot lights**
"Bright" and "hot" are both adjectives modifying the noun "lights". They are equal in strength and could be reversed in order. Thus, they are called "coordinate" (equal and reversible) adjectives. The rule is that coordinate adjectives are separated by a comma.

**33. Answer: A. No change**
The sentence is correct as it is.

**34. Answer: G. it's redundant**
The sentence repeats the same thought as the sentence before it; therefore, it is redundant and should be edited out during a revision.

**35. Answer: B. There was no television during the era, so the excellent turn-out may be attributed to that; however,**
The revision in Answer B adds "so" as a coordinating conjunction, which helps connect elements in the sentence. A semi-colon is also added to show the end of the first independent clause (which could stand alone as a sentence). The transitional word "however" helps to show the reader that the second independent clause is starting and that the sentence is changing direction. These grammatical elements clarify the sentence's meaning.

**36. Answer: J. and maintained that**
This revision corrects a sentence with mixed construction. A mixed construction brings in elements that do not make sense within the grammatical structure of an English sentence. The verb "authored" is used correctly earlier in the sentence (it is in the past tense) so the verb "maintain" should also be put in the past tense to match correctly.

**37. Answer: B. Lincoln, the self-educated frontiersman,**
"The self-educated frontiersman" is an appositive. An appositive is a noun phrase that renames a noun or pronoun that has gone before it, in this case "Lincoln". "The self-educated frontiersman" is not absolutely necessary to the sentence, however, and appositives that are not necessary to the sentence are set off by commas.

**38. Answer: J. knowledgeable, sincere, and he had a good sense of humor.**
A series is a list of three of more items or attributes. This sentence contains a series of Lincoln's attributes, so a comma between attributes is proper, as is the conjunction "and" before the last attribute.

**39. Answer: C. motion is correct; the other argues**
A semi-colon is proper punctuation joining two independent clauses (two clauses that could stand alone on their own as sentences). When a comma is used to join two independent clauses, as in underlined section 39, it is called a "comma splice" and is incorrect.

**40. Answer: J. offers and supports**
The "other" refers to the other team, which is a collective noun requiring the singular form of the verbs for subject-verb agreement: "offers and supports".

**41. Answer: B. an editorial statement**
The sentence offers an opinion and is therefore an editorial statement.

**42. Answer: H. inference**
The definition of inference is to project from the smaller to the larger.

**43. Answer: A. no, because the essay is more about the Lincoln-Douglas Debates than it is about parliamentary debates**
The essay emphasizes the Lincoln-Douglas Debates with only a little compare-and-contrast with other debate formats. The Lincoln-Douglas Debates and modern Lincoln-Douglas debates are discussed in eight out of the ten paragraphs of the essay. Parliamentary debate is only mentioned in three paragraphs (Paragraphs 7, 8, and 9).

**44. Answer: F. between the sentence beginning "Abraham Lincoln spoke against the expansion of slavery" and the sentence beginning "Douglas authored legislation allowing slavery to expand and multiply"**
This is the most logical place to insert the sentence because the sentence expands upon Lincoln's ideas about the expansion of slavery and the founding vision of the Declaration of Independence.

**45. Answer: D. Perhaps a modern-day Abraham Lincoln will reveal himself to the nation through the debate process.**
A concluding sentence both refers back to the contents of the essay and offers food for thought in a striking way. The essay is about debates in general and the Lincoln-Douglas Debates specifically. A

concluding sentence to this essay appropriately speaks of Abraham Lincoln emerging as a national figure (through the Lincoln-Douglas Debates) and offers food for thought with the idea that the debate process may reveal a similarly great modern president.

### 46. Answer: F. No change
An appositive is a noun phrase that renames a noun or pronoun that has gone before it, in this case "Quint". The appositive "captain of a fishing boat" is not absolutely necessary to the sentence, however, and appositives that are not necessary to the sentence are set off by commas.

### 47. Answer: D. an account of being
The preposition "of" is the correct one here. The idiom is to give an "account of".

### 48. Answer: G. for emphasis
"Indeed" is used for emphasis.

### 49. Answer: B. Because it was on a secretive mission to deliver nuclear bomb components,
"Because" is a dependent marker which indicates that the beginning clause of this sentence is closely related in meaning to the rest of the sentence. The word "because" indicates cause or reason. This revision shows clearly that the reason the ship was not rescued right away was that it was on a secretive mission.

### 50. Answer: J. many of the men
The sentence uses an ambiguous pronoun: "them". It is hard to tell from the sentence who "them" refers to. The ambiguity is corrected by replacing the ambiguous pronoun "them" with the phrase "of the men" to clearly show who the sentence is talking about.

### 51. Answer: A. No change
The sentence is fine as it is and adds more interest and information to the paragraph.

### 52. Answer: G. These three hundred or so men had
The pronoun "they" is incorrect in this sentence. The subject of the sentence has already been stated— "These three hundred or so men". There is no need to restate the subject by adding in the pronoun "they". All the answers remove the incorrect pronoun, but Answer B. also preserves the past tense ("had") correctly.

### 53. Answer: D. and swim off
The verb "grow" in the phrase "grow delirious" is in the present tense; "swim off" is also in the present tense, making for a correct construction.

### 54. Answer: H. they had received
The past perfect tense is used for an action already completed by the time another action in the past is completed. Since the torpedoing took place before the action being described (and the action being described is in the past), the past perfect tense is used: "had received".

### 55. Answer: B. the tone goes from one of horror and suffering to one of hope and unity
This answer is correct because the first paragraph describes the terrible situation and the suffering endured as the sailors beat off shark attacks, watched others swim off in delirium, and saw their comrades eaten by sharks or die of wounds. The second paragraph shows how heroically the men coped by tying themselves together with ropes to keep together, helping one another into lifejackets, and encouraging one another not to give up.

### 56. Answer: H. Surprisingly,
Many words become adverbs by adding an "ly" to the end. "Surprisingly" modifies the word "found", which is a verb. Adverbs are needed to modify verbs, so the "ly" is needed to turn the word "Surprising" into an adverb.

**57. Answer: B. the most awful incident of their lives.**
"Their" is a plural pronoun, so the sentence is talking about plural "lives": "their lives". The proper plural form of "life" is "lives" not "lifes".

**58. Answer: G. Adversity, Unity, and Victory**
This title captures the scope and essence of the essay better than the alternatives. The essay contains Shark Attacks, but the essence of the story is the men's unity and victory in the face of terrible adversity. "Futility" implies hopelessness, and while the men were fighting against nature, they were not fighting against one another. Answer B. covers the tragic situation and how some of the men overcame it by sticking together.

**59. Answer: D. move the second sentence, starting with "They won that battle" to the end of the paragraph as the concluding sentence**
This sentence summarizes both the paragraph and the essay and restates the theme, so it is a fitting way to provide a stronger conclusion.

**60. Answer: G. to show that even in the midst of a horrible situation, people can help one another and salvage some good out of it**
The purpose of the essay is to demonstrate the heroism and efficacy of people supporting one another, even in a bad situation. This is shown by the descriptions of how the men from Ensign Twible's group distinguished themselves through helping one another, and how the survivors banded together years later to clear their captain's name.

**61. Answer: A. things that abate or relieve discomfort temporarily**
Answer A. is the dictionary definition of "palliatives", but the meaning of the word can be derived from the context of the sentence. The sentence lists things that are comforting and produce a temporary sense of well-being, such as alcohol, drugs, and food.

**62. Answer: J. already have suffered**
The present perfect verb phrase "have suffered" should not be interrupted by the word "already". In general, verb phrases should not be interrupted except by their negative form, as in "have not suffered." Moving the word "already" to a place after the verb phrase "have suffered" does not make sense with the rest of the sentence, but placing it before the verb phrase does.

**63. Answer: B. it is a cliché**
The phrase is a cliché, meaning it is a phrase or word that has been used many times before. Good writers avoid clichés and try to express things in new, original ways.

**64. Answer: G. Al-Anon addresses**
There is no need for a comma between the subject of a sentence (in this case "Al-Anon") and the verb ("addresses"). Answer B. removes the comma. In addition, since Al-Anon names an organization, it is considered a collective, singular noun. A singular noun takes a singular verb for subject-verb agreement, so "addresses" in Answer B. is correct.

**65. Answer: D. June 10, 1935**
In a date that includes month, day, and year, a comma is needed after the day, before the year.

**66. Answer: G. eliminate the sentence as it is repetitive**
The sentence expresses the same thought as the sentence before it in almost the same terms; it simply uses synonyms to say the same thing as was said before. Therefore, the sentence is repetitive and should be eliminated.

**67. Answer: C. The two men introduced also**
"They" is an ambiguous pronoun. It is unclear who "They" are. "They" could be referring to the Twelve Steps. Thus, the reader does not know what the subject of the sentence is. "The two men" clarifies who took the action in the sentence and makes the subject of the sentence clear.

### 68. Answer: G. Thus, to this day
"Thus" is a transition word like "Hence" but it is more modern. "Thus" is also the most succinct expression. The question asks for a "modern" way to express the thought, and modern writing calls for succinctness.

### 69. Answer: C. in general covering up, protecting, and shielding the addict
This answer achieves parallel construction. The rest of the sentence uses the gerund ("ing") verb form, so in order to match, "protected" should be put into the "ing" form "protecting".

### 70. Answer: J. neither helpful nor loving.
"Neither" requires "nor" (not "or") as its partner in a sentence.

### 71. Answer: B. affected
"Affect" and "effect" are sometimes confused. "Affect" or a form of this verb is proper if the meaning is "to influence". "Effect" is usually a noun meaning "result", but it can be used as a verb when the meaning is "to bring about". ("The manager effected change when she posted the new policy; this affected all the employees.")

### 72. Answer: J. to lend emphasis and emotion to the concluding sentence
A concluding sentence should be powerful and memorable, and the use of alliteration helps emphasize the sentence and dramatize the emotions involved.

### 73. Answer: C. paragraph 7
Paragraph 7 is where the origins of Al-Anon, the organization for friends and family members of addicts, is discussed. Paragraph 7 includes friends' and family members' self-examination processes, so the new sentence logically fits there.

### 74. Answer: H. yes, because both the origins and purpose are covered
Both the origins and purposes of the organizations are covered. After introductory paragraph 1, paragraph 2 names the organizations and whom they serve; paragraphs 3-6 name the founders and describe how and why they developed the organization and its principles; paragraphs 7 and 8 discuss how Bill W.'s wife founded Al-Anon and Al-Anon's general principles and purpose, while paragraph 9 concludes the essay and restates the organizations' purposes.

### 75. Answer: A. after paragraph 1
Paragraph 1 has set up a conflict: money may be an issue with addicts and their associates. Paragraph 2 presents the solution. Logically, a paragraph after paragraph 1 could expand upon how out-of-reach many expensive clinics and treatment centers may be for addicts and their families.

# MATHEMATICS PRACTICE TEST 2

60 Minutes - 60 Questions

Directions: Each question has five answer choices. Choose the best answer for each question.

1. **Two positive integers have a greatest common factor (GCF) of 4 and a least common multiple of 40. Which pair of positive integers satisfy these conditions?**

    A. 6 and 10
    B. 8 and 10
    C. 8 and 20
    D. 10 and 20
    E. 10 and 40

2. **A jacket originally costing $40 is discounted by 20%. When the jacket fails to sell, the new cost is reduced by 30%. What is the cost of the jacket after the 30% reduction?**

    F. $28.00
    G. $26.80
    H. $22.40
    J. $20.00
    K. $18.60

3. **Which of the following is greater than $\dfrac{6}{7}$ ?**

    A. 0.86
    B. $\dfrac{19}{23}$
    C. 0.78
    D. $\dfrac{17}{25}$
    E. 0.625

4. **If $(2^x)^3 = 64$, what is the value of x?**

    F. 0
    G. 1
    H. 2
    J. 3
    K. 4

5. **Silver is currently valued at $31.00 per ounce. What is the value of $1\dfrac{1}{4}$ pounds of silver (one pound = 16 ounces)?**

    A. $620.00
    B. $840.00
    C. $960.00
    D. $1,080.00
    E. $1,200.00

6. Find the endpoint, *A*, of a segment with midpoint *M* (6,-4) and endpoint *B* (-5,2).

    F.  (0.5,-1)
    G.  (-1,0.5)
    H.  (17,-10)
    J.  (-17,10)
    K.  $(-\dfrac{6}{11},0)$

7. Simplify the following expression: $\sqrt{6}(\sqrt{10}-\sqrt{14})$

    A.  -12
    B.  $-2\sqrt{6}$
    C.  $-2\sqrt{2}$
    D.  $2(\sqrt{5}-\sqrt{7})$
    E.  $2(\sqrt{15}-\sqrt{21})$

8. What is the measure of $\angle EBA$ in the figure below?

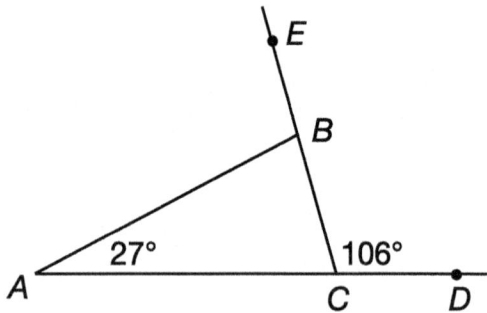

    F.  47°
    G.  51°
    H.  81°
    J.  91°
    K.  101°

9. If m > 0, then $\dfrac{2}{m}+\dfrac{1}{7}=?$

    A.  $\dfrac{3}{7+m}$

    B.  $\dfrac{14+m}{7m}$

    C.  $\dfrac{2}{7m}$

D. $\dfrac{2m}{7}$

E. 2

10. If $a$ and $b$ are positive integers such that $a^3b^2 = 576$, what is the value of $2a - 3b$?

    F. 2
    G. 1
    H. 0
    J. -1
    K. -2

11. If $\angle A$ measures 87°, what is the total measure of the other four angles?

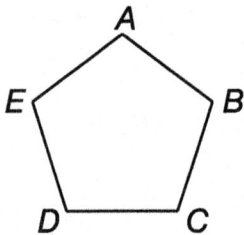

    A. 93
    B. 108
    C. 377
    D. 428
    E. 453

12. Which of the following CANNOT be the graph of the f(x)?

F.

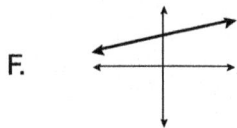

G.

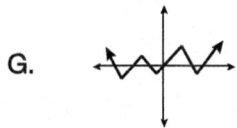

H.

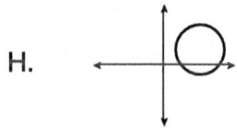

J.

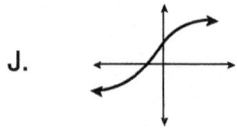

K.

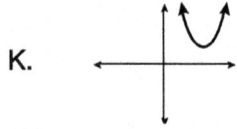

**13. The chart below represents a linear function. What is the measure of *y* when *x* = -4?**

| X | y |
|---|---|
| 0 | -7 |
| 2 | -3 |
| -1 | -9 |
| 6 | 5 |
| -4 | ? |

    A.  15
    B.  12
    C.  0
    D.  -12
    E.  -15

**14. Which of the following must be true about ⬜       pictured below?**

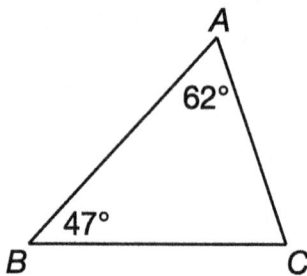

    F.  $\overline{BC} > \overline{AB} > \overline{AC}$
    G.  $\overline{AC} > \overline{AB} > \overline{BC}$
    H.  $\overline{BC} > \overline{AC} > \overline{AB}$
    J.  $\overline{AB} > \overline{BC} > \overline{AC}$
    K.  $\overline{AC} > \overline{BC} > \overline{AB}$

**15. What is 12% of 15% of 2000?**

    A.  3.6
    B.  36
    C.  180
    D.  360
    E.  540

**16. For all non-zero values for x, y, and z:**

$$\frac{(2x^3yz)^3(3xy^2z)^2}{-6xy^3z^5} = ?$$

    F.  $-2xy^3z$

    G.  $2xy^3z^2$

    H.  6xyz

    J.  $x^6y^{10}z^4$

    K.  $12x^{10}y^4$

**17. Which of the following CANNOT be the sides of a triangle?**

    A.  1,3,3

    B.  2,4,6

    C.  3,7,9

    D.  5,5,5

    E.  7,4,10

**18. What is the solution set to the inequality |6 − 2x | < 8?**

    F.  -1 < x < 7

    G.  x > 7 or x < -1

    H.  x < 4

    J.  -1 < x ≤7

    K.  $-1 \le x < 7$

**19. If the tangent of an angle in a right triangle is $\dfrac{7}{24}$, what is the cosine of that angle?**

    A.  $\dfrac{24}{25}$

    B.  $\dfrac{7}{25}$

    C.  $\dfrac{25}{24}$

    D.  $\dfrac{24}{7}$

    E.  $\dfrac{25}{7}$

**20. If the f(x) = x² and the g(x) = 7 – 2x, what is the f(g(x))?**

    F.  $49 - 4x^2$
    G.  $49 - 28x + 4x^2$
    H.  $x^2 - 2x + 7$
    J.  $7 - 2x^2$
    K.  $14 - 4x$

**21. What is one-half of one-sixth of 48?**

    A.  12
    B.  8
    C.  4
    D.  2
    E.  1

**22. Simplify the following expression.**

    $3(2 - 5)^3 - |-12|$

    F.  69
    G.  27
    H.  -39
    J.  -69
    K.  -93

**23. What is the measure of $\overline{AB}$ in the triangle pictured below?**

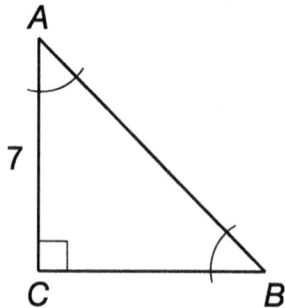

    A.  3.5
    B.  $3.5\sqrt{2}$
    C.  $3.5\sqrt{3}$
    D.  $7\sqrt{2}$
    E.  $7\sqrt{3}$

**24. In ☐ , what is the value of x?**

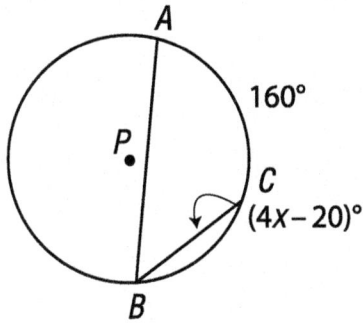

F. 85
G. 65
H. 45
J. 25
K. 20

**25. If $[x] = x^2$ when x is odd and $[x] = \sqrt{x}$ when x is even, what is the product of $[3] \times [4]$?**

A. $[324]$

B. $[288]$

C. $[18]$

D. $[12]$

E. $[6]$

**26. The average weight of 4 students is 121 pounds. When a fifth student's weight is added to the weights of the other four students, the average weight is 115 pounds. What is the weight of the fifth student?**

F. 128
G. 125
H. 115
J. 110
K. 91

**27. What is the circumference of a circle inscribed in a square which has an area of 64 square units?**

A. 8
B. 8π
C. 16π
D. 64
E. 32π

28. If the two lines represented by the two equations below do NOT intersect, what is the value of k?

    2x + 3y = 7

    y = kx – 1

    F.  3
    G.  2
    H.  $\dfrac{3}{2}$
    J.  $-\dfrac{2}{3}$
    K.  $-\dfrac{3}{2}$

29. In the equation (2x + 7)(x – 4)= 0, which of the following could be the value of x?

    A.  7
    B.  5
    C.  4
    D.  $\dfrac{7}{2}$
    E.  -4

30. What is the value of $\log_9 27$ ?

    F.  243
    G.  81
    H.  36
    J.  3
    K.  $\dfrac{3}{2}$

31. If $f(x) = x - 3x^2$ , what is the value of f(-6)?

    A.  -128
    B.  -114
    C.  -102
    D.  36
    E.  102

32. What is the vertex of the parabola in the equation y = 2x² – 6x + 7?

    F.  (-4,1.75)
    G.  (-2.5,2.5)
    H.  (0,0)
    J.  (2.5,1.5)
    K.  (1.5,2.5)

33. In right ⊔    , the tangent of $\angle A = \dfrac{5}{12}$. Which of the following could be the perimeter of

⊔

   A.   18
   B.   36
   C.   54
   D.   72
   E.   90

34. If *c* cans of mixed vegetables cost *d* dollars, in terms of *c* and *d*, what would be the cost of 7 cans of vegetables?

   F.   $\dfrac{cd}{7}$

   G.   $\dfrac{7d}{c}$

   H.   $\dfrac{c}{7d}$

   J.   7dc
   K.   7(d − c)

35. What is the solution set of the following inequality?

$$\sqrt{x-7}+3>6$$

   A.   x < -16
   B.   x ≤ 10
   C.   x ≥ 16
   D.   x > 16
   E.   x = 16

36. Three of the vertices of a rectangle have the coordinates (3,-3), (-8,3), and (3,3). What are the coordinates of the fourth vertex?

   F.   (-8,-3)
   G.   (-3,-8)
   H.   (-3,-3)
   J.   (8,-3)
   K.   (3,8)

37. What is the locus of points that are 7 units away from the point (-5,2)?

   A.   $(x+5)^2 +(y-2)^2 = 49$

   B.   $(x-5)^2 +(y+2)^2 = 49$

   C.   $(x+5)^2 +(y-2)^2 = 14$

   D.   $(x-5)^2 +(y+2)^2 = 14$

   E.   $y = -\dfrac{2}{5}x+7$

**38. What is the value of $-\left|(2-5)\right| \times (-4-(-3))^3$ ?**

    F. 147
    G. 49
    H. 3
    J. -21
    K. -49

**39. What is the value of x in the diagram of ▢ ?**

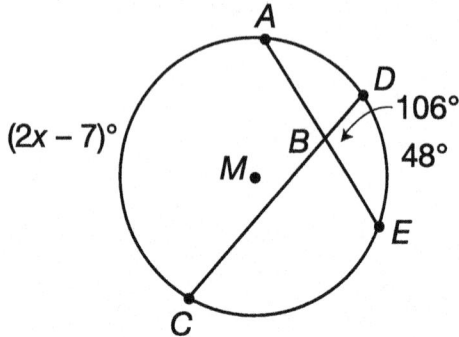

    A. 80
    B. 81
    C. 85.5
    D. 159
    E. 188

**40. The following quantities represent the times for the 50 yard freestyle for a middle school swimming team.**

**28.2, 29.4, 28, 30.6, 34.2, 28**

**What is the mode less the mean from this data? (Express your answer to the nearest tenth.)**

    F. -2.6
    G. -1.7
    H. 0.8
    J. 2.8
    K. 6.2

**41. A kite is flying at an angle of elevation of 43°. If the kite is flying 117 feet above the ground, what is the length of the string that is attached to the kite? (Express your answer to the nearest tenth.)**

    A. 211.4
    B. 171.4
    C. 107.2
    D. 79.8
    E. 66.2

**42. What is the measure of m + n?**

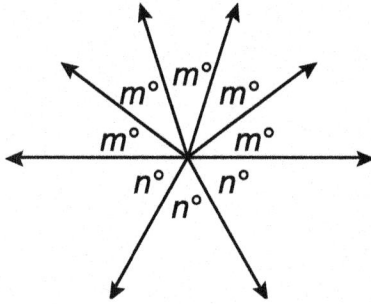

   F.  96°
   G.  90°
   H.  72°
   J.  66°
   K.  60°

**43. What number can you add to the numerator and denominator of $\frac{11}{17}$ to get $\frac{3}{4}$ ?**

   A.  -3
   B.  -2
   C.  2
   D.  6
   E.  7

**44. Four times the quantity of three and some number is the same as the number squared. What is the unknown number?**

   F.  -12 only
   G.  6 only
   H.  -4 only
   J.  6 or -2
   K.  2 or -6

**45. If the ratio of the angles in a quadrilateral is 2:3:5:8, what is the measure of the largest angle?**

   A.  200°
   B.  160°
   C.  100°
   D.  60°
   E.  40°

**46. What is the area of a triangle with vertices at (-2,0), (4,0), and (3,10)?**

   F.  60
   G.  30
   H.  20
   J.  12
   K.  5

**47. If x > 0 and y < 0, which of the following must be FALSE?**

A. $\dfrac{x}{y^2} > 0$

B. $\dfrac{x^2}{y^3} < 0$

C. $\dfrac{2x^3}{y^2} > 0$

D. $(\dfrac{x^2}{y^3})^2 < 0$

E. $2xy < 0$

**48. A skyscraper shown on a television with a 26-inch diagonal measures 16 inches on the screen. To the nearest inch, what would be the measure of the same skyscraper if it were shown on a television screen with a 45-inch diagonal?**

F. 73
G. 37
H. 31
J. 28
K. 20

**49. The graph of a portion of y = 2sin(bx + m), where x, b, and m are positive, is shown below. What is the period of the function?**

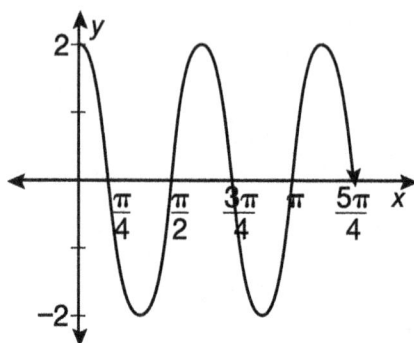

A. 2π
B. 1.5π
C. π
D. $\dfrac{\pi}{2}$
E. 1.5

**50. The distance between the points (4,-1) and (x,3) in the standard coordinate plane (x,y) is 4. What is the value of x?**

F. 4

G. $3\sqrt{2}$

H. $3\sqrt{3}$

J. 5

K. $4\sqrt{2}$

**51. What is the area of $\square$ ?**

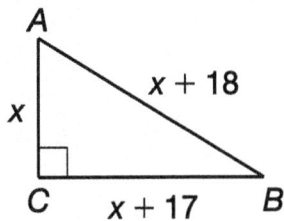

A. 192

B. 180

C. 168

D. 84

E. 24

**52. If $i^2 = -1$, what is the value of $(7-2i)^2$ ?**

F. 51

G. 47

H. $14-4i$

J. $45i-28$

K. $45-28i$

**Use the following information to answer questions 53 and 54.**

**The parents and alumnae of Bristol Western High School are completing their Spring semester charity drive for 2011. The chart below compares the results in 2011 with the Spring semester results in 2010.**

Charity Report for Bristol Western High School
($ in thousands)

|     | 2011 | 2010 |
|-----|------|------|
| Jan | 5.38 | 6.01 |
| Feb | 7.11 | 7.13 |
| Mar | 6.75 | 4.26 |
| Apr | 3.88 | 4.74 |
| May | 7.56 | 6.86 |

**53. Which percentage represents the increase in donations in 2011 compared to 2010?**

    A.  5.8%
    B.  6.2%
    C.  7.3%
    D.  7.5%
    E.  8.4%

**54. If the charity drive increases at the same percentage as it did in 2011, what would be the projected collections for 2012?**

    F.  $30,913
    G.  $32,459
    H.  $33,308
    J.  $47,414
    K.  $51,193

**55. What is the supplement of the complement of an angle measuring 64°?**

    A.  14°
    B.  26°
    C.  36°
    D.  116°
    E.  154°

**56. Two bicycle tires with diameters of 30 inches and 24 inches make four revolutions. To the nearest foot, how much farther does the larger wheel travel compared to the smaller wheel?**

    F.  6
    G.  9
    H.  22
    J.  31
    K.  47

**57. A great circle of a sphere is a circle on the sphere that shares the sphere's center point. If the volume of a sphere is 288π cubic inches, what is the area of a great circle of the sphere?**

**(Volume of a sphere = $\dfrac{4}{3}\pi r^3$)**

    A.  81π
    B.  64π
    C.  36π
    D.  25π
    E.  16π

**58. If x varies directly with y, and y = 14 when x = 6, find x when y = 45.5.**

    F.  18
    G.  18.5
    H.  19.5
    J.  28
    K.  34

**59.** The point (7,-3) is reflected across the x-axis and then the y-axis. What are the coordinates of the point after the two reflections?

    A.  (-3,-7)
    B.  (3,-7)
    C.  (-3,7)
    D.  (7,-3)
    E.  (-7,3)

**60.** In the standard coordinate plane (x,y), the points (0,0), (2,4), (10,4), and (8,0) are the vertices of the parallelogram shown below. What is the area of the parallelogram?

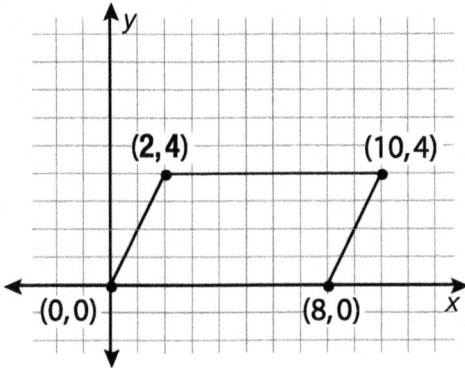

    F.  20
    G.  32
    H.  $32\sqrt{2}$
    J.  $32\sqrt{3}$
    K.  $40\sqrt{3}$

# MATHEMATICS PRACTICE TEST 2 ANSWER KEY

| | | | |
|---|---|---|---|
| 1. C | | 31. B | |
| 2. H | | 32. K | |
| 3. A | | 33. E | |
| 4. H | | 34. G | |
| 5. A | | 35. D | |
| 6. H | | 36. F | |
| 7. E | | 37. A | |
| 8. K | | 38. H | |
| 9. B | | 39. C | |
| 10. J | | 40. G | |
| 11. E | | 41. B | |
| 12. H | | 42. F | |
| 13. E | | 43. E | |
| 14. J | | 44. J | |
| 15. B | | 45. B | |
| 16. K | | 46. G | |
| 17. B | | 47. D | |
| 18. F | | 48. J | |
| 19. A | | 49. D | |
| 20. G | | 50. F | |
| 21. C | | 51. D | |
| 22. K | | 52. K | |
| 23. D | | 53. A | |
| 24. J | | 54. G | |
| 25. A | | 55. E | |
| 26. K | | 56. F | |
| 27. B | | 57. C | |
| 28. J | | 58. H | |
| 29. C | | 59. E | |
| 30. K | | 60. G | |

# MATHEMATICS PRACTICE TEST 2 RATIONALES

### 1. Answer: C. 8 and 20
The greatest common factor (GCF) of two or more numbers is the largest factor that divides evenly into the numbers. Find the factors of 8 and 20.

8: 1, 2, 4, 8
20: 1, 2, 4, 5, 10, 20

The greatest common factor of 8 and 20 is 4.

The least common multiple (LCM) of 8 and 20 is the smallest number that has 8 and 20 as factors. Since 8 and 20 are relatively small numbers, an easy way to find the LCM is by listing the multiples of each number. You can find the multiples of any number simply by multiplying by 1, then 2, and so on.

8: 8, 16, 24, 32, 40
20: 20, 40

The least common multiple of 8 and 20 is 40.

### 2. Answer: H. $22.40
Find the cost of the jacket after the 20% reduction. Expressing the percent as a decimal, 0.20, facilitates calculation.

$40.00 − (0.20)(40) = $32.00

Discount the new cost, $32.00, by an additional 30%.

$32.00 − (0.30)(32.00) = $22.40

### 3. Answer: A. 0.86
Convert all the fractions, including $\frac{6}{7}$, to decimals to make them uniform.

$$\frac{6}{7} = 0.857$$

$$\frac{19}{23} = 0.826$$

$$\frac{17}{25} = 0.68$$

Selection A is correct because 0.86 > 0.857

**4. Answer: H. 2**

When raising a power to another power, multiply the exponents.

$$(2^x)^3 = 2^{(3)(x)} = 2^{3x}$$

In the example $a^x = a^4$, x must be 4 because the base, *a*, is the same on both sides of the equation. However, in the expression $(2^x)^3 = 64$, the bases are different. Therefore, change 64 into a power of 2.

$$64 = 2^6$$

Now set $2^{3x} = 2^6$.

$$2^{3x} = 2^6$$

3x = 6

x = 2

**5. Answer: A. $620.00**

Silver's listed value is given per ounce, yet the problem requests the value of $1\frac{1}{4}$ pounds. It is therefore necessary to convert $1\frac{1}{4}$ pounds into ounces. Since 1 pound = 16 ounces, multiply $1\frac{1}{4}$ by 16 to find the number of ounces in $1\frac{1}{4}$ pounds.

$$16 \times 1\frac{1}{4} = 20$$

Next multiply 20 by 31, the value of an ounce of silver, to find the value of $1\frac{1}{4}$ pounds of silver.

$31.00 \times 20 = \$620.00$

**6. Answer: H. (17,-10)**

The midpoint formula, $\frac{x_1 + x_2}{2}, \frac{y_1 + y_2}{2}$, can also be used to find endpoints when the coordinates of the midpoint are known. Input the known data and set the equations equal to the coordinates of the midpoint.

$x_1 = -5$
$x_2 = ?$
$y_1 = 2$
$y_2 = ?$

$$\frac{-5+x_2}{2} = 6 \qquad \frac{2+y_2}{2} = -4$$

Multiply both sides by 2 to arrive at:

$$-5+x_2 = 12 \qquad 2+y_2 = -8$$

$$x_2 = 17 \qquad y_2 = -10$$

The coordinates of the endpoint $B$ are (17,-10)

## 7. Answer: E. $2(\sqrt{15} - \sqrt{21})$

Square roots can be multiplied or divided directly; they need not be like terms. Use the Distributive Property to start the problem.

$$\sqrt{6}(\sqrt{10} - \sqrt{14}) = \sqrt{60} - \sqrt{84}.$$

$\sqrt{60}$ and $\sqrt{84}$ can both be simplified by dividing out the largest factor that is a perfect square.

$$\sqrt{60} = \sqrt{4} \times \sqrt{15} = 2\sqrt{15}$$
$$\sqrt{84} = \sqrt{4} \times \sqrt{21} = 2\sqrt{21}$$

$$\sqrt{60} - \sqrt{84} = 2\sqrt{15} - 2\sqrt{21}$$

Square roots can only be added or subtracted if the numbers under the radicals are the same. For example, $2\sqrt{3} + 5\sqrt{3} = 7\sqrt{3}$. However, $2\sqrt{15} - 2\sqrt{21}$ has a common factor, 2, that can be divided:

$$2\sqrt{15} - 2\sqrt{21} = 2(\sqrt{15} - \sqrt{21})$$

## 8. Answer: K. 101°

An exterior angle of a triangle equals the sum of the two remote interior angles.

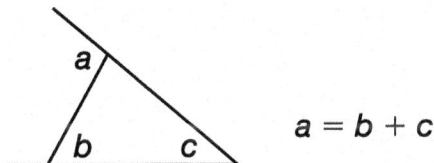

$$a = b + c$$

$$m\angle DCB = m\angle CBA + m\angle CAB$$

106 = 27 + m $\angle CBA$

79 = m $\angle CBA$

$\angle EBA$ and $\angle CBA$ are a linear pair. A linear pair is a pair of adjacent, supplementary angles; their sum is 180°. Therefore:

$m\angle EBA + 79 = 180$

$m\angle EBA = 101$

**9. Answer: B.** $\dfrac{14+m}{7m}$

Find the lowest common denominator for both fractions and add the two expressions.

The lowest common denominator for the quantities 7 and $m$ is 7m.

$$\frac{2}{m} \times \frac{7}{7} = \frac{14}{7m}$$

$$\frac{1}{7} \times \frac{m}{m} = \frac{m}{7m}$$

Add the two fractions:

$$\frac{14}{7m} + \frac{m}{7m} = \frac{14+m}{7m}$$

**10. Answer: J. -1**

Small numbers can grow large quickly when cubed and squared. Use trial and error to test a few numbers.

a = 3    b = 4          $(3)^3(4)^2 = 27 \times 16 = 432$          Too small

a = 5    b = 3          $(5)^3(3)^2 = 125 \times 9 = 1125$          Too big

a = 4    b = 3          $(4)^3(3)^2 = 64 \times 9 = 576$          Correct values for a and b

Replace a and b with 4 and 3 respectively in the expression $2a - 3b$.

$2(4) - 3(3) = 8 - 9 = -1$

**11. Answer: E. 453**

The sum of the measures of the interior angles of any polygon is found by using the formula (n − 2)(180) where $n$ is the number of sides. Since ABCDE is a pentagon, substitute 5 for $n$ in the formula.

(5 − 2)(180) = 540.

Subtract 87 from 540 to find the sum of the measures of the remaining interior angles.

540 − 87 = 453

## 12. Answer: H.
The f(x), called "the function of x", is a special relation of numbers that allow for only one input per output. In the standard coordinate plane (x,y), x is considered the input and y the output.

An easy way to discern if a graph is of a function is to use the vertical line test. Pass several vertical lines through a graph; if each vertical line intersects the graph at only one point, then the graph is of a function. If a vertical line intersects the graph at more than one point, then graph is not of a function.

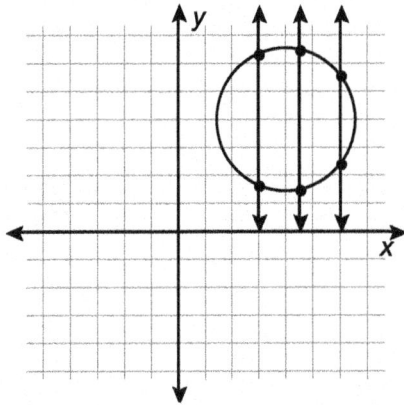

Vertical lines intersect the circle at more than one point so it cannot be the graph of a function.

## 13. Answer: E. -15
A linear function can be written in slope-intercept form, y = mx + b, where $m$ is the slope of the line and $b$ its y-intercept. Use the following steps to derive the line's equation from the data in the table.

1. Find the slope of the line using the formula $m = \dfrac{y_2 - y_1}{x_2 - x_1}$. You can use any two points in the chart, so let's use (2,-3) and (0,-7).

$$x_1 = 2$$
$$y_1 = -3$$
$$x_2 = 0$$
$$y_2 = -7$$

$$m = \frac{-7-(-3)}{0-2} = \frac{-4}{-2} = 2$$

Replace $m$ with 2.

2. Find the y-intercept by substituting any point in the chart into the equation for $x$ and $y$. Let's use (0,-7) again.

$$y = 2x + b$$

-7 = 2(0) + b
-7 = b

The equation for the linear function, in slope-intercept form, is y = 2x – 7.

3. Find the value of y when x = -4.

y = 2x – 7

y = 2(-4) – 7 = -15

## 14. Answer: J. $\overline{AB} > \overline{BC} > \overline{AC}$
In any triangle, there is a correspondence between the angles and their opposite sides. The largest angle will always be opposite the largest side and the smallest angle will always be opposite the smallest side.

In ⌴ , it is necessary to calculate the measure of $\angle C$ so the relative sizes of the sides can be found. The sum of the measures of the angles in a triangle is 180°, so subtract the known angles, 47° and 62°, from 180.

180 – (47 + 62) = 180 – 109 = 71.

The measure of $\angle C$ is 71°, so $m\angle C > m\angle A > m\angle B$. $\angle C$ is opposite $\overline{AB}$, $\angle A$ is opposite $\overline{BC}$, and $\angle B$ is opposite $\overline{AC}$. Therefore, $\overline{AB} > \overline{BC} > \overline{AC}$.

## 15. Answer: B. 36
"Of" means multiply. Change each percent into a decimal to facilitate calculation.

12% = 0.12

15% = 0.15

(0.12)(0.15)(2000) = 36

## 16. Answer: K. $12x^{10}y^4$
When raising one power to another, remember to multiply the exponents. For example, $(x^3)^2 = x^{3\times2} = x^6$

$(-2x^3yz)^3 = -8x^9y^3z^3$
$(3xy^2z)^2 = 9x^2y^4z^2$

Multiply the two expressions. Remember to add the exponents when multiplying numbers with the same bases. For example, $(x^2)(x^3) = x^{2+3} = x^5$.

$(-8x^9y^3z^3)(9x^2y^4z^2) = -72x^{11}y^7z^5$

Divide the remaining expressions. Remember to subtract the exponents when dividing numbers with similar bases. For example, $\dfrac{x^5}{x^2} = x^{5-2} = x^3$

$$\frac{-72x^{11}y^7z^5}{-6xy^3z^5} = 12x^{10}y^4$$

## 17. Answer: B. 2,4,6
The sum of the lengths of any two sides of a triangle must exceed the length of the third side.

$$2+4 \not> 6$$

## 18. Answer: F. -1 < x < 7
"| |" means the absolute value. Regardless of the quantity inside the bars, the result is positive. For example, if |x| < 7, then x < 7 and x > -7.

Solve the inequality.

|6 – 2x| < 8

6 – 2x < 8 and 6 – 2x > -8
-2x < 2 and -2x > -14
x > -1 and x < 7

Remember to reverse the direction of the inequality sign when dividing or multiplying the inequality by a negative number.

Express the inequality as a composite inequality.

-1 < x < 7

## 19. Answer: A. $\frac{24}{25}$
The tangent of an angle in a right triangle is the ratio of the side opposite the angle to the side adjacent to the angle. A useful mnemonic to remember the ratios of the three basic trigonometric ratios is **sohcahtoa** where:

$$\sin = \frac{opposite\ side}{hypotenuse}$$

$$\cos = \frac{adjacent\ side}{hypotenuse}$$

$$\tan = \frac{opposite\ side}{adjacent\ side}$$

Find the hypotenuse of a right triangle with tangent $\alpha = \frac{7}{24}$

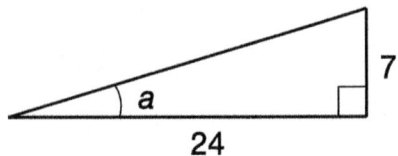

Use the Pythagorean Theorem, $a^2 + b^2 = c^2$, to find c, the hypotenuse.

$$7^2 + 24^2 = c^2$$

$$49 + 576 = c^2$$

$$625 = c^2$$

$$\sqrt{625} = \sqrt{c^2}$$

$$c = 25$$

The $\cos \alpha$ can now be found by the ratio of the side adjacent to $\alpha$ and the hypotenuse.

$$\cos \alpha = \frac{7}{25}$$

**20. Answer: G. 49 – 28x + 4x²**
The f(g(x)) is called a composite function. Knowing the correct order in which to execute operations in this problem is necessary to yield the correct answer.

The g function is adjacent to (x); take its value, 7 – 2x, and substitute it in for x in the f function.

f(g(x)) = f(7 – 2x)

The f(x) = x². Replace x with (7 – 2x) to find the value of f(g(x)).

f(7 – 2x) = (7 – 2x)² = $49 - 28x + 4x^2$

**21. Answer: C. 4**
"Of" means multiply.

$$\frac{1}{2} \times \frac{1}{6} \times \frac{48}{1} = \frac{1}{12} \times \frac{48}{1} = 4$$

**22. Answer: K. -93**
Use the order of operations to simplify the expression. The acronym PEMDAS is a useful way to remember the correct order.

P   Parentheses
E   Exponents
M   Multiplication
D   Division
A   Addition
S   Subtraction

If a line in the problem contains solely multiplication and division or addition and subtraction, proceed from left to right.

Simplify the parentheses: $3(2-5)^3 - |-12| = 3(-3)^3 - |-12|$
Simplify the exponents: $3(-3)^3 - |-12| = 3(-27) - |-12|$
Multiply: $3(-27) - |-12| = -81 - |-12|$
Subtract: $-81 - |-12| = -81 - 12 = -93$

It is important to remember |-12|, the absolute value of -12, equals 12.

## 23. Answer: D. $7\sqrt{2}$

A right triangle with congruent acute angles is called a 45-45-90 triangle. Since the right angle measures 90°, the remaining angles, if congruent, must each measure 45°. A 45-45-90 triangle has the following ratio of sides:

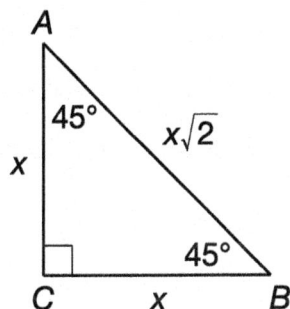

Given that 7 corresponds to x, the length of $\overline{AB}$ in $\square$ must be $7\sqrt{2}$.

## 24. Answer: J. 25

$\angle ABC$ is called an inscribed angle because it has its vertex on the circle (a central angle has its vertex on the center). An inscribed angle equals one-half of the measure of the arc it intercepts. Since $mAC = 160°$, $m\angle ABC = 80°$. Set 4x – 20 equal to 80 to solve for x.

4x – 20 = 80
4x = 100
x = 25

## 25. Answer: A. $[324]$

Notice that in both rules, $[x] = x^2$ and $[x] = \sqrt{x}$, once the operation is performed, *the result is no longer in the brackets.*

$[3] = 3^2 = 9$

$[4] = \sqrt{4} = 2$

$[3] \times [4] = 9 \times 2 = 18$

Selection A, $[324]$, is even, so find its square root.

$$\sqrt{324} = 18$$

Thus,

$$[3] \times [4] = 18 \qquad [324] = 18$$

so $[3] \times [4] = [324]$.

## 26. Answer: K. 91
The average weight of the five students is found by dividing the sum of the five weights by 5. Find the sum of the first four students' weights by multiplying their average weight, 121, by 4.

121 x 4 = 484

Although the fifth student's weight is unknown, the average of all five students' weights, 115, is known. Let $x$ represent the fifth student's weight and use the model $\dfrac{total\ weight}{number\ of\ students}$ = average weight per student.

$$\frac{484 + x}{5} = 115$$
$$(5)(\frac{484 + x}{5}) = (115)(5)$$
$$484 + x = 575$$
$$x = 91$$

## 27. Answer: B. 8π
The area of a square is found by using the formula Area = s², where $s$ represents a side of the square. Substitute 64 for the area to find the length of the square.

$$64 = s^2$$
$$\sqrt{64} = \sqrt{s^2}$$
$$s = 8$$

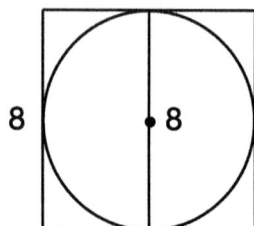

The circumference of a circle can be found by using either of two formulas:

Circumference = 2πr                    Circumference = πD

r represents the radius, which is a segment that starts at the circle's center and ends on the circle. D represents the diameter of a circle which is segment with endpoints on the circle and which intersects the center of the circle.

Note that the diameter of the circle is equal to 8, the same length as a side of the square. Use the formula C = πD to find the inscribed circle's circumference.

C = π8 = 8π

**28. Answer: J.** $-\dfrac{2}{3}$

Lines that do not intersect are parallel lines. Lines that are parallel have the same slope but different y-intercepts. The line y = kx − 1 is in slope-intercept form. Use the general formula, y = mx + b, where *m* represents the slope and *b* the y-intercept, to find the slope and y-intercept of the line. In the line y = kx − 1, the slope is k and the y-intercept is -1.

The line 2x + 3y = 7 is in standard form. The standard form of a line is in the form of Ax + By = C, where A, B, and C are all integers and A is positive. Transform the equation into slope-intercept form to examine its slope and y-intercept.

$$2x + 3y = 7$$
$$3y = -2x + 7$$
$$\frac{3}{3}y = \frac{-2}{3}x + \frac{7}{3}$$
$$y = -\frac{2}{3}x - \frac{7}{3}$$

Since parallel lines have the same slope, then k must equal $-\dfrac{2}{3}$.

**29. Answer: C. 4**

If the product (2x + 4) and (x − 4) is 0, then either 2x + 7 = 0 or x − 4 = 0. Set each quantity equal to 0 and solve for x.

2x + 7 = 0
2x = -7
$x = -\dfrac{7}{2}$
x − 4 = 0
x = 4

Selection C offers x = 4

**30. Answer: K.** $\dfrac{3}{2}$

$\log_9 27$ means "the logarithm of 9 equals 27". To solve this problem we need to know what power of 9 yields 27. These problems can be solved using exponential notation.

$9^x = 27$

If $7^x = 7^4$, we know x = 4 because the bases, 7, are equal. However, in the problem $9^x = 27$, the bases are different. Express both numbers, 9 and 27, as powers of 3.

$9 = 3^2$

$27 = 3^3$

Substitute 3² and 3³ for 9 and 27 respectively.

$9^x = 27$
$(3^2)^x = 3^3$

Multiply the exponents when raising one power to another.

$(3^2)^x = 3^3$
$3^{2x} = 3^3$

Ignore the bases and set the exponents equal to one another and solve for x.

$2x = 3$
$x = \dfrac{3}{2}$

**31. Answer: B. -114**
The f(x) is called "the function of x". To find the f(-6), "the function of -6", replace each x with -6 and simplify.

$$f(-6) = -6 - 3(-6)^2 =$$
$$-6 - 108 =$$
$$-114$$

## 32. Answer: K. (1.5,2.5)

The vertex of a parabola is its minimum point (when the coefficient of x² is positive) or its maximum point (when the coefficient of x² is negative). The vertex of the equation y = 2x² – 6x +7 is a minimum.

To find the vertex, first find the equation of the axis of symmetry. The axis of symmetry, in this graph, is a vertical line crossing the x-axis. Use the formula $x = -\dfrac{b}{2a}$ to find its equation.

In the equation y = 2x² – 6x + 7, a = 2, b = -6, c = 7

$$x = \frac{-(-6)}{(2)(2)} = 1.5$$

The vertex of the parabola lies on the axis of symmetry, so substitute 1.5 for each x in the equation to find the y-coordinate of the vertex.

y = 2(1.5)² – 6(1.5) + 7 = 2.5

The coordinates of the vertex are (1.5,2.5).

## 33. Answer: E. 90

In any right triangle, the tangent of an angle is the ratio of its opposite side to its adjacent side.

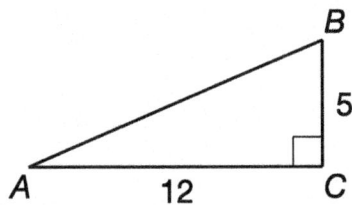

Find the length of $\overline{AB}$ by using the Pythagorean Theorem.

5² + 12² = c²
25 + 144 = c²
169 = c²
c = 13

Add up the sides to find the perimeter.

5 + 12 + 13 = 30

Although the tangent of $\angle A = \dfrac{5}{12}$, it does not necessarily mean that $\overline{BC} = 5$ and $\overline{AC} = 12$. For example, if $\overline{BC} = 15$ and $\overline{AC} = 36$, the tangent of $\angle A$ would still be $\dfrac{5}{12}$.

$$\tan \angle A = \frac{15}{36} = \frac{5}{12}$$

Mathematics Practice Test 2 Rationales

We do know, however, if the sides are not 5, 12, and 13, they must be some common multiple of each. Thus, the perimeter of ⊔ must be 30 or some multiple of 30. Selection E, 90, is a multiple of 30.

$$30 \times 3 = 90$$

**34. Answer: G.** $\dfrac{7d}{c}$

Substitute values for the variables and see which selection makes sense. Let the number of cans, c, equal 6 and the cost for the cans, d, be $12.00. By dividing the cost for the cans by the number of cans, we arrive at a cost of $2.00 per can. Multiply the number of cans desired, 7, by $2.00 per can, and we arrive at a cost of $14.00. In terms of the variables, we get:

$$7(\frac{d}{c}) = \frac{7d}{c}$$

**35. Answer: D. x > 16**
Isolate the radical to solve for x.

$$\sqrt{x-7} + 3 > 6$$
$$\sqrt{x-7} > 3$$

Square both sides of the equation to eliminate the variable.

$$(\sqrt{x-7})^2 > (3)^2$$
$$x - 7 > 9$$

Solve for x.

x − 7 > 9
x > 16

**36. Answer: F. (-8,-3)**
Rectangles are quadrilaterals that have opposite sides congruent and parallel and have four right angles. Graph the three known vertices to find the coordinates of the missing vertex.

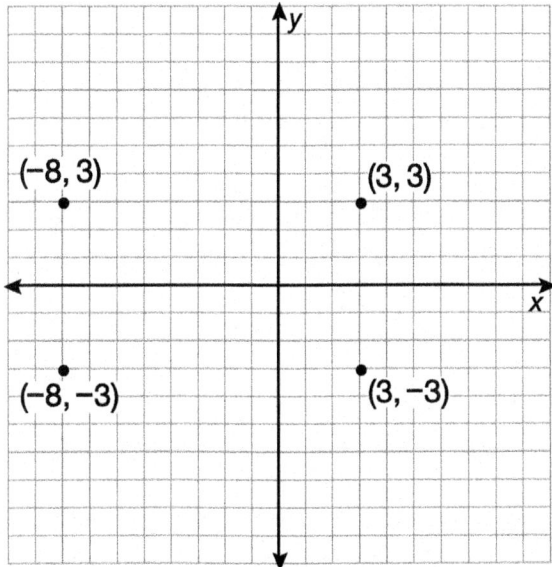

By inspection, we find the length of the rectangle, from (-8,3) to (3,3) is 11 units. Thus, the coordinates of a point that is 11 units away from (3,-3) is (-8,-3). Alternatively, we see the distance from (3,3) to (3,-3) is 6 units. Therefore, the width of the rectangle is 6 units. Count down 6 units from (-8,3) to arrive again at the coordinates (-8,-3).

**37. Answer: A.** $(x+5)^2 + (y-2)^2 = 49$

A locus of points is those points that satisfy a given condition. In this case, the locus of points that are 7 units away from (-5,2) is a circle with a radius measuring 7.

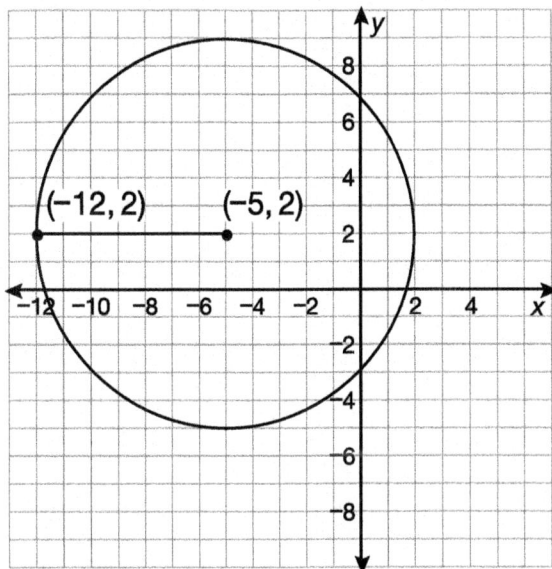

The general equation for a circle is $(x-h)^2 + (y-k)^2 = r^2$ where (h,k) represents the circle's center and r = the radius of the circle. Replace h with -5, k with 2, and r with 7.

$$(x-(-5))^2 + (y-2)^2 = 7^2$$
$$(x+5)^2 + (y-2)^2 = 49$$

**38. Answer: H. 3**

Use the order of operations to simplify the expression. The acronym PEMDAS helps us remember the order.

| | |
|---|---|
| P | Parentheses |
| E | Exponents |
| M | Multiplication |
| D | Division |
| A | Addition |
| S | Subtraction |

When performing multiplication and division or addition and subtraction, proceed from left to right and perform the operation accordingly.

Parentheses: $-|(2-5)| \times (-4-(-3))^3 = -|-3| \times (-1)^3$
Exponents: $-|-3| \times (-1)^3 = -|-3| \times (-1)$

The symbol "$||$" means the absolute value of a quantity. The absolute value of a quantity is its distance from 0 on the number line and is expressed as a positive number.

$-|-3| \times (-1) = -3 \times -1 = 3.$

**39. Answer: C. 85.5**

In $\square$ , the average of the measures of $DE$ and $AC$ is equal to the measure of either $\angle ABC$ or $\angle DBE$.

$$\frac{2x-7+48}{2} = 106$$
$$\frac{2x+41}{2} = 106$$
$$2(\frac{2x+41}{2}) = 106(2)$$
$$2x+41 = 212$$
$$2x = 171$$
$$x = 85.5$$

**40. Answer: G. -1.7**
The mean of a set of data (also known as the average) is found by adding all the values in the set and then dividing by the number of members in the set.

$$\frac{28.2 + 29.4 + 28 + 30.6 + 34.2 + 28}{6} =$$

$$\frac{178.4}{6} = 29.7$$

The mode of a set of data is the quantity that appears the most frequently. In this set of data, the mode is 28. Therefore, the mode less the mean equals $28 - 29.7 = -1.7$

**41. Answer: B. 171.4**
The kite, the string attached to the kite, and the height of the kite above the ground form a right triangle.

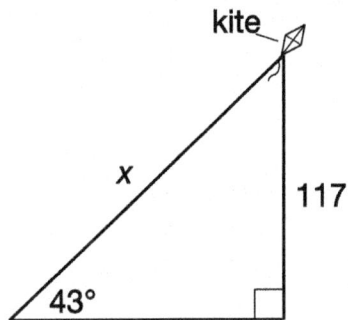

The angle of elevation, 43°, and its opposite side, 117, are known. The unknown side, the length of the string, forms the hypotenuse of the right triangle. Use the sin 43° to find the hypotenuse because the

$$\sin\theta = \frac{opposite\ side}{hypotenuse}.$$

$$\sin 43 = \frac{117}{x}$$

$$0.682 = \frac{117}{x}$$

$$x = 171.6$$

**42. Answer: F. 96°**
The number of degrees in a straight line is 180. The sum of the 5 angles that measure m° each is 180. Similarly, the sum of the 3 angles that measure n° each is also 180.

$$m + m + m + m + m = 180$$
$$5m = 180$$
$$m = 36$$
$$n + n + n = 180$$
$$3n = 180$$
$$n = 60$$
$$m + n = 36 + 60 = 96$$

**43. Answer: E. 7**
Let x = the unknown number to be added to the numerator and denominator of the fraction.

$$\frac{11 + x}{17 + x} = \frac{3}{4}$$

Cross-multiply the fractions and set the products equal to one another.

$$3(17 + x) = 4(11 + x)$$
$$51 + 3x = 44 + 4x$$
$$7 = x$$

Replace x with 7 in the equation.

$$\frac{11 + 7}{17 + 7} = \frac{18}{24} = \frac{3}{4}$$

**44. Answer: J. 6 or -2**
Let x represent the unknown number.

$$4(x + 3) = x^2$$
$$4x + 12 = x^2$$

Set the equation equal to 0 and factor the resulting expression.

$$x^2 - 4x - 12 = 0$$

Find two numbers with sum -4 and product -12.

-6 + 2 = -4        (-6)(2) = -12

Use the factors -6 and 2 to solve the equation.

(x − 6)(x + 2) = 0

Since $(x-6)(x+2) = 0$, then $x-6 = 0$ or $x+2 = 0$
$x-6 = 0$        $x+2 = 0$
$x = 6$ or $x = -2$

## 45. Answer: B. 160º
The sum of the measures of the angles in a quadrilateral is 360º. Let x represent the common multiple of: 2, 3, 5, and 8 that has a sum of 360º.

$2x + 3x + 5x + 8x = 360$
$18x = 360$
$x = 20$

In the ratio, 2:3:5:8, 8 represents the largest angle in the quadrilateral. Multiply 8 by 20 to find the measure of the largest angle.

$8 \times 20 = 160º$

## 46. Answer: G. 30
Graph the vertices of the triangle.

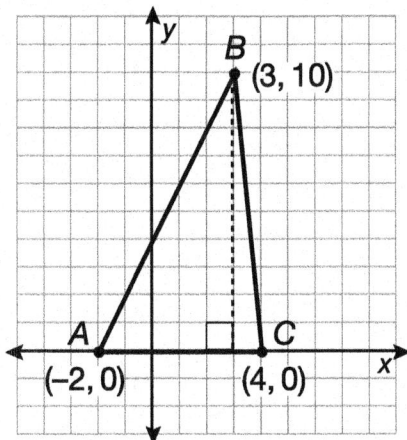

The area of a triangle is found by using the formula Area = $\frac{1}{2}(base)(height)$. By inspection, the length of the base, between (-2,0) and (4,0) is 6 units. The height of a triangle is found by extending a line from a vertex to the opposite side such that the line is perpendicular to the opposite side. Extend a line from $\angle B$; the y-coordinate of B, 10, is the height of the triangle.

Area = $\frac{1}{2}(base)(height)$

Area = $\frac{1}{2}(6)(10) = 30$

**47. Answer: D.** $(\dfrac{x^2}{y^3})^2 < 0$

Set x and y equal to manageable numbers that satisfy the inequalities x > 0 and y < 0. Let x and y equal 2 and -1 respectively. Simplify the quantity $(\dfrac{x^2}{y^3})^2$ by raising the numerator and the denominator to the second power. When raising one power to another, multiply the exponents.

$$(\dfrac{x^2}{y^3})^2 = \dfrac{x^{2\times2}}{y^{3\times2}} = \dfrac{x^4}{y^6}$$

Substitute 2 for x and -1 for y.

$$\dfrac{2^4}{(-1)^6} = \dfrac{16}{1} = 16$$

Selection D suggests $(\dfrac{x^2}{y^3})^2 < 0$, but 16 > 0. Therefore, selection D must be false.

**48. Answer: J. 28**

The ratio of the skyscraper's height to the television's diagonal, $\dfrac{16}{26}$, is provided in the question. A proportion, which compares equal ratios, can be used to solve the problem. Use the proportion $\dfrac{skyscraper\,height}{diagonal\,length} = \dfrac{skyscraper\,height}{diagonal\,length}$.

$$\dfrac{16}{26} = \dfrac{x}{45}$$

Cross-multiply and set the products equal to each other.

$26 \times x = 16 \times 45$

$26x = 720$

$x = 27.7$

Rounded to the nearest inch, the skyscraper on the television with the 45-inch diagonal will measure 28 inches.

**49. Answer: D.** $\dfrac{\pi}{2}$

The graph of any trigonometric graph in the form of y = a sin(bx + c) is cyclical. In other words, the basic shape of the graph will be identical for all values of x. The period of the graph will be the length along the x-axis of the function as it completes one complete cycle.

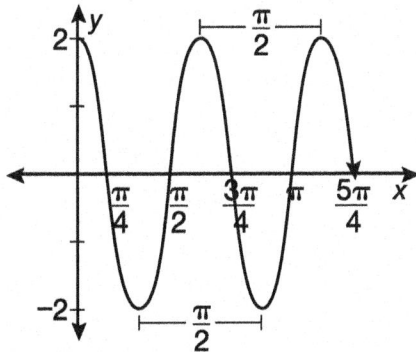

In the graph of y = 2 sin(x + m), the width of one cycle of the graph, its period, is highlighted. The graph completes one full cycle between $\dfrac{\pi}{4}$ and $\dfrac{3\pi}{4}$ and again between $\dfrac{3\pi}{4}$ and $\dfrac{5\pi}{4}$. The distance between either of these cycles is $\dfrac{\pi}{2}$.

**50. Answer: F. 4**

The distance between two points in a standard coordinate plane is found by using the distance formula.

Distance = $\sqrt{(x_1 - x_2)^2 + (y_1 - y_2)^2}$

Input the known data and solve for x.

$\sqrt{(4-x)^2 + (-1-3)^2} = 4$

Square both sides to eliminate the square root.

$(\sqrt{(4-x)^2 + (-1-3)^2})^2 = 4^2$

$(4-x)^2 + (-1-3)^2 = 4^2$

$(4-x)^2 + 16 = 16$

$(4-x)^2 = 0$

Find the square root of both sides of the equation to eliminate the exponent.

$\sqrt{(4-x)^2} = \sqrt{0}$

$4 - x = 0$

$4 = x$

**51. Answer: D. 84**

Use the Pythagorean Theorem, $a^2 + b^2 = c^2$, to find the value of x in right triangle ABC.

$$x^2 + (x+17)^2 = (x+18)^2$$
$$x^2 + (x^2 + 34x + 289) = x^2 + 36x + 324$$
$$2x^2 + 34x + 289 = x^2 + 36x + 324$$
$$x^2 - 2x - 35 = 0$$

Factor the expression $x^2 - 2x - 35 = 0$.

(x – 7)(x + 5) = 0

Set the factors x – 7 and x + 5 equal to 0 to solve for x.

x – 7 = 0          x + 5 = 0
x = 7               x = -5

The value x = -5 is called an extraneous solution. Since the length of a side in a triangle cannot be negative, discard that solution and use x = 7.

The area of a triangle is found by using the formula Area = $\frac{1}{2}$ (base)(height). Replacing 7 for x, we find the height of the triangle is 7 and the base is 24.

Area = $\frac{1}{2}(7)(24) = 84$

**52. Answer: K. 45 – 28i**

The letter i represents an imaginary number. It is shown by the equation $i = \sqrt{-1}$. The expression 7 – 2i is called a complex number because it has a real component, 7, and an imaginary component, 2i.

Expand $(7 - 2i)^2$ by using the model $(a - b)^2 = a^2 - 2ab + b^2$. In this problem, a = 7 and b = 2i.

$$(7 - 2i)^2 =$$
$$7^2 - 2(7)(-2i) + (-2i)^2 =$$
$$49 - 28i + 4i^2$$

Replace i² with -1 and simplify.

49 – 28i + 4(-1)
49 – 28i – 4
45 – 28i

**53. Answer: A. 5.8%**

To find a percent increase, use the formula $\dfrac{increase}{original} = \dfrac{n}{100}$. To find the increase in 2011 over 2011, find the sum of both and subtract the smaller figure from the larger.

2011: 5.38 + 7.11 + 6.75 + 3.88 + 7.56 = 30.68
2010: 6.01 + 7.13 + 4.26 + 4.74 + 6.86 = 29

Increase: 30.68 − 29 = 1.68

Input the data into the formula to find the percent increase.

$$\frac{1.68}{29} = \frac{n}{100}$$

Cross-multiply the fractions and solve for n.

29n = 168
n = 5.79

Selection A, 5.8%, is the closest to the answer.


**54. Answer: G. $32,459**
The increase in donations in 2011 compared to 2010 was about 5.8%. Find 5.8% of $30,680 and add it to $30,680. Expressing 5.8% as a decimal will facilitate calculations.

$30,680 + (0.058)(30,680) =
$30,680 +1779 = $32,459


**55. Answer: E. 154°**
Two angles are supplementary if their sum is 180°. Two angles are complementary if their sum is 90°. Find the complement of an angle measuring 64° by subtracting 64 from 90.

90 − 64 = 26

Find the supplement of an angle measuring 26° by subtracting 26 from 180.

180 − 26 = 154.


**56. Answer: F. 6**
One revolution of each wheel is equivalent to the circumference of each circle. Find the circumference of each circle by using the formula Circumference = diameter × π. (π is approximately equal to 3.14).

Find the circumference of the larger circle.

30 x 3.14 = 94.2

Multiply 94.2 by 4 to find the total inches the tire traveled in 4 revolutions.

4 x 94.2 = 376.8

Divide 376.8 by 12 to find the number of feet in 376.8 inches.

$376.8 \div 12 = 31.4 \approx 31$ feet

Multiply 24 by 3.14 to find the circumference of the tire with the 24 inch diameter.

24 x 3.14 = 75.36

Multiply 75.36 by 4 to find the total inches the tire traveled in 4 revolutions.

75.36 x 4 = 301.44

Divide 301.44 by 12 to find the number of feet in 301.44 inches.

$301.44 \div 12 = 25.12 \approx 25$

Subtract 25 feet from 31 feet to find out how much farther the larger tire traveled compared to the smaller tire.

31 – 25 = 6

**57. Answer: C. 36π**
A great circle of a sphere has a radius equal in measure to the radius of the sphere. Input 288π for the volume of the sphere to find the radius.

$$288\pi = \frac{4}{3}\pi r^3$$
$$\frac{3}{4\pi}(288\pi = \frac{4}{3}\pi r^3)\frac{3}{4\pi}$$
$$216 = r^3$$
$$\sqrt[3]{216} = \sqrt[3]{r}$$
$$6 = r$$

The area of a circle is found by using the formula Area = $\pi r^2$. Substitute 6 for r to find the area of the great circle.

$$Area = \pi(6)^2 = 36\pi$$

**58. Answer: H. 19.5**
Direct variation is a linear function in the form of y = kx, where k is called the constant of variation. Input the known data for x and y to solve for k.

$$14 = k(6)$$

$$k = \frac{7}{3}$$

Replace k with $\frac{7}{3}$ and solve for x.

$$45.5 = (\frac{7}{3})x$$

$$(\frac{3}{7})(45.5) = (\frac{3}{7})(\frac{7}{3}x)$$

$$x = 19.5$$

This problem could also have been solved by using the proportion $\dfrac{x_1}{x_2} = \dfrac{y_1}{y_2}$

$$\frac{6}{x_2} = \frac{14}{45.5}$$

$$14x_2 = 273$$

$$x_2 = 19.5$$

**59. Answer: E. (-7,3)**
A reflection of a point across an axis maps that point (called a translation) an equal distance from the axis to its alternate side. For example, note that the point (7,-3) is three units lower than the x-axis. Its reflection across the x-axis would be the point along the line x = 7 that is three units above the x-axis.

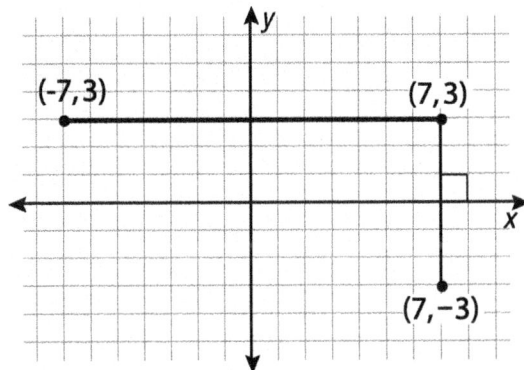

An algebraic way to visualize a reflection is to use the following rules:

Reflection across the x-axis: (x,y) → (x,-y)

Reflection across the y-axis: (x,y) → (-x,y)

Use both rules to answer the question. First, find the reflection of (7,-3) across the x-axis:

$(x,y) \rightarrow (x,-y) : (7,-3) \rightarrow (7,3)$

Reflect (7,3) across the y-axis:

$(x,y) \rightarrow (-x,y) : (7,3) \rightarrow (-7,3)$

When (7,-3) is reflected across the x-axis and the y-axis, the coordinates of the new point are (-7,3).

### 60. Answer: G. 32

The area of a parallelogram is found by using the formula Area = (base)(height). The length of the base can be found by using the distance formula:

Distance = $\sqrt{(x_1 - x_2)^2 + (y_1 - y_2)^2}$

Use the points (0,0) and (8,0) to find the length of the base.

Distance = $\sqrt{(0-8)^2 + (0-0)^2} = \sqrt{64} = 8$

The height of the parallelogram can be found by drawing a line or segment from one base such that it is perpendicular to the other base. The vertex at (2,4) can be used to discern the height.

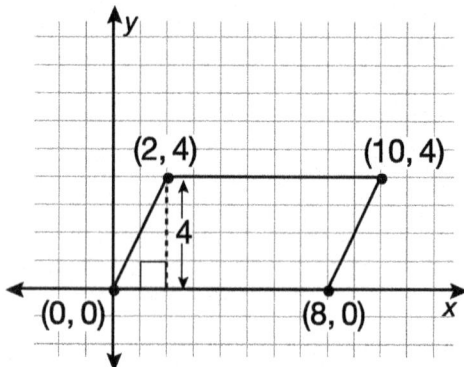

The y-coordinate, 4, is also the height of the parallelogram. Input 8 and 4 for the base and the height to find the area of the parallelogram.

Area = (base)(height) = $8 \times 4 = 32$

# READING PRACTICE TEST 2

35 Minutes - 40 Questions

Directions: Each of the four reading passages in this section is followed by ten reading questions. Choose the best answer for each question.

## The Time Machine

Excerpts from *The Time Machine* by H. G. (Herbert George) Wells, first published in 1895

The Time Traveller smiled round at us. Then, still smiling faintly, and with his hands deep in his trousers pockets, he walked slowly out of the room, and we heard his slippers shuffling down the long passage to his laboratory.

5   The Psychologist looked at us. "I wonder what he's got?"

"Some sleight-of-hand trick or other," said the Medical Man, and Filby tried to tell us about a conjurer he had seen at Burslem; but before he had finished his preface the Time Traveller came back, and Filby's anecdote collapsed.

10

The thing the Time Traveller held in his hand was a glittering metallic framework, scarcely larger than a small clock, and very delicately made. There was ivory in it, and some transparent crystalline substance. And now I must be explicit, for this that follows—unless his explanation is to be accepted—is an absolutely unaccountable thing. He took one of the small octagonal tables that

15   were scattered about the room, and set it in front of the fire, with two legs on the hearthrug. On this table he placed the mechanism. Then he drew up a chair, and sat down. The only other object on the table was a small shaded lamp, the bright light of which fell upon the model. There were also perhaps a dozen candles about, two in brass candlesticks upon the mantel and several in sconces, so that the room was brilliantly illuminated. I sat in a low arm-chair nearest the fire, and I drew this

20   forward so as to be almost between the Time Traveller and the fireplace. Filby sat behind him, looking over his shoulder. The Medical Man and the Provincial Mayor watched him in profile from the right, the Psychologist from the left. The Very Young Man stood behind the Psychologist. We were all on the alert. It appears incredible to me that any kind of trick, however subtly conceived and however adroitly done, could have been played upon us under these conditions.

25

The Time Traveller looked at us, and then at the mechanism. "Well?" said the Psychologist.

"This little affair," said the Time Traveller, resting his elbows upon the table and pressing his hands together above the apparatus, "is only a model. It is my plan for a machine to travel through time.

30   You will notice that it looks singularly askew, and that there is an odd twinkling appearance about this bar, as though it was in some way unreal." He pointed to the part with his finger. "Also, here is one little white lever, and here is another."

The Medical Man got up out of his chair and peered into the thing. "It's beautifully made," he said.

35

"It took two years to make," retorted the Time Traveller. Then, when we had all imitated the action of the Medical Man, he said: "Now I want you to clearly understand that this lever, being pressed over, sends the machine gliding into the future, and this other reverses the motion. This saddle represents the seat of a time traveler. Presently I am going to press the lever, and off the machine

40   will go. It will vanish, pass into future Time, and disappear. Have a good look at the thing. Look at the table too, and satisfy yourselves there is no trickery. I don't want to waste this model, and then be told I'm a quack."

45　There was a minute's pause perhaps. The Psychologist seemed about to speak to me, but changed his mind. Then the Time Traveller put forth his finger towards the lever. "No," he said suddenly. "Lend me your hand." And turning to the Psychologist, he took that individual's hand in his own and told him to put out his forefinger. So that it was the Psychologist himself who sent forth the model Time Machine on its <u>interminable</u> voyage. We all saw the lever turn. I am absolutely certain there was no trickery. There was a breath of wind, and the lamp flame jumped. One of the
50　candles on the mantel was blown out, and the little machine suddenly swung round, became indistinct, was seen as a ghost for a second perhaps, as an eddy of faintly glittering brass and ivory; and it was gone -- vanished! Save for the lamp the table was bare.

　　******
55
　　"Would you like to see the Time Machine itself?" asked the Time Traveller. And therewith, taking the lamp in his hand, he led the way down the long, draughty corridor to his laboratory. I remember vividly the flickering light, his queer, broad head in silhouette, the dance of the shadows, how we all followed him, puzzled but incredulous, and how there in the laboratory we beheld a larger edition of
60　the little mechanism which we had seen vanish from before our eyes. Parts were of nickel, parts of ivory, parts had certainly been filed or sawn out of rock crystal. The thing was generally complete, but the twisted crystalline bars lay unfinished upon the bench beside some sheets of drawings, and I took one up for a better look at it. Quartz it seemed to be.

65　"Look here," said the Medical Man, "are you perfectly serious? Or is this a trick—like that ghost you showed us last Christmas?"

　　"Upon that machine," said the Time Traveller, holding the lamp aloft, "I intend to explore time. Is that plain? I was never more serious in my life."
70
　　None of us quite knew how to take it.

　　I caught Filby's eye over the shoulder of the Medical Man, and he winked at me solemnly.

75　I think that at that time none of us quite believed in the Time Machine. The fact is, the Time Traveller was one of those men who are too clever to be believed: you never felt that you saw all round him; you always suspected some subtle reserve, some ingenuity in ambush, behind his lucid frankness. Had Filby shown the model and explained the matter in the Time Traveller's words, we should have shown *him* far less scepticism. For we should have perceived his motives; a pork
80　butcher could understand Filby. But the Time Traveller had more than a touch of whim among his elements, and we distrusted him. Things that would have made the frame of a less clever man seemed tricks in his hands. It is a mistake to do things too easily. The serious people who took him seriously never felt quite sure of his deportment; they were somehow aware that trusting their reputations for judgment with him was like furnishing a nursery with egg-shell china. So I don't think
85　any of us said very much about time travelling in the interval between that Thursday and the next, though its odd potentialities ran, no doubt, in most of our minds: its plausibility, that is, its practical incredibleness, the curious possibilities of anachronism and of utter confusion it suggested. For my own part, I was particularly preoccupied with the trick of the model. That I remember discussing with the Medical Man, whom I met on Friday at the Linnaean. He said he had seen a similar thing
90　at Tubingen, and laid considerable stress on the blowing out of the candle. But how the trick was done he could not explain.

1. **From the passage the reader can infer that the narrator is:**

   A. A person who heard the story secondhand from someone who was at the gathering.
   B. The author himself, telling the story in third person.
   C. The Psychologist, who was present at the gathering.
   D. A person who was invited to the gathering and is recounting the story of what he witnessed.

2. **From the passage the reader can make the assumption that the character of Filby is:**

   F. A practical everyman who can be trusted and understood easily by other men.
   G. A complex individual that always seems to mean something other than what he says.
   H. A character that is always trying to insinuate himself into the business of others by trying to be overly friendly.
   J. A fellow scientist who has invited the rest of the gentlemen in the room to view another scientist's extraordinary invention.

3. **With the exception of Filby and 'The Very Young Man', the narrator identifies each character by his occupation. In addition to the narrator, Filby, and the 'The Very Young Man', the other characters present at the gathering are:**

   A. The Medical Man, the Provincial Mayor, the Burslem Conjurer, the Time Traveller, and the Psychologist
   B. The Provincial Mayor, the Time Traveller, the Medical Man, and the Psychologist
   C. The Psychologist, the Medical Man, the Time Traveller, the Provincial Mayor, and the Pork Butcher
   D. The Medical Man, the Pork Butcher, the Time Traveller, and the Psychologist

4. **The Time Traveller prepares the room for his demonstration by:**

   F. Providing as much light as possible so that his guests can see there isn't a trick involved.
   G. Gathering his guests in a dark room lit by dim lamps and mystical candles in order to lend a magical atmosphere.
   H. Diverting his guests' attention to a handmade model constructed with crystals and ivory.
   J. Telling a detailed story about how time travelling works in order to set the stage for what his guests are about to see.

5. **From the passage the reader can infer that the character of the Time Traveller is:**

   A. A gentleman who was once highly esteemed but is now deemed, by his peers, to be a madman.
   B. A jovial man who likes to joke around and put on a good show for his friends.
   C. An aloof individual who is self-absorbed and is only tolerating the other men in order to display his work.
   D. A person who is dissatisfied with his own time and would rather escape his world to live in other eras.

6. **The Time Traveller makes the Psychologist push the lever of the model that sends it into the future. The most likely reason the Time Traveller does this is:**

   F. The Psychologist was simply the closest person in the room and the Time Traveller wanted another person to have the experience of sending the model into the future.
   G. The Psychologist represents the idea of a healthy mind; if the Psychologist sets the time machine into the future, then everyone must believe the experience is real, rather than a trick of the mind.
   H. Like a performing magician, the Time Traveller is attempting to eradicate skepticism from the room by picking an audience member to help with the trick.
   J. The Psychologist seemed to be the most skeptical of the professionals in the room and the Time Traveller picked him because of that reason alone.

7. As stated in the passage, "it was the Psychologist himself who sent forth the model Time Machine on its interminable voyage" (line 48). In this context, the word *interminable* means:

    A. To come to a bad end
    B. Intolerable
    C. Unending
    D. To end abruptly

8. The setting for the gathering is most likely:

    F. The Time Traveller's home
    G. The narrator's home
    H. The home of the Provincial Mayor
    J. The offices of the Psychologist

9. After the Time Traveller reveals his plans for the Time Machine, the narrator catches Filby's eye and Filby gives him a "solemn" wink. The narrator is implying that:

    A. Filby knows that the Time Traveller is a madman and he wants the narrator to understand that fact.
    B. Filby knows the Time Traveller is dead serious about his plans.
    C. Filby wants the narrator to know he has the same doubts that the narrator has.
    D. Filby is amused by the whole scene and wants the narrator to know how absurd the situation actually is.

10. In summarizing the aftermath of that evening, the narrator recalls that:

    F. None of the professional men were able to understand what they had seen and sought further explanation by recounting the demonstration to others.
    G. All of the professional men felt that they couldn't trust the Time Traveller and wanted to put the episode of the demonstration behind them.
    H. None of the professional men wanted to risk their reputations by recounting to others what they had seen, but all were intrigued by the possibilities of time travel.
    J. All of the professional men wondered what would happen next and also wondered what might happen if they, themselves, went time travelling.

## Nonverbal Communication

The interplay between verbal and nonverbal communication is an area of great interest to both linguists and anthropologists, as it sheds light on how humans convey and interpret meaning both consciously and subconsciously. Many people understand that the unspoken messages between us define our private and professional communication: our facial expressions, our body language,
5    our eye contact, and even our choice of clothing or hairstyle. However, many experts would expand the definition of nonverbal communication to also include the *nonverbal* elements of speech such as speaking rate, pitch, tone, volume, style, and intonation. This expansive definition makes sense when you consider that subconscious messages emanating from a persuasive speech depend not only upon the spoken word, but also on the speaker's tone and volume levels. In this way,
10   nonverbal communication can be understood to include a wide range of messages we unwittingly convey as we interact with others.

Nonverbal cues certainly supplement our verbal expression and can be delivered and received through any of the senses of sight, sound, smell, touch, or taste. These cues can range from a
15   clearing of the throat to an individual's way of standing in relation to another, to the amount or type of cologne one prefers. As humans, we send nonverbal messages all the time, both deliberately and subconsciously. It is believed that as much as 60-70% of all meaning is communicated nonverbally. This is certainly an interesting fact, especially for a <u>loquacious</u> species such as ours! In fact, it is nonverbal communication that tends to convey our true emotions and attitudes and as
20   such, it can either reinforce our spoken words or can contradict them.

If what we are saying and what we are feeling are two different things, our nonverbal cues can betray our true feelings. For example, when someone is telling an untruth, they often fidget or avoid eye contact. Their spoken words may be asserting that they are telling the truth, but their nonverbal
25   communication—their *body language* —is indicating that they are not being completely honest. Another example is that people often cross their arms or legs when they are in an uncomfortable situation or conversation. Their spoken words may indicate that they are perfectly at ease, but their body language indicates otherwise. This contradiction between the meaning that is conveyed verbally and the meaning that is conveyed nonverbally is often referred to as sending *mixed*
30   *messages*. When mixed messages occur, the receiver tends to rely primarily on nonverbal cues (most often, the sender's eyes) to clarify the true message.

There are many forms of nonverbal communication that anthropologists and psychologists consider to be universal: smiling when happy, or frowning when sad; but, some nonverbal communication is
35   culturally specific. A gesture, for instance, that may hold a positive meaning in one culture could have a negative or even offensive connotation in another culture. Eye contact is an excellent example of a culturally-specific form of nonverbal communication. In the United States, direct eye contact is valued during conversations and we often infer that someone is being evasive, untruthful, or insincere if they do not make eye contact with us when speaking. In more traditional Asian
40   countries, by contrast, direct eye contact, especially between an employer and employee, or a teacher and a student, can be interpreted as confrontational.

A salesman, or a service engineer, doing business with members of another culture will benefit greatly from learning about the specific norms of nonverbal communication within that culture. Yet,
45   anyone can benefit from learning more about nonverbal communication. Improving your understanding of how you, personally, send nonverbal cues as well as honing your ability to accurately read the nonverbal cues of others will enhance your connection with those around you. It is to your advantage to better understand the true feelings and intentions of others by pinpointing nonverbal cues.
50

Certainly, the first place where most people take their nonverbal cues from is the face. There are ten muscle groups in the scalp and face that create forty-three distinct, recognizable movements. Combinations of these movements give humans over ten thousand facial expressions. Normally functioning humans scan faces for the meaning they need in order to relate to others. Many of our

55    facial expressions are involuntary, especially when we feel extreme emotions of happiness,
       sadness, anger, or surprise and fear. These involuntary expressions help parents know what is
       right or wrong with their children, and they help mates and friends to remain close and supportive.
       The face is what people look at to discern the true nature of a person's emotional state, or even
       what that person might be thinking.
60
       There are some people who have difficulty, even an inability, with reading faces and other
       nonverbal cues. This problem is a symptom of the condition called *autism*. People who are autistic
       have difficulty with empathy, or putting themselves in someone else's shoes, a key social skill in
       understanding another's facial expressions and body language. Autistic people take the words of
65    others literally and are unable to judge from the tone of another's voice the hidden meanings which
       might be crucial to complete understanding. People with autism also don't look at the cues that
       emanate from the eyes of a speaker and will often miss subtle looks that enrich the speaker's
       verbal communication. For these reasons, interestingly enough, those who study autism have
       contributed as much to our understanding of the intricacies of nonverbal communication as the
70    scientists specialized in the field.

       The 21st century study of nonverbal communication requires us, as humans, to see ourselves as
       quantifiable, even predictable, machines. Some people might not be comfortable with research
       outcomes that provide such cut and dry evaluations. Psychologists have broken down nonverbal
75    communications, especially facial expressions, and have categorized them well enough to
       understand when someone is lying or telling the truth. Techniques derived from these studies are
       now used by detectives during police interrogations. As well, politicians and other public figures
       study their own nonverbal tendencies in order to mask emotional conflicts in front of an audience.
       Remarkably, closer inspection of nonverbal cues is now leading humans to quicker attachments
80    and closeness as in, for instance, the present practice of *speed-dating*, where men and women
       looking for companions come to hold six minute personal interviews with each other. Can one truly
       know whether or not they will deeply care for another within the first six minutes of meeting? In this
       instance, nonverbal communication makes a vital, lasting impression. For, as it has often been
       said, the most powerful human emotions truly cannot be expressed in words.

**11. The author's main point in paragraph 1 is that:**

   A.  Nonverbal communication is delivered both consciously and subconsciously.
   B.  The definition of nonverbal communication includes the nonverbal elements of speech such as
       tone and volume.
   C.  Both traditional linguists and anthropologists study the interplay of verbal and nonverbal
       communication.
   D.  Nonverbal communication is of more interest than the interplay between verbal and nonverbal
       communication.

**12. The author asserts that nonverbal communication:**

   F.  Is a small but crucial part of our conscious and unconscious communication experience.
   G.  Is a large and crucial part of our conscious communication experience.
   H.  Can be heard and seen only by our conscious selves as we communicate.
   J.  Can be sent and received by all of the senses, both consciously and unconsciously.

**13. From the context of the passage, the word *loquacious* (line 18) most likely means:**

   A.  Especially contemplative
   B.  Hyperactive
   C.  Quite talkative
   D.  Extremely nonverbal

**14. The statement that best summarizes paragraph 3 is:**

F. When our body language and our verbal language do not agree, we can send mixed messages to others.
G. When mixed messages occur, we place greater emphasis on trying to interpret the verbal cues.
H. When people are communicating an untruth, their body language almost always gives this away.
J. Skilled communicators can suppress their body language in order to hide their true feelings.

**15. According to the passage, scientists generally agree that nonverbal communication is:**

A. Culturally-specific
B. Universal
C. Unchanging across the centuries
D. A mixture of universal and culturally-specific cues

**16. The study of the human face has revealed that:**

F. The ten muscle groups of the face and scalp are only capable of producing forty-three distinct facial expressions.
G. Involuntary facial expressions occur during moments of heightened emotion.
H. Voluntary facial expressions communicate meaning more effectively than involuntary facial expressions.
J. Voluntary facial expressions help people to discern other's true emotional states.

**17. People with the condition of autism:**

A. Have difficulty reading nonverbal cues.
B. Have a greater ability than others to read nonverbal cues.
C. Have a greater ability to feel empathy for others.
D. Have taught us that nonverbal cues aren't as important as we once believed.

**18. According to the passage, knowledge of how nonverbal communication works can be used for all of the following except:**

F. To mask emotional conflicts.
G. To detect lies and deceitful communication.
H. To determine someone's past behavior.
J. To establish personal bonds.

**19. According to the passage, the author believes that a better understanding of nonverbal communication will:**

A. Benefit anyone wishing to make closer connections with others.
B. Benefit mostly business people traveling to foreign countries.
C. Benefit only those wishing to understand foreign cultures in detail.
D. Benefit mostly anthropologists and psychologists in their field studies.

**20. According to the passage, which of the following is the most reliable indicator of someone's true emotional state?**

F. Spoken words
G. Body posture
H. Hand gestures that accompany speech
J. Facial expressions

## The Pueblo Revolt

Many view the Conquistador as the Spanish conqueror of the New World, the pacifier of both the mighty Aztecs and Inca cultures. This was true in the 16th century territories of New Spain, modern Mexico, and Central and South America. However, in the 17th century (the 1600s), the northern territories comprising the present day Southwest region of the United States became the delegated
5 responsibility of another invader from Spain: the Catholic Church. Committing themselves to the task of civilizing and reforming the indigenous people, the priests of Spain developed into the most important European colonizing influence in America; but their religious zeal would often bedevil them as it did, in 1680, in the Rio Grande Valley of Mexico.

10 The massive and sparsely populated wasteland that was to become Arizona, New Mexico, and western Texas held so little promise of material reward to King Philip III of Spain that, in 1608, he was, at first, content to leave it as a buffer against the French Louisiana Territory. Yet, as increasing numbers of woebegone natives were brought to kneel before the Cross and convert, the pious royal court began to see that there were priceless spiritual gains possible. The King
15 ultimately decided that the region would be called *New Mexico*, would be turned into a royal province and the Crown itself would devote funds and energy to its Spanish settlement.

The friars of the Franciscan, Jesuit, and Dominican orders delved into these northern hinterlands establishing the mission/presidio system that came to typify the center of every Spanish settlement.
20 The *presidio* was the fort that was built to protect the Spanish and loyal Indians from marauders. The *mission* was to teach the native peoples to farm, convert them to Christianity, and create a civilization from which both Spaniard and native alike could benefit. Missions were first set up throughout New Mexico's Rio Grande Valley where less than 50,000 indigenous people had inhabited, for centuries, their own well-planned agriculturally-oriented towns of adobe structures the
25 Spanish called *pueblos*. Although these Indians were divided by cultural idiosyncrasies and differences in language, they all shared the same problems: continuous drought and persistent attacks by nomadic Navajo and Apache. The new firearms, agricultural technology, and domesticated animals brought by the Spanish were at first bewildering. Nonetheless, many of the Pueblo cultures came to grudgingly accept the newcomers and their book-oriented religion. The
30 illiterate native peoples became familiar with Christianity through liturgical biblical stories and were, at first, happy to incorporate these lessons into their own ways of seeing the world.

By 1611, the Spanish had established their capital presidio, Santa Fe, and native peoples were helping to raise horse, cattle, goats, sheep, fruit trees and crops all along the Rio Grande. Indians
35 fused European carpentry and masonry with their own native methods and resources and churches began rising up alongside the old pueblos. By 1630, friars of the various priestly orders were converting and ministering in over 90 villages. Over one thousand Spaniards had come to settle in the valley and the new royal province appeared, on the surface, to be flourishing.

40 Yet success and abundance brought jealousy and dysfunction to the province's Spanish administrators. The secular governors of New Mexico felt that, as representatives of royal power, theirs was the final word on all public matters. After all, they were in charge of everything from enforcing the law to protecting the people from marauders. The priests, however, felt that God, in His omnipotence, had naturally given the shepherds of His flock the final word. Native populations
45 were soon caught in the crossfire of this struggle for final provincial authority. By the 1660s Indians were being flogged and tortured by civil authorities for helping priests to farm and labor, or even if found participating in church services. Many Indians were persuaded by these same civil authorities to leave the Church and return to their own religion. The priests would then punish the Indians for their lack of faith. Who could blame the Puebloans if they had become increasingly
50 disillusioned and angry toward the Spanish?

Inevitably, in 1675 his Most Catholic Majesty, King Charles II, appointed a governor in New Mexico who made the Church his priority. The new Governor moved to prohibit Indian religious practice. In one instance, forty-seven Indians were arrested on the charge of engaging in witchcraft; four of

55     them were hanged, the rest publically flogged. Many natives had seen enough, including a middle-aged Pueblo Indian named Popé, who began to secretly plan a revolt against the Spanish authorities. Because recent drought conditions had caused widespread famine and the Apache raids on the pueblos were becoming more frequent, Indians fervently listened to Popé's message of insurrection. Amidst all this trouble, Popé exclaimed, the Spanish compelled the Indians to
60     deliver food and work as slaves. Between the evil governor and his soldiers and the hypocritical friars, there was just no relief from these invaders. It was time to drive them out! The Pueblo people united for the first time under Popé.

    On August 10, 1680, Indians from all across the Rio Grande Valley to hundreds of miles west to the
65     Zuñi and Hopi villages were given the signal for revolt. Everywhere presidios were methodically attacked, churches set aflame, priests and hundreds of Spanish civilians were killed. Spanish survivors attempted to escape to Santa Fe and, by August 13th, over 2,000 Spaniards were gathered together in the capital. One hundred-fifty Spanish soldiers battled against well over a thousand Indian warriors. Parleys with Spanish speaking Indians achieved little and, by the 16th of
70     August, almost 4,000 Indians controlled everything but the central plaza, cutting off the water supply and making life miserable for Santa Fe's defenders. The impasse was broken when a surprise counterattack by the remaining Spanish soldiers stunned the Indians long enough to allow the trapped contingent to escape. With little food and water, the Spaniards composed a slow, ragged line south to the mission of El Paso, leaving a third of their number behind in the Rio
75     Grande Valley, dead or missing.

    The Spanish mission into the northern borderlands to convert the Indians to Christianity had failed, but only for a while. Popé had his followers destroy all the remnants of Spanish influence, both spiritual and secular, except for the governor's palace. Popé wanted that for himself and,
80     predictably, he became a corrupt ruler who allowed the region to be over-run by raiding Apache tribes aided now by captured Spanish horses. The Pueblos had never before had a single leader and they soon became disenchanted with Popé. He died just eight years after the Spanish left, in 1688, with the violence-torn region still facing pervasive famine and worse off than before the insurrection. By 1692, when the Spanish friars returned, the Indians were ready to receive them
85     and their Christianity with open arms in a bloodless *Reconquista*.

**21. From the context of the passage, it can be inferred that the word *secular* (line 41) means:**

    A.   Belonging to a particular sect, or group
    B.   Not religious or spiritual in nature
    C.   Extremely powerful
    D.   Derived from royal authority

**22. The main idea of paragraph 2 is that:**

    F.   The indigenous populations of America were so lost spiritually that converting them to Christianity would make the Spanish world famous.
    G.   The Spanish saw the northern territories as a wasteland and regarded the natives as not worth the Crown's time.
    H.   The Spanish Court believed that the opportunity to convert Native Americans to Christianity was a priceless opportunity.
    J.   The rich natural resources of the northern territories could be harvested and then sold to other nations for profit.

**23. In paragraph 3, the author implies that:**

A. The mission of the Spanish priests was to bring a spiritual and self-sustaining way of life to a group of people that already enjoyed both.
B. The mission of the Spanish priests was to bring a spiritual and self-sustaining way of life to a group of people that were in desperate need of both.
C. The indigenous people of the Rio Grande Valley had been waiting for the Spaniards to come and welcomed them with open arms.
D. The mission/presidio system created an "us against them" separation between the Spaniards and the indigenous population.

**24. From the context in <u>line 25</u>, it can be inferred that the word *idiosyncrasies* means:**

F. All the Pueblo Indian groups were basically the same in ways of spiritual worship, leadership, and family mores.
G. Each Pueblo Indian group had cultural ways of living that made them seem extremely odd to other Indian groups.
H. Each Indian group had cultural mores that could never be changed, even by an outside group such as the Spaniards.
J. Each Pueblo Indian group had their own particular way of spiritual worship, leadership, and family mores.

**25. The mission/presidio system of early Spanish settlements is best summarized by which two words?**

A. Secular and religious
B. Conversion and redemption
C. Protection and conversion
D. Jesuit and Dominican

**26. In paragraphs 4 and 5, the author's main point is:**

F. The relationship between the Spanish and the Native populations was always tempestuous and seething under the surface.
G. At first, the interaction between the Spanish and Native populations was somewhat harmonious but, because of Spanish inconsistencies, the relationship turned sour.
H. The relationship between the Spanish and the Native Americans was soured by the priests and their expectations.
J. The Spanish government's use of torture was a complete surprise to the Native populations and this created an atmosphere of rebellion in the Rio Grande Valley.

**27. In the passage, the author implies that the historical figure of Popé:**

A. Is a Pueblo Indian who becomes the first true leader of his people and an incorruptible hero.
B. Is a Pueblo Indian who was a criminal at first, but later became a powerful hero to his people.
C. Is a shadowy figure and there is little historical evidence to speak of his life.
D. Is a Pueblo Indian who, at first, leads his people against Spanish injustice but, later, becomes a self-serving ruler.

**28. Paragraph 7 relates that the Pueblo Revolt of 1680 was:**

   F.  A successful, choreographed attack by the Pueblo people that ultimately drove the Spanish from the northern territories.

   G.  An unsuccessful series of isolated attacks against Spanish settlers that did nothing but create hatred and distrust between two cultural groups.

   H.  An isolated incident that changed nothing between the two cultural groups.

   J.  A famous event that contributed to the birth of America's oldest town, Santa Fe, New Mexico.

**29. In the final paragraph of the passage, the author writes about a bloodless *Reconquista*. The *Reconquista*, or reconquest, of the Northern Territories was bloodless because:**

   A.  The Pueblo Indians had died off and left little opposition to the returning Spaniards.

   B.  The power of the friars was such that Pueblo Indians must have been frightened by their return and dared not resist the Spanish again.

   C.  The Pueblo Indian leader, Popé, failed to advance the gains made by his people during the Revolt and the situation in the territories worsened to the point that the Indians were receptive to the Spaniards' return.

   D.  The Pueblo Indian leader, Popé, had died, so that there was little effective leadership to resist the returning Spanish soldiers twelve years after the Revolt.

**30. The main idea of this passage is that:**

   F.  The Spanish mission was to conquer the northern territories in much the same way the Spanish had conquered the Aztec and the Inca.

   G.  The Pueblo Revolt was the event that halted Spanish influence in the present-day Southwest United States.

   H.  The integration of Spanish and Pueblo Indian culture was born from an idea of mutual respect that continues to this day.

   J.  The Spanish mission to the northern territories was to convert the Indians to Christianity but, ultimately, this mission failed due to the inflexibility of the Spanish.

## Trends and Rising Threats from Invasive Species

The following passage is adapted from the United States Forest Service Research Position Paper: *Invasive Species.*

### What Is An Invasive Species?

An invasive species is defined as a species that is nonnative to the ecosystem under consideration and whose introduction causes or is likely to cause economic or environmental harm or harm to human health. Thousands of invasive exotic plants, insects, fish, mollusks, crustaceans, diseases,
5  mammals, birds, reptiles, and amphibians have infested hundreds of millions of acres of lands and waters across the nation, causing massive disruption in ecosystem function, reducing biodiversity, and degrading ecosystem health. Forests, prairies, mountains, wetlands, rivers, and oceans have each been infested by these aggressive exotic species.

10  ### Trends and Rising Threats from Invasive Species

Humans intentionally and unintentionally spread invasive species. The foundations of agriculture and animal husbandry are based on ancient habits of selectively favoring some plant and animal species and their habitats over others for food, fiber, and medicine. About 50,000 non-native species have been introduced in the United States. Many nonnative species have been deliberately
15  introduced for erosion control (kudzu), food animals and fish (brown trout), agricultural crops (Johnson grass), and ornamental trees and landscape plants (purple loosestrife). Some insects and diseases have been introduced in ignorance, as was the Gypsy Moth, or as the unintentional result of a global economy, as with the West Nile virus and Zebra mussels.

20  Many invasive plants in the United States were originally introduced for food, fiber or erosion control, or as ornamentals. For example, purple loosestrife was introduced as an ornamental in the early 19th century. Loosestrife is present in riparian areas throughout the continental United States and control costs are an estimated $45 million per year. Riparian areas are extremely valuable to native plants and animals, and the wholesale invasion by Loosestrife poses a serious threat of
25  eventual extinction to numerous riparian-dependent species.

Other plant species, such as European Cheatgrass, have almost entirely displaced sagebrush-grassland plants and associated animals. Cheatgrass has also seriously altered the fire regime from an average return interval of 60-110 years to 0-3 years. Cheatgrass is an example of the
30  adverse impacts an introduced species can have on the environment. Some scientists estimate that Cheatgrass is present on 100 million acres of grassland-steppe in the western United States. Cheatgrass forms a dense, uniform carpet that out-competes native grasses and shrubs. It greens quickly and produces a very flammable cover that often burns completely, without allowing native plants to reestablish. In pinyon-juniper woodlands, the combination of Cheatgrass and fire may
35  effectively prevent the re-establishment of the original woodlands.

Invasive species cost the public approximately $137 billion per year in damage, loss, and control. The economic losses are significant but the ecological and cultural losses of native flora and fauna are equally important. For example, the bullfrog, a nonnative species in California, has almost
40  completely replaced the native California red-legged frog—the famed jumping frog of Calaveras County. Another introduced plant, the Giant Reed, eliminates native streamside vegetation and dries up creeks that provide habitat for four endangered species: least bell's vireo, southwestern willow flycatcher, California red-legged frog, and unarmored three-spine stickleback. Approximately 46% of the plants and animals federally listed as endangered species have been negatively
45  impacted by invasive species.

Introduced insects and disease have also taken their toll on the environment. Chestnut Blight and Dutch elm disease are two well-known examples. Gypsy moth was intentionally introduced in the 1800s as a possible source of silk production. As a result of these well-known pests, the American
50  chestnut and American elm have virtually disappeared from the US landscape and numerous other eastern trees are at risk from Gypsy moth.

### Invasive Plants

The United States has about 2,000 nonnative invasive plant species, which are concentrated in
55   California, Florida, and Hawaii. On non-croplands in the Midwestern states, one Forest Service
researcher estimates that 14 percent of the plant species are nonnative invasive plants. Trend data
from the 19th century to the present indicates a significant escalation in the percentages of
nonnative invasive plants in the last half of the 20th century.

60   An estimated 3.5 million acres of National Forest System lands are infested with invasive weeds,
according to the 2000 RPA assessment, which summarized local estimates from individual national
forests. However, local estimates vary widely, and the agency lacks a comprehensive inventory for
either terrestrial or aquatic areas infested with invasive species. The Framework for Invasive
Species calls for expanding inventory and monitoring activities to identify more invasive insects,
65   pathogens and plants. Some species of particular concern to Forest Service managers are leafy
spurge, knapweeds and starthistles, saltcedar, non-indigenous thistles, purple loosestrife, and
cheatgrass in the West and garlic mustard, kudzu, Japanese knotweed, Tree-of-heaven, and
purple loosestrife and hydrilla in the East.

### 70   Insect Damage and Disease

Insect damage and plant disease are natural disturbances that are part of a healthy, functioning
ecosystem, along with fire and wind damage. However, both native and nonnative insects and
diseases have caused above normal mortality rates on forested lands in the United States. Some
58 million acres or 8 percent of forested land are at risk for mortality rates that exceed the norm by
75   25 percent or more. High mortality rates can accelerate the development of high fuel-loading in fire-
dependent forests, effectively remove important ecosystem elements, and reduce private property
values.

The highest profile exotic insects and diseases include Dutch elm disease, chestnut blight, white
80   pine blister rust, Port-Orford cedar root disease, European gypsy moth, hemlock wooly adelgid,
and beech bark disease. Aside from the potential economic loss from timber volume, many wildlife
and fish species are dependent on the ecosystems affected by these invasive insects and
diseases.

### 85   International Context

Invasive species negatively affect natural ecosystems throughout the world by out-competing
native flora and fauna for resources and growing space. Because there are often no biological
controls on their growth, invasive species spread quickly and negatively impact threatened and
endangered species. At least 4,500 nonnative plant, animal, and microbe species were established
90   in the United States during the 19th century, and about 15 percent of these are considered harmful.

Many invasive species arrive in the United States through international trade. Therefore, the Forest
Service must work with the international partners to (1) stem the flow of invasive species into the
country, (2) discern and apply biological controls for invasives that have already established and
95   spread, and (3) protect island ecosystems, which are especially vulnerable due to their high
percentage of unique species and evolutionary isolation.

**31. When describing the distribution of invasive species in North America, the passage reports
that:**

A. Invasive species are a widespread problem but prevalent only in riparian areas.
B. Invasive species are a widespread problem but prevalent only in the Neotropics, where
intraspecific competition occurs.
C. Invasive species are a widespread problem and not exclusive to one type of ecosystem.
D. Invasive species are not exclusive to one section of the biosphere, and are a relatively minor
threat to North American ecosystems.

**32. The passage states that one of the biggest reasons for the arrival of invasive species in North America is that:**

- F. Non-native species arrived solely through international commercial transactions.
- G. Humans have unintentionally spread over 50,000 non-native species throughout North America through agricultural endeavors.
- H. Most non-native species are brought into North America through the migration of insects and birds.
- J. Many non-native species were introduced because humans thought that they might be beneficial.

**33. Invasive species are limited to which of the following categories:**

- A. Invasive species can come from all categories of living creatures
- B. Birds, plants, and mammals only
- C. Plants, insects, and birds only
- D. Plants, insects, birds, and mammals only

**34. In paragraph 4, European Cheatgrass is described as an invasive plant in the grassland-steppe areas of the western United States. In what way does Cheatgrass affect these ecosystems?**

- F. Cheatgrass out-competes native species and, because of its density and flammability, leads to more fires.
- G. Cheatgrass improves the fire regime from an average return interval of 0-3 years to 60-110 years.
- H. Cheatgrass forms a dense and uniform carpet that protects native species from fire.
- J. Cheatgrass improves the fire regime from an average return interval of 60-110 years to 0-3 years.

**35. The main point of paragraph 5 is that:**

- A. Invasive species cost the public $137 billion per year in damage and loss.
- B. The ecological and cultural losses are as significant as the economic losses.
- C. The non-native bullfrog has almost completely replaced the native jumping frog of Calaveras County.
- D. The non-native Giant Reed plant has eliminated native streamside vegetation that provides habitats for four endangered species.

**36. The authors of the passage report that the percentages of non-native invasive plants species in the United States increased significantly from the 19th to the 20th century. The most likely reason for this is:**

- F. The failure of the U.S. government to implement eradication strategies.
- G. The expansion of international trade.
- H. The lack of inventory and monitoring frameworks to identify invasive insects, pathogens, and plants.
- J. The popularity of non-native plants in ornamental landscaping and agriculture.

**37. The effects of invasive species on federally listed endangered species could be described as:**

- A. Limited
- D. Limited to moderate
- C. Moderate to significant
- D. Significant

**38.** In paragraph 9, the authors write that non-native insects and diseases can destroy native plants and that when these plants die it "can accelerate the development of high fuel-loading in fire-dependent forests." The main point of the paragraph is that:

F. Non-native species benefit fire-dependent forests by increasing the fuel-load.
G. Fire-dependent forests require both native and non-native species in order to have sufficient fuel-loads for natural fires to occur.
H. Insect damage and plant disease are natural disturbances in a healthy, fire-dependent forest.
J. Non-native species increase the mortality rate of forested land, which adds to the fuel-load and increases the number of fires.

**39.** Which of the following is NOT given as an example of a *deliberately* introduced invasive species?

A. American chestnut
B. Gypsy moth
C. Purple loosestrife
D. Brown trout

**40. The authors of the passage conclude that:**

F. There is little hope in eradicating non-native species of any kind once these species take root.
G. Invasive plant and animal species have many benefits that far outweigh the negative aspects of their arrival in North America.
H. One critical factor in eradicating new invasive species is international cooperation.
J. Invasive non-native species spread quickly due to a low level of competition but can be eradicated just as quickly.

# READING PRACTICE TEST 2 ANSWER KEY

| | |
|---|---|
| 1. D | 21. B |
| 2. F | 22. H |
| 3. B | 23. A |
| 4. F | 24. J |
| 5. C | 25. C |
| 6. G | 26. G |
| 7. C | 27. D |
| 8. F | 28. F |
| 9. B | 29. C |
| 10. H | 30. J |
| 11. B | 31. C |
| 12. J | 32. J |
| 13. C | 33. A |
| 14. F | 34. F |
| 15. D | 35. B |
| 16. G | 36. G |
| 17. A | 37. D |
| 18. H | 38. J |
| 19. A | 39. A |
| 20. J | 40. H |

# READING PRACTICE TEST 2 RATIONALES

**1. Answer: D. A person who was invited to the gathering and is recounting the story of what he witnessed.**
The narrator tells the story from the point of view of someone who was present at the gathering and is recounting what he observed directly, rather than what he overheard from someone else. In <u>line 1</u>, the narrator states that "The Time Traveller smiled round at us", indicating that the narrator was at the gathering. There are several similar sentences where the narrator puts himself directly in the setting of the gathering. If he had not been present and was only retelling a story he overheard or was told by someone else, he would not refer to himself as present.

The Psychologist was also present at the gathering but is not the narrator; we know this because the narrator refers to the Psychologist as another attendee.

**2. Answer: F. A practical everyman who can be trusted and understood easily by other men.**
Filby seems to be a character without a mentioned profession, therefore, we don't know enough from the passage to choose answer D. We can make certain assumptions about Filby's character both from what the narrator says about him directly, as well as how he contrasts Filby's nature with that of the Time Traveller. By the narrator's direct description, we can see that Filby is easy to understand, transparent in his intentions, and trustworthy. In <u>lines 78-80</u>, the narrator says, "Had Filby shown the model and explained the matter in the Time Traveller's words, we should have shown *him* far less scepticism. For we should have perceived his motives; a pork butcher could understand Filby". By comparison, the Time Traveller is described as being complex and untrustworthy.

**3. Answer: B. The Provincial Mayor, the Time Traveller, the Medical Man, and the Psychologist**
A careful reading of the passage indicates that in addition to the narrator, Filby, and 'The Very Young Man', there are four other individuals present at the gathering. The Burslem Conjurer is mentioned in <u>line 8</u>, but not as an attendee of the meeting. A Pork Butcher is mentioned in <u>line 79</u> when the narrator contrasts Filby's character with that of the Time Traveller's, but no actual butcher is present at the meeting.

**4. Answer: F. Providing as much light as possible so that his guests can see there isn't a trick involved.**
In addition to the many candles already in the room and the small lamp that cast bright light directly on the model (<u>lines 16-19</u>), the Time Traveller makes it a point to place the table directly in front of the fire (<u>lines 15-16</u>) for better lighting. From the facts provided in the passage, we can assume that the Time Traveller wanted to create a neutral atmosphere for his demonstration so that his guests have no doubt as to what has occurred. He implores his guests to study the area upon which his model rested, "Have a good look at the thing. Look at the table too, and satisfy yourselves there is no trickery." (<u>lines 40-41</u>)

**5. Answer: C. An aloof individual who is self-absorbed and is only tolerating the other men in order to display his work.**
It is possible that answer D could be correct, however, the passage does not delve into the Time Traveller's reasons for wanting to travel in time. He only says, "I intend to explore time. Is that plain? I was never more serious in my life." (<u>lines 68-69</u>) While the Time Traveller does smile faintly in the first paragraph before he gets his model for demonstration, there is not much evidence in the passage for him being a jovial and joking man (eliminating answer B). The Time Traveller is best described as an aloof and self-absorbed character. He isn't overly friendly with any of his guests, seems abrupt when he explains his plans, and wants to make sure that those present know he is extremely serious about his invention and his plans for his invention.

**6. Answer: G. The Psychologist represents the idea of a healthy mind; if the Psychologist sets the time machine into the future, then everyone must believe the experience is real, rather than a trick of the mind.**

After the time machine was set on the table, everyone in the room came forward to inspect it, so we do not know from the passage what person was closest to the machine (lines 34-37). It is possible that the Time Traveller was playing a trick on his guests and wanted someone from the audience to pull the lever in order to build further credibility, however, the passage states that the Time Traveller wanted to dispel doubt by allowing everyone to inspect the model closely (lines 40-41). This suggests there is no trick involved.

There is no direct evidence in the passage that the Psychologist was the most skeptical, therefore we can assume that the Psychologist is meant to represent some ideal. Since psychology is the study of the mind and its processes, it is safe to assume the Psychologist represents the rational mind. If someone who is an expert on sanity can be persuaded that something fantastic has truly happened, then won't the others also be persuaded?

**7. Answer: C. Unending**

The word interminable means to never end. The root of the word, terminable, means to have the ability to end. The prefix changes the meaning of the root word to its opposite. Since the time machine is sent on a journey through time, with no known destination, answer choice C is the best choice.

**8. Answer: F. The Time Traveller's home**

There are two rooms mentioned in the passage. In paragraph 1, the Time Traveller walks out of the meeting room and is described in line 3 as walking down the hallway into "his laboratory". When the Time Traveller returns from his laboratory with his model of the time machine, he prepares for the demonstration by pulling up a table and placing it in front of the fire on a hearthrug (lines 14-15). The Time Traveller's comfort with rearranging the furniture in the meeting room and the fact that the meeting room is down the hall from his laboratory suggest that the gathering is taking place in his own home.

**9. Answer: B. Filby knows the Time Traveller is dead serious about his plans.**

After the Time Traveller states plainly and seriously that he intends to "explore time", the narrator relates that no one in the room really knew how to react to this statement (line 71). While the passage does not explain what Filby is thinking, the narrator describes his wink as solemn, not furtive or playful. This implies that Filby understands the gravity of the situation and the seriousness of the Time Traveller's intentions.

**10. Answer: H. None of the professional men wanted to risk their reputations by recounting to others what they had seen, but all were intrigued by the possibilities of time travel.**

It is clear from the passage that, although no one in the room quite believed or understood what they had witnessed, they did not recount the demonstration to others for fear of how this would affect their reputations. This is conveyed in lines 83-85: "they were somehow aware that trusting their reputations for judgment with him was like furnishing a nursery with egg-shell china. So I don't think any of us said very much about time travelling in the interval between that Thursday and the next".

Even given their doubts, though, the passage suggests that all of the men were intrigued by the possibilities of time travel. In lines 86-87 the narrator states that "though its odd potentialities ran, no doubt, in most of our minds: its plausibility, that is, its practical incredibleness, the curious possibilities of anachronism and of utter confusion it suggested."

**11. Answer: B. The definition of nonverbal communication includes the nonverbal elements of speech such as tone and volume.**

In paragraph 1, the author contrasts the typical definition of nonverbal communication with the more expansive, expert definition. In lines 4-5, the author states that most people would understand nonverbal communication to include "our facial expressions, our body language, our eye contact, and even our choice of clothing or hairstyle". While this is true, the author makes the point in paragraph 1 that a more expansive definition is more accurate; that nonverbal communication is best defined to include "the nonverbal elements of speech such as speaking rate, pitch, tone, volume, style, and intonation" (lines 6-7).

**12. Answer: J. Can be sent and received by all of the senses, both consciously and unconsciously.**
The author, in lines 13-14 of paragraph 2, states that nonverbal communication "can be delivered and received through any of the senses of sight, sound, smell, touch, or taste." Additionally, in lines 16-17, the author states that "As humans, we send nonverbal messages all the time, both deliberately and subconsciously."

**13. Answer: C. Quite talkative**
Paragraphs 1 and 2 describe the important role that nonverbal communication plays in how we send and receive messages. In lines 17-18, the author underscores this point by stating that "It is believed that as much as 60-70% of all meaning is communicated nonverbally." Then, the author points out with exclamation that "This is certainly an interesting fact, especially for a loquacious species such as ours!" (line 18). The author is implying that it is ironic or funny that an extremely talkative species is more dependent on nonverbal cues than verbal cues for the majority of its meaningful communication.

**14. Answer: F. When our body language and our verbal language do not agree, we can send mixed messages to others.**
The main point of paragraph 3 is stated in lines 22-23: "If what we are saying and what we are feeling are two different things, our nonverbal cues can betray our true feelings." This means that if there is a contradiction between what we are expressing verbally and what we are really thinking or feeling, then our nonverbal expression will often reveal this contradiction, leading to "mixed messages".

**15. Answer: D. A mixture of universal and culturally-specific cues**
According to paragraph 4, nonverbal communication has both universal elements and culturally-specific elements. Lines 33-34 identify some elements considered universal, such as smiling while happy and frowning while sad, whereas the remainder of the paragraph discusses highly culturally-specific elements, such as when and with whom it is appropriate to make direct eye contact. People of each culture use a combination of universal, or innate, nonverbal cues as well as nonverbal cues specific to their own culture.

**16. Answer: G. Involuntary facial expressions occur during moments of heightened emotion.**
In lines 54-56, the author states that many of our facial expressions happen involuntarily, "especially when we feel extreme emotions of happiness, sadness, anger, or surprise and fear." At first glance, answer A looks like it could be correct, but a careful read of paragraph 6 indicates that there are over ten thousand possible facial expressions that can be made from the ten muscle groups of the face and scalp and the forty-three movements that these muscle groups can make.

**17. Answer: A. Have difficulty reading nonverbal cues.**
In paragraph 7, the author writes that people with autism "have difficulty, even an inability, with reading faces and other nonverbal cues" (lines 61-62).

**18. Answer: H. To determine someone's past behavior.**
Paragraph 8 gives many specific examples of how the study of nonverbal communication can be used to one's advantage. Lines 75-76 state that knowledge of facial expressions can be used to determine whether someone is telling the truth. Lines 77-78 indicate that public figures evaluate their own nonverbal cues in order to mask their emotional conflict and to avoid sending mixed messages. Lines 79-81 reveal that close inspection of nonverbal cues can assist people in making quick evaluations of potential mates. Only answer C is unsupported by the passage. While there is some indication that nonverbal cues can point to future behavior (for example, an extremely agitated person may be about to commit an act of violence), it cannot be used to determine past behavior.

**19. Answer: A. Benefit anyone wishing to make closer connections with others.**
The author does state in paragraph 5 that those doing business in foreign countries will benefit from learning culturally-specific nonverbal cues. However, the author goes on to say in <u>lines 44-45</u> that, "anyone can benefit from learning more about nonverbal communication." As well, in <u>lines 46-47</u>, the author writes that, "honing your ability to accurately read the nonverbal cues of others will enhance your connection with those around you." This makes answer A the best choice.

**20. Answer: J. Facial expressions**
While nonverbal communication can take many forms ranging from posture to tone of voice to choice of clothing, the passage indicates that facial expressions are a very reliable indicator of one's true feelings. As facial expressions are often involuntary (<u>lines 54-55</u>), they are more difficult to suppress or control. The passage suggests that it is innate for people to search the face for clues as to a speaker's intent. As stated in <u>lines 58-59</u>, "the face is what people look at to discern the true nature of a person's emotional state, or even what that person might be thinking."

**21. Answer: B. Not religious or spiritual in nature**
The word secular means temporal and worldly, or not religious and spiritual in nature. This meaning can be inferred from the context of paragraph 5 by examining how the author contrasts the secular authorities with the religious authorities. In <u>lines 41-43</u>, the secular authorities are described as representatives of the King who are responsible for enforcing royal laws. These secular authorities were engaged in a power struggle with the religious authorities who in <u>lines 43-44</u> are described as believing they should hold power because they saw their authority as coming directly from God. Finally, in paragraph 8, <u>lines 78-79</u> we see a direct contrast between the word secular and spiritual when the author describes the Pueblo Revolt as having destroyed all Spanish influence "both spiritual and secular". From all of this evidence, we can infer that secular means not of a spiritual nature.

**22. Answer: H. The Spanish Court believed that the opportunity to convert Native Americans to Christianity was a priceless opportunity.**
The Spaniards had long believed that it was their duty under God to convert the rest of the world's people to what they believed to be the one true religion: Christianity. Although secondary to the procurement of gold, silver, and land, most Spanish believed that through the spiritual conversion of others lay their own salvation. <u>Line 14</u> mentions that the "pious royal court began to see that there were priceless spiritual gains possible." Being "pious" means having an earnest wish to fulfill religious obligations. According to paragraph 2, the possibilities for converting Native Americans outweighed the lack of material wealth that the northern territories offered.

**23. Answer: A. The mission of the Spanish priests was to bring a spiritual and self-sustaining way of life to a group of people that already enjoyed both.**
In <u>lines 23-25</u>, the passage states that native people "had inhabited, for centuries, their own well-planned agriculturally-oriented towns of adobe structures." These native civilizations existed well before the Spanish introduced their mission/presidio system to protect, teach, and convert the Indians. It can be inferred from this that although the Spanish viewed the native peoples as needing the teachings, technology, and religion of the Spanish, the Pueblo Indians already had a well-established and sophisticated culture of their own.

**24. Answer: J. Each Pueblo Indian group had their own particular way of spiritual worship, leadership, and family mores.**
An idiosyncrasy is defined as a mannerism or characteristic peculiar to an individual or a group. In <u>lines 25-26</u>, the passage mentions that, "these Indians were divided by cultural idiosyncrasies and differences in language," implying that each group was unique and different in these ways. This division contrasts with ways they are described as similar, for example, they all shared problems with drought and attacks by nomadic tribes. From this context, it can be inferred that idiosyncrasies means a type of difference or uniqueness.

**25. Answer: C. Protection and conversion**
As described in lines 18-22, every Spanish settlement was set up in a mission/presidio system that came to typify new world Spanish towns. The presidio was a fort built to protect both the Spanish and their native allies from hostile tribes and outside invasion. The mission was the Spanish commitment to converting native peoples to Christianity.

**26. Answer: G. At first, the interaction between the Spanish and Native populations was somewhat harmonious but, because of Spanish inconsistencies, the relationship turned sour.**
Lines 33-34 tell of how "native peoples were helping to raise horse, cattle, goats, sheep, fruit trees and crops," and how natives were also fusing their own skills with European influenced techniques, illustrating an initial, harmonious relationship. However, by line 40, the passage explains that "jealousy and dysfunction" became the norm in the Rio Grande Valley. The competitive relationship between the Spanish civil and religious authorities sent mixed messages to the natives of New Mexico. This is evidenced by lines 41-43, which explain that the secular governors felt they should have the final authority and lines 43-44, which show that the priests felt the authority belonged to them. Native resentment, anger, and violent reaction grew among the Indians until the 1680 Pueblo Revolt.

**27. Answer: D. Is a Pueblo Indian who, at first, leads his people against Spanish injustice but, later, becomes a self-serving ruler.**
Paragraph 6 explains how the Pueblo Indians became increasingly frustrated by their treatment at the hands of the Spanish rulers. Lines 55-59 indicate that Popé advocated driving out the Spanish invaders and became their first true leader, uniting them in revolt. However, after the successful insurrection, Popé became a corrupt ruler, wanting to gather the symbols of power for himself. Lines 78-82 state that "Popé had his followers destroy all the remnants of Spanish influence, both spiritual and secular, except for the governor's palace. Popé wanted that for himself and, predictably, he became a corrupt ruler who allowed the region to be over-run by raiding Apache tribes aided now by captured Spanish horses. The Pueblos had never before had a single leader and they soon became disenchanted with Popé."

**28. Answer: F. A successful, choreographed attack by the Pueblo people that ultimately drove the Spanish from the northern territories.**
The paragraph indicates that the revolt was not a haphazard, disorganized, and unplanned event but rather a successful, choreographed attack. Lines 64-65 relate how "Indians from all across the Rio Grande Valley to hundreds of miles west to the Zuñi and Hopi villages" participated in a coordinated attack. Line 65 indicates that the Spanish enclaves were "methodically attacked", further supporting the description of the revolt as an organized one. The remainder of the paragraph details how the Spanish were ultimately driven out of Santa Fe, indicating a Native victory and a successful purging of the Spanish from the northern territories.

**29. Answer: C. The Pueblo Indian leader, Popé, failed to advance the gains made by his people during the Revolt and the situation in the territories worsened to the point that the Indians were receptive to the Spaniards' return.**
The corruption and ineffectiveness of Popé after the expulsion of the Spaniards (described in lines 78-82) exacerbated the already devastating famine brought on by the drought and the attacks by nomadic tribes. Lines 83-85 relate that, after twelve years of starvation and violence, the Indians were ready to receive the Spaniards back.

**30. Answer: J. The Spanish mission to the northern territories was to convert the Indian to Christianity but, ultimately, this mission failed due to the inflexibility of the Spanish.**
In paragraph 2 we learn that although the northern territories offered no material wealth to the Spanish, the King decided that the potential spiritual gains were priceless if they focused on converting the native peoples to Christianity; this became their primary mission. In paragraph 5 and 6 we learn that the power struggles between the state authorities and the church authorities resulted in a worsening relationship between the Spanish and the Pueblo people. This worsening relationship led directly to the Pueblo Revolt that drove the Spanish out of the northern territories. The entire passage leads the reader through the mistakes the Spanish made in ruling the northern territories and how these led eventually to them being driven from the region.

**31. Answer: C. Invasive species are a widespread problem and not exclusive to one type of ecosystem.**

The passage offers many pieces of evidence to indicate that the problem of invasive species is widespread. For example, lines 13-14 state that "50,000 non-native species have been introduced in the United States" and lines 37-38 indicate that the economic damage caused by invasive species has been costly. Paragraphs 2-6 then give specific examples of invasive species that affect many different types of ecosystems ranging from riparian areas, grassland-steppe areas, and pinyon-juniper woodlands, to streamside habitats. As well, paragraph 1 indicates that "forests, prairies, mountains, wetlands, rivers, and oceans" have all been affected by invasive species, showing the full range of ecosystems affected.

**32. Answer: J. Many non-native species were introduced because humans thought that they might be beneficial.**

As the passage relates in lines 13-14, about 50,000 non-native species have been introduced in the United States. Lines 14-16 state that many of these invasive species were brought into the country deliberately in order to control erosion, to provide a source of food, or to decorate property as ornamental plants. While the passage also refers to the unintentional introduction of some invasive species, it makes it clear that many were brought in on purpose, without the full understanding of the negative impact they could have to native species.

**33. Answer: A. Invasive species can come from all categories of living creatures**

As defined in paragraph 1, an invasive species is any species that is non-native to the ecosystem and that causes economic or environmental harm by its presence. An invasive species could be any creature ranging from a bird to a reptile to an insect to bacteria. In describing the wide range of invasive species, lines 4-5 refer to "plants, insects, fish, mollusks, crustaceans, diseases, mammals, birds, reptiles, and amphibians". Given the broad definition of an invasive species, it is clear that an invasive species can come from any category of living creature.

**34. Answer: F. Cheatgrass out-competes native species and, because of its density and flammability, leads to more fires.**

Cheatgrass changes the average fire return interval from 60-110 years to 0-3 years, but this is not a positive improvement—this is a dramatic increase in the number of fires (eliminating both answers B and D). As described in lines 32-34, Cheatgrass grows so quickly, densely, and uniformly that native species are essentially out-competed for space. In addition to its fast-growing nature, Cheatgrass greens quickly and becomes a highly flammable fuel source for fires, leading to considerably more fires in the grassland-steppe areas of the western United States. The combined effects of competing with Cheatgrass and being wiped out by fire on a regular basis are high hurdles for the native plant species to overcome, leading to almost complete displacement.

**35. Answer: B. The ecological and cultural losses are as significant as the economic losses.**

While the passage does state that the economic cost of invasive species is as high as $137 billion per year, this is not the main point of the passage. The main point is that while the economic damage is high, the ecological and cultural losses are equally high. This is stated directly in lines 37-39 and then supported by specific examples offered in the supporting sentences that follow. To further emphasize the main point, lines 43-45 state that "approximately 46% of the plants and animals federally listed as endangered species have been negatively impacted by invasive species".

**36. Answer: G. The expansion of international trade.**

Answer B is the best answer choice available. While invasive plants were certainly introduced as ornamentals and for other deliberate uses such as agriculture, line 92 states that "many invasive species arrive in the United States through international trade". Given that the transition from the 19th century to the 20th century represents a significant expansion in the levels of international exchange, one can infer that the increase in the numbers of invasive plant species coincided directly with the expansion of international trade.

## 37. Answer: D. Significant

Lines 43-45 state that "approximately 46% of the plants and animals federally listed as endangered species have been negatively impacted by invasive species". This level would be best described as significant, as it represents almost half of the total number of federally listed endangered plants and animals.

## 38. Answer: J. Non-native species increase the mortality rate of forested land, which adds to the fuel-load and increases the number of fires.

While paragraph 9 concedes that "insect damage and plant disease are natural disturbances that are part of a healthy, functioning ecosystem" (lines 71-72), the main point is that non-native insects and diseases increase the mortality rates of forested lands, effectively increasing the fuel load and number of fires. Lines 74-75 state that "8 percent of forested land are at risk for mortality rates that exceed the norm" because of the combined effects of both native and non-native insects and disease. The implication is that the damage from non-native insects and disease push the mortality rate past the norm for healthy forests, leading to more fires.

## 39. Answer: A. American chestnut

The brown trout is referred to in line 15 as a deliberately introduced food source. In line 16, purple loosestrife is referred to as a deliberately introduced ornamental plant. In lines 48-49 the Gypsy moth is referred to as a species deliberately introduced as a possible source of silk production. Lines 49-51 explain that the American chestnut is a native tree species that has been negatively affected by invasive species to the point of being virtually wiped out.

## 40. Answer: H. One critical factor in eradicating new invasive species is international cooperation.

There is no evidence in the passage to suggest the authors feel eradicating invasive species is a hopeless task (eliminating answer A). There is plenty of evidence in the passage to indicate that the damage done by invasive species outweighs any benefits they bring to ecosystems (eliminating answer B). In the final paragraph of the passage, the authors offer three specific steps that must be taken in order to slow the arrival of invasive species into the United States (lines 92-96). Because many non-native species enter the country through international trade, the authors conclude that one of these critical factors is for the Forest Service to "work with the international partners to stem the flow of invasive species into the country."

# SCIENCE REASONING PRACTICE TEST 2

35 Minutes - 40 Questions

Directions: Following are seven passages and questions that refer to each passage. Choose the best answer for each question.

## Radiation Exposure

An accident at a nuclear power plant released large amounts of radiation into the atmosphere. A sudden spike in power output led to a series of explosions that resulted in radioactive fallout over an area of about 100,000 sq. Km around the plant. About thirty people were killed in the accident and hundreds of thousands of people were evacuated from the area. Elevated radiation levels due to radioiodine (I-131), radiocaesium (Cs-137), and radiostrontium (Sr-90) were detected in local water bodies for several months after the disaster but fell to normal levels after that period. Twenty five years later there is disagreement between scientists over the actual long-term impact of the accident on people and the environment. Many scientific studies have been conducted but the controversy has not been resolved.

### Expert 1
Medical records over a period of twenty years since the accident show that close to a million people died prematurely as a result of the accident. This analysis is based on hundreds of scientific publications made about the disaster. The occurrence of Down's syndrome in babies peaked at 2.1 per 1000 live births in the year following the accident as opposed to the rate of 1.5 per 1000 live births observed during the five years prior to the accident. Neural tube defects increased to 20 per 1000 live births from a previously observed value of about 6 per 1000 live births.

It is true that plant and animal life has apparently flourished in the evacuated area but appearances can be misleading. Although some plant species can adapt to high levels of radiation, a detailed look at the data shows that areas with higher radiation contain fewer animals. Also, these animals have reduced lifespans and reduced reproduction rates. The rate of genetic mutations observed in the affected area is also high compared with control populations. For instance, mutations have been found in one of every ten birds. The difficulty of obtaining data has kept the sample sizes of studies small. As a result, the level of mutation found in each study is not considered statistically significant. However, the fact that 22 out of 31 studies conducted actually found genetic mutations is significant in and of itself.

### Expert 2
Over a period of twenty years since the accident, about 6000 cases of thyroid cancer, which is very treatable and has a high survival rate, have occurred in the area. The impact of any long-term genetic defects is not yet clear. Apart from this there is no evidence of long-term health impact according to an international report from a committee with 120 members from twenty countries

The incidence of leukemia or solid cancers, such as lung cancer, has not been elevated because of the radiation exposure. Nor has there been any increase in birth defects and abnormalities. Studies which claim otherwise are based on small populations or anecdotal evidence and are not rigorous, controlled studies of large populations. The effects observed by these studies are likely to be caused by factors other than radiation. People fail to realize that an average person receives a certain dose of radiation, estimated at 2.5 mSv per year, from natural and man-made sources. People who work with radiation are exposed to about 20 mSv per year without exhibiting any ill effects from these relatively high doses. Overall, one can say that there have not been serious health consequences for a majority of the population resulting from the nuclear accident.

1.  **Expert 2 contends that much of the evidence for health problems caused by radiation is anecdotal. Anecdotes about single cases do not constitute scientific evidence because of:**

    A.  The absence of controls.
    B.  Lack of objective data.
    C.  Lack of statistical significance.
    D.  All of the above.

2.  **According to Expert 1, evidence for genetic problems due to radiation is provided by:**

    F.  The large number of premature deaths.
    G.  The mutations found in birds.
    H.  Elevated levels of thyroid cancer.
    J.  Fewer animals found in the area exposed to radiation.

3.  **The main point of disagreement between Expert 1 and Expert 2 is over:**

    A.  The level of radiation that people were exposed to.
    B.  The number of premature deaths in the affected area.
    C.  The reliability of studies showing adverse effects of radiation.
    D.  The environmental effect of the radiation.

4.  **Expert 2 believes that it is reasonable to think that radiation exposure has not had major impact on health because:**

    F.  Thyroid cancer is highly treatable.
    G.  Plant life has flourished in the affected area.
    H.  People are able to tolerate a certain level of radiation without ill effects.
    J.  The incidence of birth defects has not increased.

5.  **According to the passage, it is a fact that:**

    A.  A large number of people were exposed to radiation due to the nuclear accident.
    B.  The radiation has adversely affected the health of many people.
    C.  The radiation has adversely affected the health of only a few people.
    D.  The radiation has caused mutations in birds.

6.  **A new study shows that the people in the affected area were exposed to an average radiation of about 500 mSv over the course of a year. This result supports:**

    F.  Expert 1
    G.  Expert 2
    H.  Both Expert 1 and Expert 2
    J.  Neither Expert 1, nor Expert 2

7.  **Both experts use different strategies in making their arguments. One of the strategies used is:**

    A.  Ethical considerations
    B.  Disease statistics
    C.  Emotional appeal
    D.  Economic arguments

## Energy Efficient Homes

The availability of many energy saving options in home building and the reduced cost of installing solar panels on homes has made it possible today to build homes that consume nearly zero net energy. Photovoltaic panels installed on roofs generate electricity when the sun is shining. If the amount of electricity generated at a particular time exceeds the energy requirement of the house, the excess electricity can actually be sent through the grid for use in other places, i.e., the homeowner ends up selling electricity to the utility.

Since electrical energy cannot be stored for later use, it is not possible to store the excess energy for use in the home at a later time. At night or on cloudy days the home uses energy off the grid. A home with good energy saving features such as good insulation, high performance windows, and energy efficient appliances can generate enough energy so that its net consumption of external energy from the grid is close to zero. The average energy generated and used by a near zero energy home in a typical year is shown in the graph below. Specifically how the energy is consumed is shown in the table that follows.

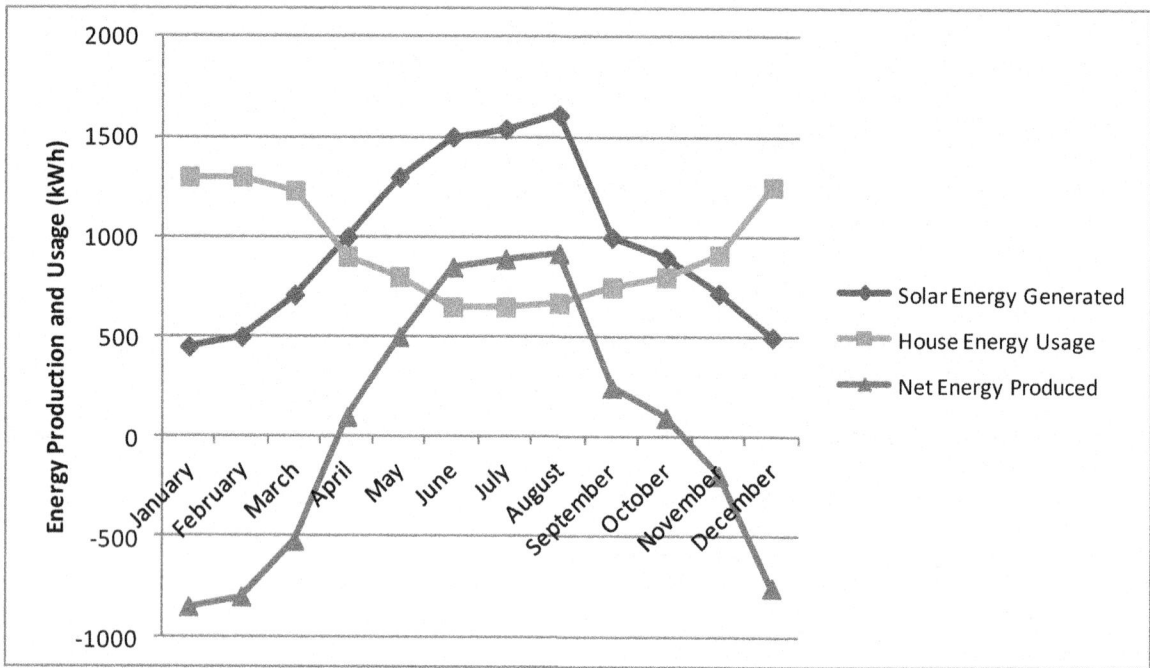

| Home Energy Usage | |
|---|---|
| Air conditioner | 32% |
| Appliances | 25% |
| Water heater | 16% |
| Lights | 11% |
| Refrigerator | 8% |
| Electronics | 8% |

8.  **The amount of energy the house draws from the grid in December is:**

    F.  500 kWh
    G.  1250 kWh
    H.  750 kWh
    J.  2000 kWh

9. **The house is powered a hundred percent by solar energy in:**

    A. January – June
    B. April – October
    C. June – August
    D. December – March

10. **If the fraction of energy used in the house for various purposes remains the same throughout the year, the energy used to run appliances in July would be about:**

    F. 600 kWh
    G. 300 kWh
    H. 150 kWh
    J. 0 kWh

11. **The house is remodeled with higher efficiency solar panels and solar energy production rises 50% all through the year. As a result, in February the energy requirement from the grid becomes:**

    A. 550 kWh
    B. 0 kWh
    C. 800 kWh
    D. 1000 kWh

12. **The water heater and lights together use approximately:**

    F. 1/10 of the total energy
    G. 1/5 of the total energy
    H. 1/3 of the total energy
    J. 1/6 of the total energy

## Boiling Point

The boiling point of water at normal atmospheric pressure is 100°C. This is the temperature at which the vapor pressure of water, which increases as temperature increases, is equal to the surrounding pressure of 1 atm. It is generally known that the boiling point of water varies as ambient pressure changes and also when sugar, salt, or other substances are dissolved in it. Several experiments are performed to measure exactly how this happens.

### Experiment 1
The boiling point of pure water is measured at different values of the ambient pressure. The data is given in the table below.

| Pressure (atm) | Boiling Point (°C) |
|----------------|--------------------|
| 0.1 | 20 |
| 0.5 | 80 |
| 1 | 100 |
| 3 | 125 |
| 5 | 150 |

A graphical view of the data:

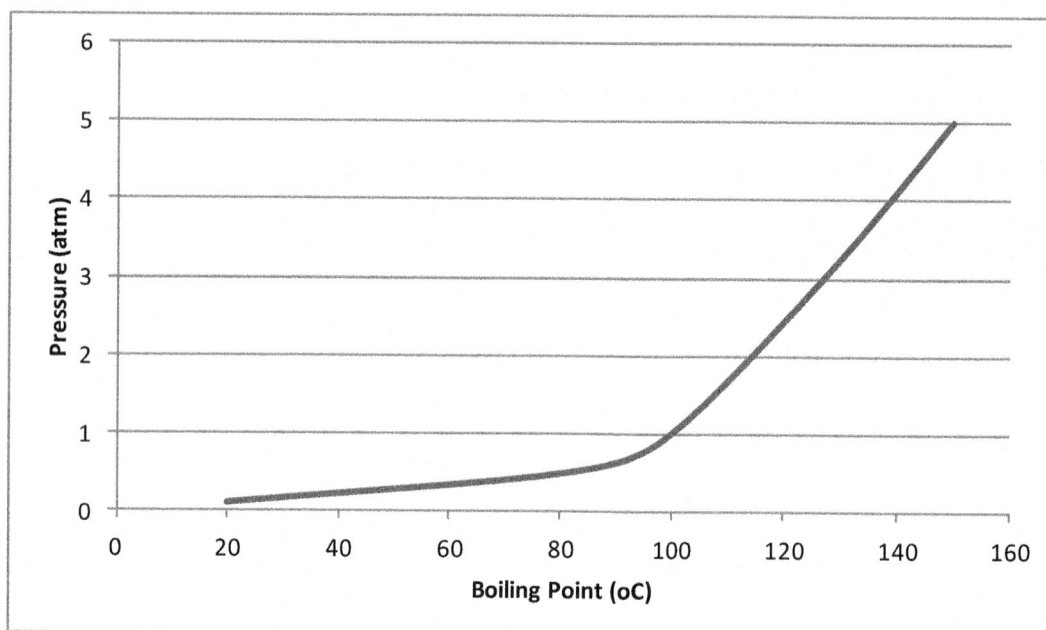

**Experiment 2**
Sugar is dissolved in water at different concentrations up to 50% by weight. The boiling point of the sugar solution at a pressure of 1 atm and at different concentrations is measured. The results are plotted below.

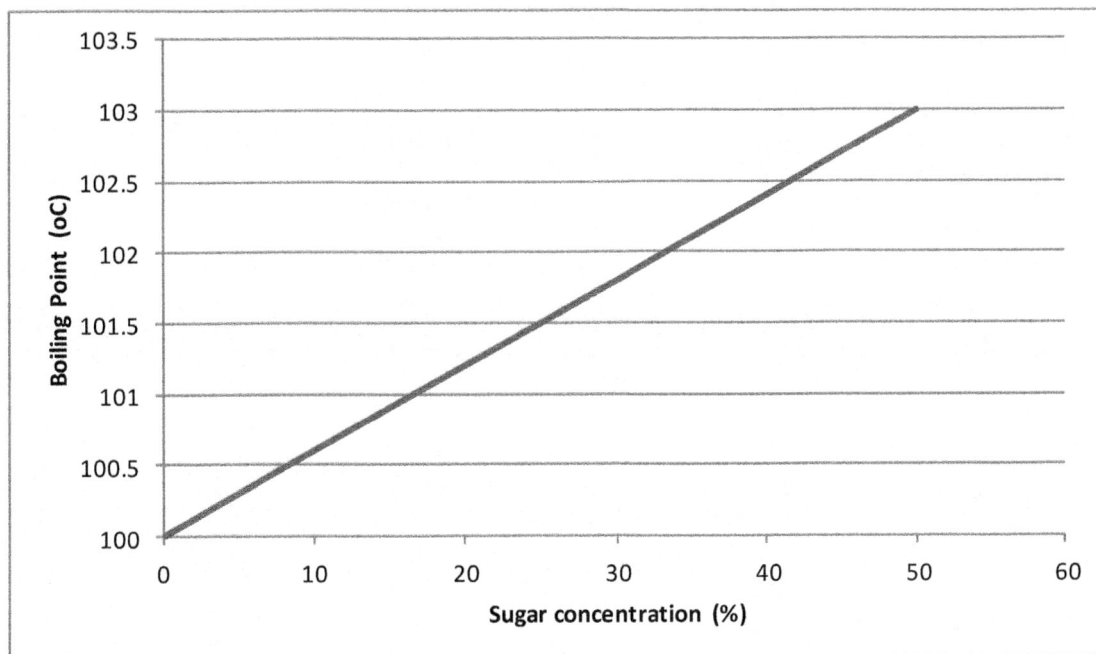

**Experiment 3**
Sugar is dissolved in water at different concentrations up to 90% by weight. The boiling point of the sugar solution at a pressure of 1 atm and at different concentrations is measured. The results are plotted below.

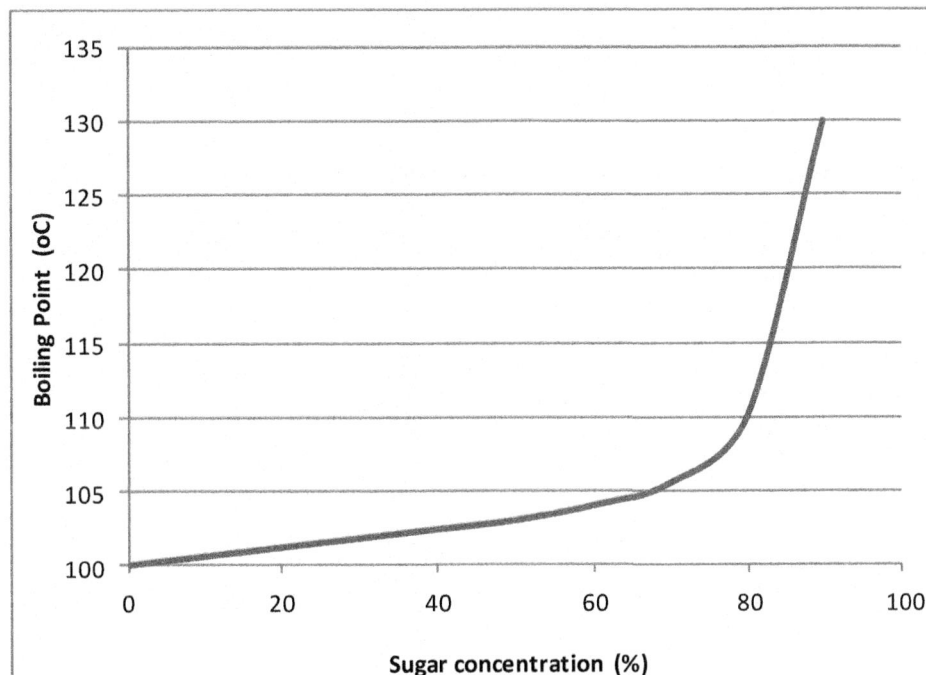

**13. As pressure is raised, the increase in the boiling point of water:**

    A. Continues at a steady rate.
    B. Starts to slow down and level off.
    C. Continues at an increasing rate.
    D. None of the above.

**14. The results of Experiments 2 and 3 are:**

    F. Contradictory because one graph is linear while the other is curved.
    G. Contradictory because the initial slope is much smaller in Experiment 3.
    H. Identical in the common range at sugar concentrations of 0 to 50%.
    J. Partly overlapping in the common range at sugar concentrations of 0 to 50%.

**15. You are camped up on a mountain and find that it's taking a really long time to cook your food because the water is not hot enough. If the ambient pressure is 0.9 atm, the water will boil at:**

    A. 60 – 70 °C
    B. 70 – 80 °C
    C. 80 – 90 °C
    D. 90 – 100 °C

**16. The elevation of the boiling point of water by adding a chemical can be used to:**

    F. Keep fuel from freezing in winter.
    G. Keep coolant from boiling away in summer.
    H. Melt ice on winter roads.
    J. Cook food in a pressure cooker.

**17. The boiling point of an 80% sugar solution in water is approximately:**

    A. 101 °C
    B. 103 °C
    C. 105 °C
    D. 110 °C

**18. The boiling point of a 40% sugar solution under 2 atm pressure is likely to be:**

    F. Less than 105 °C
    G. Approximately 110 °C
    H. Approximately 115 °C
    J. More than 120 °C

## Metabolic Syndrome

A recent study has shown that obesity may not simply be a matter of lifestyle choices; there may be a genetic component to the tendency to gain weight and develop a set of symptoms known as metabolic syndrome. In addition to obesity, this includes insulin resistance, elevated blood pressure, and elevated cholesterol and puts people at higher risk for heart disease and diabetes. The study was conducted on two sets of mice; one set with a gene that monitors immune response and one set in which this particular gene is missing.

**Experiment 1**
The body weight of the mice was monitored for several weeks after birth.

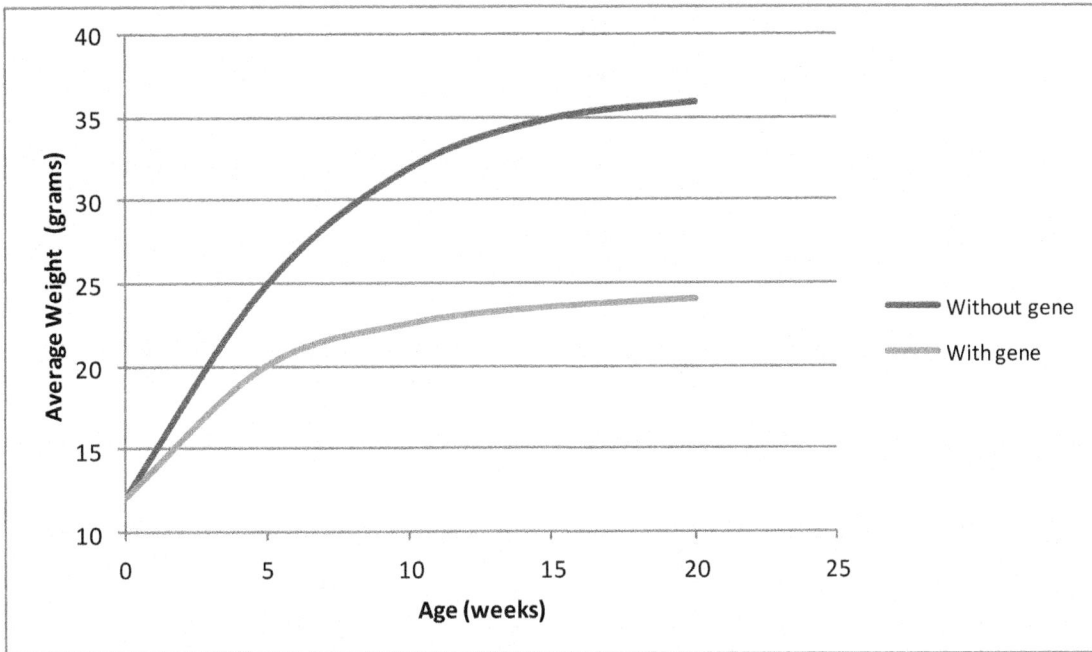

**Experiment 2**
At age 20 weeks, blood cholesterol levels were measured for the two sets of mice.

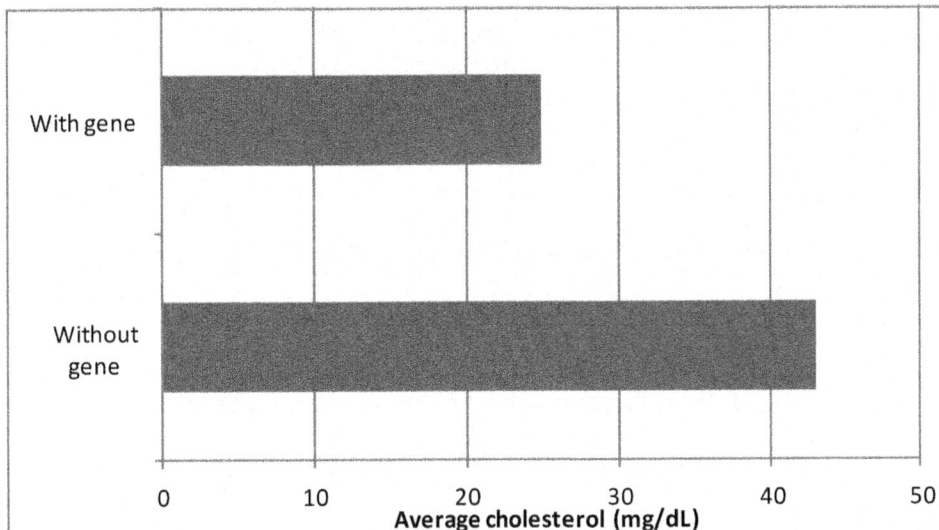

**Experiment 3**

A glucose tolerance test was performed on the two sets of mice at age 20 weeks. They were given a certain quantity of sugar solution and their blood glucose levels were monitored for two hours after the feeding.

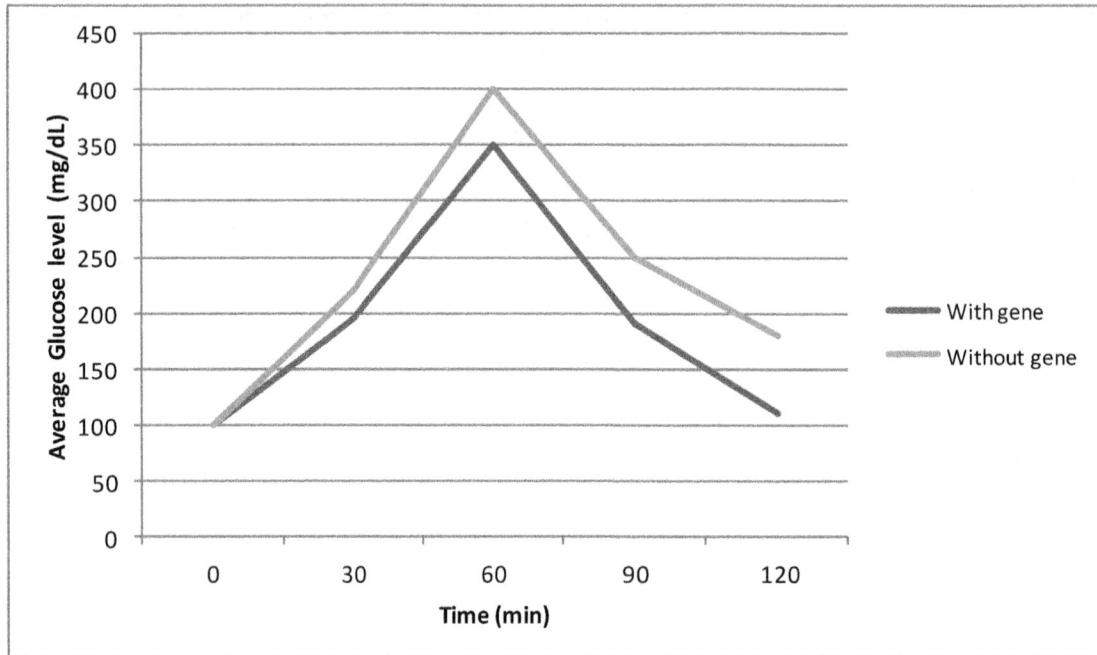

19. **At 15 weeks, the average body weight of mice without the gene that monitors immune response was approximately:**

    A. 35 oz
    B. 35 g
    C. 23 oz
    D. 23 g

20. **Experiments 1 and 2 show that mice without the immune response gene had higher body weights and higher cholesterol. From this we can conclude that:**

    F. High body weights cause mice to have high cholesterol.
    G. High cholesterol leads to obesity in mice.
    H. There is a correlation between high body weights and high cholesterol.
    J. None of the above.

21. **The results from Experiment 3 show that the average blood glucose level for mice without the immune response gene:**

    A. Is generally higher than that for mice with the gene.
    B. Rises higher and falls more slowly than for mice without the gene when sugar solution is given.
    C. Rises slower and falls more rapidly than for mice without the gene when sugar solution is given.
    D. Is generally lower than that for mice with the gene.

**22. At the age of fifty weeks we can expect that a mouse with the immune response gene will have a body weight of:**

F.  More than 40 g
G.  Approximately 35 g
H.  Approximately 25 g
J.  Approximately 15 g

**23. The control variable in Experiments 2 and 3 is:**

A.  The age of the mice.
B.  The body weight of the mice.
C.  The cholesterol level of the mice.
D.  The blood glucose level of the mice.

**24. All of the experiments in this study were performed to assess whether the absence of the immune response gene predisposed mice towards the metabolic syndrome. The following study could shed further light on this question:**

F.  Measurements of blood pressure of mice with and without the immune response gene.
G.  Measurements of bone density of mice with and without the immune response gene.
H.  Measurements of body weight of mice missing other genes.
J.  Measurements of cholesterol at age 50 weeks of mice with and without the immune response gene.

## Igneous Rocks

Igneous rocks can be classified in many different ways. One way of chemically classifying igneous rocks is by the silica content. Felsic rocks such as granite and rhyolite have high silica content. Mafic rocks such as gabbro have less silica and more iron-magnesium.

Igneous rocks can also be classified as intrusive or extrusive based on their mode of formation. Intrusive rocks are coarse-grained rocks that are formed by slow cooling and solidification of magma within the earth's crust. Extrusive rocks are fine-grained rocks formed by fast cooling of magma on the surface of the earth. The diagram and table below provide some information on different kinds of igneous rocks.

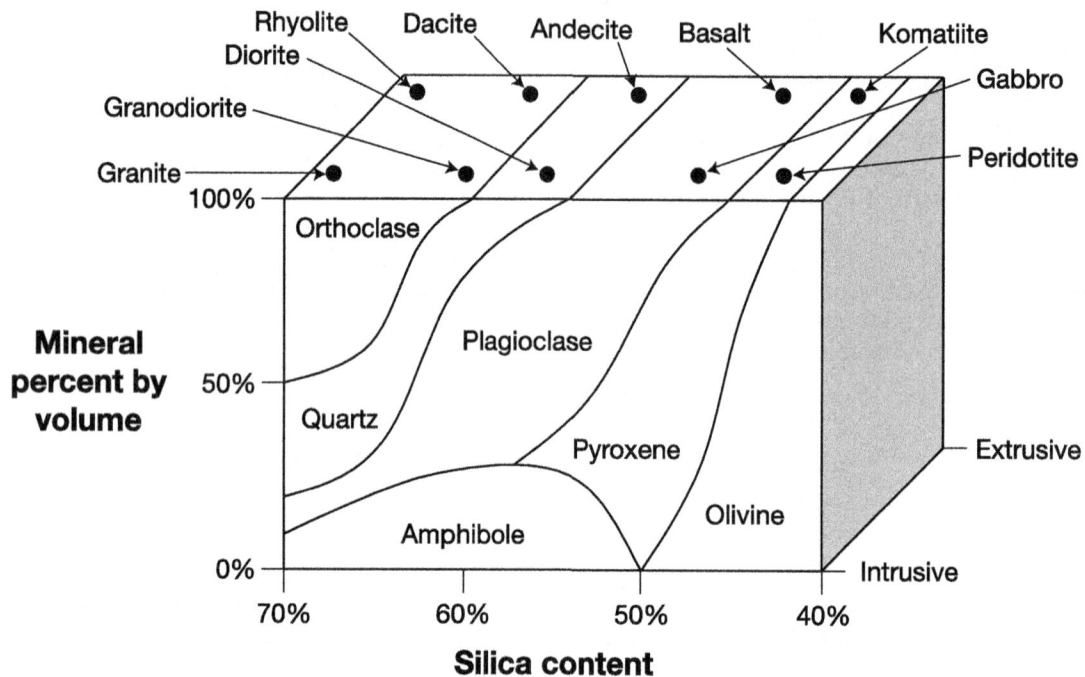

| Rock Type | Characteristics |
|---|---|
| Felsic | High silica content above 63%, viscous with lot of water vapor |
| Intermediate | Contains 52 - 63% silica |
| Mafic | 45 - 52% silica and high iron-magnesium content, less viscous |
| Ultramafic | Less than 45% silica |

**25. Compared to andecite, the rock komatiite:**

   A.  Has less silica content.
   B.  Is more viscous.
   C.  Contains more quartz.
   D.  Is more coarse-grained.

**26. A petrologist is asked to identify a coarse-grained, igneous rock. She finds that its silica content is almost 70%. This rock is most likely:**

   F.  Basalt
   G.  Granodiorite
   H.  Peridotite
   J.  Granite

**27. Gabbro is an igneous rock that is classified as:**

    A. Felsic
    B. Intermediate
    C. Mafic
    D. Ultramafic

**28. Which of the following pairs of rocks have the same chemical composition?**

    F. Granite and rhyolite
    G. Rhyolite and dacite
    H. Basalt and diorite
    J. Komatiite and andecite

**29. The following rock contains no pyroxene:**

    A. Basalt
    B. Komatiite
    C. Dacite
    D. Gabbro

## Transformation Efficiency

Transformation is a technique used in the laboratory to insert new genetic material into bacterial cells. Bacterial species that are capable of undergoing this procedure are known as competent species. Some bacteria are naturally competent; others can be made artificially competent by incubating them in a solution of divalent cations and then exposing them to a pulse of heat shock.

Transformation allows bacteria to be used as hosts for the replication of exogenous DNA. The degree to which the competent host expresses the exogenous genes is known as transformation efficiency and is measured by the number of transformants per microgram (µg) of DNA. This efficiency depends on several factors including the pH of the buffer. Studies have shown that transformation efficiency peaks in certain pH ranges. Transformation efficiency can also be enhanced by physical methods such as agitating the bacteria with glass beads.

### Experiment 1
The transformation efficiency of a colony of bacteria was measured for different pH levels of the buffer solution. The results are given in the table below.

| pH of buffer solution | Number of transformants | Quantity of DNA used (µg) | Transformation efficiency |
|---|---|---|---|
| 5.5 | 413 | 2.5 | 165 |
| 6.1 | 315 | 1.8 | 175 |
| 6.9 | 562 | 2.7 | 208 |
| 7.7 | 521 | 3.0 | 174 |
| 8.4 | 225 | 1.6 | 141 |
| 9.5 | 168 | 1.5 | 112 |

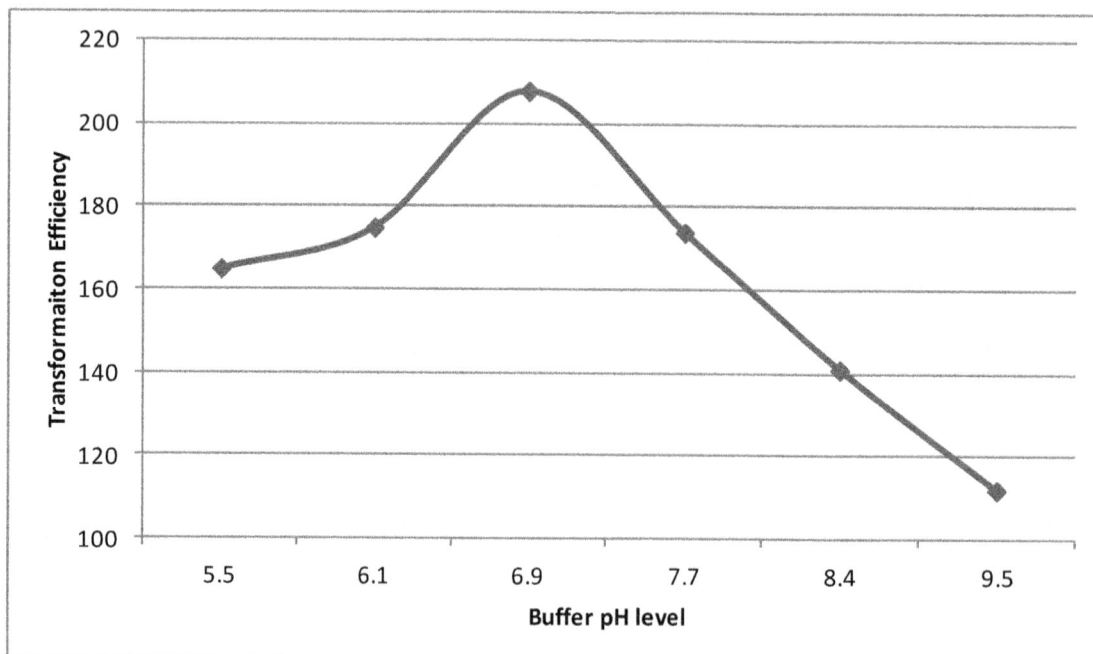

## Experiment 2

The following data was obtained under experimental conditions that were identical to those in Experiment 1:

| pH of buffer solution | Number of transformants | Quantity of DNA used (µg) | Transformation efficiency |
|---|---|---|---|
| 6.1 | 315 | 1.8 | 175 |
| 6.3 | 425 | 2.3 | 185 |
| 6.6 | 450 | 2.3 | 196 |
| 6.9 | 562 | 2.7 | 208 |
| 7.2 | 550 | 2.5 | 220 |
| 7.4 | 474 | 2.4 | 198 |
| 7.7 | 521 | 3.0 | 174 |

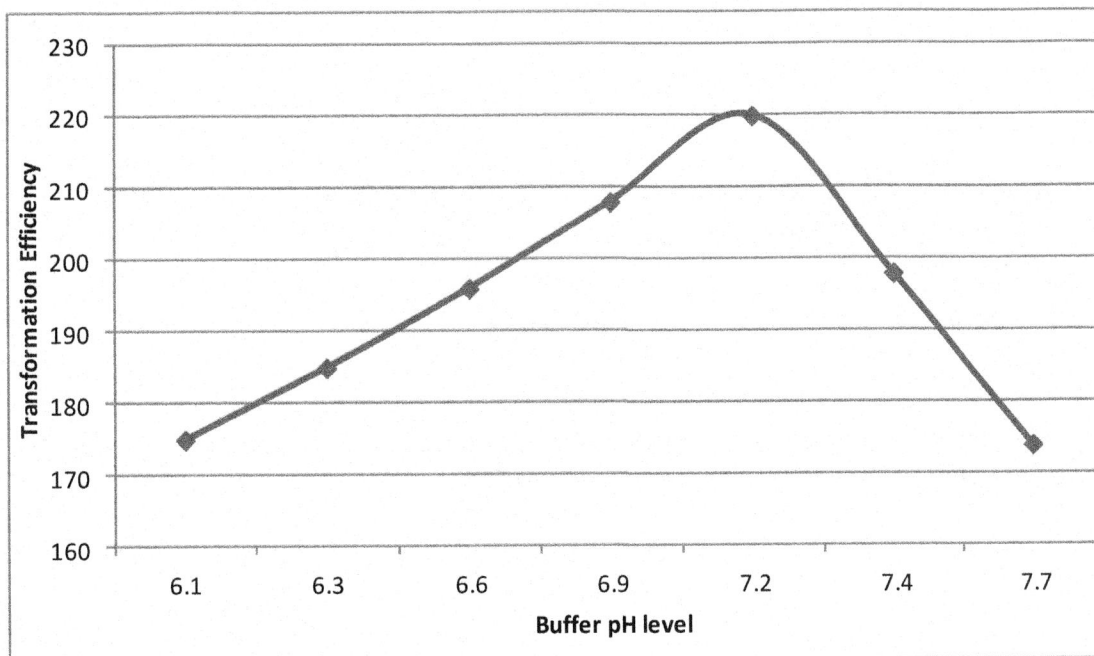

30. **The number of transformants per µg of DNA for pH 8.4 is:**

F. 225
G. 141
H. 521
J. 174

31. Experiments 1 and 2 both measure transformation efficiency of certain bacteria for different pH levels of the buffer solution. After completing Experiment 1, scientists felt the need to conduct Experiment 2 in order to:

    A. Verify that the results of Experiment 1 were accurate.
    B. Narrow down the pH range where transformation efficiency is maximum.
    C. Find transformation efficiency for a different pH range.
    D. Find transformation efficiency under different experimental conditions.

32. To get the maximum number of transformants when the bacteria is used as a host, a researcher should select a buffer solution with pH in the range of:

    F. 5.5 – 6.5
    G. 6.1 – 7.7
    H. 6.9 – 7.4
    J. 7.5 – 9.5

33. In an experiment, 5 micrograms of DNA yields 970 transformants. The pH of the buffer is approximately:

    A. 5.7
    B. 6.1
    C. 6.6
    D. 7.3

34. In both experiments, the transformation efficiency, rather than the number of transformants, was plotted against pH level because:

    F. The range was lower making it easy to create an accurate plot.
    G. The number of transformations does not depend on the pH range.
    H. The quantity of DNA used in each test is different.
    J. All of the above.

35. A researcher conducts a test with 3 micrograms of DNA and a buffer solution that has pH 7.3. The expected number of transformants is approximately:

    A. 200
    B. 350
    C. 450
    D. 600

## Cellular Energy

It is well known that adenosine triphosphate (ATP) is a source of power in human body cells. Cells use the energy stored in ATP molecules to power various cellular activities. ATP is made up of an adenosine molecule attached to three phosphates, hence the name adenosine triphosphate. Energy is stored in the bonds between the three phosphates.

ATP is manufactured in the mitochondria of a cell through a process, powered by protons, that adds a phosphate to adenosine diphosphate (ADP). It is then released into the cytoplasm where it is available to provide energy for cellular activities such as protein formation. Energy from ATP is released when an ATP molecule is broken down into ADP and a phosphate.

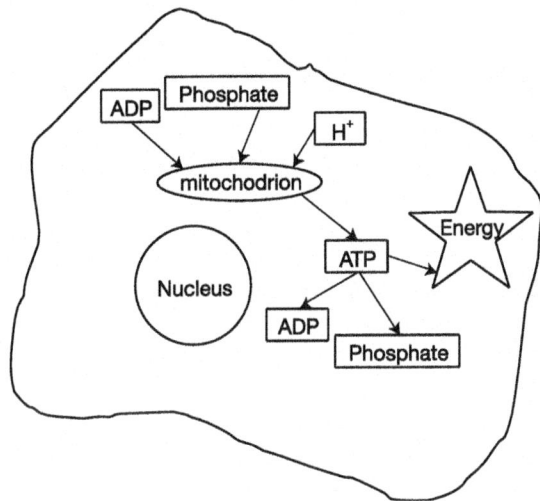

Studies have found that ATP also has another function—that of a messenger between nerve cells. Along with other neurotransmitters such as acetylcholine and dopamine, ATP is released from vesicles when a neuron fires. This ATP is broken down by enzymes into ADP, then adenosine monophosphate (AMP), and finally adenosine. ATP, ADP, AMP, and adenosine transmit messages to another cell by binding to specific receptors known as P2X, P2Y, and P1. The diagram below shows which receptors bind to which of the chemicals.

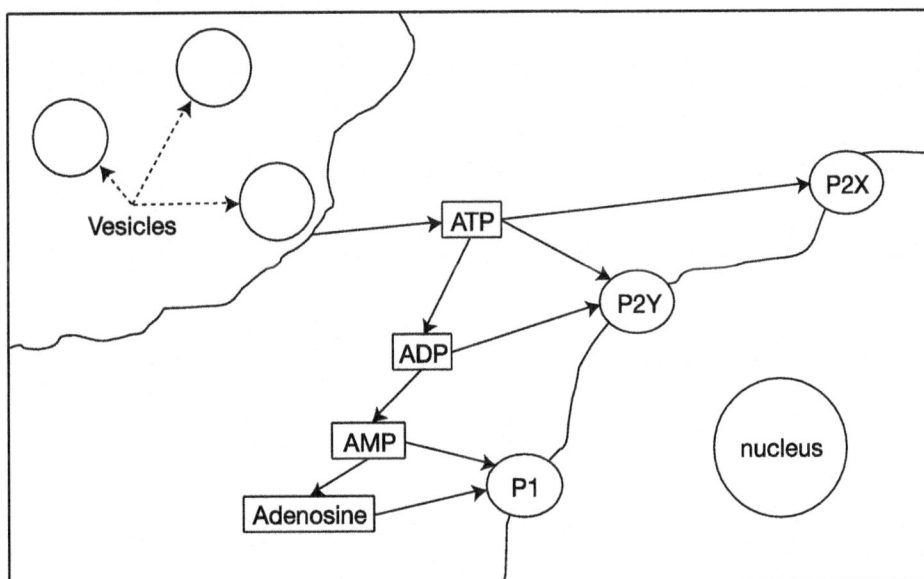

**36. Adenosine monophosphate is made up of adenosine attached to:**

    F. One phosphate
    G. Two phosphates
    H. Three phosphates
    J. Four phosphates

**37. The receptor P2Y binds to:**

    A. Adenosine and AMP
    B. AMP and ADP
    C. ADP and ATP
    D. AMP and ATP

**38. Energy for cellular processes is released through the following reaction:**

    F. ATP → ADP + phosphate
    G. AMP + phosphate → ADP
    H. ADP + phosphate → ATP
    J. AMP → adenosine + phosphate

**39. ATP is released by a vesicle along with other neurotransmitters when a neuron fires. The subsequent breakdown of ATP happens in the following sequence:**

    A. ATP > Adenosine > AMP > ADP
    B. ATP > ADP > AMP > Adenosine
    C. ATP > ADP > Adenosine > AMP
    D. ATP > AMP > ADP > Adenosine

**40. ATP is manufactured in the cell:**

    F. Nucleus
    G. Mitochondria
    H. Vesicles
    J. Receptors

# SCIENCE REASONING PRACTICE TEST 2 ANSWER KEY

| | | |
|---|---|---|
| 1. D | | 21. B |
| 2. G | | 22. H |
| 3. C | | 23. A |
| 4. H | | 24. F |
| 5. A | | 25. A |
| 6. F | | 26. J |
| 7. B | | 27. C |
| 8. H | | 28. F |
| 9. B | | 29. C |
| 10. H | | 30. G |
| 11. A | | 31. B |
| 12. H | | 32. H |
| 13. B | | 33. C |
| 14. H | | 34. H |
| 15. D | | 35. D |
| 16. G | | 36. F |
| 17. D | | 37. C |
| 18. J | | 38. F |
| 19. B | | 39. B |
| 20. H | | 40. G |

# SCIENCE REASONING PRACTICE TEST 2 RATIONALES

### 1. Answer: D. All of the above.
A genuine scientific study must include controls. For instance, a study of a population exposed to radiation must include a control population, i.e., a very similar population that was not exposed to radiation. This helps eliminate factors other than the one being studied as potential causes of the results observed. Also, anecdotes are subjective and lack precise data that can be evaluated scientifically. Thirdly, a single incident may be true but not reliable as evidence. An observation must be repeated multiple times and be statistically significant in order to constitute scientific evidence.

### 2. Answer: G. The mutations found in birds.
Mutations refer to changes in the genomic sequence of a plant or animal cell. Expert 1 states that mutations have been found in one of every ten birds in the affected area. Choices A and D refer to effects of radiation that are not necessarily genetic. Choice C is information given by Expert 2, not Expert 1.

### 3. Answer: C. The reliability of studies showing adverse effects of radiation.
Expert 1 cites many studies to support the idea that radiation from the nuclear accident has had a major effect on the health of people. Expert 2 dismisses the evidence provided by various studies saying that they are based on small populations and anecdotal evidence. Both experts agree on the points mentioned in choices A and B. Choice D is incorrect since the main issue here is human health.

### 4. Answer: H. People are able to tolerate a certain level of radiation without ill effects.
Expert 2 cites levels of radiation that people are exposed to in their everyday lives and at work without any adverse effects. This supports the idea that some level of radiation may not be harmful to health. The statements in choices A and D are points that Expert 2 makes to support the claim that the radiation was not harmful but these are not ideas that support the reasonableness of the claim.

### 5. Answer: A. A large number of people were exposed to radiation due to the nuclear accident.
Only Choice A states an indisputable fact. The other choices are opinions expressed by one or the other of the experts.

### 6. Answer: F. Expert 1
This study indirectly supports Expert 1 since it negates the implication made by Expert 2 that the people in the affected area were likely exposed to tolerable amounts of radiation not much exceeding 20 mSv. Since the radiation level mentioned by the new study is 25 times as much, it undercuts one of the points that support the argument made by Expert 2.

### 7. Answer: B. Disease statistics
Both experts refer to disease numbers in their arguments, Expert 1 in particular. Although the situation of people affected by radiation has ethical, emotional, and economic dimensions, neither expert uses these in supporting their claims.

### 8. Answer: H. 750 kWh
The graph shows that the energy usage of the house in December is close to 1250 kWh. The solar energy generated is just 500 kWh. The difference, 750 kWh, is the amount of energy the house draws from the grid.

### 9. Answer: B. April – October
The house is powered completely by solar energy when the production of solar energy equals or exceeds the house energy usage. The graph shows that this happens between April and October. Choice C is within the correct time frame but does not include the whole range of months. Hence B is the correct choice.

**10. Answer: H. 150 kWh**
The line graph shows that the house uses about 600 kWh of energy in July. According to the table showing how the home energy is used, 25% of the energy is used by appliances. Appliance usage in July would be 25% of 600, which is 150 kWh.

**11. Answer: A. 550 kWh**
The amount of solar energy produced in February before the upgrade was 500 kWh. After the upgrade, the amount of solar energy produced is 50% more, i.e., 750 kWh. The house usage stays the same at 1300 kWh. Therefore, 1300 − 750 = 550 kWh of energy will be needed from the grid.

**12. Answer: H. 1/3 of the total energy**
The water heater uses 16% of the total energy and the lights use 11% of the total energy. Together, they use 27% which is approximately 1/3 of the total energy.

**13. Answer: B. Starts to slow down and level off.**
At first glance it may seem like the increase in boiling point continues at an increasing rate but notice that pressure, the independent variable, is plotted on the vertical axis while boiling point, the dependent variable, is plotted on the horizontal axis. As pressure increases, the rate of change of boiling point falls and it levels off. Hence B is the correct answer choice.

**14. Answer: H. Identical in the common range at sugar concentrations of 0 to 50%.**
Both experiments show the exact same results over the common range which is up to 50% sugar concentration. In both cases the boiling point rises linearly from 100 at 0% sugar to 103 at 50% sugar concentration. Choice A is incorrect because in Experiment 3 the line becomes nonlinear only after the sugar concentration is increased beyond 50%, a range that is not measured in Experiment 2; therefore, there is no contradiction. Choice B is incorrect because both graphs initially have the same slope. The graph in Experiment 3 may look like it has a smaller slope but this is due to the difference in the scale of the vertical axis.

**15. Answer: D. 90 − 100 °C**
The graph from the first experiment shows that the boiling point of water at 0.9 atm is close to 100°C and a little bit less than that.

**16. Answer: G. Keep coolant from boiling away in summer.**
Mixing ethylene glycol with water elevates the boiling point of the coolant mixture to stop it from boiling. Choices A and C rely on a different property of water, the depression of the freezing point, by the addition of a chemical. Choice D relies on boiling point elevation due to pressure, not due to addition of a chemical.

**17. Answer: D. 110 °C**
The graph from Experiment 3 shows that the boiling point of an 80% sugar solution in water is approximately 110 °C.

**18. Answer: J. More than 120 °C**
Experiment 1 shows that the boiling point of pure water at 2 atm is close to 120 °C. Adding sugar to water has the effect of raising the boiling point, therefore we can expect that a 40% sugar solution at 2 atm will have a boiling point greater than 120 °C.

**19. Answer: B. 35 g**
The graph from Experiment 1 shows that mice without the gene had an average body weight of about 35 g at 15 weeks.

**20. Answer: H. There is a correlation between high body weights and high cholesterol.**
It is clear from the experiments that high body weight is correlated with high cholesterol. However, from that data we cannot conclude that there is a causal relationship between the two. Correlation is not the same as causation; therefore, C is the best choice.

**21. Answer: B. Rises higher and falls more slowly than for mice without the gene when sugar solution is given.**
The graph from Experiment 3 shows that the average blood glucose level in mice without the immune response gene rises higher (up to 400 versus 350 mg/dL) and falls more slowly than that for mice without the gene when sugar solution is given. Hence B is the correct choice. A is incorrect because both start out at the same blood sugar level.

**22. Answer: H. Approximately 25 g**
It is clear from the graph of Experiment 1 that the average body weight of the mice with the immune response gene levels off at approximately 25 g by week 20. We can therefore assume that by week 50, the weight will be the same.

**23. Answer: A. The age of the mice.**
The control variable in an experiment is the one that is held constant so that its effect on the result can be eliminated. In both Experiments 2 and 3, all the mice tested were at age 20 weeks. This ensured that variations in cholesterol and glucose level due to age would not influence the experiments. Both Experiments 2 and 3 were trying to determine the effect of the immune response gene on cholesterol and blood glucose.

**24. Answer: F. Measurements of blood pressure of mice with and without the immune response gene.**
According to the passage, elevated blood pressure is one of the symptoms of metabolic syndrome; therefore, a study of blood pressure with and without the immune response gene could shed further light on the primary topic of enquiry. Choices B and C are irrelevant to the current study. The study in Choice D would help solidify the conclusions of Experiment 2 but would not bring major new information to light.

**25. Answer: A. Has less silica content.**
Notice that in the diagram, the silica content on the horizontal axis goes from a higher number to a lower content (70% to 40%); a careful reading of the diagram shows that komatiite has less silica content (under 45%) than andecite (close to 55%). Choice B is incorrect since, according to the table, rocks with more silica content are more viscous. Choice C is incorrect since the diagram shows that andecite contains quartz but komatiite does not. Choice D is incorrect since both andecite and komatiite are fine-grained extrusive rocks (see z-axis).

**26. Answer: J. Granite**
According to the passage, coarse-grained rocks are classified as intrusive. Intrusive rocks are located in the front "half" of the diagram (granite, granodiorite, diorite, gabbro, and peridotite). Of these intrusive rocks, only granite is found near the 70% silica content end of the x-axis. Granodiorite is also an intrusive rock with high silica content but its silica content is closer to 60% than 70%. In order to interpret the diagram correctly, it is important to look at all three axes and the information they convey.

**27. Answer: C. Mafic**
The diagram shows that gabbro has almost 50% silica content. Cross-correlating this information with the table, we see that rocks with between 45-52% silica content are classified as mafic.

**28. Answer: F. Granite and rhyolite**
The diagram shows granite and rhyolite as both being close to 70% in silica content and containing some orthoclase, quartz, plagioclase, and amphibole; they have the same chemical composition. Granite is the intrusive form of the rock while rhyolite is the extrusive form.

**29. Answer: C. Dacite**
As shown in the diagram, basalt, komatiite, and gabbro are all relatively low silica content rocks that contain a certain percentage of pyroxene. Only dacite does not contain pyroxene.

**30. Answer: G. 141**
According to the passage, the number of transformants per μg of DNA is the transformation efficiency. From the table in Experiment 1, we see that for pH 8.4 this number is 141. Choice A is incorrect because 225 is the total number of transformants for 1.6 μg of DNA at pH 8.4, not for 1 microgram of DNA.

**31. Answer: B. Narrow down the pH range where transformation efficiency is maximum.**
The pH range tested in Experiment 1 is 5.5 to 9.5. The pH range tested in Experiment 2 is 6.1 to 7.7. This is the range in which the transformation efficiency peaks in Experiment 1. Experiment 2 provides several more data points within this range, allowing the range of the peak pH level to be narrowed down. Hence B is the correct answer choice. Choice A is incorrect since the pH levels in Experiment 2 are not identical to those in Experiment 1. Choice C is incorrect since the pH range for Experiment 2 lies within the pH range for Experiment 1. Choice D is incorrect since it is clearly stated in the passage that the experimental conditions for Experiment 2 were identical to that of Experiment 1.

**32. Answer: H. 6.9 – 7.4**
Looking at the graph for Experiment 2, we can see that 6.9 to 7.4 is the pH range in which the transformation efficiency is maximum. Hence C is the correct answer choice. Choice B includes the maximum efficiency range, however, it is a broader range obtained from Experiment 1 and does not pinpoint the most efficient range. Since Experiment 2 has narrowed the range down, it provides a more accurate range.

**33. Answer: C. 6.6**
The transformation efficiency is 970/5 = 194 which is close to the transformation efficiency given for pH 6.6 in the table for Experiment 2.

**34. Answer: H. The quantity of DNA used in each test is different.**
Transformation efficiency is the number of transformants per microgram of DNA. If the quantity of DNA is changed, it is reasonable to assume that the number of transformants will also change. Data tables for both experiments show that the DNA quantity for each experiment is different. In order to accurately compare the data from the two tests, the transformation efficiency is the variable that should be compared between tests. Choices A and B both give incorrect information.

**35. Answer: D. 600**
Based on the data table for Experiment 2, the transformation efficiency for pH 7.3 is approximately 200 (between 198 for 7.4 and 220 for 7.2). This represents the number of transformants for 1 microgram of DNA. Therefore, the number of transformants for 3 microgram of DNA is expected to be approximately 200 x 3 = 600.

**36. Answer: F. One phosphate**
According to the passage, adenosine triphosphate (ATP) is made up of an adenosine molecule attached to three phosphates. The passage further describes how energy is released as the bonds between these phosphates are broken. ATP becomes ADP with the release of a phosphate and ADP becomes AMP with the release of a phosphate. From this, we can conclude that adenosine monophosphate contains one phosphate.

**37. Answer: C. ADP and ATP**
From the second diagram it is clear that the receptor P2Y binds to ADP and ATP.

**38. Answer: F. ATP → ADP + phosphate**
Energy from ATP is released when an ATP molecule is broken down into ADP and a phosphate. This is mentioned in the passage and shown schematically in the first diagram.

**39. Answer: B. ATP > ADP > AMP > Adenosine**
In each step of the ATP > ADP > AMP > Adenosine sequence, one phosphate is lost.

**40. Answer: G. Mitochondria**
According to the passage, ATP is manufactured in the mitochondria of a cell through a process that adds a phosphate to ADP.

# ACT ASSESSMENT

# PRACTICE TEST THREE

# ENGLISH PRACTICE TEST 3

45 Minutes - 75 Questions

Directions: Read the provided passage. You will notice that words or phrases are underlined and numbered. Pay particular attention to these underlined words and phrases. Most questions on the test will offer you four alternatives to the underlined words or phrases, including the option of No change. Select the answer that best expresses the idea, style, or intention of the passage; is free of grammatical and punctuation errors, reflects standard usage in English, and works best within the context of the passage. Some questions may refer to parts of the passage or the whole passage rather than the underlined parts.

---

**The following passage is the basis for Questions 1-3:**

**The Sinking of the RMS Titanic—A Class Act?**

(1) Nothing in the world <u>compare to</u> the tragic story of the *RMS Titanic*. It is one of the most haunting and
         1
fascinating disasters in history.

(2) Why is this? Is it because of the glamorous passenger list, <u>which would be</u> <u>packed</u> with the rich and
         2
famous of the time? Is it the contrast between the publicity about the size and safety of the ship and the fact that all her shiny new state-of-the-art bells and whistles wound up at the bottom of the sea? Is it because *Titanic* symbolized the triumph of human ingenuity over the forces of nature, and yet was thoroughly defeated by an iceberg's sharp edges and tons of frosty ocean water? Whatever the reasons, the story of the *RMS Titanic* foundering in freezing waters off Novia Scotia on her way to New York has haunted and intrigued people ever since that fateful night of <u>April 14 1912</u> when over a thousand people
         3
went into the water to meet icy deaths.

---

1. **Which of the following changes, if any, should be applied to underlined section 1?**

    A. No change
    B. compared
    C. compares
    D. is comparing

2. **Which of the following changes, if any, should be applied to underlined section 2?**

    F. No change
    G. which was packed
    H. which had been packed
    J. which is packed

3. **Which of the following changes, if any, should be applied to underlined section 3?**

   A. No change
   B. April, 14 1912
   C. April 14 1912,
   D. April 14, 1912

---

**The following passage is the basis for Questions 4-6:**

(3) It is said that arrogance played a role in the great ship's <u>dramatic demise</u>. It is believed that there were
4
sayings about the *Titanic* that almost tempted fate.

(4) Some people said, <u>"The *Titanic* is unsinkable"</u>! (Some historians say that the claim was "almost
5
unsinkable"). Of course, no ship is unsinkable.

(5) On the subject of arrogance, the wireless radio operator of the *Titanic* told the wireless radio operator

of a nearby ship, the *California*, to "Shut up" earlier in the evening of the sinking because communications

from the *California* were jamming signal messages from *Titanic's* important and wealthy to shore. The

*California* was the closest ship to the *Titanic*—much closer than the ship that eventually came to the

rescue. Yet the *California* crew did not pay attention to the wireless distress signals from the *Titanic*, <u>as
6
the wireless radio operator went to bed soon after being told off.</u>

---

4. **In underlined section 4, what stylistic device is the author using to emphasize these words?**

   F. irony
   G. hyperbole
   H. personification
   J. alliteration

5. **Which of the following changes, if any, should be applied to underlined section 5?**

   A. No change
   B. "The *Titanic* is unsinkable!"
   C. "The *Titanic* is sinkable"!
   D. "The *Titanic* is "unsinkable!"

**6. Is there an underlying implication in the way underlined section 6 is phrased? If so, what is that implication?**

F. There is no implication.
G. Yes, it is implied that the wireless operators of the two ships had been on bad terms for a long time and there was no hope for help from the *California*.
H. Yes, it is implied that the wireless radio operator of the *California* deliberately shut down his equipment in revenge, knowing *Titanic* would soon be in trouble.
J. Yes, it is implied that the wireless radio operator of the *California* may have gone to bed because he was disheartened by arrogant treatment from the *Titanic's* radio operator.

---

**The following passage is the basis for Questions 7-9:**

(6) Much was made in the James Cameron movie *Titanic* about the snobbish class divisions that kept many third class passengers locked into the lower parts of the ship while the first class passengers escaped by lifeboat. The fence-like doors that kept the third class passengers penned in appeared many times in the movie. Although these gates did exist, they were not intended to trap third class passengers should there be an emergency. At that time, disease was a concern, and the spread of disease from poorer classes of people <u>was something the ship had to consider.</u> Health regulations required immigrants
7
to be restricted to one part of the ship.

(7) According to <u>british parliamentary papers</u> recording the survivors, the largest group of survivors of the
8
*Titanic* were women and children of all classes. On one side of the *Titanic*, the noble cry was: "Women and children only!" as crew members loaded the lifeboats. On the other side of the *Titanic*, the cry was: "Women and children first!" which allowed some men to escape via lifeboat. First class male passengers, however, had a lower survival rate than any of the classes of women and children.

(8) One hundred percent of children from both the first and the second class passenger lists survived. Ninety-seven percent of first class women survived, as did eighty-six percent of second class women and female crew members. <u>Alas, less than fifty percent of third class women survived</u>, and less than a third of
9
third class children survived.

---

**7. The way underlined section 7 is worded could imply:**

A. Nothing in particular
B. that the ship itself, rather than the ship's doctor or crew, had concerns about health
C. that health concerns were due to prejudice and ignorance
D. that this was one more example of class privilege aboard the *Titanic*

8. **Which of the following changes, if any, should be applied to underlined section 8?**

   F. No change
   G. British Parliamentary Papers
   H. British parliamentary papers
   J. british Parliamentary papers

9. **A more modern style of phrasing in underlined section 9 might be:**

   A. No change
   B. Woefully, less than fifty percent of third class women survived
   C. Less than fifty percent of third class women unfortunately survived
   D. Sadly, less than fifty percent of third class women survived

---

**The following passage is the basis for Questions 10-12:**

**(9)** However, it is to be noted that there were many more third class children aboard than there were second and first class ones, so actual numbers of third class children survivors may have been comparable to first and second class children survivors.

**(10)** Close to thirty percent of first class men survived, twenty-two percent of crew men survived (perhaps because they had ready access to the lifeboats) and third class men only survived at about 20%. However, the smallest percentage group of survivors was second class men at 8%, so third class men in general outlived second class men.

**(11)** <u>Third class women were forty percent more likely to survive than first class men.</u> Third class men
   10
were twice as likely to survive as second class men.

**(12)** Thus, it appears that a "class system" interpretation of the survival rate is more the stuff of Hollywood fiction than of fact. In fact, *Titanic's* owner, Bruce Ismay (made out to be a villain in the movie) made third class accommodations on the *Titanic* <u>on a parity</u> with second class accommodations on other ships;
   11
second class accommodations on the *Titanic* were more like first class ones on other ships. Ismay did this deliberately. He wanted people who were emigrating to the United States to feel that a better new life awaited them, beginning with their transatlantic passage. In short, his motives were democratic.

---

**(13)** This we do know: no matter what the class divisions on the *Titanic* might have been, when faced with a life or death situation, the category of people who sacrificed themselves the most were men of all classes as they followed their <u>societies code of honor</u> to protect women and children.
12

**10. Which of the following changes, if any, should be applied to underlined section 10?**

    F. No change
    G. Third class women were forty percent likeliest to survive over first class men.
    H. Third class women were surviving forty percent more than first class men.
    J. Third class women were in the fortieth percentile of survival when you compare them to first class men.

**11. In underlined section 11, the phrase "on a parity" mostly likely means:**

    A. equal or comparable to
    B. they were adjacent to one another in the ship
    C. third class accommodations on the *Titanic* were pared down second class ones
    D. third class accommodations were parallel to second class accommodations

**12. Which of the following changes, if any, should be applied to underlined section 12?**

    F. No change
    G. societie's code of honor
    H. societies' code of honor
    J. society's code of honor

**The following passage is the basis for Questions 13-15:**

## The Sinking of RMS Titanic—A Class Act?

**(1)** Nothing in the world compare to the tragic story of the *RMS Titanic*. It is one of the most haunting and fascinating disasters in history.

**(2)** Why is this? Is it because of the glamorous passenger list, which would be packed with the rich and famous of the time? Is it the contrast between the publicity about the size and safety of the ship and the fact that all her shiny new state-of-the-art bells and whistles wound up at the bottom of the sea? Is it because *Titanic* symbolized the triumph of human ingenuity over the forces of nature, and yet was thoroughly defeated by an iceberg's sharp edges and tons of frosty ocean water? Whatever the reasons, the story of the *RMS Titanic* foundering in freezing waters off Novia Scotia on her way to New York has haunted and intrigued people ever since that fateful night of April 14 1912 when over a thousand people went into the water to meet icy deaths.

**(3)** It is said that arrogance played a role in the great ship's dramatic demise. It is believed that there were sayings about the *Titanic* that almost tempted fate.

**(4)** Some people said, "The *Titanic* is unsinkable"! (Some historians say that the claim was "almost unsinkable"). Of course, no ship is unsinkable.

**(5)** On the subject of arrogance, the wireless radio operator of the *Titanic* told the wireless radio operator of a nearby ship, the *California*, to "Shut up" earlier in the evening of the sinking because communications from the *California* were jamming signal messages from *Titanic's* important and wealthy to shore. The

*California* was the closest ship to the *Titanic*—much closer than the ship that eventually came to the rescue. Yet the *California* crew did not pay attention to the wireless distress signals from the *Titanic*, as the wireless radio operator went to bed soon after being told off.

(6) Much was made in the James Cameron movie *Titanic* about the snobbish class divisions that kept many third class passengers locked into the lower parts of the ship while the first class passengers escaped by lifeboat. The fence-like doors that kept the third class passengers penned in appeared many times in the movie. Although these gates did exist, they were not intended to trap third class passengers should there be an emergency. At that time, disease was a concern, and the spread of disease from poorer classes of people was something the ship had to consider. Health regulations required immigrants to be restricted to one part of the ship.

(7) According to british parliamentary papers recording the survivors, the largest group of survivors of the *Titanic* were women and children of all classes. On one side of the *Titanic*, the noble cry was: "Women and children only!" as crew members loaded the lifeboats. On the other side of the *Titanic*, the cry was: "Women and children first!" which allowed some men to escape via lifeboat. First class male passengers, however, had a lower survival rate than any of the classes of women and children.

(8) One hundred percent of children from both the first and the second class passenger lists survived. Ninety-seven percent of first class women survived, as did eighty-six percent of second class women and female crew members. Alas, less than fifty percent of third class women survived, and less than a third of third class children survived.

(9) However, it is to be noted that there were many more third class children aboard than there were second and first class ones, so actual numbers of third class children survivors may have been comparable to first and second class children survivors.

(10) Close to thirty percent of first class men survived, twenty-two percent of crew men survived (perhaps because they had ready access to the lifeboats) and third class men only survived at about 20%. However, the smallest percentage group of survivors was second class men at 8%, so third class men in general outlived second class men.

(11) Third class women were forty percent more likely to survive than first class men. Third class men were twice as likely to survive as second class men.

(12) Thus, it appears that a "class system" interpretation of the survival rate is more the stuff of Hollywood fiction than of fact. In fact, *Titanic's* owner, Bruce Ismay (made out to be a villain in the movie) made third class accommodations on the *Titanic* on a parity with second class accommodations on other ships; second class accommodations on the *Titanic* were more like first class ones on other ships. Ismay did this deliberately. He wanted people who were emigrating to the United States to feel that a better new life awaited them, beginning with their transatlantic passage. In short, his motives were democratic.

(13) This we do know: no matter what the class divisions on the *Titanic* might have been, when faced with a life or death situation, the category of people who sacrificed themselves the most were men of all classes as they followed their societies code of honor to protect women and children.

**13. Judging by the title of the passage as well as its contents, the author's point of view is:**

    A.  that outmoded Edwardian social mores, left over from the Victorian era, doomed many *Titanic* passengers to watery graves

    B.  that the chances of survival on the *Titanic* had less to do with income or social status than they did with gender

    C.  that *Titanic* did not have enough lifeboats because the first class passengers wanted more room to promenade

    D.  that surviving the *Titanic* disaster required a combination of luck, intestinal fortitude, good relations with the second class crew members, and some knowledge of seamanship.

**14. The author wishes to add the following paragraph to the essay. Where would be the best place to insert such a paragraph?**

**In the movie *Titanic* the ship's builder says that first class passengers would not like many lifeboats crowding the decks. It is implied that the selfishness of first class passengers led to more deaths during the disaster for want of lifeboats. However, the *Titanic* had more lifeboats than were legally required. Prior to the sinking of the *Titanic*, it was assumed lifeboats would be used over and over again, ferrying passengers from a sinking ship to a rescue ship. After the *Titanic* disaster, maritime law required ships to carry enough lifeboats for every person on board in case a ship foundered in isolation from other ships.**

    F.  between paragraphs 3 and 4

    G.  between paragraphs 5 and 6

    H.  between paragraphs 10 and 11

    J.  between paragraphs 11 and 12

**15. The author's assignment was to refute the idea, popularized in culture by James Cameron's movie *Titanic*, that class snobbery contributed to a high death toll on the *Titanic*. Did the author fulfill the assignment?**

    A.  No, because the movie, which showed strong class snobbery, won a lot of Academy Awards.

    B.  No, because the essay makes several points at the beginning about arrogance being a factor in the disaster.

    C.  Yes, because the essay presents some points in favor of arrogance contributing to the disaster and some points against it, and it specifically refutes some aspects of the movie with facts and figures.

    D.  Yes, because the essay says there really were gates keeping the third class passengers confined, which confirms that the movie's depiction of class differences was accurate.

---

**The following passage, an excerpt from *Narrative of the Life of Frederick Douglass, An American Slave*, is the basis for Questions 16-18:**

## An American Slave

(1) My new mistress proved to be all she appeared when I first met her at the door,—a woman of the

kindest heart and finest feelings. She had never therein had a slave under her control previously to
                                               16

myself, and prior to her marriage she had been dependent upon her own industry for a living. She was by

trade a weaver; and by constant application to her business, she had been in a good degree preserved

from the blighting and dehumanizing effects of slavery.

**(2)** I was utterly astonished at her goodness. I scarcely knew how to behave towards her. She was entirely unlike any other white woman I had ever seen. <u>I could not approach her so as I was accustomed to approach other white ladies.</u> My early instruction was all out of place. The crouching servility, usually
17
so acceptable a quality in a slave, did not answer when manifested toward her. Her favor was not gained by it; she seemed <u>to be "disturbed"</u> by it. She did not deem it impudent or unmannerly for a slave to look
18
her in the face. The meanest slave was put fully at ease in her presence, and none left without feeling better for having seen her. Her face was made of heavenly smiles, and her voice of tranquil music.

**16. Which of the following changes, if any, should be applied to underlined section 16?**

F. No change
G. She had never therefore had a slave under her control
H. She had never thenceforth had a slave under her control
J. She had never had a slave under her control

**17. Which of the following changes, if any, should be applied to underlined section 17?**

A. No change
B. I could not approach her as I was accustomed to approach other white ladies.
C. I could not approach her so; I was accustomed to approach other white ladies.
D. I could not approach her so I did not, accustomed as I was to approach other white ladies.

**18. Which of the following changes, if any, should be applied to underlined section 18?**

F. No change
G. to be "undisturbed"
H. to be "distributed"
J. to be disturbed

The following passage, an excerpt from *Narrative of the Life of Frederick Douglass, An American Slave*, is the basis for Questions 19-25:

**(3)** But, alas! This kind heart had but a short time to remain such. <u>The fatal poison of irresponsible power</u>
19
<u>was already in her hands, and soon commenced its infernal work.</u> <u>That cheerful eye, under the influence</u>
20
<u>of slavery, soon became red with rage</u>; that voice, made all of sweet accord, changed to one of harsh and horrid discord; and that <u>angelic face gave place to that of a demon...</u>
21

**(4)** ...My mistress was, as I have said, a kind and tender-hearted woman; and in the simplicity of her soul she commenced, when I first went to live with her, to treat me as she supposed one human being ought to treat another. In entering upon the duties of a slaveholder, she did not seem to perceive that I

sustained to her the relation of a mere chattel, and that for her to <u>treat me as an human being was not</u>
<u>only wrong</u>, but dangerously so.
22

**(5)** <u>Slavery proved as injurious to her as it did to me.</u> When I went there, she was a pious, warm, and
23
tender-hearted woman. There was no sorrow or suffering for which she had not a tear. <u>She herself had</u>
24
<u>bread for the hungry</u>, clothes for the naked, and comfort for every mourner that came within her reach.

<u>Slavery soon proved its ability to divest her of these heavenly qualities. Under its influence, the tender</u>
25
heart became stone, and the lamblike disposition gave way to one of tiger-like fierceness.

**19. In the context of the whole essay, what famous saying might complement the meaning of underlined section 19?**

    A. A stitch in time saves nine.
    B. Powerful is as powerful does.
    C. Absolute power corrupts absolutely.
    D. Power to the people.

**20. Which of the following changes, if any, should be applied to underlined section 20?**

    F. No change
    G. That cheerful eye under the influence of slavery soon became red with rage,
    H. That cheerful eye under the influence of slavery, soon became red with rage;
    J. That cheerful eye under the influence of slavery, soon became red with rage;

**21. The use of an "ellipsis" (three periods) as in underlined section 21 indicates what?**

    A. that some material has been taken out
    B. that the situation is so dramatic, three periods should be used rather than one
    C. that words have failed the author
    D. that the reader is to finish the sentence in his or her mind

**22. Which of the following changes, if any, should be applied to underlined section 22?**

    F. No change
    G. treat me as a human being was not only wrong
    H. treat me as if an human being was not only wrong
    J. treat me if as an human being was not only wrong

**23. Paragraphs 3 through 5, summarized in underlined section 23, indicate that Douglass believed:**

    A. slavery was morally corrupting for slaves
    B. slavery was morally corrupting for slave-owners
    C. slavery was morally corrupting for both slaves and slave owners
    D. slavery was not morally corrupting

**24. Which of the following changes, if any, should be applied to underlined section 24?**

    F.  No change
    G.  She had bread for the hungry
    H.  She herself had bread that she did give to the hungry
    J.  She herself gave bread for the hungry

**25. What feeling is the author expressing in underlined section 25?**

    A.  fear that he is going to be punished because of his mistress's split personality
    B.  self-doubt as to whether his own behavior had wrought such changes in his mistress
    C.  wonder that a human being could change so
    D.  anger and outrage at the pernicious power of slavery to corrupt people's characters

---

**The following passage, an excerpt from *Narrative of the Life of Frederick Douglass, An American Slave*, is the basis for Questions 26-28:**

(6) The first step in her downward course was in her ceasing to instruct me. She now commenced to practice her <u>husbands' precepts</u>. She finally became even more violent in her opposition than her
                      26
husband himself. She was not satisfied with simply doing as well as he had commanded; she seemed anxious to do better.

(7) Nothing seemed to make her more angry than to see me with a newspaper. She seemed to think that here lay the danger. I have had her rush at me with a face made all up of fury, and snatch from me a newspaper, in a manner that fully revealed her apprehension. <u>She was a woman apt</u>; and a little
                                                27
experience soon demonstrated, to her satisfaction, that education and slavery were incompatible with each other.

(8) From this time I was most narrowly watched. If I was in a separate room any considerable length of time, I was sure to be suspected of having a book, and was at once called to give an account of myself. All this, however, was too late. The first step had been taken. Mistress, in teaching me the alphabet, had <u>given me the inch and no precaution could prevent me from taking the ell.</u>
                                      28

---

**26. Which of the following changes, if any, should be applied to underlined section 26?**

    F.  No change
    G.  husband's precepts
    H.  husbands precepts
    J.  husband precepts

**27. Which of the following changes, if any, should be applied to underlined section 27?**

    A. No change
    B. She was a apt woman
    C. She was an apt woman
    D. She was as apt as a woman

**28. In underlined section 28, from the context of the sentence, "ell" most likely means:**

    F. the whole length
    G. half inch
    H. dozen
    J. the most

The following passage, an excerpt from *Narrative of the Life of Frederick Douglass, An American Slave*, is the basis for Questions 29-30:

## An American Slave

**(1)** My new mistress proved to be all she appeared when I first met her at the door,—a woman of the kindest heart and finest feelings. She had never therein had a slave under her control previously to myself, and prior to her marriage she had been dependent upon her own industry for a living. She was by trade a weaver; and by constant application to her business, she had been in a good degree preserved from the blighting and dehumanizing effects of slavery.

**(2)** I was utterly astonished at her goodness. I scarcely knew how to behave towards her. She was entirely unlike any other white woman I had ever seen. I could not approach her so as I was accustomed to approach other white ladies. My early instruction was all out of place. The crouching servility, usually so acceptable a quality in a slave, did not answer when manifested toward her. Her favor was not gained by it; she seemed to be "disturbed" by it. She did not deem it impudent or unmannerly for a slave to look her in the face. The meanest slave was put fully at ease in her presence, and none left without feeling better for having seen her. Her face was made of heavenly smiles, and her voice of tranquil music.

**(3)** But, alas! This kind heart had but a short time to remain such. The fatal poison of irresponsible power was already in her hands, and soon commenced its infernal work. That cheerful eye, under the influence of slavery, soon became red with rage; that voice, made all of sweet accord, changed to one of harsh and horrid discord; and that angelic face gave place to that of a demon...

**(4)** ...My mistress was, as I have said, a kind and tender-hearted woman; and in the simplicity of her soul she commenced, when I first went to live with her, to treat me as she supposed one human being ought to treat another. In entering upon the duties of a slaveholder, she did not seem to perceive that I sustained to her the relation of a mere chattel, and that for her to treat me as an human being was not only wrong, but dangerously so.

**(5)** Slavery proved as injurious to her as it did to me. When I went there, she was a pious, warm, and tender-hearted woman. There was no sorrow or suffering for which she had not a tear. She herself had bread for the hungry, clothes for the naked, and comfort for every mourner that came within her reach. Slavery soon proved its ability to divest her of these heavenly qualities. Under its influence, the tender heart became stone, and the lamblike disposition gave way to one of tiger-like fierceness.

**(6)** The first step in her downward course was in her ceasing to instruct me. She now commenced to practice her husbands' precepts. She finally became even more violent in her opposition than her husband himself. She was not satisfied with simply doing as well as he had commanded; she seemed anxious to do better.

**(7)** Nothing seemed to make her more angry than to see me with a newspaper. She seemed to think that here lay the danger. I have had her rush at me with a face made all up of fury, and snatch from me a newspaper, in a manner that fully revealed her apprehension. She was a woman apt; and a little experience soon demonstrated, to her satisfaction, that education and slavery were incompatible with each other.

**(8)** From this time I was most narrowly watched. If I was in a separate room any considerable length of time, I was sure to be suspected of having a book, and was at once called to give an account of myself. All this, however, was too late. The first step had been taken. Mistress, in teaching me the alphabet, had given me the inch and no precaution could prevent me from taking the ell.

**29. What would be a good title for this passage?**

A. The Corrupting Effects of Slavery on Mistress and Man
B. Chronicles of Slavery from a Mistress's Perspective
C. The Effects of Reading upon Slaves
D. A Woman's Unchanging Heart

**30. Which of the following best describes the evolution of the mistress in the passage?**

F. She went from being a free woman to being a slave to slavery.
G. She went from being mild-mannered, charitable, and helpful to being temperamental and cruel.
H. She went from being an avowed slaveowner to being an abolitionist once she learned how difficult slaves were to teach.
J. She was innocent as a dove until her slave's misbehavior and rebelliousness coarsened her nature and caused her to discipline him.

**The following passage is the basis for Questions 31-33:**

## Study War No More

**(1)** According to the Human Security Report of 2009-2010, the new millennium ushered in an era of

decreased warfare. Throughout the long history of humankind, war has been the normal way to acquire

land and natural resources, which were the traditional sources of wealth. Times, to everyone's great
                                         31

relief, have changed.

**(2)** The world celebrated in style when the century turned. All over the world, people rang in the new

millennium with high hopes and dreams. Although there have certainly been setbacks, in fact, the new

millennium is living up to some of it's promises of peace.
                                                    32

(3) Since the turn of the twenty-first century, there have been one or less than one international conflicts annually. Preceding the turn of the century, six or seven international conflicts were waged per year.

Peace is breaking out!
33

**31. Which of the following changes, if any, should be applied to underlined section 31?**

A. No change
B. which were the traditional sources of wealth.
C. , that were the traditional sources of wealth.
D. , that which were the traditional sources of wealth.

**32. Which of the following changes, if any, should be applied to underlined section 32?**

F. No change
G. its promises of peace.
H. its' promises of peace.
J. it's having made promises of peace

**33. What is the tone of the passage as exemplified in underlined section 33?**

A. pessimistic
B. optimistic
C. reserved
D. doubtful

**The following passage is the basis for Questions 34-38:**

(4) There is more good news. When there are wars in the new millenium, there are far fewer casualties.
34
The Human Security Report cites figures that in the 1950s and throughout the last decades of the twentieth century, the average international conflict took a death toll of 21,000 people per year. Now, international conflicts claim the lives of 3,000 people (or less) on an annual basis.

(5) What is the reason for these positive developments? Scholars have several theories.
35

(6) One theory is that democracy is an instrument of peace. Spreading all over the globe, wars between
36
democracies are rare. Democracies do go to war with tyrannies, dictatorships, and other forms of government, but they almost never go to war with one another. As the number of democracies increases, the number of wars naturally decrease.
37

**(7)** Another theory is that capitalism, also spreading throughout the globe, encourages countries to
engage in trade with and to invest in other countries. Countries with strong economic ties rarely go to war
38
with one another, and the interconnected, global economy means that nations do not want to risk their
capital by going to war with trading or investment partners.

**34. Which of the following changes, if any, should be applied to underlined section 34?**

    F.  No change
    G.  milennium
    H.  millennia
    J.  millennium

**35. In underlined section 35, what would be a good revision of paragraph 5?**

    A.  No revision
    B.  add two sentences to make it longer
    C.  switch the two sentences to change the order
    D.  edit the paragraph out; it is unnecessary

**36. Which of the following changes, if any, should be applied to underlined section 36?**

    F.  No change
    G.  Spreading all over the globe, democracies are rare.
    H.  Spreading all over the globe, wars with democracies are rare.
    J.  Spreading all over the globe, democracies rarely go to war with one another.

**37. Which of the following changes, if any, should be applied to underlined section 37?**

    A.  No change
    B.  the number of wars naturally decrease.
    C.  the number of wars naturally decreases.
    D.  the number of war naturally decrease.

**38. In underlined section 38, the tone of paragraph 7 may be described as:**

    F.  anxious
    G.  optimistic
    H.  pragmatic
    J.  hopeful

**The following passage is the basis for Questions 39-42:**

**(8)** Technology has played a part, as it has made the world a global village. In the past, some wars were
fought simply because of a lack of communication. The War of 1812, for example, was unnecessary. The
war started even though Great Britain had agreed to all of the United States' requests. The
39
correspondence simply did not arrive in time to prevent the clash, as messages between the
governments had to travel by ship across the Atlantic Ocean.

(9) Technology has also brought about economic innovations that made traditional methods of wealth-gathering obsolete. Wealth is no longer dependent on land ownership or natural resources. Wealth is generated in new ways in a technologically advanced world. There is not as much need to go to war to order to acquire wealth through acquisition of physical assets. <u>Physical assets are no longer the basis of</u>
<u>wealth or war.</u>
                                                                                                   40

(10) Another peace-promoting innovation that democracy brought to the world was the peaceful succession of leaders chosen by majority vote. In most cases, in a democracy, the people who did not vote for a leader submit to his or her leadership until a candidate more to their liking can be elected. This makes the transition from one leader to another peaceful. Notable exceptions are civil wars—including the American Civil War, when the South seceded from the nation as soon as Abraham Lincoln was elected president. <u>Still, in modern times, there are few violent uprisings in democracies, and even civil</u>
                                                                                    41
<u>wars are on the wane.</u> People can always work "within the system" to bring about change when they are dissatisfied in a democracy.

(11) Because democracy is a system of voting, a leader may be changed by the people voting the leader out of office. This holds leaders accountable in ways military dictatorships or tyrannies cannot. As anti-war feeling grows all over the world (and the Human Security Report holds that such feeling is indeed growing) democratically elected leaders must answer to this feeling when considering waging war. <u>This</u>
                                                                                                      42
<u>acts as a break upon engaging in war.</u>

**39. Underlined section 39 has overtones of:**

    A. No feeling
    B. hilarity
    C. solemnity
    D. irony

**40. Underlined section 40 is an example of:**

    F. hyperbole
    G. personification
    H. metaphor
    J. redundancy

**41. In underlined section 41, the phrase "on the wane" may be understood to mean:**

    A.  on the rise
    B.  on the horizon
    C.  on the decrease
    D.  on the increase

**42. Which of the following changes, if any, should be applied to underlined section 42?**

    F.  No change
    G.  This acts as a brake upon engaging in war.
    H.  This breaks up acts of engaging in war.
    J.  This acts as a break-up of wars.

---

**The following passage is the basis for Questions 43-45:**

## Study War No More

**(1)** According to the Human Security Report of 2009-2010, the new millennium ushered in an era of decreased warfare. Throughout the long history of humankind, war has been the normal way to acquire land and natural resources, which were the traditional sources of wealth. Times, to everyone's great relief, have changed.

**(2)** The world celebrated in style when the century turned. All over the world, people rang in the new millennium with high hopes and dreams. Although there have certainly been setbacks, in fact, the new millennium is living up to some of it's promises of peace.

**(3)** Since the turn of the twenty-first century, there have been one or less than one international conflicts annually. Preceding the turn of the century, six or seven international conflicts were waged per year. Peace is breaking out!

**(4)** There is more good news. When there are wars in the new millenium, there are far fewer casualties. The Human Security Report cites figures that in the 1950s and throughout the last decades of the twentieth century, the average international conflict took a death toll of 21,000 people per year. Now, international conflicts claim the lives of 3,000 people (or less) on an annual basis.

**(5)** What is the reason for these positive developments? Scholars have several theories.

**(6)** One theory is that democracy is an instrument of peace. Spreading all over the globe, wars between democracies are rare. Democracies do go to war with tyrannies, dictatorships, and other forms of government, but they almost never go to war with one another. As the number of democracies increases, the number of wars naturally decrease.

**(7)** Another theory is that capitalism, also spreading throughout the globe, encourages countries to engage in trade with and to invest in other countries. Countries with strong economic ties rarely go to war with one another, and the interconnected, global economy means that nations do not want to risk their capital by going to war with trading or investment partners.

**(8)** Technology has played a part, as it has made the world a global village. In the past, some wars were fought simply because of a lack of communication. The War of 1812, for example, was unnecessary. The war started even though Great Britain had agreed to all of the United States' requests. The correspondence simply did not arrive in time to prevent the clash, as messages between the governments had to travel by ship across the Atlantic Ocean.

**(9)** Technology has also brought about economic innovations that made traditional methods of wealth-gathering obsolete. Wealth is no longer dependent on land ownership or natural resources. Wealth is generated in new ways in a technologically advanced world. There is not as much need to go to war to order to acquire wealth through acquisition of physical assets. Physical assets are no longer the basis of wealth or war.

**(10)** Another peace-promoting innovation that democracy brought to the world was the peaceful succession of leaders chosen by majority vote. In most cases, in a democracy, the people who did not vote for a leader submit to his or her leadership until a candidate more to their liking can be elected. This makes the transition from one leader to another peaceful. Notable exceptions are civil wars—including the American Civil War, when the South seceded from the nation as soon as Abraham Lincoln was elected president. Still, in modern times, there are few violent uprisings in democracies, and even civil wars are on the wane. People can always work "within the system" to bring about change when they are dissatisfied in a democracy.

**(11)** Because democracy is a system of voting, a leader may be changed by the people voting the leader out of office. This holds leaders accountable in ways military dictatorships or tyrannies cannot. As anti-war feeling grows all over the world (and the Human Security Report holds that such feeling is indeed growing) democratically elected leaders must answer to this feeling when considering waging war. This acts as a break upon engaging in war.

**43. What would be a good alternative title to this essay?**

   A.  No alternative
   B.  War on the Wane
   C.  Peace through Strength
   D.  An Anxious World

**44. What would be an effective editorial decision regarding paragraphs 1 and 2?**

   F.  No change
   G.  move them to the end of the essay
   H.  delete paragraph 2
   J.  switch their order so that paragraph 2 opens the essay

**45. The author wants to add the following paragraph to the passage. Where would be a good place to put this addition?**

**In short, the world is becoming a more peaceful place. If this trend continues (and there is no reason to believe it will not) future generations can look forward to a time when war will be a thing of the past.**

   A.  No place
   B.  between paragraphs 3 and 4
   C.  as a concluding paragraph
   D.  as the introductory paragraph

The following passage, an excerpt from *The Cask of Amontillado* by Edgar Allan Poe, is the basis for Questions 46-48:

## The Cask of Amontillado

**(1)** The thousand injuries of Fortunato I had borne as I best could, but when he ventured upon insult, I vowed revenge. You, who so well know the nature of my soul, will not suppose, however, that I gave utterance <u>at a threat.</u> At length I would be avenged; this was a point definitely settled—but the very
46
definitiveness with which it was resolved, <u>precluded </u>the idea of risk. I must not only punish, but punish
47
with impunity. <u>A wrong is unredressed when retribution overtakes its redresser. It is equally unredressed</u>
48
<u>when the avenger fails to make himself felt as such to him who has done the wrong.</u>

**46. Which of the following changes, if any, should be applied to underlined section 46?**

    F.  No change
    G.  to a threat
    H.  of a threat
    J.  by a threat

**47. In underlined section 47, what might be a synonym for the word "precluded"?**

    A.  concluded
    B.  obtruded
    C.  intruded
    D.  excluded

**48. What would be a good summary of paragraph 1?**

    F.  Fortunato is being unjustly accused by the narrator.
    G.  Fortunato has offended the narrator many times, but the narrator does not believe in vengeance for the redress of wrongs.
    H.  Fortunato has offended the narrator many times, and the narrator wants revenge. He does not want to be caught or punished for his revenge, though, and he wants Fortunato to know it was him who caused Fortunato pain.
    J.  Fortunato has offended the narrator, but the narrator would never threaten him or do any other damage, so the narrator is caught in a moral dilemma.

The following passage, an excerpt from *The Cask of Amontillado* by Edgar Allan Poe, is the basis for Questions 49-50:

**(2)** <u>It must be understood that neither by word nor deed had I given Fortunato cause to doubt my good</u>
49
will. <u>I continued, as was my wont, to smile in his face</u>, and he did not perceive that my smile now was at the thought of his <u>immolation.</u>
50

      

**49. From underlined section 49 we can understand that the narrator is a man of:**

    A. honesty
    B. cunning
    C. integrity
    D. unselfishness

**50. In underlined section 50, from the context of what has gone before in the passage, the meaning of the word "immolation" is:**

    F. destruction
    G. verification
    H. justification
    J. imitation

---

**The following passage, an excerpt from *The Cask of Amontillado* by Edgar Allan Poe, is the basis for Questions 51-55:**

**(3)** He had a weak point—this Fortunato—<u>although in other regards he was a man to be respected and</u>
51

<u>even feared.</u> He prided himself on his connoisseurship in wine. Few Italians have the true virtuoso spirit.

For the most part their enthusiasm is adopted to suit the time and opportunity—to practise imposture

upon the British and Austrian millionaires. In painting and gemmary, Fortunato, like his countrymen, was a

quack—but in the matter of old wines he was sincere. In this respect I did not differ from him materially: I

was skillful in the Italian vintages myself, and <u>bought largely whenever I could.</u>
52

**(4)** It was about dusk, one evening during the supreme madness of the carnival season, that I

encountered my friend. He accosted me with excessive warmth, for he had been drinking much. The man

wore motley. He had on a tight-fitting parti-striped dress, and his head was surmounted by the conical cap

and bells. <u>I was as pleased to see him</u>, that I thought I should never have done wringing his hand.
53

**(5)** I said to him—"My dear Fortunato, you are luckily met. How remarkably well you are looking to-day!

But I have received a pipe [cask] of what passes for Amontillado, and I have my doubts."

**(6)** "How?" said he. "Amontillado? A pipe [cask]? Impossible! And in the middle of the carnival!"

**(7)** "I have my doubts," I replied; "and I was silly enough to pay the full Amontillado price without consulting

you in the matter. You were not to be found, and I was fearful of losing a bargain."

**(8)** "Amontillado!"

---

**(9)** "I have his doubts."
54

**(10)** "Amontillado!"

**(11)** "And I must satisfy them."

**(12)** "Amontillado!"
55

**51. Which of the following changes, if any, should be applied to underlined section 51?**

- A.  No change
- B.  although in other regards he was a man to be respected and feared even.
- C.  even although in other regards he was a man to be respected and feared.
- D.  although in other regards he was an even man to be respected and feared.

**52. From the context of the sentence, the meaning of underlined section 52 may be understood to be:**

- F.  the narrator rarely bought wine
- G.  the narrator spent generously on wine whenever he could
- H.  the narrator only bought when his bank balance was large
- J.  the narrator bought wine with grand gestures and much bragging

**53. Which of the following changes, if any, should be applied to underlined section 53?**

- A.  No change
- B.  I was as pleased as punch to see him
- C.  I was pleased so as to see him
- D.  I was so pleased to see him

**54. Which of the following changes, if any, should be applied to underlined section 54?**

- F.  No change
- G.  I have my doubts.
- H.  I have much doubts.
- J.  I have had doubts.

**55. Which of the following changes, if any, should be applied to underlined section 55?**

- A.  No change
- B.  delete it as unnecessary repetition
- C.  "Amontillado! Good heavens, man!"
- D.  "Amontillado."

---

**The following passage, an excerpt from *The Cask of Amontillado* by Edgar Allan Poe, is the basis for Questions 56-57:**

(13) "As you are engaged, I am on my way to Luchesi. If any one has a critical turn, it is he. He will tell me—"

(14) "Luchesi cannot tell Amontillado from Sherry."

(15) "And yet some fools will have it that his taste is a match for your own."

(16) "Come, let us go."

(17) <u>"Whither?"</u>
      56

(18) "To your vaults."

(19) "My friend, no; I will not impose upon your good nature. <u>I percieve you have an</u> engagement.
                                                                                        57
Luchesi—"

(20) "I have no engagement;—come."

---

56. **From the context of the passage, the meaning of underlined section 56 may be understood to be:**

   F.  Who?
   G.  When?
   H.  What?
   J.  Where?

57. **Which of the following changes, if any, should be applied to underlined section 57?**

   A.  No change
   B.  I perceive you have an
   C.  I percieve you have a
   D.  It is to be perceived that you have an

**The following passage, an excerpt from *The Cask of Amontillado* by Edgar Allan Poe, is the basis for Questions 58-60:**

# The Cask of Amontillado

**(1)** The thousand injuries of Fortunato I had borne as I best could, but when he ventured upon insult, I vowed revenge. You, who so well know the nature of my soul, will not suppose, however, that I gave utterance at a threat. At length I would be avenged; this was a point definitely settled—but the very definitiveness with which it was resolved, precluded the idea of risk. I must not only punish, but punish with impunity. A wrong is unredressed when retribution overtakes its redresser. It is equally unredressed when the avenger fails to make himself felt as such to him who has done the wrong.

**(2)** It must be understood that neither by word nor deed had I given Fortunato cause to doubt my good will. I continued, as was my wont, to smile in his face, and he did not perceive that my smile now was at the thought of his immolation.

**(3)** He had a weak point—this Fortunato—although in other regards he was a man to be respected and even feared. He prided himself on his connoisseurship in wine. Few Italians have the true virtuoso spirit. For the most part their enthusiasm is adopted to suit the time and opportunity—to practise imposture upon the British and Austrian millionaires. In painting and gemmary, Fortunato, like his countrymen, was a quack—but in the matter of old wines he was sincere. In this respect I did not differ from him materially: I was skillful in the Italian vintages myself, and bought largely whenever I could.

**(4)** It was about dusk, one evening during the supreme madness of the carnival season, that I encountered my friend. He accosted me with excessive warmth, for he had been drinking much. The man wore motley. He had on a tight-fitting parti-striped dress, and his head was surmounted by the conical cap and bells. I was as pleased to see him, that I thought I should never have done wringing his hand.

**(5)** I said to him—"My dear Fortunato, you are luckily met. How remarkably well you are looking to-day! But I have received a pipe [cask] of what passes for Amontillado, and I have my doubts."

**(6)** "How?" said he. "Amontillado? A pipe [cask]? Impossible! And in the middle of the carnival!"

**(7)** "I have my doubts," I replied; "and I was silly enough to pay the full Amontillado price without consulting you in the matter. You were not to be found, and I was fearful of losing a bargain."

**(8)** "Amontillado!"

**(9)** "I have his doubts."

**(10)** "Amontillado!"

**(11)** "And I must satisfy them."

**(12)** "Amontillado!"

**(13)** "As you are engaged, I am on my way to Luchesi. If any one has a critical turn, it is he. He will tell me—"

**(14)** "Luchesi cannot tell Amontillado from Sherry."

**(15)** "And yet some fools will have it that his taste is a match for your own."

**(16)** "Come, let us go."

**(17)** "Whither?"

**(18)** "To your vaults."

**(19)** "My friend, no; I will not impose upon your good nature. I percieve you have an engagement. Luchesi—"

**(20)** "I have no engagement;—come."

58. **In the passage, the narrator is luring Fortunato by playing on Fortunato's weak point. From the text, we can infer this weak point is:**

    F. Fortunato's pride
    G. Fortunato's alcoholism
    H. Fortunato's respect for Luchesi
    J. Fortunato's affection for the narrator

59. **This passage is written in what style?**

    A. third person narrative
    B. second person narrative
    C. first person narrative
    D. third person singular narrative

60. **From whose point of view is the story told and is this a reliable or unreliable point of view?**

    F. the story is told from the point of view of an omniscient narrator
    G. the story is told from the point of view of an unreliable narrator
    H. the story is told from the point of view of a reliable narrator
    J. the story is told from the point of view of Fortunato

The following passage, an 1851 letter from Abraham Lincoln to a step-brother who was continually borrowing from him, is the basis for Questions 61-66:

## "You Shall Go to Work"

(Abraham Lincoln, a successful lawyer who had raised himself out of poverty, responded to a poor relative's frequent pleas for loans)

**(1)** Dear Johnston: Your request for eighty dollars I do not think it best to comply at now. At the various
                                                                                        61
times when I have helped you a little you have said to me, "We can get along very well now"; but in a very

short time I find you in the same difficulty again. Now, this can only happen by some defect in your

conduct.

**(2)** I doubt whether, since I saw you, you have done <u>a good whole days work</u> in one day. You do not very
                                                                                    62

much dislike to work, and still you do not work much, merely because it does not seem to you that you

could get much for it. <u>This habit of uselessly wasting time is the whole difficulty; it is vastly important to</u>
                                                                    63

<u>you, and still more to your children, that you should break the habit.</u> It is more important to them, because

they have longer to live, and can keep out of an idle habit before they are in it, easier than they can get

out after they are in.

**(3)** <u>You are now in need of some money</u>; and what I propose is, that you shall go to work, <u>"tooth and nail,"</u>
                                          64                                                                                    65

for somebody who will give you money for it. Let father <u>and you're boys take care of your things at home,</u>
                                                                                    66

prepare for a crop, and make the crop, and you go to work for the best money wages, or in discharge of

any debt you owe, that you can get; and to secure you a fair reward for your labor, I now promise you,

that for every dollar you will, between this and the first of May, get for your own labor, either in money or

as your own indebtedness, I will then give you one other dollar.

**61. Which of the following changes, if any, should be applied to underlined section 61?**

    A. No change
    B. to comply with now
    C. to comply as now
    D. to comply by now

**62. Which of the following changes, if any, should be applied to underlined section 62?**

    F. No change
    G. a good wholedays work
    H. a good whole days' work
    J. a good whole day's work

**63. In underlined section 63, why did Lincoln use a semi-colon to attach these sentences rather than break them up into two shorter sentences?**

    A. to show that, although they are independent clauses and can stand alone as sentences, the two thoughts are closely related to one another.
    B. to show that, because they are dependent clauses, they need this punctuation to tie them together.
    C. in the old days people used much longer sentences and used semi-colons as pauses
    D. he wanted to emphasize his point by using this exclamation point of punctuation

**64. Which of the following changes, if any, should be applied to underlined section 64?**

    F.  No change
    G.  You are now as often you are in need of some money
    H.  Again, you are now in need of some money again
    J.  You are not now in need of some money, but

**65. What alternative phrase might Lincoln have used that would be the same in meaning and style as underlined section 65?**

    A.  like a laggard
    B.  as hard as you can
    C.  betwixt and between
    D.  tiger and claw

**66. Which of the following changes, if any, should be applied to underlined section 66?**

    F.  No change
    G.  and your boys take care of your things at home,
    H.  and yore boys take care of your things at home,
    J.  and yours boys take care of your things at home,

---

**The following passage, an 1851 letter from Abraham Lincoln to a step-brother who was continually borrowing from him, is the basis for Questions 67-72:**

**(4)** By this, if you hire yourself at ten dollars a month, from me <u>you will get ten more making twenty dollars</u>
67
<u>a month</u> for your work. In this I do not mean <u>you are go</u> off to St. Louis, or the lead mines, or the gold
68
mines in California, but I mean for you <u>to go at it</u> for the best wages you can get close to home in Coles
69
County.

**(5)** Now, if you will do this, you will be soon out of debt, and what is better, you will have a habit that will keep you from getting in debt again. But, if I should now clear you out of debt, <u>next year you would be just</u>
70
<u>as deep in as ever.</u>

**(6)** You say you would almost give your place in heaven for seventy or eighty dollars. Then you value your place in heaven very cheap, for I am sure you can, with the offer I make, get the seventy or eighty dollars for four of five months' work. You say if I will furnish you the money you will deed me the land, and, if you don't pay the money back, you will deliver possession. <u>Nonsense!</u> If you can't now live with the
71
land, how will you then live without it?

(7) You have always been kind to me, and I do not mean to be unkind to you. On the contrary, if you will

but follow my advice, <u>you will find it worth more than eighty times eighty dollars to you.</u>
72

**67.** Which of the following changes, if any, should be applied to underlined section 67?

  A. No change
  B. you will get ten more making, twenty dollars a month
  C. you will get ten more making twenty dollars, a month
  D. you will get ten more, making twenty dollars a month

**68.** Which of the following changes, if any, should be applied to underlined section 68?

  F. No change
  G. you shall go
  H. you would have gone
  J. you are going

**69.** In underlined section 69, choosing the phrase "to go at it", Lincoln is trying to urge his stepbrother to:

  A. go for it
  B. make an attempt at it
  C. give it a try
  D. demand employment

**70.** Which of the following changes, if any, should be applied to underlined section 70?

  F. No change
  G. next year you are going to have been
  H. next year you will have been just as deep in as ever.
  J. next year you are just as deep in as ever

**71.** Which of the following changes, if any, should be applied to underlined section 71?

  A. No change
  B. Nonsense.
  C. Nonsense?
  D. Nonsense;

**72.** In underlined section 72, Lincoln is speaking:

  F. rhetorically
  G. categorically
  H. literally
  J. figuratively

> **The following passage, an 1851 letter from Abraham Lincoln to a step-brother who was continually borrowing from him, is the basis for Questions 73-75:**
>
> ## "You Shall Go to Work"
>
> (Abraham Lincoln, a successful lawyer who had raised himself out of poverty, responded to a poor relative's frequent pleas for loans)
>
> **(1)** Dear Johnston: Your request for eighty dollars I do not think it best to comply at now. At the various times when I have helped you a little you have said to me, "We can get along very well now"; but in a very short time I find you in the same difficulty again. Now, this can only happen by some defect in your conduct.
>
> **(2)** I doubt whether, since I saw you, you have done a good whole days work in one day. You do not very much dislike to work, and still you do not work much, merely because it does not seem to you that you could get much for it. This habit of uselessly wasting time is the whole difficulty; it is vastly important to you, and still more to your children, that you should break the habit. It is more important to them, because they have longer to live, and can keep out of an idle habit before they are in it, easier than they can get out after they are in.
>
> **(3)** You are now in need of some money; and what I propose is, that you shall go to work, "tooth and nail," for somebody who will give you money for it. Let father and you're boys take care of your things at home, prepare for a crop, and make the crop, and you go to work for the best money wages, or in discharge of any debt you owe, that you can get; and to secure you a fair reward for your labor, I now promise you, that for every dollar you will, between this and the first of May, get for your own labor, either in money or as your own indebtedness, I will then give you one other dollar.
>
> **(4)** By this, if you hire yourself at ten dollars a month, from me you will get ten more making twenty dollars a month for your work. In this I do not mean you are go off to St. Louis, or the lead mines, or the gold mines in California, but I mean for you to go at it for the best wages you can get close to home in Coles County.
>
> **(5)** Now, if you will do this, you will be soon out of debt, and what is better, you will have a habit that will keep you from getting in debt again. But, if I should now clear you out of debt, next year you would be just as deep in as ever.
>
> **(6)** You say you would almost give your place in heaven for seventy or eighty dollars. Then you value your place in heaven very cheap, for I am sure you can, with the offer I make, get the seventy or eighty dollars for four of five months' work. You say if I will furnish you the money you will deed me the land, and, if you don't pay the money back, you will deliver possession. Nonsense! If you can't now live with the land, how will you then live without it?
>
> **(7)** You have always been kind to me, and I do not mean to be unkind to you. On the contrary, if you will but follow my advice, you will find it worth more than eighty times eighty dollars to you.

### 73. What old saying most exemplifies the theme of this letter?

    A. I must being cruel to be kind
    B. a penny saved is a penny earned
    C. he who laughs last laughs best
    D. four score and seven years ago

**74. What is the emotional tone of Lincoln's letter?**

    F.  secretly rejoicing at his stepbrother's misfortune
    G.  superiority from one who has succeeded over one who has failed
    H.  stern yet caring
    J.  regretful that he cannot help more and hopeless about the future

**75. What can the reader glean about Johnston from the passage?**

    A.  he is a hard-working man who has fallen on hard times
    B.  he has some attitudes and habits that have led him into financial trouble
    C.  he is an evil man who is mortgaging his children's future to pay for his own excesses
    D.  he helped Lincoln succeed and is only now asking for some compensation

# ENGLISH PRACTICE TEST 3 ANSWER KEY

| | |
|---|---|
| 1. C | 39. D |
| 2. G | 40. J |
| 3. D | 41. C |
| 4. J | 42. G |
| 5. B | 43. B |
| 6. J | 44. J |
| 7. B | 45. C |
| 8. H | 46. G |
| 9. D | 47. D |
| 10. F | 48. H |
| 11. A | 49. B |
| 12. J | 50. F |
| 13. B | 51. A |
| 14. J | 52. G |
| 15. C | 53. D |
| 16. J | 54. G |
| 17. B | 55. A |
| 18. J | 56. J |
| 19. C | 57. B |
| 20. F | 58. F |
| 21. A | 59. C |
| 22. G | 60. G |
| 23. C | 61. B |
| 24. G | 62. J |
| 25. D | 63. A |
| 26. G | 64. F |
| 27. C | 65. B |
| 28. F | 66. G |
| 29. A | 67. D |
| 30. G | 68. G |
| 31. A | 69. A |
| 32. G | 70. F |
| 33. B | 71. A |
| 34. J | 72. J |
| 35. A | 73. A |
| 36. J | 74. H |
| 37. C | 75. B |
| 38. H | |

# ENGLISH PRACTICE TEST 3 RATIONALES

## 1. Answer: C. compares
"Nothing", which is the subject of the sentence, is a singular noun and requires the singular form of the verb "compares" for subject-verb agreement.

## 2. Answer: G. which was packed
"Was packed" is a past participle. Past participles may be used to form the passive voice. In this case, "was packed" is referring to "the passenger list" and is appropriate.

## 3. Answer: D. April 14, 1912
Commas are placed between the day of the month and the year in dates.

## 4. Answer: J. alliteration
Alliteration is the use of the same or similar initial consonant sounds in words close to one another in a sentence. It is used for emphasis and drama.

## 5. Answer: B. "The *Titanic* is unsinkable!"
This is a direct quotation of what some people said; therefore, the punctuation goes inside the closing quotation mark.

## 6. Answer: J. Yes, it is implied that the wireless radio operator of the *California* may have gone to bed because he was disheartened by arrogant treatment from the *Titanic's* radio operator.
The fact that the wireless operator went to bed soon after being told off implies, within the context of the paragraph about arrogance, that he might have been affected by the rudeness of *Titanic's* radio operator.

## 7. Answer: B. that the ship itself, rather than the ship's doctor or crew, had concerns about health
The words "The ship had to consider" implies that the ship itself had to take health concerns into consideration. Of course, a ship cannot do such things. The sentence should be corrected to include people or a person.

## 8. Answer: H. British parliamentary papers
"British" is a proper noun and needs capitalization; the other nouns are not proper nouns and do not require capitalization.

## 9. Answer: D. Sadly, less than fifty percent of third class women survived
Question 9 calls for a modern style of phrasing. "Sadly" is modern in that it is succinct and commonly used.

## 10. Answer: F. No change
The sentence is correct as it is.

## 11. Answer: A. equal or comparable to
The dictionary definition of "parity" is equal or equivalent. Gleaning meaning from the context of the sentence and paragraph, third class accommodations on the *Titanic* were the same quality as second class accommodations on other ships.

## 12. Answer: J. society's code of honor
"Society" is a collective noun. Collective nouns, even though they refer to a plurality, are punctuated to show possession the same way singular nouns are: with an apostrophe "s".

## 13. Answer: B. that the chances of survival on the *Titanic* had less to do with income or social status than it did with gender
The title of the passage ends with a question mark, indicating that the author is questioning whether class determined the survival rates on the *Titanic*. The description of the accommodations being comparable to

higher classes on other ships, as well as the statistics from the British parliamentary papers show that women and children of all classes survived at higher rates than did men of all classes. This shows that Answer B. is correct for it notes that gender was the greatest indicator for survival on the *Titanic*.

### 14. Answer: J. between paragraph 11 and 12
Paragraph 11 ends the recounting of the percentage of survivors from each class, and Paragraph 12 sums up the idea that class differences were more important to Hollywood than in reality. Between these two paragraphs is the best place to introduce more argument that class differences were not as pronounced in reality as in the movie.

### 15. Answer: C. Yes, because the essay presents some points in favor of arrogance contributing to the disaster and some points against it, and it specifically refutes some assertions of the movie with facts and figures.
This is correct because the essay attempts balance through acknowledging some arrogance surrounding the *Titanic* yet refutes with facts and figures the idea that third class passengers were marked for death by class snobbery.

### 16. Answer: J. She had never had a slave under her control
There is no need for any transition words like therein, therefore, or thenceforth, as the sentence is a complete thought without these words.

### 17. Answer: B. I could not approach her as I was accustomed to approach other white ladies.
There is no need for the word "so" in the sentence. It does not connect equal elements of the sentence as a coordinating conjunction; it does not serve as a transitional word to indicate a logical relationship between parts of the sentence. The other choices either leave the incorrect "so" in the sentence or, as in Answer A., they do not remove it.

### 18. Answer: J. to be disturbed
There is no need for quotation marks in this sentence. The author is not quoting anyone, directly or indirectly. The word is not an unusual word used in an unusual way and requires no quotation marks to distinguish it.

### 19. Answer: C. Absolute power corrupts absolutely.
Douglass is clearly saying that having too much power in her hands under a system with no accountability (slavery) turned a kind mistress into a cruel one. The sentence "The fatal poison of irresponsible power was already in her hands, and soon commenced its infernal work" demonstrates this.

### 20. Answer: F. No change
In the sentence, the words "under the influence of slavery" are not absolutely necessary to the meaning of the sentence. They are there for emphasis, but the meaning would be unchanged without them. This is called a "nonrestrictive element". Nonrestrictive elements (nonessential elements) are set off with commas. This sentence does this, so no change is necessary.

### 21. Answer: A. that some material has been taken out
An ellipsis or ellipses (three periods) always indicates that some material from the original text has been edited out.

### 22. Answer: G. treat me as a human being was not only wrong
"a" is used before consonants; "an" is used before vowels, so "a human being" is correct.

### 23. Answer: C. slavery was morally corrupting for both slaves and slave owners
Douglass makes the point several times in these paragraphs that slavery corrupted his mistress and changed her from a kind person into a cruel one. His words about "crouching servility" and his surprise at the fact that his mistress initially treated him like a human being imply that slavery was morally corrupting for slaves as well.

**24. Answer: G. She had bread for the hungry**
Pronouns like myself, yourself, himself, herself, ourselves, and yourselves are sometimes used as intensive pronouns. They are used for emphasis: "The President himself visited the wounded soldier." However, in this sentence, there is no need for the emphasis. The straightforward sentence "She had bread for the hungry" is correct.

**25. Answer: D. anger and outrage at the pernicious power of slavery to corrupt people's characters**
Douglass's strong language of contrast (a tender heart becoming like stone, a lamb-like personality becoming one of tiger-like fierceness) expresses anger and outrage at slavery's "ability" to "influence" human nature in a negative way.

**26. Answer: G. husband's precepts**
The "precepts" in the sentence belong to the husband, showing possession. "Husband" is a singular noun. The singular possessive form is apostrophe "s" after the noun that has possession.

**27. Answer: C. She was an apt woman**
Usually adjectives are placed before the noun they modify, so "apt woman" is better than "woman apt"; "an" is used before a word starting with a vowel.

**28. Answer: F. the whole length**
"Give him an inch and he takes a yard" is a common expression; "ell" may be surmised from the context of the sentence to mean a measurement of a whole length.

**29. Answer: A. The Corrupting Effects of Slavery on Mistress and Man**
As discussed previously, this portion of Douglass's book focuses on how a kind mistress became a cruel one once the unchecked power of slavery was in her hands. Douglass's initial shock at being treated well by her, described at the beginning of the passage, shows that slaves expected ill treatment and groveled to try to avoid it, corrupting their own characters.

**30. Answer: G. She went from being mild-mannered, charitable, and helpful to being temperamental and cruel.**
Words such as "This kind heart had but a short time to remain such. The fatal poison of irresponsible power was already in her hands...That cheerful eye, under the influence of slavery, soon became red with rage; that voice, made all of sweet accord, changed to one of harsh and horrid discord" show that Answer B. is the most accurate description of the mistress's evolution.

**31. Answer: A. No change**
"Which" is a relative pronoun introducing an adjective clause describing the nouns "land and natural resources". The descriptive adjective clause is not absolutely necessary to the sentence (it could be removed without significantly altering the meaning) so it is set off with commas.

**32. Answer: G. its promises of peace.**
"Its" is a possessive pronoun that needs no apostrophe. "It's" is a contraction of "it is" and is incorrect.

**33. Answer: B. optimistic**
The tone of the passage is optimistic as it is talking about a reduction in the numbers of international conflicts per year. This is exemplified in underlined section 33 as a joyful announcement emphasized with an exclamation point.

**34. Answer: J. millennium**
"Millennium" is the correct spelling of the word.

**35. Answer: A. No revision**
Two sentences is the minimum length for a paragraph, so the paragraph is correct in length. Switching the sentences or editing the paragraph out interrupts the sense of the paragraph and the essay.

**36. Answer: J. Spreading all over the globe, democracies rarely go to war with one another.**
A dangling modifier is when a phrase such as "spreading all over the globe" lacks a proper subject or is unrelated to the subject of the sentence. It is "dangling" because it has nothing to attach itself to with any meaning. In this case, democracies, not wars, are spreading all over the globe, so moving democracies into the subject position, as in Answer D., corrects the dangling modifier.

**37. Answer: C. the number of wars naturally decreases.**
"Number" is the subject of the sentence, and it is a collective singular noun, so for subject-verb agreement, "decreases" is correct.

**38. Answer: H. pragmatic**
When something is "pragmatic" it is down-to-earth and practical. Paragraph 7 discusses pragmatic reasons why democracies do not go to war with one another: they have strong economic ties and do not want to risk them.

**39. Answer: D. irony**
One meaning of irony is that there is contrast or incongruity between two things that is somewhat humorous or sardonic. It is ironic in our electronic, information age to contemplate the idea that a war started because messages had to be carried from nation to nation by transatlantic shipping.

**40. Answer: J. redundancy**
The sentence repeats the same thought as has gone previously and is therefore a redundancy.

**41. Answer: C. on the decrease**
To "wane" means to recede, decrease, or lose power. This can be determined from the context of the section, as it states that there are fewer violent uprisings now.

**42. Answer: G. This acts as a brake upon engaging in war.**
In the context of the sentence, the word "brake" shows that war is stopped or prevented, so the mechanical device that stops momentum, a "brake", is the right word to use.

**43. Answer: B. War on the Wane**
The essay is about the decrease of wars in the new millennium, therefore "War on the Wane" is more appropriate than the other answer choices.

**44. Answer: J. switch their order so that paragraph 2 opens the essay**
Going from the general to the specific is a good way to begin an essay.

**45. Answer: C. as a concluding paragraph**
This paragraph sums up the essay's points and argument and draws a reasonable and thought-provoking conclusion.

**46. Answer: G. to a threat**
We give utterance "to" a pronouncement. "To" is the correct preposition in this sentence.

**47. Answer: D. excluded**
Answer D. is the closest to a synonym, for the definition of precluded is "ruled out" or "ruled out in advance".

**48. Answer: H. Fortunato has offended the narrator many times, and the narrator wants revenge. He does not want to be caught or punished for his revenge, though, and he wants Fortunato to know it was him who caused Fortunato pain.**
The words "The thousand injuries of Fortunato" show that the narrator was offended many times. The phrase "I vowed revenge" show the narrator wants revenge. Yet the narrator does not feel wrong is redressed "when the avenger fails to make himself felt" to the one who wronged him, so the narrator wants Fortunato to know it was him who caused Fortunato's pain.

**49. Answer: B. cunning**
The narrator is hiding his desire for revenge under a smile; he does not indicate by word or deed that he is plotting revenge. From this, we may say that the narrator is cunning.

**50. Answer: F. destruction**
The narrator is clearly planning to do something vengeful to Fortunato to his destruction. None of the other answers make sense in the context of the passage.

**51. Answer: A. No change**
The sentence is correct as it is; all the other choices are incorrect.

**52. Answer: G. the narrator spent generously on wine whenever he could**
"Largely" is a synonym for "generously", so if he bought "largely" it means he spent generously whenever he could.

**53. Answer: D. I was so pleased to see him**
"So" is an adverb modifying "pleased"; it tells how pleased the narrator was to see Fortunato. "As" would set up a comparison, which is not the point of the sentence, so the sentence must be revised. Adding in words as in Answer B. does not benefit the sentence and the word addition in Answer C. is incorrect.

**54. Answer: G. I have my doubts.**
The possessive pronoun "my" fits with the subject of the sentence, which is "I". The possessive pronoun "he" is wrong.

**55. Answer: A. No change**
Poe deliberately used repetition here in order to impress on the reader how rare and enticing this wine would be. The wine is the "bait" for his revenge.

**56. Answer: J. Where?**
Fortunato has suggested they "go"; this implies they should go to some place. He also says "to your vaults" so they are going to a definite place. "Where" is the relative pronoun used to indicate place, as in "Where should we go?" "Where are we going?" "Where did you put the pencil?"

**57. Answer: B. I perceive you have an**
The rule "i before e except after c" makes Answer B. correct. Answer B. also correctly uses "an" before the word "engagement". If the word being modified starts with a vowel, "an" rather than "a" is used.

**58. Answer: F. Fortunato's pride**
In paragraph 3, the narrator mentions that Fortunato has a weak point; he prides himself on his good taste in wine. The narrator appeals to Fortunato's pride by saying he has a rare wine that requires discerning taste. He also plays upon Fortunato's pride by saying he will ask a rival of Fortunato's to taste the wine instead.

**59. Answer: C. first person narrative**
The first person narrative is always characterized by the author using the pronoun "I".

**60. Answer: G. the story is told from the point of view of an unreliable narrator**
The narrator is full of vengeance and cunning, and he is determined to bring about Fortunato's destruction. As such, he is an unreliable narrator. If the story were told from Fortunato's or someone else's point of view, the reader might see things quite differently.

**61. Answer: B. to comply with now**

In common usage, the preposition that is used following the verb "comply" is "with", as in "The company required the workers to wear hardhats to comply with state and federal safety policies."

**62. Answer: J. a good whole day's work**

The work referred to is "of the day". The work belongs to the day, so it takes the possessive case. The possessive case for a singular noun requires an apostrophe between the noun and the "s".

**63. Answer: A. to show that, although they are independent clauses and can stand alone as sentences, the two thoughts are closely related to one another.**

Lincoln uses a semi-colon here to tie two independent clauses together, as is grammatically correct. Stylistically, he did this because the two thoughts are closely related and important for the reader to consider together.

**64. Answer: F. No change**

The phrase is correct as it is.

**65. Answer: B. as hard as you can**

The expression "tooth and nail" means to fight for something as hard as a person can.

**66. Answer: G. and your boys take care of your things at home,**

Lincoln is using imperative sentences (command sentences) to advise his stepbrother what to do. The implied subject is "you". "You're" as in underlined section 66, is the contraction of "you are", so it is incorrect. "Your" is the correct possessive form used with "you".

**67. Answer: D. you will get ten more, making twenty dollars a month**

A comma usually precedes a participial phrase like "making twenty dollars a month" if the phrase is non-essential to the meaning of the sentence. "Making twenty dollars a month" makes things more clear, but it is not necessary to the meaning of the sentence.

**68. Answer: G. you shall go**

The sentence does not make sense as it is, so it must be corrected. Lincoln is speaking of future actions, so the tense should be the future tense: "you shall go".

**69. Answer: A. go for it**

The entire letter is urging his stepbrother to try harder ("go for it") in his work life. "Go at it" is a stylistic choice, urging his stepbrother to try harder.

**70. Answer: F. No change**

"Would" is used in sentences where something is contingent upon certain conditions in the future. Paired with "if", which sets up such a condition in the future ("if I should now clear you out of debt") it is appropriate to use "would be", so the sentence is correct as it is.

**71. Answer: A. No change**

Lincoln's use of an exclamation point is proper to emphasize the absurdity of the idea.

**72. Answer: J. figuratively**

Lincoln is not attaching a literal or specific and real monetary amount to his advice; he is simply saying that, if heeded, it will multiply his stepbrother's financial benefits many times over. He is speaking figuratively.

**73. Answer: A. I must be cruel to be kind**

Lincoln must perform the "cruelty" of refusing a loan in order to urge his stepbrother to change his bad habits. However, this is a kindness, because, as Lincoln points out, his stepbrother and his whole family suffer from his bad habits. It is an example of "tough love" or being "cruel" in order to help someone take more responsibility and ultimately have a better life.

**74. Answer: H. stern yet caring**
Lincoln firmly refuses the loan and tells his stepbrother why in very clear terms. The emotional tone is stern with such utterances as "Nonsense!" and the firmness and honesty of the refusal. However, Lincoln also offers concrete help in that he will match his stepbrother's earnings. He also expresses care for his stepbrother's family and his stepbrother's future.

**75. Answer: B. he has some attitudes and habits that have led him into financial trouble**
Lincoln feels his stepbrother has some attitudes and habits he must change in order to succeed. Lincoln says, "You do not work much, merely because it does not seem to you that you could get much for it." This is an attitude Lincoln thinks his stepbrother must change in order to succeed. Lincoln also says that his stepbrother's habits are the problem: "This habit of uselessly wasting time is the whole difficulty."

# MATHEMATICS PRACTICE TEST 3

60 Minutes - 60 Questions

Directions: Each question has five answer choices. Choose the best answer for each question.

1. **A 6 foot fence post casts a 4 foot shadow. On level ground, what would be the height of a nearby building if its shadow is 28 feet long?**

   A. 18
   B. 21
   C. 32
   D. 42
   E. 56

2. **The cost to join a movie rental club is $80.00 for annual dues and $12.00 per month for unlimited rentals. If Arnie has paid the club $164.00, how many monthly payments has he made?**

   F. 7
   G. 6
   H. 5
   J. 4
   K. 3

3. **If $\dfrac{2x}{5} + 3 = -11$, then x =?**

   A. $-\dfrac{7}{2}$
   B. -7
   C. -14
   D. -32.5
   E. -35

4. $4x^5 \times 7x^2 = ?$

   F. $28x^{10}$
   G. $28x^7$
   H. $11x^{10}$
   J. $11x^7$
   K. $3x^3$

5. **A rectangle has a width that measures 8 units and a length that measures 12 units. If P represents the perimeter of the rectangle and A represents the area of the rectangle, what is the value of P – A?**

   A. -76
   B. -66
   C. -56
   D. 56
   E. 96

6. For what value of n is the equation $\frac{n}{18} = \frac{8}{12}$ true?

   F. 2
   G. 6
   H. 8
   J. 12
   K. 16

7. In the figure below, D, A, and C are collinear and $\overline{BA} = \overline{BC}$. What is the value of $x$?

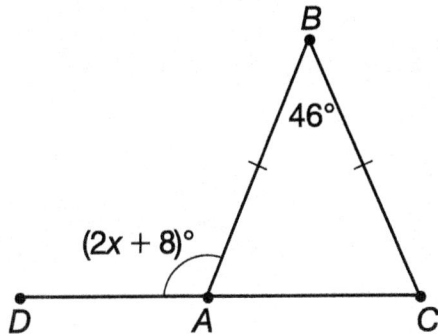

   A. 53
   B. 52.5
   C. 52
   D. 46
   E. 21.6

8. If $f(x) = -2x^2 + 3x - 7$, then $f(-4)$ = ?

   F. -67
   G. -51
   H. -4
   J. 4
   K. 13

9. The histogram below shows the number of students who attend a certain elementary school. What is the median of the histogram?

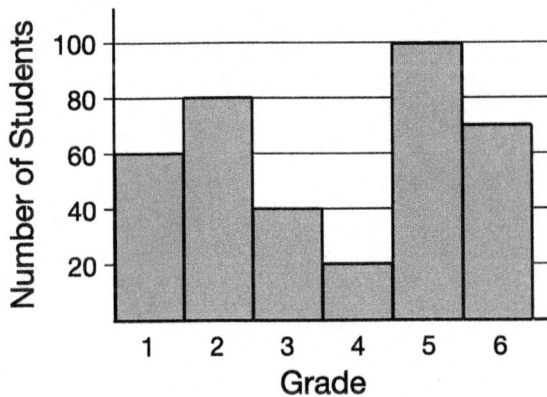

A. 80
B. 65
C. $61\dfrac{2}{3}$
D. 40
E. 25

**10. A lunch special at a certain restaurant offers the following choices:**

**Entrée: pizza slice, cheeseburger, or burrito**
**Side order: cole slaw, french fries, or cooked vegetable**
**Drink: soda, water, iced tea, or coffee**

**How many combinations of entrée, side order, and drink are available to the customer?**

F. 48
G. 36
H. 24
J. 10
K. 3

**11. What regular polygon has an exterior angle that measures 72°?**

A. Parallelogram
B. Square
C. Pentagon
D. Hexagon
E. Octagon

**12. For all values of $r$, what is the value of $(4r+5)^2$ ?**

F. $16r+25$
G. $16r^2+25$
H. $16r^2+40r+25$
J. $81r^2$
K. $400r^2$

**13. Factor the expression $x^4-81$ completely.**

A. $(x-9)^2$
B. $(x+9)(x-9)$
C. $x^2(x+9)(x-9)$
D. $(x^2+9)(x^2-9)$
E. $(x^2+9)(x+3)(x-3)$

**14. If -7(n – 8) = 14, then n = ?**

    F.  6

    G.  $\dfrac{15}{7}$

    H.  $\dfrac{11}{7}$

    J.  $-\dfrac{4}{7}$

    K.  -6

**15. What is the value of** $-6\begin{pmatrix} -9 & 6 \\ 4 & -4 \end{pmatrix}$ **?**

    A.  -72

    B.  -36

    C.  12

    D.  18

    E.  72

**16. Squares ABCD and CEFG are adjacent. If ABCD has an area measuring 16 square units and CEFG has an area measuring 8 square units, what is the perimeter of the figure below?**

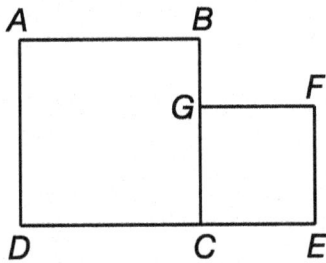

    F.  $16+8\sqrt{2}$

    G.  $16+4\sqrt{2}$

    H.  $12+6\sqrt{2}$

    J.  24

    K.  12

17. The slope of the line containing points (7,-2) and (5,y) is $-\dfrac{2}{3}$. What is the value of y?

    A.   $-\dfrac{2}{3}$

    B.   $-\dfrac{1}{3}$

    C.   $\dfrac{1}{3}$

    D.   $\dfrac{2}{3}$

    E.   $\dfrac{3}{2}$

18. What is the quotient of $6\dfrac{2}{3}$ and $5\dfrac{1}{6}$ ?

    F.   $\dfrac{11}{9}$

    G.   $\dfrac{13}{11}$

    H.   $\dfrac{27}{23}$

    J.   $\dfrac{40}{31}$

    K.   $\dfrac{310}{9}$

19. Federal law requires that all public facilities be handicapped-accessible. If a wheelchair ramp in front of a public building has an angle of elevation of 3° and is 36 feet long, what is its height above the parking lot? (Express your answer to nearest tenth of a foot.)

    A.   1.7
    B.   1.8
    C.   1.9
    D.   2.4
    E.   4.7

**20.** A rectangle has an area measuring 168 square units and a width that measures 7 units. What is the length of the diagonal of the rectangle?

    F.  12
    G.  13
    H.  17
    J.  24
    K.  25

**21.** The vertices of rectangle ABCD in a standard coordinate plane are (3,7), (3,0), (7,0), and (7,7). What are the coordinates of the point where the diagonals intersect?

    A.  (3,5.5)
    B.  (5,3.5)
    C.  (4,7)
    D.  (2.5,2.5)
    E.  (-2,2.5)

**22.** If $a = 2b^2$ and $b = c^3$, which equation expresses a in terms of c?

    F.  a = 8bc

    G.  $a = 2c^6$

    H.  $a = 2b^3 c^3$

    J.  $a = 2bc^3$

    K.  $a = c\sqrt[3]{2b}$

**23.** Each term after 3 is found by adding 1 to the term and then doubling the result. What is the sixth term in this series?

    **3, 8, 18, 38...**

    A.  39
    B.  78
    C.  152
    D.  158
    E.  168

**24.** In ⬜  , PC = 5 and AB = 24. What is the circumference of ⬜  ?

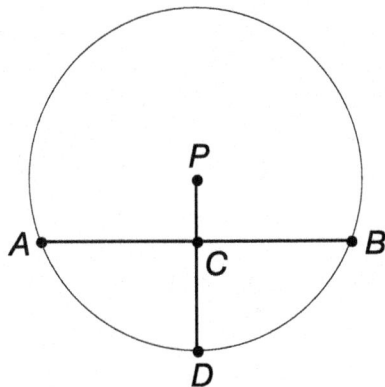

F. 13π
G. 26π
H. 169π
J. 676π
K. Cannot be determined from the information provided.

25. **James wants to put stone tiles in his patio area. The rectangular patio is 4 feet wide and 6 feet long. If each square tile has a perimeter of 1 foot, how many tiles will James need to purchase?**

    A. 576
    B. 384
    C. 64
    D. 32
    E. 24

26. **In the figure below, line l is parallel to line m. If** $m\angle 2 = (4x - 20)°$ **and** $m\angle 7 = (2x + 40)°$, **what is the measure of** $\angle 4$?

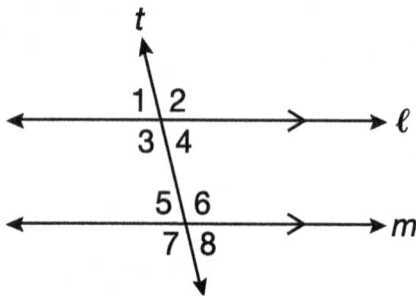

    F. 15°
    G. 25°
    H. 30°
    J. 60°
    K. 80°

27. **What does** $\dfrac{-2x^2 y^3}{-z^2}$ **equal if x =** $\dfrac{1}{2}$, **y = -2 and z = -4?**

    A. -2
    B. $-\dfrac{1}{4}$
    C. $\dfrac{3}{8}$
    D. 6
    E. 8

**28.** What is the equation of a line that is perpendicular to $y = -\dfrac{2}{3}x + 6$ and passes through (-6,3)?

F. $y = -\dfrac{2}{3}x - 1$

G. $y = \dfrac{3}{2}x + 12$

H. $y = -\dfrac{3}{2}x + 12$

J. $y = \dfrac{2}{3}x + 2$

K. $x = \dfrac{2}{3}y - 2$

**29.** $3\left[2 + 5(2 - b^2)\right]$ is equivalent to:

A. $15b^2 - 36$
B. $18b^2 + 15$
C. $36 - 15b^2$
D. $36 + 15b^2$
E. $21$

**30.** In the diagram below, $\overline{AB}$ is a radius of ⬚ and $\overline{BC}$ is tangent to the circle at point B. What is the value of x?

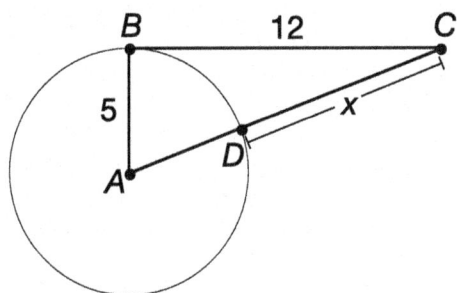

F. 5
G. 6
H. 6.5
J. 8
E. 13

**31. Simplify the following:** $\dfrac{x^3 - 1}{x^2 - 7x + 6}$

A. $\dfrac{x}{-7x + 6}$

B. $\dfrac{x}{7x - 6}$

C. $\dfrac{x^2 + x + 1}{x - 6}$

D. $\dfrac{x + 1}{x - 6}$

E. $\dfrac{x - 1}{x + 6}$

**32.** $\overline{AB}$ **has endpoints at A(6,-4) and B(2,-12) and midpoint M. What are the coordinates of the point that is** $\dfrac{1}{4}$ **of the distance from A to B?**

F.  (4,-8)
G.  (8,-4)
H.  (-10,3)
J.  (5,-6)
E.  (-6,4)

**33. If the** $\sin\theta = \dfrac{5}{13}$ **and** $\dfrac{\pi}{2} \le \theta < \pi$ **, what is** $\sec\theta$?

A. $\dfrac{5}{12}$

B. $\dfrac{5}{13}$

C. $-\dfrac{5}{12}$

D. $-\dfrac{12}{13}$

E. $-\dfrac{13}{12}$

**34.** The point A(-5,6) is translated using the rule $(x, y) \rightarrow (x-7, y+5)$. **What are the coordinates of A´, the coordinates of A after the translation?**

    F.  (-12,11)
    G.  (2,11)
    H.  (2,1)
    J.  (-7,5)
    K.  (7,-5)

**35.** One afternoon, Jenny ran at a rate of 5 miles per hour, rode her bicycle at a rate of 17 miles per hour, and rested. The graph below indicates that the order of resting, riding her bicycle, and running was:

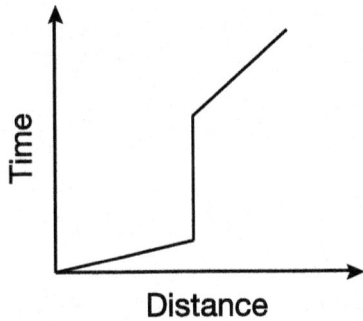

    A.  Rested, ran, rode
    B.  Rested, rode, ran
    C.  Ran, rested, rode
    D.  Rode, rested, ran
    E.  Ran, rode, rested

**36. Which of the following CANNOT be the slope of $\overline{OM}$?**

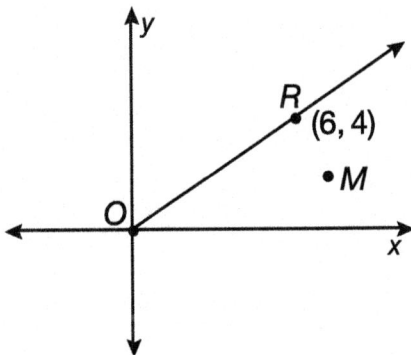

F. $\dfrac{1}{4}$

G. $\dfrac{1}{2}$

H. $\dfrac{3}{5}$

J. $\dfrac{5}{8}$

K. $\dfrac{17}{25}$

**37. What is the area of** $\sqcup$ **? (Express your answer to the nearest tenth of a square unit.)**

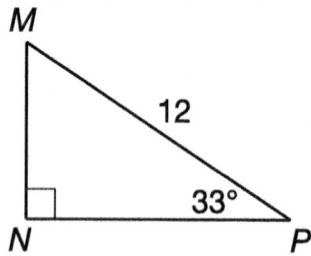

A. 14.8
B. 22.1
C. 29.4
D. 32.8
E. Cannot be determined from the information provided.

**38. Which of the following is the solution to the inequality** $11 - 6x > -2$ **?**

F. $x > \dfrac{13}{6}$

G. $x < \dfrac{13}{6}$

H. $x > \dfrac{3}{2}$

J. $x < \dfrac{3}{2}$

K. $x < -\dfrac{3}{2}$

39. ☐ has a radius that measures 8 units. If the circumference of the circle is subtracted from its area, what is the result?

    A. 6π
    B. 12π
    C. 24π
    D. 36π
    E. 48π

40. If C is the midpoint of $\overline{BD}$ and $\overline{AE}$, which congruence postulate proves ☐ ☐ ?

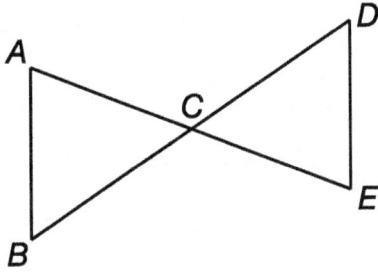

    F. SAS
    G. AAA
    H. ASA
    J. AAS
    K. SSS

41. In the target below, each ring is 2 inches wide and the bull's eye is 4 inches wide. What is the geometric probability of hitting the bull's eye?

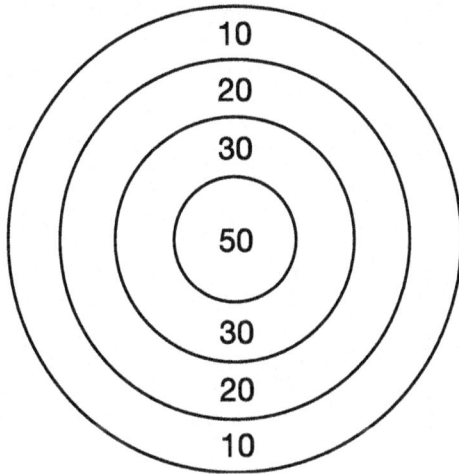

A. $\dfrac{1}{32}$

B. $\dfrac{1}{16}$

C. $\dfrac{1}{8}$

D. $\dfrac{1}{4}$

E. $\dfrac{1}{2}$

**Use the following information to answer questions 42-44.**

The attendance at the Boys Water Polo Team games was as follows:

| Date | Attendance |
|------|------------|
| 2/4  | 174 |
| 2/6  | 176 |
| 2/8  | 174 |
| 2/10 | 172 |
| 2/11 | 168 |
| 2/12 | 144 |

**42. Which number represents the mode of the data?**

F. 174
G. 173
H. 172
J. 170
K. 168

**43. What figure was the median of the attendance figures listed in the table?**

A. 173
B. 174
C. 176
D. 178
E. 180

**44. If M is the mean of the data and R is the range of the data, what is the value of M − R?**

F. 136
G. 142
H. 162
J. 168
K. 172

**45. What is the value of** $\log_3 81 + 2\log_5 125$ **?**

    A. 1,254
    B. 57
    C. 36
    D. 13
    E. 11

**46. What is the perimeter of the figure below?**

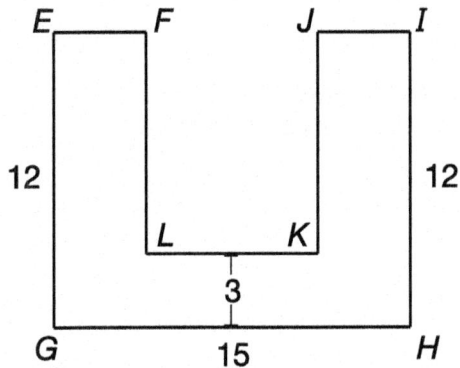

    F. 48
    G. 60
    H. 72
    J. 84
    K. 96

**47. In a particular class, one-half of the students dropped the class after the first test. After the second test, one-third of the remaining students dropped the class. If 16 students went on to take the third test, how many students were originally enrolled in the class?**

    A. 80
    B. 60
    C. 56
    D. 48
    E. 36

**48. Which of the following inequalities is the solution to the number line below?**

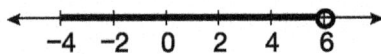

    F. $x > 6$ or $x < -4$
    G. $-4 < x \leq 6$
    H. $-4 < x < 6$
    J. $-4 \leq x < 6$
    K. $x > 6$ and $x \leq -4$

**49.** If $x = \dfrac{1}{8}$ and y = -6, what is the value of $(2x^{-2}y^{-3})^2$ ?

    A. -81
    B. -63
    C. $\dfrac{256}{729}$
    D. 0.6
    E. $\dfrac{5}{8}$

**50.** Maria earns $8.60 per hour and works 35 hours each week. Her employer gave her a raise, increasing her weekly pay to $315. On an hourly basis, how much was Maria's raise?

    F. $1.50
    G. $1.20
    H. $0.85
    J. $0.55
    K. $0.40

**51.** The pie chart below represents the majors of the incoming freshman class at a small college. What is the measure of the central angle formed by the fraction of students who will be Sociology majors?

Total Students = 480

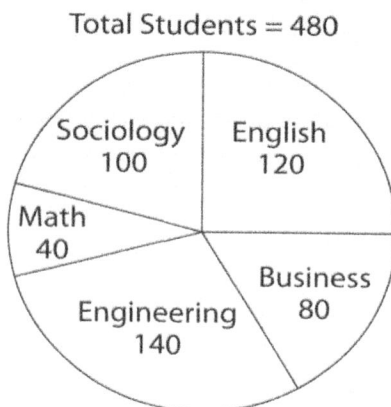

    A. 90°
    B. 75°
    C. 72°
    D. 64°
    E. 60°

**52.** Evaluate the following expression: cos[tan(csc) $\theta$ ]

    F. $\theta$
    G. $2\theta$
    H. $\cos\theta$
    J. $\sin\theta$
    K. $\sec\theta$

**53. What translations are needed to transform the graph of** $y = x^2$ **into** $y = (x+2)^2 - 5$**?**

    A. Shift 2 units to the left and 5 units down.
    B. Shift 5 units to the left and 2 units down.
    C. Shift 2 units to the right and 5 units down.
    D. Shift 2 units to the right and 5 units up.
    E. Shift 5 units to the right and 2 units up.

**54. If the following system of equations has an infinite number of solutions, what is the value of m?**

$$2x - 4y = 13$$
$$-4x + 8y = m$$

    F. 26
    G. 13
    H. 0
    J. -13
    K. -26

**55. A school bus can transport 48 students for a field trip. There are 156 students in the seventh grade of a middle school. How many busses are needed to transport all of the students?**

    A. 2
    B. 3
    C. $3\frac{1}{4}$
    D. 4
    E. 5

**56. What value for k is needed to make** $x^2 + \frac{7}{6}x + k$ **a binomial square?**

    F. $\dfrac{49}{12}$

    G. $\dfrac{49}{6}$

    H. $\dfrac{49}{12}$

    J. $\dfrac{49}{144}$

    K. $\dfrac{7}{144}$

**57. PRTS is a square and is adjacent to** ⊔ **. RV = 12 and** $m\angle VRT = 45°$ **. In square units, what is the area of square PRTS?**

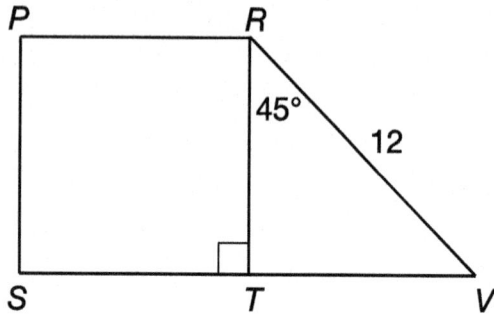

A. $6\sqrt{2}$
B. $24\sqrt{2}$
C. 72
D. $48\sqrt{3}$
E. 96

**58. If 140% of a number is 70, what is 80% of the number?**

F. 105
G. 65
H. 62.5
J. 50
K. 40

**59. Place the fractions in descending order:** $\dfrac{7}{29}, \dfrac{5}{26}, \dfrac{11}{37}$

A. $\dfrac{7}{29}, \dfrac{11}{37}, \dfrac{5}{26}$

B. $\dfrac{11}{37}, \dfrac{7}{29}, \dfrac{5}{26}$

C. $\dfrac{11}{37}, \dfrac{5}{26}, \dfrac{7}{29}$

D. $\dfrac{7}{29}, \dfrac{5}{26}, \dfrac{11}{37}$

E. $\dfrac{5}{26}, \dfrac{7}{29}, \dfrac{11}{37}$

**60.** In the equation $\dfrac{12}{x} + x = 13$, **x = ?**

    F.  x = 1
    G.  x = 12
    H.  x = 13
    J.  x = 1 or x = 12
    K.  x = 2 or x = 6

# MATHEMATICS PRACTICE TEST 3 ANSWER KEY

| | |
|---|---|
| 1. D | 31. C |
| 2. F | 32. J |
| 3. E | 33. E |
| 4. G | 34. F |
| 5. C | 35. D |
| 6. J | 36. K |
| 7. B | 37. D |
| 8. G | 38. G |
| 9. B | 39. E |
| 10. G | 40. F |
| 11. C | 41. B |
| 12. H | 42. F |
| 13. E | 43. A |
| 14. F | 44. F |
| 15. A | 45. D |
| 16. G | 46. H |
| 17. A | 47. D |
| 18. J | 48. J |
| 19. C | 49. C |
| 20. K | 50. K |
| 21. B | 51. B |
| 22. G | 52. F |
| 23. D | 53. A |
| 24. G | 54. K |
| 25. B | 55. D |
| 26. K | 56. J |
| 27. B | 57. C |
| 28. G | 58. K |
| 29. C | 59. B |
| 30. J | 60. J |

# MATHEMATICS PRACTICE TEST 3 RATIONALES

## 1. Answer: D. 42

The height of the fence post and its shadow form the ratio $\dfrac{6}{4}$. When two ratios are equal, they are called a proportion. We can use a proportion to find a missing component.

Use the proportion $\dfrac{height}{shadow} = \dfrac{height}{shadow}$.

$$\frac{6}{4} = \frac{x}{28}$$

Cross-multiply the fractions and set the products equal to each other.

$$(6)(28) = (4)(x)$$
$$168 = 4x$$
$$x = 42$$

## 2. Answer: F. 7

The movie rental membership can be modeled using a linear function in the form of y = mx + b where:

y = all payments made
m = the monthly fee
x = the number of months paid
b = the annual dues

164 = 12x + 80

Use the model to find the number of months for which Arnie has paid the fee.

164 = 12x + 80
84 = 12x
x = 7

## 3. Answer: E. -35

Subtract 3 from both sides of the equation to begin isolating the variable.

$$\frac{2}{5}x + 3 - 3 = -11 - 3$$

$$\frac{2}{5}x = -14$$

Multiply both sides of the equation by the reciprocal of $\dfrac{2}{5}$ to ensure the coefficient of x is 1. The reciprocal of $\dfrac{2}{5}$ is $\dfrac{5}{2}$.

$$(\dfrac{5}{2})(\dfrac{2}{5}x) = (-14)(\dfrac{5}{2})$$
$$x = -35$$

### 4. Answer: G. $28x^7$
Begin this problem by multiplying the coefficients 4 and 7.

$$4x^5 \times 7x^2 = 28(x^5)(x^2)$$

When multiplying like terms, add the exponents.

$$28(x^5)(x^2) = 28x^{5+2} = 28x^7$$

### 5. Answer: C. -56
The perimeter of a rectangle is found by using the formula Perimeter = $(2 \times length) + (2 \times width)$. Input the values 12 and 8 to find the perimeter of the rectangle.

Perimeter = $(2 \times 12) + (2 \times 8) = 40$

The area of a rectangle is found by using the formula Area = (length)(width).

Input 12 and 8 for the length and width to find the area.

Area = (12)(8) = 96

Subtract 96 from 40 to find the value of P – A.

P – A = 40 – 96 = -56

### 6. Answer: J. 12
Solve the equation by cross-multiplying the fractions and setting the products equal.

$$\dfrac{n}{18} = \dfrac{8}{12}$$
$$(18)(8) = (12)(n)$$
$$144 = 12n$$
$$12 = n$$

**7. Answer: B. 52.5**

⊔⃝      is an isosceles triangle because it has two congruent sides. When two sides of a triangle are congruent, the angles opposite those sides are also congruent.

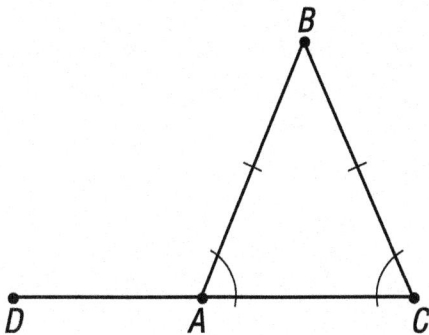

In the diagram, $m\angle BAC = m\angle BCA$. Begin solving this problem by finding the measures of $\angle BAC$ and $\angle BCA$. Since the sum of the measures of the angles in a triangle is 180°, create an equation by letting $n$ equal the measures of $\angle BAC$ and $\angle BCA$.

$$46 + n + n = 180$$
$$46 + 2n = 180$$
$$2n = 134$$
$$n = 67$$

$\angle DAB$ and $\angle BAC$ form a linear pair. A linear pair is a pair of adjacent, supplementary angles. Since the sum of supplementary angles is 180°, set the sum of the measures of $\angle DAB$ and $\angle BAC$ to 180°.

$$67 + 2x + 8 = 180$$
$$2x + 75 = 180$$
$$2x = 105$$
$$x = 52.5$$

**8. Answer: G. -51**
The f(x) is called "the function of x". To find f(-4), the function of -4, replace each x with -4.

$$f(-4) = -2(-4)^2 + 3(-4) - 7$$
$$= -2(16) - 12 - 7$$
$$= -32 - 12 - 7$$
$$= -51$$

### 9. Answer: B. 65

The median of a data set is the middle value. Array the data from least to greatest to find the middle term.

| 20 | 40 | 60 | 70 | 80 | 100 |

Since 60 and 70 are both in the middle, find their mean (the mean is the average).

$$\frac{60 + 70}{2} = 65$$

### 10. Answer: G. 36

Using the counting principle, the number of combinations of entrée, side order, and drink can be visualized by using the following diagram.

E = entree    S = side order    D = drink

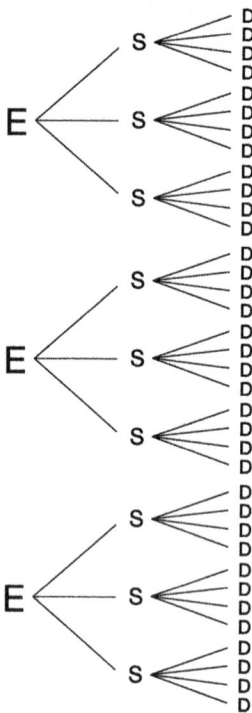

There are 36 combinations of entrée, side order, and drink available to the customer.

An easier way to answer the question is to simply multiply the number of entrees by the number of side orders by the number of drinks.

(3)(3)(4) = 36

### 11. Answer: C. Pentagon

The sum of the measures of the exterior angles of a polygon is 360°. A regular polygon has these additional properties:

A. all sides are congruent
B. all interior angles are congruent
C. all exterior angles are congruent

Since each exterior angle measures 72º, divide 72 into 360 to find the number of sides, interior angles, and exterior angles.

$$360 \div 72 = 5$$

A regular polygon with five sides is a pentagon.

**12. Answer: H.** $16r^2 + 40r + 25$

Expand the expression $(4r+5)^2$ by using the model $(a+b)^2 = a^2 + 2ab + b^2$. In this exercise, a = 4r and b = 5.

$$(4r+5)^2 = (4r)^2 + 2(4r)(5) + 5^2$$
$$= 16r^2 + 40r + 25$$

$(4r+5)^2$ can also be expanded by using the FOIL method of multiplication.

F:    First
O:    Outer
I:    Inner
L:    Last

Rewrite $(4r+5)^2$ as $(4r+5)(4r+5)$ and multiply.

First: $(4r)(4r) = 16r^2$
Outer: (4r)(5) = 20r
Inner: (5)(4r) = 20r
Last: (5)(5) = 25

Combine like terms.

$$16r^2 + 20r + 20r + 25 = 16r^2 + 40r + 25$$

**13. Answer: E.** $(x^2+9)(x+3)(x-3)$

The model for factoring the difference of squares is $a^2 - b^2 = (a+b)(a-b)$. The expression $x^4 - 81$ can be factored using this model because $x^4$ and 81 are both squares.

$$a^2 = x^4$$
$$a = x^2$$
$$b^2 = 81$$
$$b = 9$$

$$x^4 - 81 = (x^2+9)(x^2-9)$$

Notice that the second factor, $x^2 - 9$, can also be factored as the difference of squares.

$$x^2 - 9 = (x+3)(x-3)$$

Therefore: $x^4 - 81 = (x^2 + 9)(x^2 - 9) = (x^2 + 9)(x+3)(x-3)$

## 14. Answer: F. 6
Use the Distributive Property to find an equivalent equation.

$$-7(n-8) = 14$$
$$-7n + 56 = 14$$

Subtract 56 from both sides of the equation.

$$-7n + 56 - 56 = 14 - 56$$
$$-7n = -42$$

Divide both sides of the equation by -7.

$$\frac{-7}{-7}n = \frac{-42}{-7}$$
$$n = 6$$

## 15. Answer: A. -72
The configuration of numbers in this problem is called a matrix. A matrix is a rectangular array of numbers. Matrices are configured with rows, such -9 and 6 in this problem, and columns, such as 6 and -4.

A matrix that has two rows and two columns can be simplified using the following model:

$$\begin{pmatrix} a & b \\ c & d \end{pmatrix} = ad - bc$$

The result of ad – bc is called the determinant of the matrix.

In this exercise, a = -9, b = 6, c = 4, and d = -4. Input these values into the model.

(-9)(-4) – (6)(4) = 36 – 24 = 12

The determinant of this matrix is 12. Multiply by -6 to solve the problem.

(-6)(12) = -72

**16. Answer: G.** $16 + 4\sqrt{2}$

The perimeter of a figure is its measure around. A square has four congruent sides and the formula for its perimeter is Perimeter = 4s, where s represents the length of one side. The area of a square measures its interior. The formula for the area of a square can be found by using the formula Area = s². Use both formulas to derive the perimeter of the square.

$$16 = s^2$$

$$\sqrt{16} = \sqrt{s^2}$$

$$4 = s$$

Input 4 for s into the perimeter formula.

Perimeter = (4)(4) = 16

The perimeter of ABCD is 16.

Square CEFG has an area that equals 8. Find the perimeter of CEFG by using the area and perimeter formulas once again.

$$8 = s^2$$

$$\sqrt{8} = \sqrt{s^2}$$

$$2\sqrt{2} = s$$

Input $2\sqrt{2}$ for s into the perimeter formula.

Perimeter = 4($2\sqrt{2}$) = $8\sqrt{2}$

The sum of the perimeters of ABCD and CEFG is 16 + $8\sqrt{2}$.

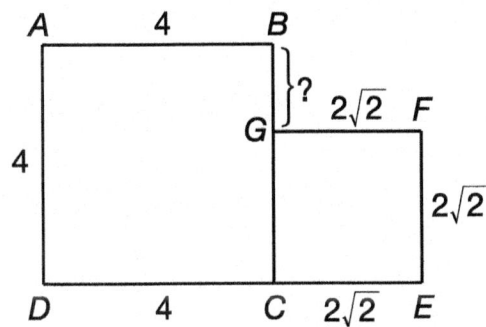

$\overline{GC}$ is in the interior of the figure and should not be included in the perimeter. Since $\overline{GC}$ is eliminated from the perimeter, add solely the length of $\overline{BG}$ into the final sum. Find $\overline{BG}$ by subtracting the length of $\overline{GC}$, $2\sqrt{2}$, from the length of $\overline{BC}$, which is 4.

$$4 - 2\sqrt{2} = 4 - 2\sqrt{2}$$

Add all the sides that are part of the perimeter of the figure.

$$4+4+4+2\sqrt{2}+2\sqrt{2}+2\sqrt{2}+(4-2\sqrt{2})=16+4\sqrt{2}$$

**17. Answer: A.** $-\dfrac{2}{3}$

The slope of a line can be determined if the coordinates of two of the points on the line are known. The formula to determine the slope of a line is:

$$m=\frac{y_2-y_1}{x_2-x_1}$$

Although either point can be deemed $(x_1,y_1)$, let's assume the following:

$x_1=7$
$y_1=-2$
$x_2=5$
$y_2=?$
$m=-\dfrac{2}{3}$

Input the known data and solve for $y_2$.

$$\frac{y_2-(-2)}{5-7}=-\frac{2}{3}$$

$$\frac{y_2+2}{-2}=-\frac{2}{3}$$

Cross-multiply the fractions and set the products equal to each other.

$-3(y_2+2)=2(-2)$
$-3y_2-6=-4$
$-3y_2=2$
$y_2=-\dfrac{2}{3}$

**18. Answer: J.** $\dfrac{40}{31}$

The quotient is the answer to a division problem. Divide $6\dfrac{2}{3}$ by $5\dfrac{1}{6}$.

$$6\frac{2}{3}\div5\frac{1}{6}=?$$

Convert $6\dfrac{2}{3}$ and $5\dfrac{1}{6}$ into improper fractions to begin the problem.

$$6\frac{2}{3} = \frac{3 \times 6 + 2}{3} = \frac{20}{3}$$

$$5\frac{1}{6} = \frac{6 \times 5 + 1}{6} = \frac{31}{6}$$

When dividing a number by a fraction, multiply by the reciprocal of that fraction. The reciprocal of $\dfrac{31}{6}$ is $\dfrac{6}{31}$.

$$\frac{20}{3} \times \frac{6}{31} =$$

$$\frac{20}{\cancel{3}} \times \frac{\cancel{6}}{31} =$$

$$20 \times \frac{2}{31} = \frac{40}{31}$$

**19. Answer: C. 1.9**

The ramp forms a right triangle with an angle of elevation of 3°.

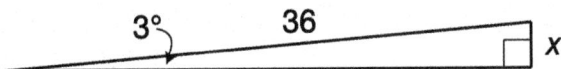

When a side and an angle of a right triangle are known, use right triangle trigonometry to solve for an unknown measure. A useful mnemonic to remember the three basic trigonometric ratios is **sohcahtoa.**

$$\sin = \frac{opposite\ side}{hypotenuse}$$

$$\cos = \frac{adjacent\ side}{hypotenuse}$$

$$\tan = \frac{opposite\ side}{adjacent\ side}$$

In this question, the hypotenuse and opposite angle are known and the side opposite is the variable. Therefore, use the sine ratio to solve for x. The sin of 3° is 0.0523 and is found by pressing "sin 3" on your calculator (make sure your calculator is in **degree** mode).

$$\sin 3° = \frac{x}{36}$$

$$36(\sin 3°) = (\frac{x}{36})36$$

$$36(0.0523) = x$$

$$x = 1.88$$

To the nearest tenth, 1.88 becomes 1.9.

## 20. Answer: K. 25

The diagonal, length, and width of a rectangle form a right triangle within the rectangle. Once the length has been found, use the Pythagorean Theorem to calculate the length of the diagonal.

The formula for the area of a rectangle is found by using the formula Area = (length)(width). Use this formula to calculate the measure of the length.

$$168 = (length)(7)$$

$$\frac{168}{7} = \frac{(length)(7)}{7}$$

$$24 = length$$

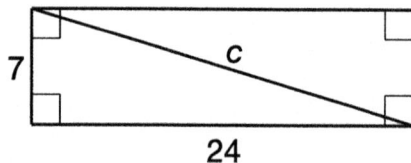

Use the Pythagorean Theorem $a^2 + b^2 = c^2$, to calculate the measure of the diagonal.

$$7^2 + 24^2 = c^2$$

$$49 + 576 = c^2$$

$$625 = c^2$$

$$\sqrt{625} = \sqrt{c^2}$$

$$25 = c$$

**21. Answer: B. (5,3.5)**
Like all parallelograms, the diagonals of a rectangle bisect each other. That means the diagonals intersect at their midpoints.

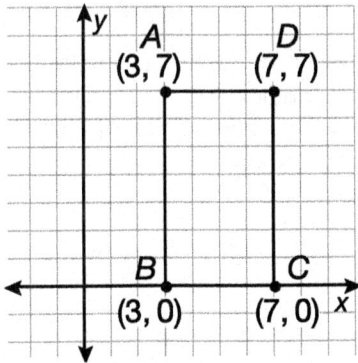

To find the midpoint of either segment, use the midpoint formula.

Midpoint formula: $\dfrac{x_1 + x_2}{2}, \dfrac{y_1 + y_2}{2}$

Find the midpoint of $\overline{AC}$ with endpoints located at (3,7) and (7,0)

$$\frac{3+7}{2}, \frac{7+0}{2} = (5,3.5)$$

You can check your answer by seeing whether the midpoint of $\overline{BD}$ is also (5,3.5).

$$\frac{3+7}{2}, \frac{0+7}{2} = (5,3.5)$$

**22. Answer: G.** $a = 2c^6$
Use the substitution principle by replacing b in the first equation with $c^3$ .

$b = c^3$
$a = 2b^2$
$a = 2(c^3)^2$
$a = 2c^{3 \times 2} = 2c^6$

When raising one power to another, remember to multiply the exponents.

**23. Answer: D. 158**
Find the fifth term by adding 1 to 38 and then doubling the result.

(38 + 1)(2) = 78

Add 1 to 78 and then double it to find the sixth term.

$(78 + 1)(2) = 158$

## 24. Answer: G. 26π

$\overline{AB}$ is a chord of ⬚ because its endpoints lie on the circle. When a radius or diameter intersects a chord, the radius or diameter is the perpendicular bisector of the chord. A perpendicular bisector divides a segment into two congruent segments and forms a right angle with the chord. Use these two properties to find $\overline{PA}$ or $\overline{PB}$, which are radii of the circle. Once the radius is known, use the formula $circumference = 2\pi r$ to find the circumference of the circle.

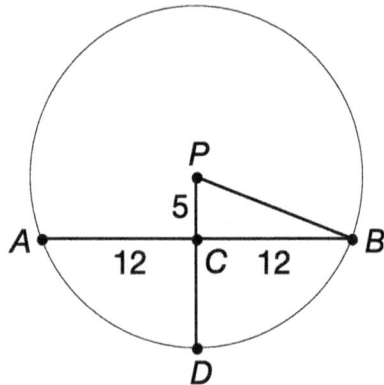

Radius $\overline{PD}$ bisects $\overline{AB}$. Therefore, AC = BC = 12. $\overline{PD}$ is also perpendicular to $\overline{AB}$, creating right triangle PCB. Since the lengths of $\overline{PC}$ and $\overline{CB}$ are known, use the Pythagorean Theorem, $a^2 + b^2 = c^2$, to find the length of $\overline{PB}$.

$$5^2 + 12^2 = c^2$$
$$25 + 144 = c^2$$
$$169 = c^2$$
$$\sqrt{169} = \sqrt{c^2}$$
$$13 = c$$

$\overline{PB}$ is a radius of the circle, so use the circumference formula to find the circumference of ⬚.

Circumference = 2πr
= 2(π)(13)
= 26π

## 25. Answer: B. 384

The square tiles, each with a perimeter of 1 foot, are 0.25 foot long on a side because a square has 4 equal sides. Find how many tiles will line the length of the patio by dividing the length by 0.25.

$$6 \div 0.25 = 24$$

Next, find how many tiles line the width of the patio by dividing the width by 0.25.

$4 \div 0.25 = 16$

The area of a rectangle is found by using the formula Area = (length)(width). Replace the length and width by 24 and 16 respectively to find the number of tiles James must purchase to cover the patio.

Area = (24)(16) = 384

**26. Answer: K. 80°**
When parallel lines are intersected by a transversal (line t in the diagram), groups of congruent and supplementary angles are formed. $\angle 2$ and $\angle 7$ are called alternate exterior angles and they have equal measures. Set their measures equal to each other and solve for x.

$4x - 20 = 2x + 40$

$2x = 60$

$x = 30$

Replace 30 for x in either equation to find the measure of $\angle 2$ or $\angle 7$.

4(30) − 20 = 100

$m\angle 2 = m\angle 7 = 100°$

$\angle 2$ and $\angle 4$ form a linear pair of angles. A linear pair of angles is a pair of adjacent, supplementary angles. Since the sum of supplementary angles is 180°, add 100° to the measure of $\angle 4$ and set the sum equal to 180.

$100 + m\angle 4 = 180$

$m\angle 4 = 80.$

**27. Answer: B.** $-\frac{1}{4}$

Replace the variables with their values and use the rules of the order of operations to simplify the expression.

Order of Operations

Parentheses
Exponents
Multiplication
Division
Addition
Subtraction

$$\frac{-2(\frac{1}{2})^2(-2)^3}{-(-4)^2}$$

The quantities in the parentheses are in simplest form, so work with the exponents next.

$$\frac{-2(\frac{1}{4})(-8)}{-(16)}$$

Multiply the numbers in the numerator.

$$\frac{4}{-16}$$

Simplify the fraction.

$$\frac{4}{-16} = -\frac{1}{4}$$

**28. Answer: G.** $y = \frac{3}{2}x + 12$

Perpendicular lines have slopes that are the opposite reciprocals of each other. In the equation $y = -\frac{2}{3}x + 6$, the slope is $-\frac{2}{3}$ and the y-intercept is 6. The slope of a line that is perpendicular to $-\frac{2}{3}$ is $\frac{3}{2}$. Replace $-\frac{2}{3}$ with $\frac{3}{2}$ and replace 6 with b, the general term for the y-intercept.

$$y = \frac{3}{2}x + b$$

Replace x and y with -6 and 3 respectively to find b.

$$y = \frac{3}{2}x + b$$
$$3 = \frac{3}{2}(-6) + b$$
$$3 = -9 + b$$
$$12 = b$$

The equation of the line perpendicular to $y = -\frac{2}{3}x + 6$ that passes through (-6,3) is $y = \frac{3}{2}x + 12$ .

**29. Answer: C.** $36 - 15b^2$
Use the order of operations to simplify the expression.

Parentheses
Exponents
Multiplication
Division
Addition
Subtraction

The parentheses cannot be simplified, so multiply each term in the parentheses by 5.

$$3\left[2 + 5(2 - b^2)\right] = 3(2 + 10 - 5b^2)$$

Combine like terms in the parentheses.

$$3(2 + 10 - 5b^2) = 3(12 - 5b^2)$$

Finally, multiply each term in the parentheses by 3.

$$3(12 - 5b^2) = 36 - 15b^2$$

**30. Answer: J. 8**
A segment that is tangent to a circle is perpendicular to the radius of the circle. Therefore, $\angle B$ is a right angle and $\sqcup$ is a right triangle. Given that AB = 5, and BC = 12, use the Pythagorean Theorem to find the length of AC.

$$a^2 + b^2 = c^2$$
$$5^2 + 12^2 = c^2$$
$$25 + 144 = c^2$$
$$169 = c^2$$
$$\sqrt{169} = \sqrt{c^2}$$
$$13 = c$$

Note that $\overline{AD}$ is a radius of $\sqcup$ . All radii in a circle have equal measures so AB = AD = 5.

Find x by subtracting the length of AD from the length of AC.

$$13 - 5 = 8$$

**31. Answer: C.** $\dfrac{x^2 + x + 1}{x - 6}$
Factor the numerator and denominator of the fraction and divide any common factors.

The expression $x^3 - 1$ can be factored using the difference of cubes model because $x^3$ and 1 are cubes.

$$a^3 - b^3 = (a-b)(a^2 + ab + b^2)$$
$$x^3 - 1 = (x-1)(x^2 + x + 1)$$

The expression $x^2 - 7x + 6$ can also be factored. Because its leading coefficient is 1, a quick way to factor the expression is to find two factors of 6 that add to -7.

(-1)(-6) = 6      -1 + -6 = -7

We can now factor $x^2 - 7x + 6$ as $(x-1)(x-6)$. Finally, replace $x^3 - 1$ and $x^2 - 7x + 6$ with their factored forms and divide common factors.

$$\frac{x^3 - 1}{x^2 - 7x + 6} = \frac{\cancel{(x-1)}(x^2 + x + 1)}{\cancel{(x-1)}(x-6)} = \frac{x^2 + x + 1}{x - 6}$$

**32. Answer: J. (5,-6)**

The point that is $\frac{1}{4}$ the distance from A to B is the midpoint of $\overline{AM}$. Find the coordinates of M by using the midpoint formula to find the midpoint of $\overline{AB}$.

Midpoint formula: $\frac{x_1 + x_2}{2}, \frac{y_1 + y_2}{2}$

$$\frac{6 + 2}{2} = 4, \quad \frac{-4 + -12}{2} = -8$$

The coordinates of M are (4,-8) and at A are (6,-4). Now find the midpoint of $\overline{AM}$.

$$\frac{4 + 6}{2} = 5 \quad \frac{-8 + -4}{2} = -6$$

The coordinates of the point that is $\frac{1}{4}$ the distance from A to B are (5,-6).

**33. Answer: E.** $-\dfrac{13}{12}$

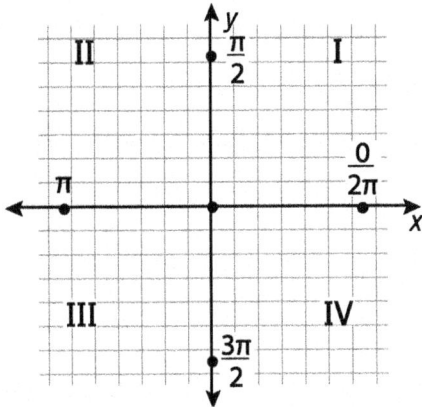

By inspection of the graph above, we see that $\dfrac{\pi}{2} \le \theta < \pi$ means that $\theta$ is in Quadrant II. The sine of an angle in a right triangle is the ratio of the side opposite the angle to the hypotenuse.

$$\sin \theta = \frac{opposite\ side}{hypotenuse}$$

Construct a right triangle in Quadrant II with the side opposite equal to 5 and the hypotenuse equal to 13.

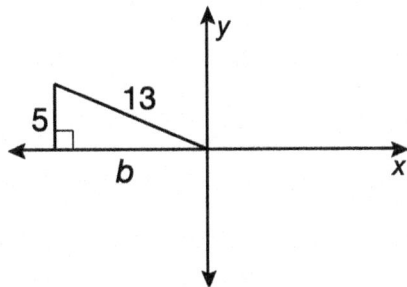

The question asks for $\sec \theta$ which is the ratio of the hypotenuse to the adjacent side.

$$\sec \theta = \frac{hypotenuse}{adjacent\ side}$$

Since the adjacent side is unknown, use the Pythagorean Theorem to find its measure.

$a^2 + b^2 = c^2$

$5^2 + b^2 = 13^2$

$25 + b^2 = 169$

$b^2 = 144$

$b = 12$

Because side b is located where the x-axis is negative, change b = 12 to b = -12.

Given that the hypotenuse is 13 and the adjacent side is -12, $\sec\theta = -\dfrac{13}{12}$.

## 34. Answer: F. (-12,11)

The rule $(x, y) \rightarrow (x-7, y+5)$ means move the point 7 units to the left and 5 units up. An easy way to find the coordinates after the translation is to subtract 7 from the x-coordinate and to add 5 to the y-coordinate.

x: -5 – 7 = -12

y: 6 + 5 = 11

The coordinates of A′ are (-12,11).

## 35. Answer: D. Rode, rested, ran

The first portion of the graph, starting at time 0, indicates much distance was covered in a small amount of time. The vertical component indicates time passed but no distance was covered. The third component indicates that less distance per unit of time was covered when compared to the first component. Since the first component of the graph implies a greater velocity, it represents the bicycle ride. The vertical component that shows the passage of time without any distance covered is the rest period. Finally, the third component, which shows more time passing per unit of distance (compared to the first component), must be the running portion of the graph.

## 36. Answer: K. $\dfrac{17}{25}$

M is in the interior of the region between $\overrightarrow{OR}$ and the x-axis. Therefore, the slope of $\overrightarrow{OM}$ must be less than the slope of $\overrightarrow{OR}$ but greater than the slope of the x-axis. Find the slope of $\overrightarrow{OR}$ by using the slope formula $m = \dfrac{y_2 - y_1}{x_2 - x_1}$ where m represents the slope. Point R, (6,4) and the origin, (0,0) are both on $\overrightarrow{OR}$, so input their values into the slope formula.

$$\frac{4-0}{6-0} = \frac{4}{6} = \frac{2}{3}$$

The slope of $\overrightarrow{OR}$ is $\dfrac{2}{3}$.

The slope of the x-axis is 0. You can check this by using any two points on the x-axis. Let's use (3,0) and (0,0).

$$\frac{0-0}{0-3} = \frac{0}{-3} = 0$$

Any value that falls outside the parameters $0 < m < \dfrac{2}{3}$ cannot be the slope of $\overrightarrow{OR}$. Choice E, $\dfrac{17}{25}$, is

0.68 when expressed as a decimal. $\dfrac{2}{3}$, when expressed as a decimal, is 0.666... Therefore, the slope of

$\overrightarrow{OM}$ cannot be $\dfrac{17}{25}$.

## 37. Answer: D. 32.8

The area of a triangle is found by using the formula Area = $(\dfrac{1}{2})(base)(height)$. In the figure provided,

neither the base nor the height are known. However, since $\angle P$ and the hypotenuse are known, we can use trigonometry to find the missing sides. The mnemonic **sohcahtoa** is a useful device to remember the trigonometric ratios.

$$\sin\theta = \frac{side\ opposite}{hypotenuse}$$

$$\cos\theta = \frac{side\ adjacent}{hypotenuse}$$

$$\tan\theta = \frac{side\ opposite}{side\ adjacent}$$

Although any of the three ratios can be used to solve this problem, we can start by showing $\sin 33° = \dfrac{x}{12}$.

$$\sin 33° = \frac{x}{12}$$

$$12(\sin 33 = \frac{x}{12})12$$

$$12(.5446) = x$$

$$6.5 = x$$

Here is what we now know about $\square\quad\quad$:

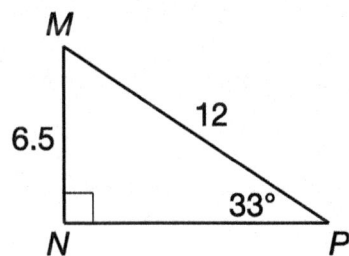

Use the Pythagorean Theorem to find NP.

$$a^2 + b^2 = c^2$$
$$6.5^2 + b^2 = 12^2$$
$$42.3 + b^2 = 144$$
$$b^2 = 101.7$$
$$\sqrt{b^2} = \sqrt{101.7}$$
$$b = 10.1$$

$\square$   has a base that measures 10.1 and height equal to 6.5. Input both into the area formula to find the area of $\square$   .

$$Area = (\frac{1}{2})(10.1)(6.5) = 32.8$$

**38. Answer: G.** $x < \dfrac{13}{6}$

Isolate the variable as you would when solving an equation. First, subtract 11 from both sides of the inequality.

$$11 - 6x - 11 > -2 - 11$$
$$-6x > -13$$

When dividing or multiplying an inequality by a negative number, reverse the direction of the inequality sign.

$$-6x > -13$$
$$\frac{-6}{-6}x > \frac{-13}{-6}$$
$$x < \frac{13}{6}$$

**39. Answer: E. 48π**

The area of a circle is found by using the formula $Area = \pi r^2$. Find the area of $\square$   .

$$Area = \pi(8^2) = 64\pi$$

The circumference of a circle is found by using the formula Circumference = 2πr. Find the circumference of $\square$   .

$$Circumference = 2(\pi)(8) = 16\pi$$

Find the difference between the area and the circumference.

$$64\pi - 16\pi = 48\pi$$

## 40. Answer: F. SAS

A midpoint divides a segment into two congruent segments. Therefore, $\overline{BC} \cong \overline{DC}$ and $\overline{AC} \cong \overline{EC}$. $\angle ACB \cong \angle ECD$ because they are vertical angles. Therefore, $\square$ $\square$ by way of the SAS postulate.

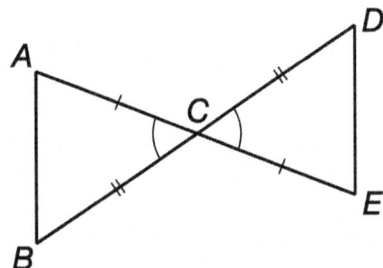

## 41. Answer: B. $\dfrac{1}{16}$

The geometric probability of hitting the bull's eye can be found by using the ratio of the bull's eye's area to the area of the entire target. Since both the target and the bull's eye are circles, use the formula Area = $\pi r^2$ to find the area of both circles.

The bull's eye is 4 inches wide, so its radius is 2 inches.

Area = $\pi(2)^2 = 4\pi$

Starting from the target's center, add the 2 inch radius of the bull's eye to the width of the 3, two-inch rings to create a radius of 8 inches for the entire target.

Area = $\pi(8)^2 = 64\pi$

The ratio of the bull's eye's area to the area of the target is $\dfrac{4\pi}{64\pi}$. Simplify this fraction to get $\dfrac{1}{16}$, the geometric probability of hitting the bull's eye.

## 42. Answer: F. 174

The mode is the number that appears most frequently in the data set. The attendance figures show that on two dates, 174 spectators were at the water polo games. On all other dates, attendance figures did not repeat. Therefore, the mode of the data is 174.

## 43. Answer: A. 173

The median of the attendance figures is the number that is in the middle. Array the data from least to greatest to find the middle term.

144     168     172     174     174     176

In the data array, note that both 172 and 174 occupy the middle positions. When two numbers are in the middle, find their mean (the average) which will be the median.

$$\frac{172+174}{2}=173$$

## 44. Answer: F. 136
The mean of the data is its average. Add all the attendance figures and divide their sum by the number of games.

$$\frac{174+176+174+172+168+144}{6}=\frac{1008}{6}=168$$

The range of the data is found by subtracting the smallest value from the largest value.

176 – 144 = 32

If M = 168 and R = 32, then subtract 32 from 168 to find the value of M – R.

168 – 32 = 136

## 45. Answer: D. 13
Logs, or more formally, logarithms, express numbers by their exponents. You can simplify logs by expressing them as exponential equations. For example, $\log_3 81$ is simplified by asking "what power of 3 is 81"?

$3^x = 81$

$3^4 = 81$

$x = 4$

In this example, x = 4, so $\log_3 81 = 4$.

The second term, $2\log_5 125$, is different because it is being multiplied by 2. Solve $\log_5 125$ first as we did earlier.

$5^z = 125$

$x = 3$

$\log_5 125 = 3$

The 2 in $2\log_5 125$ means "square the result of $\log_5 125$". Since $\log_5 125 = 3$, 3² = 9.

Finally, add the results of both logarithmic terms.

4 + 9 = 13

**46. Answer: H. 72**

Note that the measures of $\overline{EF}, \overline{FL}, \overline{LK}, \overline{JK}$ and $\overline{JI}$ are not given in the figure. Each measure, however, can be deduced from the information provided. For example, the sum of the lengths of $\overline{EF}, \overline{LK},$ and $\overline{JI}$ are equal in measure to $\overline{GH}$ which is 15. $\overline{FL}$ and $\overline{JK}$ must each equal 9 because each segment is 3 less than $\overline{EG}$ which is 12.

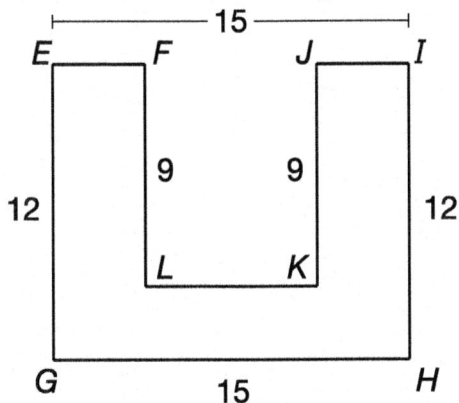

Find the perimeter by adding the measures of the sides.

$15 + 12 + 12 + 15 + 9 + 9 = 72$

**47. Answer: D. 48**

Let x = the number of students originally enrolled in the class. Those who dropped the class after the first test were one-half of x, or $\frac{1}{2}x$. If one-half of the class dropped the class at this point, then $\frac{1}{2}x$ went on take the second test.

$$x - \frac{1}{2}x = \frac{1}{2}x$$

Of the number of students who took the second test, one-third of that number dropped the class after the second exam.

$$\frac{1}{2}x - (\frac{1}{3})(\frac{1}{2})x = \frac{1}{2}x - \frac{1}{6}x = \frac{1}{3}x$$

After two exams, 16 students remained in the class. Set 16 equal to $\frac{1}{3}x$ to find how many students were originally enrolled in the class.

$$\frac{1}{3}x = 16$$

$$(3)(\frac{1}{3})x = (3)(16)$$

$$x = 48$$

**48. Answer: J.** $-4 \leq x < 6$

The shaded area shows values that are between -4 and 6. The dot at -4 is closed, indicating that -4 is a part of the graph. The point at 6, however, is not a part of the graph because it is open. The inequality sign $\leq$ means that one value is greater than or equal to another value. The inequality sign $<$ indicates one value is greater than but not equal to another value.

The graph shows numbers that are less than but not equal to 6. The graph also shows numbers that are larger than or equal to -4. Therefore the graph shows the following composite inequality:

$-4 \leq x < 6$

**49. Answer: C.** $\dfrac{256}{729}$

Input the values of x and y and calculate the value in the parentheses.

$2(\dfrac{1}{8})^{-2}(-6)^{-3}$

Calculating with negative exponents can be done by replacing the base with its reciprocal and then changing the exponent from negative to positive.

$2(\dfrac{1}{8})^{-2}(-6)^{-3} = 2(8)^{2}(-\dfrac{1}{6})^{3} = 2(64)(-\dfrac{1}{216}) = -\dfrac{16}{27}$

Square $-\dfrac{16}{27}$ to finish the problem.

$(-\dfrac{16}{27})^{2} = \dfrac{256}{729}$

**50. Answer: K. $0.40**

Maria earned $8.60 per hour and worked 35 hours a week. Find Maria's weekly pay before she received her raise by multiplying her hourly rate by the number of hours she worked each week.

$8.60 × 35 = $301

Find out how much Maria's weekly pay increased by subtracting her old weekly pay from her new weekly pay.

$315 − 301 = $14

Divide $14 by 35 to find Maria's hourly increase.

$14 ÷ 35 = $.40.

**51. Answer: B. 75°**

A central angle in a circle is any angle with its vertex on the center. In the pie chart shown, all of the chart's components are created by using central angles.

A circle measures 360°. Find the fraction of the circle that is composed of Sociology majors.

$$\frac{sociology \ majors}{all \ students} = \frac{100}{480} = \frac{5}{24}$$

The Sociology majors represent $\frac{5}{24}$ of the circle's 360°. Multiply $\frac{5}{24}$ by 360 to find the measure of the central angle.

$$(\frac{5}{24})(360) = 75°$$

**52. Answer: F. $\theta$**

Simplify the expression by expressing the tangent (tan) and the cosecant (csc) in terms of the sine (sin) and cosine (cos).

$$\tan = \frac{\sin}{\cos}$$

$$\csc = \frac{1}{\sin}$$

Input the new values into the expression.

$$\cos[\tan(\csc \theta)] =$$
$$\cos[\frac{\sin}{\cos}(\frac{1}{\sin}\theta)] =$$
$$\cos(\frac{1}{\cos}\theta) =$$
$$\theta$$

**53. Answer: A. Shift 2 units to the left and 5 units down.**

The graph of $y = x^2$ is a parabola that opens up and has its vertex at (0,0). The graph of $y = (x+2)^2 - 5$ is in the form of $y = a(x-h)^2 + k$ where h and k represent the vertex in the form of (h,k). In this example, $(x-h)^2 = (x+2)^2$.

$$x - h = x + 2$$
$$-h = 2$$
$$h = -2$$

The x-coordinate of the vertex is -2.

Find the y-coordinate of the vertex by letting k equal -5. The vertex of the parabola $y = (x+2)^2 - 5$ is (-2,-5). The vertex of the parabola has moved from (0,0) to (-2,-5) by shifting 2 units to the left and moving 5 units down.

## 54. Answer: K. -26

Two lines can intersect at one point, no points, or infinite points. If the two lines have different slopes, they intersect at one point and have one solution. Two lines that have the same slope but different y-intercepts are parallel, do not intersect, and have no solutions. Lines that have the same slope and the same y-intercept are the same line and therefore
intersect at every point and have an infinite number of solutions.

If the system of equations has an infinite number of solutions, the lines must be equivalent equations.

$$2x - 4y = 13$$
$$-4x + 8y = m$$

We see that each term in the second equation results from multiplying the top equation by -2. Therefore, m = -26.

$$-2(2x - 4y = 13) = -4x + 8y = -26$$

## 55. Answer: D. 4

Find how many busses are needed to transport all the students by dividing the number of students by the capacity of each bus.

$$156 \div 48 = 3\frac{1}{4}$$

or

$$156 \div 48 = 3 \text{ remainder } 12$$

The school can fill up 3 busses completely. The remaining 12 students will need to ride in a fourth bus. Therefore, the school needs to arrange for 4 busses to transport all of the seventh graders.

## 56. Answer: J. $\dfrac{49}{144}$

A binomial square is a special trinomial in the form of $(a+b)^2 = a^2 + 2ab + b^2$. The expression $x^2 + \dfrac{7}{6}x + k$ can be transformed into a binomial square by using a technique called completing the square. To complete the square, multiply the coefficient of x by $\dfrac{1}{2}$ and square the product.

$$(\frac{1}{2})(\frac{7}{6}) = \frac{7}{12}$$
$$(\frac{7}{12})^2 = \frac{49}{144}$$

When $k = \dfrac{49}{144}$, we get :

$$x^2 + \dfrac{7}{6}x + \dfrac{49}{144} = (x + \dfrac{7}{12})^2$$

**57. Answer: C. 72**

The area of a square is found by using the formula $Area = s^2$, where s is a length of a side. In the figure, the triangle and the square share $\overline{RT}$. Find the length of $\overline{RT}$ in ⊔ and then input that value into the area formula for a square.

$\angle RTS$ and $\angle RTV$ are supplementary angles. The sum of the measures of supplementary angles is $180°$. Given that $\angle RTS$ is a right angle, then $\angle RTV$ is also a right angle because $180 - 90 = 90$.

The sum of the measures of the angles in a triangle is $180°$. Add the measures of $\angle RTV$ and $\angle TRV$ and subtract their sum from 180 to find the measure of $\angle V$.

$180 - (90 + 45) = 45$.

The $m\angle V = 45°$, making ⊔ a 45-45-90 triangle. The ratio of the sides of a 45-45-90 triangle is shown below.

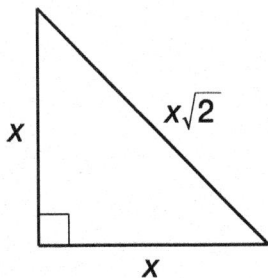

Find $\overline{RT}$ by setting 12, the hypotenuse in ⊔ , to $x\sqrt{2}$, the hypotenuse in the general model for a 45-45-90 triangle.

$$x\sqrt{2} = 12$$
$$\dfrac{x\sqrt{2}}{\sqrt{2}} = \dfrac{12}{\sqrt{2}}$$

$$x = \dfrac{12}{\sqrt{2}} \times \dfrac{\sqrt{2}}{\sqrt{2}} = \dfrac{12\sqrt{2}}{2} = 6\sqrt{2}$$

$$x = RT = 6\sqrt{2}$$

Input $6\sqrt{2}$ into the area formula for a square.

$$Area = s^2$$

$$Area = (6\sqrt{2})^2 = (36)(2) = 72$$

### 58. Answer: K. 40

Let x = the unknown number. Convert the percentages in the question into decimals to facilitate calculation.

140% of x = 1.4x

$$1.4x = 70$$

$$\frac{1.4x}{1.4} = \frac{70}{1.4}$$

$$x = 50$$

Find 80% of 50.

(0.8)(50) = 40

### 59. Answer: B. $\dfrac{11}{37}, \dfrac{7}{29}, \dfrac{5}{26}$

This question can be answered using common denominators. However, the numbers are relatively large and unwieldy. Use a calculator to convert each fraction into a decimal.

$$\frac{7}{29} = 0.241$$

$$\frac{5}{26} = 0.192$$

$$\frac{11}{37} = 0.297$$

Arrange the values from greatest to least.

0.297, 0.241, 0.192

Replace each decimal with its equivalent fraction.

$$\frac{11}{37}, \frac{7}{29}, \frac{5}{26}$$

**60. Answer: J. x = 1 or x = 12**

Eliminate the denominator in the term $\dfrac{12}{x}$ by multiplying the entire equation by x.

$$\frac{12}{x} + x = 13$$

$$x(\frac{12}{x} + x = 13)x$$

$$12 + x^2 = 13x$$

$$x^2 - 13x + 12 = 0$$

Factor $x^2 - 13x + 12$. Since the coefficient of $x^2$ is 1, we find factors of 12 that add to -13.

(-1)(-12) = 12          -1 + -12 = -13

$$x^2 - 13x + 12 = (x - 1)(x - 12)$$

Since $x^2 - 13x + 12 = 0$, then $(x-1)(x-12) = 0$. Solve for x by setting x – 12 and x – 1 equal to 0.

x – 12 = 0
x = 12

x – 1 = 0
x = 1

In the equation $\dfrac{12}{x} + x = 13$, x = 1 or x = 12

# READING PRACTICE TEST 3

35 Minutes - 40 Questions

Directions: Each of the four reading passages in this section is followed by ten reading questions. Choose the best answer for each question.

## My Antonia

Excerpt from *My Ántonia* by Willa Cather, first published in 1918

No wagon could be got to the Shimerdas' until a road was broken, and that would be a day's job. Grandfather came from the barn on one of our big black horses, and Jake lifted grandmother up behind him. She wore her black hood and was bundled up in shawls. Grandfather tucked his bushy white beard inside his overcoat. They looked very Biblical as they set off, I thought. Jake and
5  Ambrosch followed them, riding the other black and my pony, carrying bundles of clothes that we had got together for Mrs. Shimerda. I watched them go past the pond and over the hill by the drifted cornfield. Then, for the first time, I realized that I was alone in the house.

I felt a considerable extension of power and authority, and was anxious to acquit myself creditably.
10  I carried in cobs and wood from the long cellar, and filled both the stoves. I remembered that in the hurry and excitement of the morning nobody had thought of the chickens, and the eggs had not been gathered. Going out through the tunnel, I gave the hens their corn, emptied the ice from their drinking-pan, and filled it with water. After the cat had had his milk, I could think of nothing else to do, and I sat down to get warm. The quiet was delightful, and the ticking clock was the most
15  pleasant of companions. I got 'Robinson Crusoe' and tried to read, but his life on the island seemed dull compared with ours. Presently, as I looked with satisfaction about our comfortable sitting-room, it flashed upon me that if Mr. Shimerda's soul were lingering about in this world at all, it would be here, in our house, which had been more to his liking than any other in the neighborhood. I remembered his contented face when he was with us on Christmas Day. If he could have lived with
20  us, this terrible thing would never have happened.

I knew it was homesickness that had killed Mr. Shimerda, and I wondered whether his released spirit would not eventually find its way back to his own country. I thought of how far it was to Chicago, and then to Virginia, to Baltimore—and then the great wintry ocean. No, he would not at
25  once set out upon that long journey. Surely, his exhausted spirit, so tired of cold and crowding and the struggle with the ever-falling snow, was resting now in this quiet house.

I was not frightened, but I made no noise. I did not wish to disturb him. I went softly down to the kitchen which, tucked away so snuggly underground, always seemed to me the heart and centre of
30  the house. There, on the bench behind the stove, I thought and thought about Mr. Shimerda. Outside I could hear the wind singing over hundreds of miles of snow. It was as if I had let the old man in out of the tormenting winter, and were sitting there with him. I went over all that Ántonia had ever told me about his life before he came to this country; how he used to play the fiddle at weddings and dances. I thought about the friends he had mourned to leave, the trombone-player,
35  the great forest full of game—belonging, as Ántonia said, to the 'nobles'—from which she and her mother used to steal wood on moonlight nights. There was a white hart (deer) that lived in that forest, and if anyone killed it, he would be hanged, she said. Such vivid pictures came to me that they might have been Mr. Shimerda's memories, not yet faded out from the air in which they had haunted him.
40

It had begun to grow dark when my household returned, and grandmother was so tired that she went at once to bed. Jake and I got supper, and while we were washing the dishes he told me in loud whispers about the state of things over at the Shimerdas'. Nobody could touch the body until the coroner came. If anyone did, something terrible would happen, apparently. The dead man was

45  frozen through, "just as stiff as a dressed turkey you hang out to freeze," Jake said. The horses and oxen would not go into the barn until he was frozen so hard that there was no longer any smell of blood. They were stabled there now, with the dead man, because there was no other place to keep them. A lighted lantern was kept hanging over Mr. Shimerda's head. Antonia and Ambrosch and the mother took turns going down to pray beside him. The crazy boy went with them, because he
50  did not feel the cold. I believed he felt cold as much as anyone else, but he liked to be thought insensible to it. He was always coveting distinction, poor Marek!

1. **The narrator of the passage is most likely:**

   A. A neighbor
   B. An adult friend of the family
   C. A young child
   D. Antonia

2. **The setting of the passage is most likely:**

   F. A crowded, urban tenement district.
   G. A mercantile crossroads town.
   H. A lonely outpost in the wilderness area of Northern Canada.
   J. A rural outpost in the United States.

3. **Paragraph 1 implies that the characters are:**

   A. Setting out, stoically, on a mission of mercy to help out their neighbor.
   B. Heading to their neighbor's house to help them clear a road through the snow.
   C. Attempting to quickly reach their neighbor before a disaster happens.
   D. Breaking a path through the snow to prepare for a future visit with their neighbor.

4. **Once her family leaves for the Shimerdas' house, the narrator is all alone in her house. It is evident that the narrator feels:**

   F. A fair amount of trepidation and anxiety over this unusual circumstance of being left alone.
   G. Indifferent about being alone; she reads *Robinson Crusoe* to pass the time and relax until her family returns.
   H. Exhilarated by this unusual circumstance; she wants to prove to herself and her family that she can handle the experience.
   J. She has plenty of chores to keep her busy while the family is gone and is too preoccupied to give much thought to being left alone.

5. **The character of Mr. Shimerda seems to have been:**

   A. A friend of the family and, having spent much time at the narrator's house, will be sorely missed.
   B. A casual acquaintance of the family and, even though he lived far away, will be sadly missed.
   C. A member of an immigrant family that could not speak English and most likely needed constant assistance to survive in their new American homeland.
   D. A musician who often played music for the weddings and celebrations attended by the narrator and her family.

6. **The narrator felt that Mr. Shimerda's soul:**

   F. Had returned to his homeland to play his trombone and hunt in the forest.
   G. Was taking refuge from the cold in her house.
   H. Had left this world and had gone to a peaceful resting place.
   J. Had stayed to keep a constant vigil next to his still-frozen body.

7. **From the passage we can presume that Antonia is:**

    A. The narrator's sister and was acquainted with the Shimerdas through some reason not mentioned in the passage.
    B. Mr. Shimerda's wife and long-time companion from the old country.
    C. A close friend of the Shimerda family who lives nearby and has known the Shimerdas since they arrived in America.
    D. A close friend of the narrator and related to the Shimerda family.

8. **An accurate summary of the chronological order of the passage would be:**

    F. Mr. Shimerda went out to fetch a stray calf. Mr. Shimerda froze to death. Antonia told the narrator's family what happened to her father. Antonia's brother, Ambrosch, brought the narrator's family to the funeral after breaking a road through the snow.
    G. A road is broken through the snow. The narrator's parents and brother went to the Shimerda's home to help. The narrator did chores to keep herself busy and thought about Mr. Shimerda's soul. The narrator's family came back home cold and tired.
    H. The narrator saw her family off as they went to visit and help the Shimerdas. The narrator engaged in chores and went down into the basement kitchen to read *Robinson Crusoe*. The narrator fell asleep until her family came back cold and tired. Her family related all that had happened to Mr. Shimerda.
    J. Mr. Shimerda's son, Ambrosch, came to tell the narrator's family what happened. The narrator saw her family off as they went to visit and help the Shimerdas. The narrator engaged in chores and went down into the basement kitchen to read *Robinson Crusoe*. The narrator fell asleep until her family came back cold and tired. Jake related the story about what was happening at the Shimerdas' farm.

9. **It is clear from the passage that of all of Mr. Shimerda's family, Marek was:**

    A. A child with an obvious mental disability.
    B. A man who knew that the responsibility of the family now rested upon his shoulders.
    C. Suffered from a physical disability.
    D. Was a frequent companion to the narrator and received much sympathy from her family.

10. **From the passage, one can make the assumption that the relationship between the narrator, her family, and the Shimerdas:**

    F. Was initiated by the friendship between the narrator and Antonia.
    G. Came about when the narrator's father and Mr. Shimerda began working together.
    H. Revolved around the relationship built by Mr. Shimerda's presence in the narrator's home and later involved Antonia.
    J. Was brought about by the friendship between the two boys, Jake and Ambrosch.

## The Evolving Art of Printmaking

It is1690 and the Japanese artist, Katsushika Hokusai, is hard at work in his candle-lit studio. He carefully plans where wood will be cut away and where raised ridges in the wood will stand above the carved background. He rolls a colored ink over the finished carved woodblock, and in one deft movement, places paper face down upon the inked block. He takes another piece of wood and
5  gently rubs the back of the paper to transfer the ink to the paper. Pulling the paper away, he turns it over to inspect the initial image while it dries. Later, he coats a second carved woodblock with a different color of ink and transfers the image onto the original print. After a pre-planned sequence of multiple woodblocks with different colors, Hokusai adds the final woodblock with the black ink to give the final structure to his work of art. As it dries, he inspects what will become the most
10  recognizable *ukiyo-e* style print in history: *The Great Wave*, an image of lush blues defined by a huge, foamy wave overcoming two long fishing boats filled with frightened passengers. Mount Fuji, in the middle background looks as if it too will be swallowed forever. Katsushika Hokusai was a master of the ancient, artistic process called printmaking and over his lifetime created many beautiful and iconic works of art using these techniques.
15

Woodcut printing, like that practiced by Hokusai, is most likely the earliest form of printmaking. It has an ancient history in the Far East and was likely first developed to print patterns on cloth. By the 5th century, Chinese artisans were using woodblock printing for placing text and images together on another Chinese invention: paper. The basic techniques of woodblock printing are
20  simple. The artist draws a design directly on a wooden block, or transfers the design from paper to a wooden block, and then cuts away the parts of the block that will not receive ink. The desired color of ink is then rolled onto the surface of the block. The artist places paper on the inked block and presses the paper by hand or with a machine to transfer the ink to the paper. Separate blocks are used for each color or the artist may use a more complicated technique called reduction
25  printing. In reduction printing, the same woodblock is used for all of the colors; the lines for each successive color are carved and then printed one after the other. The number of layers for one print can number from two to dozens, depending upon the creativity and the goals of the artist, however, this technique requires careful planning as one cannot go back and print one color after the next color has been carved and printed.
30

The works of art created by printmaking are called impressions, not copies, since each piece produced is technically an original, not a reproduction of another work of art. Printmaking has many variations, but is most commonly created by transferring ink from a matrix (a solid piece of wood, stone, or metal), or through a prepared screen such as silk, to a medium, such as a sheet of paper
35  or other material. Multiple impressions made from the same matrix create what is called an edition. Artists generally sign individual impressions from an edition and number the impressions to create a limited edition. For example, a notation such as 1/100 means that the print is the first print out of a hundred that were made from the original matrix.

40  Printmaking revolutionized the world of art because it allowed artists to produce multiple 'copies' of their artwork; they could now sell, display, and distribute their work more widely. For the first time in East Asia, and in other parts of the world where the technique thrived, people no longer had to be wealthy to experience or own beautiful art. For example, the *ukiyo-e* style of printmaking in medieval Japan allowed even the middle class to purchase art made by expert craftsman.
45

Intaglio printing, a form of printmaking developed in renaissance Italy, is the opposite of the woodcut technique. Instead of the raised areas holding the ink and creating the design, in intaglio printing the cuts in the matrix hold the ink and produce the art. By the early 15th century the most common type of intaglio printing, called engraving, was developed by German goldsmiths, who
50  were masters of carving metal. The techniques of intaglio have changed little over time: An artist uses a variety of specialized sharp tools called burin to gouge lines into the surface of a smooth polished metal; the most common matrix material is a sheet of copper. Ink is pressed into the lines of the design and then the surface is wiped clean by a cloth so that only the cut lines retain the ink. A water-soaked sheet of paper, placed upon the inked surface, is then run through a printing press.

55    The pressure applied by the press forces the pliable paper into the small cut lines and the result is a piece of art that has the detail of an exquisite pen and ink drawing.

60    The engraved metal sheets could be used hundreds of times to make hundreds of prints, making them perfect for large editions and book illustrations. The burgeoning middle class of Europe began to collect fine art in the way that only the nobility could just decades before. Demand surged for fine artwork that could be easily reproduced and made those who could deliver such works wealthy craftsmen. Masters of engraving, such as the artist Albrecht Dürer, produced timeless works of art using the intaglio method, many of which are valued today in the millions of dollars.

65    Etching, another intaglio technique, is an offshoot of engraving. Instead of carving directly into the metal, the artist carves into a material coating the metal. The artist covers the metal plate with a waxy or acrylic material and then draws into this material with an etching needle. The finished plate is dipped into a bath of etchant (nitric acid or ferric chloride) which bites into the exposed metal, leaving behind lines in the plate where the artist has drawn into the coating. Etching can produce
70    more subtle tone gradations than engraving and is perfect for single color, or monotone, reproductions and decorating metals.

    By the early 1800s, printmaking took another creative turn with the development of lithography, a simple and inexpensive method of printmaking, as well as one of the most interesting. Lithography
75    begins with a smooth, flat slab of limestone rock. An artist draws their design directly onto the limestone surface with a wax-based marker or crayon and then applies water to the stone. Because of the natural repulsion between oil and water, the water moves to the places with an absence of oil. An oil-based ink is then applied to the stone with a roller and adheres only to the oiled, marked areas. Paper is pressed to the stone and the ink is transferred to the surface of the
80    paper, creating the image. Henri de Toulouse-Lautrec created his posters for the famous Moulin Rouge nightclub in late 19th century Paris using the inexpensive lithograph technique.

    Screen printing is another form of printmaking that is almost as old as woodblock printing. Also from medieval China, this technique was patented over a thousand years later in early 20th century
85    England as a method for making wallpaper. In screen printing, ink or paint is pushed through a prepared screen or stencil made of silk or synthetic fibers stretched tightly across a frame. Glues, paper, or other materials are used to keep the ink or paint from passing through selected areas; wherever these materials are applied, no ink passes through. Multiple screens and different colors can be used to create intricate designs; screen printing is used to create everything from fine art to
90    posters to t-shirts. Two American artists of the 1960s became especially famous for their screen prints: Andy Warhol and Robert Indiana. Warhol constructed images of famous icons like Marilyn Monroe, China's Chairman Mao Tse Tung, and Campbell's Soup cans using screen printing. Indiana created one of the most famous images in history with his red and green screen print of the word, LOVE.
95

    Printmaking as an art form has been around since ancient times and has evolved from woodblock carving and screen printing to intaglio printing, metal etching, and lithography as artists have experimented with its basic techniques and principles. Even today, old techniques are put into service by modern artists to create cutting-edge art that resonates with people. Whether it is the
100   masterful woodcut art of Hokusai or the popular art of Andy Warhol, printmaking has played an undeniable role in the history of the visual arts.

**11. From the description of the making of *The Great Wave* in paragraph 1, the author is primarily establishing for the reader that:**

    A. The printmaker, Hokusai, was like many other traditional Japanese printmakers in that he worked in isolation.

    B. The techniques of woodcut printing required careful planning and skillful execution.

    C. *The Great Wave* was an early type of mass produced art that even the Japanese middle class could afford to own.

    D. *The Great Wave* was produced using the iterative method of woodblock printing rather than the reduction method.

**12. The goal of the author in writing this passage is most likely to:**

    F. Introduce the reader to the key figures in printmaking history, such as Hokusai, Dürer, Henri de Toulouse-Lautrec, Andy Warhol, and Robert Indiana.

    G. Explain the key differences between raised matrix and cut matrix printmaking.

    H. Underscore the importance of the Far East in the development of printmaking.

    J. Educate the reader on the basic techniques, history, and importance of printmaking.

**13. Works of art created using printmaking techniques are called an 'impressions' because:**

    A. Printmaking was most fully embraced by the Impressionist artists of 19th century Paris.

    B. Each piece produced is a lasting and faithful reproduction of the original.

    C. Each piece produced is technically an original work of art.

    D. Printmakers have created some of the most impressive and iconic images in the history of visual arts.

**14. In the printmaking process, the matrix is:**

    F. The material the ink is applied to.

    G. The first edition, or impression, made.

    H. The object to be printed upon.

    J. The type of ink or paint used.

**15. According to the passage, the oldest style of printmaking is:**

    A. Intaglio style printing

    B. Woodblock printing

    C. Silk screen printing

    D. Lithographic printing

**16. The major difference between woodcut printing and intaglio printing is that:**

    F. In woodcut printing, the raised portions of the matrix hold the ink; in intaglio printing, the cut-away surfaces of the matrix hold the ink.

    G. Woodcut printing only uses a wood matrix, while intaglio printing only uses a stone matrix.

    H. In intaglio printing, the raised portions of the matrix hold the ink; in woodcut printing, the cut-away surfaces of the matrix hold the ink.

    J. Woodcut printing follows specific rules passed down from ancient Japanese masters. Intaglio printing has no strict rules or boundaries.

**17. The most common style of intaglio printing in the early part of the 15ᵗʰ century was:**

    A.  Etching
    B.  Engraving
    C.  Lithographic printing
    D.  Silk screen printing

**18. An advantage of metallic intaglio printing over woodcuts is that:**

    F.  Less ink is required when using a metallic matrix.
    G.  The metal matrix can be re-used hundreds of times.
    H.  Engraving a metal matrix requires less skill than carving a wooden matrix.
    J.  The impressions made by a wooden matrix are of higher quality than those made by a metallic matrix.

**19. According to the passage, the popularity of lithography can be attributed to:**

    A.  Its simplicity and low cost.
    B.  The prestige associated with the difficulty of its techniques.
    C.  The uniqueness and originality of using stone as a matrix.
    D.  The ease with which soft limestone rock can be etched.

**20. The author states that "printmaking has played an undeniable role in the history of the visual arts". What, according to the passage, is its most significant contribution?**

    F.  Its basic techniques allowed for more experimentation than any other medium of expression.
    G.  It allowed artists to create works of art with no limit to the number of colors used.
    H.  It empowered both master craftsmen as well as pop culture artists to create cutting edge art.
    J.  It lowered the cost, and thus the availability, of art.

# Leo Durocher

Imagine meeting one person who could tell you about all the greatest players of the golden age of baseball. A personality so well placed through 50 years of our national past-time that he could not only explain what made these players from the 1920s to the 1970s tick, but do it in a way that made you laugh out loud, gasp incredulously, and shake your head in amazement. Leo "the Lip"
5 Durocher was that story-teller and what made Durocher so compelling and thought-provoking was that he spent fifty years as a top baseball player, manager, and entertainment personality.

Born in 1905, to a poor French-Catholic family in West Springfield, Massachusetts, Leo learned to field baseballs from local hero and Hall of Fame shortstop Rabbit Maranville. By the time he was
10 twenty years old in 1925, Leo was breaking into the major leagues with the powerful New York Yankees. Tempestuous with both opponents and his teammates, especially the legendary Babe Ruth who labeled the light-hitting Durocher, "the All-American Out," Leo chattered incessantly on the field as a loud-mouthed fly to be swatted. His smart-aleck remarks brought him his most famous moniker of all: "the Lip." He would make hitters so mad that they became violent.
15 Lumbering to the plate, the weight-conscious Fatty Fothergill was hitting in a crucial situation when, in the middle of Fothergill's at bat, Durocher leaned in from second base, pointed at Fothergill and screamed, "Hey Taxi!" Fothergill took three quick strikes and then chased Durocher around the field until he was restrained by both teams.

20 Already a member of two World Champion Yankees teams, it was as a member of the renowned St. Louis Cardinals "Gas House Gang" from 1933 to 1937 that Leo would peak as a player. The Cardinals were a coarse mixture of hillbillies and blue collar bowery bums that could play serious baseball. Out onto the field unshaven, in unwashed, smelly uniforms came a motley collection that reminded audiences of 1930s gashouse refinery workers. However, the Cards were stacked with
25 Hall of Famers like their player-manager Frankie Frisch, Joe "Ducky" Medwick, and pitcher Dizzy Dean. Iconic players of the day like Pepper Martin and Rip Collins, whose talents had already helped the Cards win the World Series in 1931, entertained fans before games by doing rapid acrobatic tosses, hits, and catches with baseballs. By 1934, Leo Durocher was the nationally famous shortstop of the Gashouse Gang and having one of his best seasons. Again, "the Lip" was
30 whipping up fervor on and off the field angering opposing squads with insults and underhanded tactics. St. Louis went on to win the World Series that year in seven games over the powerful Detroit Tigers.

In 1938, Leo Durocher became a player-manager for the Brooklyn Dodgers, known as "Dem Bums"
35 at their home park, Ebbets Field. The Dodgers had not won a pennant, or a championship flag, in many years. Now, having been a part of three World Champion teams, Durocher knew the type of tough and talented players he wanted and got them: hard-hitting Joe Medwick from the Cardinals, fleet centerfielder Pete Reiser, and Hall of Fame shortstop Pee Wee Reese from the Dodgers' farm system. Leo "The Lip" instantly gained notoriety, delighting the working class Brooklyn fans as he
40 scrapped with umpires and opposing players. Arguments could be heard quite clearly in intimate parks like Ebbets and Leo routinely kicked dirt on an umpire's shoes then dramatically exited through the outfield to the clubhouse after being ejected from the game. The Dodgers faithful went crazy and, because he was fighting for them, it usually fired up his players. Each year the Dodgers improved until, in 1941, they won 100 games and their first National League championship in over
45 two decades.

Leo was the manager of the Brooklyn Dodgers during Jackie Robinson's initial years breaking the major league's color barrier. Although Durocher was suspended by Major League Baseball in 1947, Robinson's rookie season, he had defended Jackie's right to play with his team during Robinson's
50 time in the minors and became an advocate for other famous African American players like Dodgers Roy Campanella, and Don Newcombe. Durocher used his "Lip" to coax white players into giving players of color a chance by appealing to their wallets. Talented players, black, white, or brown, would get them World Series shares.

55 Leo was a hero in Brooklyn for nine years, but in 1948 he became a scoundrel by becoming manager of the rival New York Giants. Ebbets Field, in the Flatbush section of Brooklyn, was only eleven and a half miles away from the Polo Grounds, the Manhattan home of the Giants. The historic subway rivalry had raged since the late 19th century. The Giants, however, had fallen on hard times and Leo Durocher was called upon to right the ship. Durocher began to gather players
60 that he knew could win games like veteran infielder Alvin Dark, pitcher Sal Maglie, and one of the all-time greatest players in history, Willie Mays. As well, "the Lip" began to get the skeptical Giants fans on his side by displaying the same type of fire that he had for years as the Dodgers' skipper: needling opposing teams from his bench in the dugout and always keeping umpires and opposing managers alike guessing with his acumen and caustic wit. In August, 1951, the Giants under
65 Durocher were thirteen and a half games behind first place in the standings when they began to go on a tear to capture the National League pennant. It all came down to the final day of a three game, winner take all series where the Giants faced the team that Durocher had previously helped build into a winner, the Brooklyn Dodgers. In the final game, the Giants were down to their last out, behind by three runs when, in the ninth inning, Bobby Thomson hit a homerun that won the game
70 and the National League championship. Although they were beaten by the New York Yankees in the World Series that year, the New York Giants under Leo Durocher, later went on to win the 1954 World Championship.

Leo's colorful personality <u>transcended</u> the game of baseball. He became an NBC television
75 commentator for the Baseball Game of the Week in the 1950s and, in the early 1960s, made guest appearances as himself in cornball TV comedy shows like *The Munsters*, *Mr. Ed*, and the *Beverly Hillbillies*. He also sang with Judy Garland on her 1963 variety show. In the 1960s and 70s, Durocher was an assistant coach for the World Champion Los Angeles Dodgers and then managed the Chicago Cubs and Houston Astros. As a manager, he won over 2000 games, and is
80 seventh on the all-time list for victories. Leo passed away in October of 1991, three years before he was enshrined in the Baseball Hall of Fame in 1994. The Hall's Veterans Committee saw fit to honor what they called Leo's "combative and swashbuckling style, brilliant baseball mind, uncanny memory and fiery disposition." To the rest of the baseball world, and to his fans, Leo will simply be remembered as "the Lip."

(Note to the reader: There are two leagues in Major League Baseball: The American League and the National League. American League teams compete to win the American League Championship flag, or pennant, and the National League teams do the same within their league. The National League and American League Champions then compete for the World Championship in the World Series.)

**21. The main idea of this passage is:**

A. Leo Durocher was a strange success story in Major League Baseball because he showed how dysfunctional behavior could win championships.
B. Leo Durocher fought for the underdog everywhere he was a player or manager and the world should remember him for this.
C. Leo Durocher personifies the Golden Age of Baseball both because of his personal experiences and his larger than life personality.
D. Leo Durocher profited from his legacy as "the Lip" through acting on television and being a commentator on NBC's Game of the Week.

**22. As used in paragraph 1, the word *incredulously* (<u>line 4</u>) means:**

F. Skeptical
G. Unbelieving
H. Eager for more
J. Disdainfully

**23. The author infers paragraph 2 that Leo may have used his *tempestuous* nature in order to:**

A. Make friends using reverse psychology.
B. Fit in with his teammates.
C. Create a distraction away from his inability to hit a baseball.
D. Gain a competitive edge against opponents.

**24. From the context of <u>lines 13-14</u>, the meaning of the word *moniker* can be inferred as:**

F. A quote attributable to a specific person.
G. A memorable experience.
H. A personal name or nickname.
J. A smart-aleck response to a remark.

**25. The Gas House Gang was able to win a World Championship because:**

A. Leo Durocher became shortstop for the team.
B. Despite their rough outward appearance and feisty disposition, the team held a lot of talent.
C. The slovenly outward appearance of the team consistently distracted opponents from playing their best game.
D. The methods used by the Gas House Gang were often intimidating to opposing teams.

**26. In paragraph 4, the author is trying to show that:**

F. Leo Durocher used his experience as a player to put together a winning team in Brooklyn.
G. Leo Durocher had a hard time translating his experience as a player into the job of managing a team.
H. Leo Durocher knew that the only way he could win was to have his old Cardinals teammates on the Brooklyn Dodgers with him.
J. Despite Leo Durocher's dysfunctional behavior, which angered fans, umpires and opposing managers, his team still won 100 games and a championship in 1941.

**27. According to paragraph 5, Leo Durocher defended the rights of African Americans to play Major League Baseball by:**

A. Convincing white players that all players were equal regardless of whether they were black, white, or brown.
B. Convincing white players that sharing the feeling of a World Series championship was the only thing that mattered.
C. Convincing white players that talent, not race, was the only thing that mattered when evaluating players.
D. Convincing white players that, regardless of color, better players would benefit everyone by making members of the team more World Series money.

**28. In comparing Durocher's management of the Brooklyn Dodgers with his management of the New York Giants, one could say that:**

F. He was more successful managing the New York Giants because he won both a National League pennant and a World Series Championship.
G. He was never as successful as when he managed the Brooklyn Dodgers and he will always be remembered by Dodger fans as a scoundrel for leaving to manage their rival.
H. Giant fans quickly became disenchanted with Durocher; he displayed the same dysfunctional behaviors he had displayed earlier with the Cardinals and Dodgers.
J. Durocher never won as many games with the Giants as he had with the Brooklyn Dodgers.

**29. When the author writes that Leo Durocher was "always keeping umpires and opposing managers alike guessing with his acumen and caustic wit," it shows that:**

A. Leo's baseball decisions were often made impulsively; opponents never knew if he was serious or not.
B. Leo's excellent baseball knowledge was often undermined by his habit of getting into tirades with umpires and opposing managers.
C. Leo's smart-aleck goading and dramatic tirades made umpires and opposing managers wary that he was trying to play mind games in order to get a win.
D. Leo was, on the outside, all business; but on the inside, he was laughing at opposing managers and umpires.

**30. What does the author mean when he says that 'Leo's colorful personality *transcended* the game of baseball' (line 74)?**

F. Durocher's personality on and off the baseball field made him famous even to non-baseball fans.
G. Baseball fans knew who Leo Durocher was and followed his exploits in the entertainment world.
H. Durocher contributed to the world outside of baseball.
J. Durocher's stature as a baseball player and manager made him famous to baseball fans all over the world.

## Habitat Population Distributions

The following passage is adapted from the United States Forest Service Research and Development publication titled "Multiple space-use strategies and their divergent consequences in a nonbreeding migratory bird (Parkesia noveboracensis). 2011. Smith, Joseph A.M.; Reitsma, Leonard R.; Marra, Peter P. The Auk. 128(1):53-60.

The distribution of individuals within and among habitats has important implications for survival and reproduction. Distribution patterns that result from intraspecific competition are often described using theoretical models proposed by Fretwell and Lucas. These include the ideal-free and the ideal-despotic distribution. In the ideal-free distribution, individuals are free to select any habitat
5   patch without interference from other individuals and density is a function of habitat quality, so that all individuals have equal success regardless of the habitat they choose. Conversely, with the ideal-despotic distribution, density is limited by competitive interactions (i.e., despotism), and less competitive individuals are excluded from high-quality habitats.

10  Understanding which of these two models describe animals in the field is important because each model has distinct implications for the role of habitat availability in influencing population dynamics. If the ideal-free distribution underlies spacing patterns, then individual birds are not territorial, resources are not limited, and habitat availability is not likely to be a primary driver of population processes. If patterns consistent with the ideal-despotic distribution are revealed, this suggests that
15  habitat is limiting and that through territoriality some individuals can secure a greater amount of resources than others. Furthermore, population processes can be greatly affected if excluded individuals are of a distinct age or sex class.

Territoriality in nonbreeding migratory songbirds is evidenced by aggression toward conspecifics,
20  defense of small home ranges, and fidelity to a site both within and between years. If territoriality occurs during the nonbreeding season, we would expect differential consequences for individuals across habitats and home ranges, with more competitive individuals maintaining better body condition than less competitive individuals. Furthermore, we would expect that ecological determinants of fitness such as habitat quality would vary correspondingly, with more competitive
25  individuals maintaining higher-quality territories.

For nonbreeding migratory birds in the Neotropics, key ecological determinants are moisture and resulting food availability. Throughout much of the nonbreeding range of migratory birds, a dry season sets in from December through mid-April, just prior to spring migration, which changes the
30  distribution and availability of fruit, nectar, and invertebrate food resources. Such changes to habitats and their food resources may further intensify competition for high-quality sites that are often buffered from the effects of the dry season. These changes may also lead less competitive individuals to disperse as habitat conditions deteriorate.

35  We studied patterns of territoriality and overwinter site-persistence in a population of Northern Waterthrushes that occupied a mosaic of nonbreeding habitats in Puerto Rico. Previous studies of territoriality in this species have led to different conclusions regarding patterns of winter space use. Schwartz (1964) showed Northern Waterthrushes to be site-faithful and territorial in a botanical garden, with agonistic behavior of color-marked birds at territorial boundaries described in detail.
40  Conversely, mist-netting and resighting studies in Black Mangrove have reported overlapping home ranges and low within-season site fidelity. No studies have yet compared space use across multiple habitat types as a possible explanation for the conflicting results.

To that end, we examined evidence for defense of exclusive areas by individual Northern
45  Waterthrushes by measuring aggression, estimating home-range overlap, and documenting overwinter site-persistence across multiple habitat types. We also examined whether a territorial space-use strategy resulted in the acquisition of higher-quality sites and tested whether this had consequences for the physical condition of individual birds by monitoring mass change over the later-winter dry season.

50

Our findings indicate that the space-use patterns of Northern Waterthrushes are consistent with the ideal-despotic distribution rather than the ideal-free distribution. As predicted by the ideal-despotic model, we observed that more competitive individuals, which were more aggressive and territorial, acquired higher-quality home ranges and were in better body condition than less aggressive
55    individuals. Previous studies that concluded that Northern Waterthrushes were not territorial described patterns of low-overwinter site fidelity similar to that which we observed in Black Mangrove and dry forest. Schwarz, on the other hand, showed that Northern Waterthrushes were territorial in an irrigated botanical garden. Our work reconciles these disparate findings by documenting a continuum of space-use strategies that is dependent on competitive ability and
60    habitat selection. It is likely that in high-quality, seasonally stable habitats, territoriality is more common whereas in lower-quality or seasonally dynamic habitat, alternative strategies are more prevalent.

**31. In the ideal-free distribution model, the population density of a species is dependent on:**

A. Competitive interactions
B. Territoriality
C. Physical fitness
D. Habit quality

**32. A ruby-throated hummingbird drives off another of its species from a nectar-laden flower. A group of ducks lands in a pond and begins to feed. These are examples of:**

F. First, ideal-free distribution then, ideal-despotic distribution.
G. First, ideal-despotic distribution then, ideal-free distribution.
H. Interspecific competition
J. Multiple space-use strategies

**33. According to the passage, understanding the intraspecific competition model of a particular species will help humans to understand:**

A. Which animals within a population are most vulnerable to the loss of habitat.
B. Which animal populations are distributed in Neotropical areas.
C. The diversity of various animal populations within Black Mangrove.
D. The ability of an animal to find food within a specific area.

**34. When speaking of conspecific aggression in paragraph 3, the characteristic of *territoriality* is:**

F. A negative trait that does not benefit individual members of the species.
G. A co-existence strategy where members of a species band together to protect their area against invaders from their own species.
H. A despotic characteristic that means members of a species in the best shape and fitness will get the best territory.
J. Influenced by climatic events and phenomena such as earthquakes or floods.

**35. The authors of the passage state that intraspecific territoriality and competition can be intensified by:**

A. A natural dry season that sets in from April to mid-December, affecting the availability of food.
B. Human predation, which disrupts normal intraspecific competition and distribution patterns.
C. Seasonal climatic changes that set in before spring migration, affecting the availability of food.
D. The introduction of non-native species to the ecosystem, which increases the competition for available resources.

**36.** In paragraph 5, the authors use the term *agonistic behavior.* **Given the context of the sentence, the likely meaning of this phrase is:**

   F.  Behavior of an almost 'religious nature' by members of the same species.
   G.  Aggressive behavior by members of the same species who are in competition for food, territory, or mates.
   H.  Behavior of an aggressive type between members of different species populations.
   J.  Passive behavior by members of the same species competing for food, territory, or mates.

**37. The naturally occurring dry season affects bird habitats by:**

   A.  Changing the location and amount of food resources.
   B.  Decreasing the total amount of food resources.
   C.  Increasing the availability of fruit, nectar, and invertebrate food resources.
   D.  Decreasing the amount of fruit and nectar food sources and increasing the amount of invertebrate food resources.

**38. What is the primary mission of the authors in conducting their study of Northern Waterthrushes?**

   F.  To show that no previous study of the Northern Waterthrush has provided valid conclusions regarding territoriality.
   G.  To show that the studies performed in Black Mangrove have provided the most consistent and reliable results thus far.
   H.  To prove that the findings of the1964 Schwartz studies should be accepted over studies that found conflicting results.
   J.  To explore whether a comparison of space use across multiple habitats can explain the conflicting results of previous studies.

**39. In their study of the Northern Waterthrush, the authors conclude that:**

   A.  Within high-quality habitats, territoriality decreased due to the great availability of resources. In lower-quality habitats, aggressive behaviors increased due to the limited availability of resources.
   B.  Within high-quality, seasonally stable habitats, ideal-despotic behaviors are more commonly observed. In low-quality or seasonally dynamic habitats, alternative strategies are more common.
   C.  There was no scientifically valid way to harmonize the conflicting results of the 1964 Schwartz study and the Black Mangrove studies.
   D.  Fewer and fewer birds were found in the same territories every year, leading to the conclusion that the Northern Waterthrush populations were diminishing due to low-quality habitats.

**40. The tone of the author's writing can best be described as:**

   F.  Neutral and dispassionate
   G.  Passionate and engaging
   H.  Argumentative
   J.  Defensive

# READING PRACTICE TEST 3 ANSWER KEY

| | |
|---|---|
| 1. C | 21. C |
| 2. J | 22. G |
| 3. A | 23. D |
| 4. H | 24. H |
| 5. A | 25. B |
| 6. G | 26. F |
| 7. D | 27. D |
| 8. G | 28. F |
| 9. A | 29. C |
| 10. H | 30. F |
| 11. B | 31. D |
| 12. J | 32. G |
| 13. C | 33. A |
| 14. F | 34. H |
| 15. B | 35. C |
| 16. F | 36. G |
| 17. B | 37. A |
| 18. G | 38. J |
| 19. A | 39. B |
| 20. J | 40. F |

# READING PRACTICE TEST 3 RATIONALES

## 1. Answer: C. A young child
In paragraph 1 the narrator speaks of her grandmother and grandfather which eliminates answer choice B; a friend of the family would not refer to these members of the household in this way. The narrator also speaks of Antonia in the passage so answer D is not a possible answer choice; a narrator would not refer to herself in the third person. A powerful piece of evidence that the narrator is a young child is that in line 7, she refers to herself as being alone in the house in a way that makes it clear this was not a normal situation. This makes sense only if the narrator is a young, non-adult age person.

## 2. Answer: J. A rural outpost in the United States.
Answers A and B can be eliminated because there is clear evidence in the passage to support that this is a rural location, not an urban center or a busy trading town. In paragraph 2, the chores of feeding the chickens and gathering eggs are described; these are chores typical of a rural household. In line 1, the characters have to spend an entire day clearing a road to the Shimerdas' house. This suggests a remote location where one has to rely upon themselves. Could this rural location be a lonely outpost in the wilderness area of Northern Canada (answer C)? In lines 23-24, the narrator mentions the names of U.S. towns such as Chicago and Baltimore, and the state of Virginia. If the passage was set in Canada, it is unlikely the narrator would mention locations in the United States.

## 3. Answer: A. Setting out, stoically, on a mission of mercy to help out their neighbor.
We know that the trip to the neighbor's house is a serious mission, not a joyful one. In line 3, the grandmother is described as being dressed in a black hood and bundled in shawls, which suggests a state of mourning. As the grandfather tucks his beard inside his overcoat, the narrator describes the party of four as looking "very Biblical as they set off", implying a time of trial and seriousness.

The characters are breaking a path through the snow, but they are doing it for immediate reasons, not for future visits (eliminating D). The family is trying to reach their neighbor as quickly as possible (answer C), but the disaster has already happened in Mr. Shimerda's death. Because the family is bringing bundles of clothes for Mrs. Shimerda after the death of her husband (lines 5-6), answer A is the best choice.

## 4. Answer: H. Exhilarated by this unusual circumstance; she wants to prove to herself and her family that she can handle the experience.
At the beginning of paragraph 2, the narrator relates that she felt a "considerable extension of power and authority" and that she was "anxious to acquit" herself creditably as able to handle being alone in such unusual circumstances (line 9). From this, we know that she was excited at being alone, not anxious or indifferent. She also speaks in line 14 of enjoying the quiet of the house, another indication that she is enjoying her experience.

While she does try to read *Robinson Crusoe*, she finds that it won't hold her attention. She says in lines 15-16 that "I got 'Robinson Crusoe' and tried to read, but his life on the island seemed dull compared with ours." She does perform the chores forgotten by the others (answer D), but she does them with enthusiasm and in order to show her independence and maturity.

## 5. Answer: A. A friend of the family and, having spent much time at the narrator's house, will be sorely missed.
The information gradually released by the narrator throughout the passage leads us to believe that Mr. Shimerda was more than just a casual acquaintance and had been welcome often (including Christmas, line 19) inside the narrator's home. Since the narrator's family has set out in difficult winter conditions in order to bring clothes to the Shimerda widow, it implies closeness between the two families.

We know from the passage (lines 22-23, 32-33) that Mr. Shimerda was an immigrant (answer C), but there is no indication that he could not speak English or that his family needed constant assistance from the narrator's family. The narrator also relates that Mr. Shimerda was a fiddler who loved to play music (lines 33-34), but mentions nowhere that she herself has attended any functions where he was performing (answer D). Considering the tone and information of the passage, answer A is the best choice.

### 6. Answer: G. Was taking refuge from the cold in her house.
In paragraph 2 the narrator tells us that, "if Mr. Shimerda's soul were lingering about in this world at all, it would be here, in our house." (lines 17-18) Then, in paragraph 3, she mentions that, "surely, his exhausted spirit, so tired of cold and crowding and the struggle with the ever-falling snow, was resting now in this quiet house." (lines 25-26)

### 7. Answer: D. A close friend of the narrator and related to the Shimerda family.
Antonia and Mr. Shimerda's wife are characterized by the narrator as two different people. In lines 35-36, the narrator describes how Antonia and her mother used to steal wood from the nobles in their old homeland. From this we can assume that Mrs. Shimerda is Antonia's mother. Another piece of evidence comes from lines 48-49 that states "Antonia and Ambrosch and the mother took turns going down to pray beside" Mr. Shimerda's body. This supports the assumption that Antonia is a member of the Shimerda family.

### 8. Answer: G. A road is broken through the snow. The narrator's parents and brother went to the Shimerda's home to help. The narrator did chores to keep herself busy and thought about Mr. Shimerda's soul. The narrator's family came back home cold and tired.
The best answer choice is B. Line 1: A road is broken through the snow. Paragraph 1: The narrator's parents and brother went to the Shimerda's home to help. Paragraph 2 and 3: The narrator did chores to keep herself busy and thought about Mr. Shimerda's soul. Paragraph 5: The narrator's family came back home cold and tired.

### 9. Answer: A. A child with an obvious mental disability.
The passage does not mention that Marek has a physical disability (answer C). The narrator does not mention Marek until the final sentences of the last paragraph of the passage and never mentions that they are friends (answer D); the last paragraph simply refers to Marek as "the crazy boy." The narrator is implying that he has a mental deficiency.

### 10. Answer: H. Revolved around the relationship built by Mr. Shimerda's presence in the narrator's home and later involved Antonia.
Using evidence found *only* in the passage itself, one could assume that the relationship between the two families evolved from Mr. Shimerda's relationship with the family. We know from lines 17-20 that Mr. Shimerda made frequent visits to the narrator's house: "…it flashed upon me that if Mr. Shimerda's soul were lingering about in this world at all, it would be here, in our house, which had been more to his liking than any other in the neighborhood. I remembered his contented face when he was with us on Christmas Day. If he could have lived with us, this terrible thing would never have happened." So it is clear that Mr. Shimerda was no stranger. We can assume from this that the relationship between the adults fostered a relationship between the children in the families.

### 11. Answer: B. The techniques of woodcut printing required careful planning and skillful execution.
In paragraph 1, the author imagines the night that Katsushika Hokusai created his masterful work, *The Great Wave*. Since we know that the author wasn't present when the art was made, we can infer that his description is illustrative of what occurred, rather than being a detailed description of actual events. The author recounts this scene in order to establish for the reader that Katsushika Hokusai and other woodblock printmakers had to go through an intricate series of steps, each involving careful planning, in order to execute their work.

### 12. Answer: J. Educate the reader on the basic techniques, history, and importance of printmaking.
The author takes the reader through each of the key developments in printmaking history, from the origins of early woodblock and screen printing to the later invention of intaglio printing, engraving, and lithography. The author also gives the reader a brief description of the techniques unique to each new

subset of printmaking and ends the passage with a declaration of the importance of printmaking in the history of the visual arts. Although the author does give specific examples of important printmaking artists, this is not the primary concern of the passage. Rather, the author wants the reader to come away from the passage knowing the basic history of printmaking, its basic techniques, and its importance in the history of the arts.

### 13. Answer: C. Each piece produced is technically an original work of art.
In lines 31-32, the author states that "the works of art created by printmaking are called impressions, not copies, since each piece produced is technically an original, not a reproduction of another work of art".

### 14. Answer: F. The material the ink is applied to.
The matrix is defined in lines 33-34 as "a solid piece of wood, stone, or metal". The ink is applied directly onto the matrix and transferred to a chosen object, usually paper, by applying light pressure. The object to be printed upon is called the medium.

### 15. Answer: B. Woodblock printing
The author states in line 16 that woodcut printing "is most likely the earliest form of printmaking", although screen printing is mentioned as being almost as old and also originating in medieval China. Intaglio printing is stated as developing in renaissance Italy (line 46) and lithographic printing is said to have begun in the early 1800s (line 73).

### 16. Answer: F. In woodcut printing, the raised portions of the matrix hold the ink; in intaglio printing, the cut-away surfaces of the matrix hold the ink.
Lines 46-47 state that the technique of intaglio printing "is the opposite of the woodcut technique". In lines 47-48, the author further explains that "instead of the raised areas holding the ink and creating the design, in intaglio printing the cuts in the matrix hold the ink and produce the art."

### 17. Answer: B. Engraving
Engraving is described in paragraph 5 as being a form of intaglio printing developed in the early 15th century by skilled German goldsmiths. This subset of intaglio is described as engraving designs onto a metal plate, most often copper.

### 18. Answer: G. The metal matrix can be re-used hundreds of times.
In speaking of the metallic matrices used in intaglio printmaking, the author explains that "the engraved metal sheets could be used hundreds of times to make hundreds of prints, making them perfect for large editions and book illustrations." (lines 58-59)

### 19. Answer: A. Its simplicity and low cost.
While the use of a stone matrix (limestone) is described as a creative development in printmaking, the author states that lithography was "a simple and inexpensive method of printmaking" (line 74). One can infer that its simplicity and low cost led to its popularity and adoption by artists.

### 20. Answer: J. It lowered the cost, and thus the availability, of art.
The only answer choice that is explicitly expressed by the author is that printmaking expanded the availability of art (answer D), which we can infer from the passage is due the lower cost of printmaking versus making original art. In paragraph 4, the author states that "printmaking revolutionized the world of art because it allowed artists to produce multiple 'copies' of their artwork; they could now sell, display, and distribute their work more widely" (lines 40-41). Before printmaking, the artist had to create each original work separately and could only sell each work to one person. Once printmaking was developed, the author indicates that even middle class people could purchase art. Lines 42-43 state that "people no longer had to be wealthy to experience or own beautiful art" and lines 59-60 state that "the burgeoning middle class of Europe began to collect fine art in the way that only the nobility could just decades before". Answer D is the best choice.

**21. Answer: C. Leo Durocher personifies the Golden Age of Baseball both because of his personal experiences and his larger than life personality.**

Leo's behavior might have been seen as dysfunctional at times (answer A), and he did often portray himself and his teams as underdogs (answer B). Leo Durocher did also profit from his renown as a Major League Baseball personality while making a living on television (answer D). However, the consistent idea throughout the passage is that Leo Durocher was a prominent player and manager who experienced a high level of success throughout fifty years and he was able to get to know, and compete with and against some of the greatest baseball players of the 20th century.

**22. Answer: G. Unbelieving**

The sentence containing the word incredulously also contains references to laughter and amazement. This would imply that the word is being used in a light-hearted way, not in a manner of disdain or with a skeptical reaction.

**23. Answer: D. Gain a competitive edge against opponents.**

We can infer that Leo was not an incredible hitter (answer C) from Babe Ruth's nickname for him in line 12, "The All-American Out", but the passage does not imply that he used his tempestuous and smart-aleck nature to distract from his average hitting skills. Leo had more practical reasons for creating distractions on the baseball diamond. As described in lines 14-18, Durocher baits Fatty Fothergill into striking out in a crucial situation; this is an example of how Leo used his mind and his mouth to gain a competitive edge against opponents.

**24. Answer: H. A personal name or nickname.**

A moniker is a personal name or nickname different from someone's given name. Lines 12-14 describe how it was Durocher's smart-aleck remarks and verbal goading of opposing players that led directly to him being called 'the Lip'.

**25. Answer: B. Despite their rough outward appearance and feisty disposition, the team held a lot of talent.**

Lines 28-29 indicate that Leo Durocher played the shortstop position for the Gas House Gang, but the passage does not indicate that this was why they won the World Championship. Paragraph 3 describes the team as a rough looking bunch; line 23 states that they would come "onto the field unshaven, in unwashed, smelly uniforms" but the paragraph makes it clear that it was their raw talent that led to their win. Line 22 says they "could play serious baseball" and line 24 says they "were stacked with Hall of Famers", indicating a deep talent pool.

**26. Answer: F. Leo Durocher used his experience as a player to put together a winning team in Brooklyn.**

While it is true that Leo Durocher brought Joe Medwick from the Cardinals to the Dodgers (answer C), Leo's success as a player-manager came from his long experience as a player. As conveyed by lines 36-37, Leo had the experience of winning three World Championships as a player and knew something about what it took to be a successful team. He put together a team by choosing the "type of rough and talented players" that shared his view of the sport, recruiting old teammates and players from the Dodgers farm system.

**27. Answer: D. Convincing white players that, regardless of color, better players would benefit everyone by making members of the team more World Series money.**

Lines 51-53 state that Durocher appealed to player's wallets when discussing the issue of the color barrier in baseball. He felt that having the best players, regardless of color, would benefit all players by helping them win more championships and thus, make more money.

**28. Answer: F. He was more successful managing the New York Giants because he won both a National League pennant and a World Series Championship.**

From paragraph 4 that describes Durocher's management of the Brooklyn Dodgers, we know that they only went as far as winning the National League Championship in 1941 (lines 43-45). From paragraph 6 that describes his management of the rival New York Giants team, we know that he won both a 1951

National League Championship (lines 68-70) and eventually a World Series Championship in 1954 (lines 70-72). In this way, his management of the Giants can be considered more successful than his management of the Dodgers.

**29. Answer: C. Leo's smart-aleck goading and dramatic tirades made umpires and opposing managers wary that he was trying to play mind games in order to get a win.**
As the passage illustrates, the genius of Leo Durocher as a baseball player and a manager was that he was able to goad others into making mistakes and was able to win some games just with his mind and mouth. In describing how he verbally taunted and distracted batter Fothergill during a game, lines 13-14 state that "His smart-aleck remarks brought him his most famous moniker of all: 'the Lip'. He would make hitters so mad that they became violent." His behavior on the field was always calculated for winning ballgames. This makes answer C the best choice.

**30. Answer: F. Durocher's personality on and off the baseball field made him famous even to non-baseball fans.**
Leo Durocher was extremely well-known to baseball fans all over the world. Yet, because Durocher was such an interesting personality in a popular sport, he also appealed to those who were only casual baseball fans or not fans at all. Paragraph 7 indicates that he became notorious outside of the baseball world, appearing on popular television shows ranging from *The Munsters* to the *Beverly Hillbillies*. In this way, his popularity extended beyond the game of baseball.

**31. Answer: D. Habitat quality**
Paragraph 1 offers definitions of both the ideal-free distribution model and the ideal-despotic distribution model. Lines 4-5 state that in the ideal-free model "individuals are free to select any habitat patch without interference from other individuals and density is a function of habitat quality". This means that instead of competitive interactions determining which individuals get which patch of territory, the only limiting factor is the quality of the habitat itself. A high-quality habitat can support more individuals than a lower-quality habitat, leading to a higher population density.

**32. Answer: G. First, ideal-despotic distribution then, ideal-free distribution.**
Competition between members of the same species group would be *intra*specific, not *inter*specific, so answer C cannot be correct as it would only apply to the actions of the ruby-throated hummingbird. Aggressive display and competitive interactions between members of the same species during a confrontation over resources is a characteristic of animals that adhere to ideal-despotic distribution (lines 6-8). Non-competitive behavior within a species group is typical of animals that exist within an ideal-free distribution model (lines 4-5). Thus, given the examples above, answer B is the best choice.

**33. Answer: A. Which animals within a population are most vulnerable to the loss of habitat.**
In paragraph 2, the authors state that understanding the two basic models of intraspecific competition (ideal-free distribution and ideal-despotic distribution) "is important because each model has distinct implications for the role of habitat availability in influencing population dynamics" (lines 10-11). In an ideal-despotic distribution, some individuals within a population gain more resources through territoriality while others within that population lose territory and the resources that come with it.

**34. Answer: H. A despotic characteristic that means members of a species in the best shape and fitness will get the best territory.**
We know from paragraph 1 that territoriality is consistent with the ideal-despotic distribution. Paragraph 3 indicates that territoriality leads to an unequal distribution of resources, with more competitive individuals "maintaining better body condition" (line 22) and "maintaining higher-quality territories" (line 25).

**35. Answer: C. Seasonal climatic changes that set in before spring migration, affecting the availability of food.**
According to the authors of the passage, their studies show that natural climactic changes increase territoriality and competition in nonbreeding migratory birds in the Neotropics. They give as an example the dry season that sets in "from December through mid-April, just prior to spring migration" (line 29). This

natural climatic change decreases the amount of available resources and leads to increased competition for these limited resources.

### 36. Answer: G. Aggressive behavior by members of the same species who are in competition for food, territory, or mates.

In addition to describing the Northern Waterthrushes as "site-faithful and territorial" (line 38), which we know from paragraph 1 are ideal-despotic behaviors, the authors also say the birds display 'agonistic behavior' at territorial boundaries. In this context, we can assume that agonistic behavior is also despotic in nature and therefore aggressive. We can assume that this aggressive behavior is between members of the same species because the authors are discussing only one species: the Northern Waterthrush.

### 37. Answer: A. Changing the location and amount of food resources.

It may be true that the total amount of food resources decreases during the dry season (answer B), however, the passage states only that the dry season "changes the distribution and availability" of food (lines 29-30). The most accurate interpretation of this wording is that the location (distribution) and amount (availability) of food resources is different (changes) during the dry season than during the other seasons.

### 38. Answer: J. To explore whether a comparison of space use across multiple habitats can explain the conflicting results of previous studies.

The authors explain in paragraph 5 that previous studies of Northern Waterthrush have provided conflicting results. The 1964 Schwartz studies have shown the birds to be despotic in a botanical garden habitat. The Black Mangrove studies have shown the birds to be ideal-free in their behavior. In lines 41-42, the authors convey that their primary goal is to examine whether or not a multiple space use strategy across habitats can explain these conflicting results. They want to explore whether these conflicting results can be explained by different behavior strategies at different habitat sites.

### 39. Answer: B. Within high-quality, seasonally stable habitats, ideal-despotic behaviors are more common. In low-quality or seasonally dynamic habitats, alternative strategies are more commonly observed.

According to lines 60-62, answer B is the correct choice. In lines 32-33 that describe the reaction of migratory birds to climatic changes, the authors state that "these changes may also lead less competitive individuals to disperse as habitat conditions deteriorate". The implication is that with a less stable habitat, the birds create alternative strategies for survival.

### 40. Answer: F. Neutral and dispassionate

The overall tone of the author's writing can best be described as neutral and dispassionate. The passage is a scientific article written by researchers; they present background information, previous studies, their own findings, and their conclusions in a neutral manner. They do not present their position or conclusions in an argumentative or defense manner. This tone of writing is consistent with scientific writing.

# SCIENCE REASONING PRACTICE TEST 3

35 Minutes - 40 Questions

Directions: Following are seven passages and questions that refer to each passage. Choose the best answer for each question.

## Genetically Modified Foods

The development of recombinant DNA technology has made it possible for genes from one organism to be inserted into another in order to control some characteristic such as growth rate or resistance to disease. Some transgenic or genetically modified (GM) organisms have been introduced into the human food chain. This has created controversy since not all people are convinced that GM foods are safe for consumption. This controversy has reached new levels with a proposal for farming a particular variety of transgenic fish that includes genes from two other species of fish and grows five times faster than the unmodified variety. One of the genes introduces a growth hormone into the fish and the other turns on a genetic switch that allows the fish to continue growing all year round. It is expected that this will increase the production and consumption of fish.

### Expert 1
The use of technology to solve the problem of food availability for a growing world population is exciting news. Rigorous testing has confirmed that the nutritional profile of a portion of GM fish is the same as that of an equivalent portion of unmodified fish. Tests have also shown that the levels of known toxins and allergens in the transgenic fish are within acceptable levels.

Farming this variety of fish will reduce the market price and make healthy fish protein more widely available to a larger population. It has also been shown that omega-3 fatty acids found in this species of fish improve cardiovascular health. Safety concerns regarding this fish are exaggerated. Horticulturists and animal breeders have been controlling the genetic makeup of organisms for thousands of years. Modern genetic methods are doing essentially the same thing using different processes. The concerns regarding interbreeding of this fish with wild populations are also misplaced. The fish will be farmed in land-based facilities and 99.5% of the fish will be sterile. They will be raised in areas with warm tropical ocean water and will not be able to survive at those temperatures even if they escape. It is important that the farming of this fish be approved without delay.

### Expert 2
The parameters of safety testing performed on the transgenic fish were too narrow. It is not enough to just demonstrate that the fish is safe to eat. Wider nutritional and environmental impact of the release of large quantities of this fish on the market should also be considered. Nutritional considerations should not only include the benefits of eating more fish but also the effect of not eating other kinds of protein that the fish is likely to replace.

The potential environmental impact is also huge. Farming of large numbers of these fish will increase pollution due to waste and the harvesting of wild fish needed to feed the farmed fish. The proposed containment measures are not foolproof. Land-based fish farming is expensive and there is no guarantee that some fish farmers will not try to use offshore cages in the ocean to raise the fish. Even though most of the fish will be sterile, the escape of even one fertile fish into the environment can have disastrous consequences due to the Trojan gene effect. This effect is a result of the larger fish having a mating advantage while their offspring are weaker and less fit for survival. This can lead to rapid extinction of wild species that mate with the genetically modified fish. It is necessary to proceed with caution and not approve farming of this fish too soon.

1.  **In tests evaluating the safety of transgenic fish for consumption, the control group used was:**

    A.  Fish of a different species.
    B.  Unmodified fish of the same species.
    C.  Other protein sources to be replaced by the modified fish.
    D.  Fish that does not contain omega-3 fatty acids.

2.  **Expert 2 has the following objection to safety tests conducted on the GM fish:**

    F.  The tests did not prove conclusively that the GM fish was safe to eat.
    G.  The containment measures designed to keep the fish from interbreeding were not tested.
    H.  The tests did not evaluate wider health and environmental impacts of eating the GM fish.
    J.  The tests did not verify the Trojan gene effect.

3.  **Expert 1 thinks that concerns about the negative environmental impact of genetically modified fish are unfounded because:**

    A.  Fish containing omega-3 fatty acids are known to be good for health.
    B.  Tests have confirmed that genetically modified fish is as nutritious as unmodified fish.
    C.  The fish will be farmed in land-based facilities and will be 99.5% sterile.
    D.  The fish do not contain high levels of toxins and allergens.

4.  **The method used to insert a gene from one organism into another is called:**

    F.  Recombinant DNA technology
    G.  Animal breeding
    H.  Trojan gene effect
    J.  Horticulture

5.  **Expert 1 and Expert 2 agree that:**

    A.  The GM fish is safe to eat.
    B.  The containment measures for farming GM fish are adequate.
    C.  No further evaluation is needed before the fish is approved for farming.
    D.  The escape of a fertile fish can be disastrous for the environment.

6.  **The Trojan gene effect is:**

    F.  Sterility in fish caused by genetic manipulation.
    G.  An effect that causes a larger fish to have a higher mating advantage.
    H.  Genetic weakness in the offspring of fish.
    J.  The combined effect of higher mating advantage with weakness of offspring.

7.  **A new study shows that the genetically modified fish has twice as much omega-3 fatty acid as the unmodified fish. In light of the fact that heart disease is a leading killer of people all over the world, this information supports:**

    A.  Expert 1
    B.  Expert 2
    C.  Both Expert 1 and Expert 2
    D.  Neither Expert 1, nor Expert 2

## Ordovician Limestone

Geologists studying Ordovician limestone in a certain area found that it consists of limestone, dolomite, and cherty dolomitic limestone formed as a result of variation in depositional environments and subsequent physical and chemical transformations. This limestone was deposited in an epicontinental sea that covered the area during the Ordovician period. Observations conducted in several wells bored for oil and gas exploration in the area have yielded the following stratigraphic profile of the petrographic characteristics and fossil content of different layers of rock.

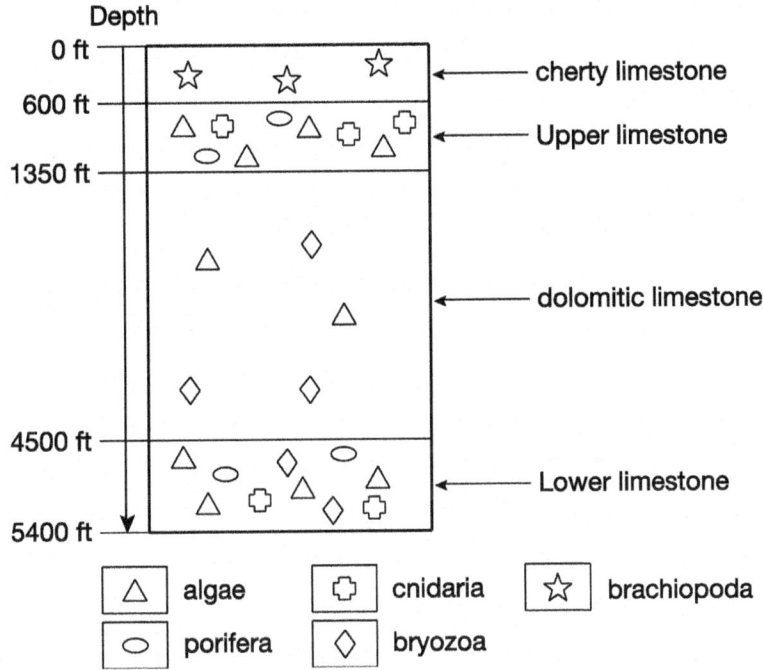

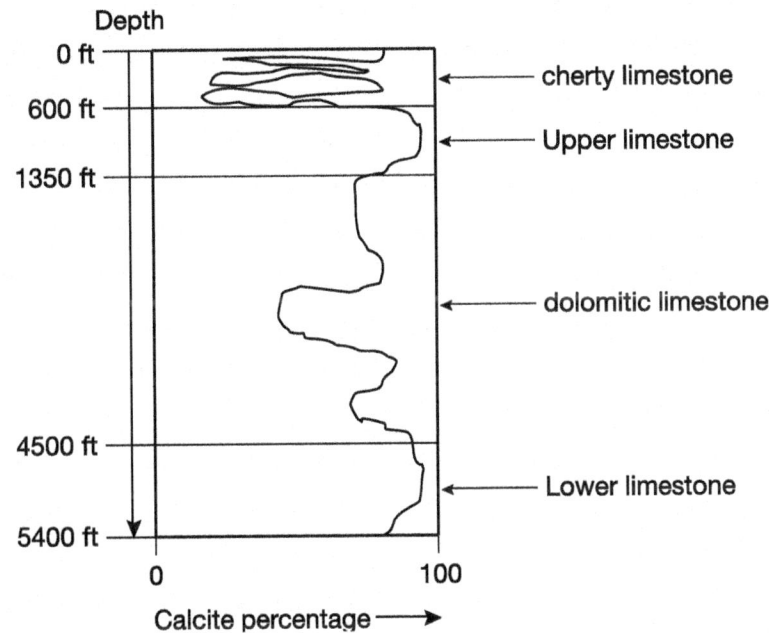

Calcite percentage ⟶

8.  **The fossils found in the upper limestone layer include:**

    F.  Cnidaria, algae, and porifera
    G.  Cnidaria, bryozoa, and porifera
    H.  Algae, porifera, and brachiopoda
    J.  Algae, bryozoa, and porifera

9.  **A paleontologist, an expert in the study of bryozoa, is digging for fossils in the area. To find samples of bryozoa, she has to dig at least to the depth of:**

    A.  300 ft
    B.  600 ft
    C.  1350 ft
    D.  4500 ft

10. **For the different layers of Ordovician limestone under study, calcite content is:**

    F.  Highest in limestone
    G.  Lowest in limestone
    H.  Highest in dolomitic limestone
    J.  Highest in cherty limestone

11. **The difference between the upper limestone and lower limestone layers is that:**

    A.  Only the upper limestone layer contains bryozoa.
    B.  The lower limestone layer is thicker than the upper limestone layer.
    C.  The calcite content in the lower limestone layer is significantly less.
    D.  The upper limestone layer does not contain algae.

12. **Narrow, alternating layers of high calcite and low calcite content are found in the:**

    F.  Upper limestone layer
    G.  Lower limestone layer
    H.  Dolomitic limestone layer
    J.  Cherty limestone layer

# Hearing Loss

The human ear can detect sounds that range in frequency from 20 Hz to 20,000 Hz. As people age, this range narrows and the threshold intensity at which a person can hear sound of a certain frequency increases, i.e., some degree of hearing loss occurs. In addition to age, another factor that can damage the ear's ability to detect sound is prolonged exposure to loud noise. The longer the exposure and the louder the noise, the greater the hearing loss experienced. Naturally, people in professions that require them to be near loud noises for long periods of time are at greater risk for hearing loss than the general population.

Sound intensity is measured using the decibel (dB) scale. The decibel level of a sound refers to ten times the logarithm of the ratio of its intensity to a reference level (usually the threshold of hearing). This scale is not linear. A sound that is at a level 10 dB higher than another is 10 times the intensity of the first one. For instance, a 50 dB sound is 10 times louder than a 40 dB sound. A change in intensity by a factor of two is about a 3 dB change.

## Experiment 1
An experiment was performed to measure the percentage of hearing loss in people exposed to loud noises over a period of time. The graph below shows average hearing loss observed in people exposed several hours a day to noise at 80 dB, 90 dB, and 100 dB for period of about 30 years.

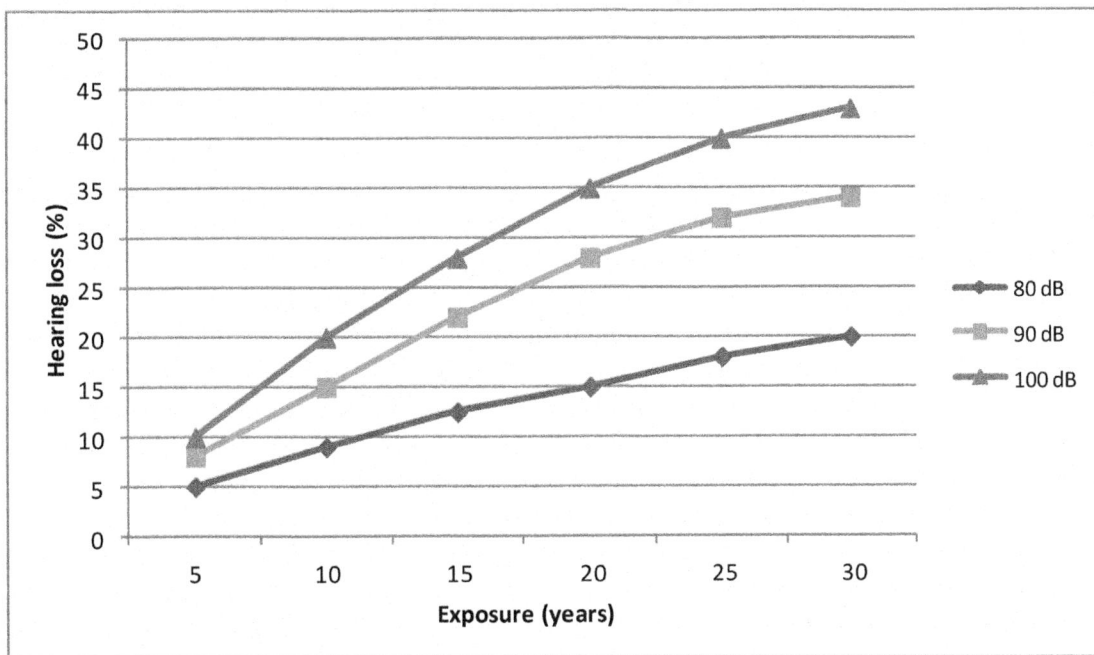

The data obtained in this experiment was sorted by profession. The graph below shows the percentage hearing loss observed after 30 years in people belonging to different professions.

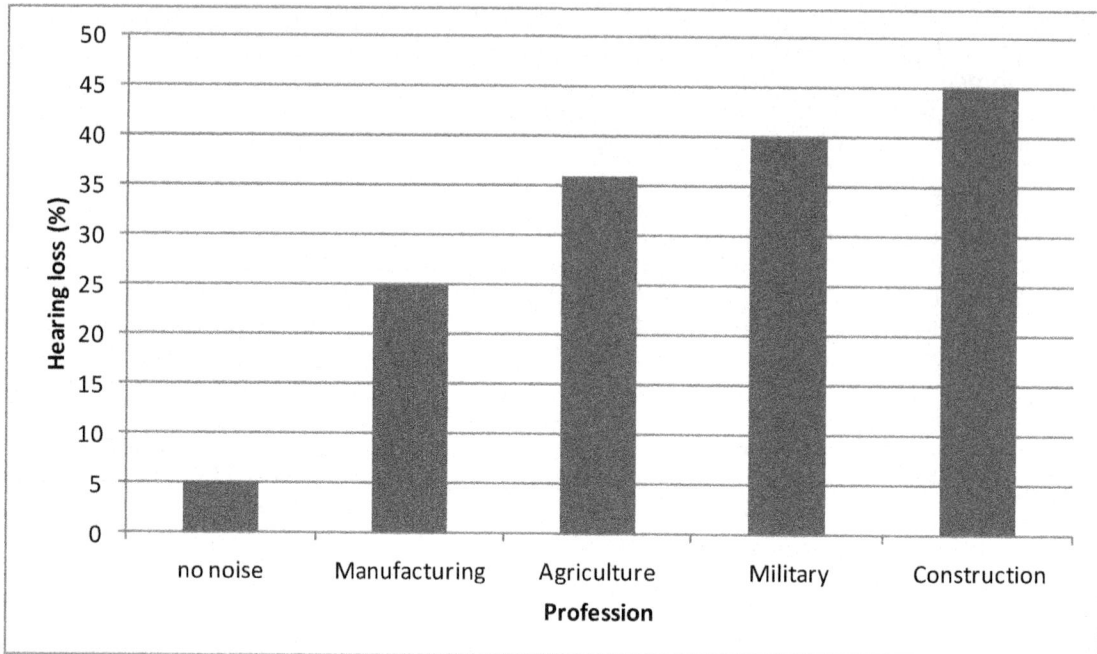

## Experiment 2

A second experiment tracked hearing loss at three different frequencies, 1000 Hz, 3000 Hz, and 5000 Hz after consistent exposure to a noise level of 100 dB for a range varying from 0 to 40 years. The results are plotted below.

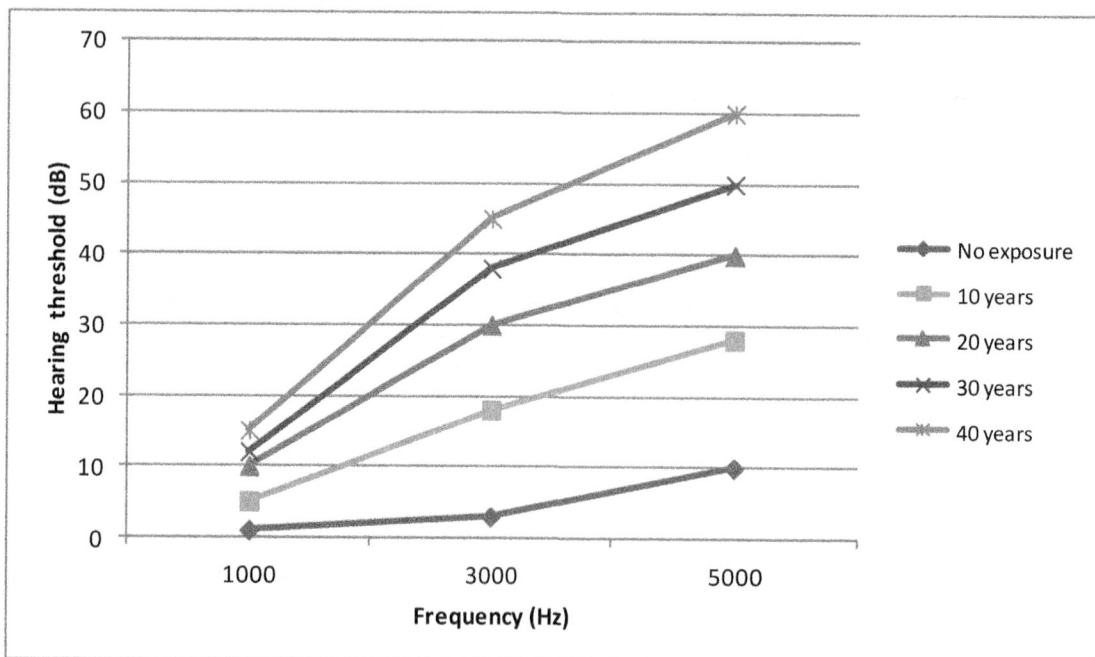

13. **Regular exposure over 20 years to a 90 dB sound results in average hearing loss of approximately:**

    A. 5 - 10%
    B. 25 - 30%
    C. 35 - 40%
    D. 40 - 50%

14. **Based on the results of Experiment 1, we can conclude that a person working in manufacturing is regularly exposed to a noise level of at least:**

    F. 80 dB
    G. 90 dB
    H. 100 dB
    J. 110 dB

15. **Hearing loss with exposure to loud noise is:**

    A. Higher at higher frequencies.
    B. Lower at higher frequencies.
    C. The same at all frequencies.
    D. Cannot be measured by frequency.

16. **All three experiments taken together point to the conclusion that:**

    F. People experience hearing loss as they grow older.
    G. People experience greater hearing loss when they are exposed to louder noises.
    H. The degree of hearing loss can depend on a person's profession.
    J. All of the above.

17. **In Experiment 2, the control variable is:**

    A. The frequency of the sound.
    B. The level of hearing loss.
    C. The exposure noise level.
    D. The profession of the people tested.

18. **Compared to a person who has been exposed to a noise level of 100 dB for 30 years, a person exposed to a noise level of 100 dB for 40 years has a hearing threshold at 5000 Hz that is:**

    F. Double
    G. Triple
    H. 10 times
    J. 100 times

## Calorie Restriction and Lifespan

Researchers have known for decades that judicious calorie restriction, i.e., eating fewer calories, without deficiency of essential nutrients, can extend lifespan in mice. It also reduces the incidence of diseases in late life. Additionally, the long-living older mice actually have bodily responses that are similar to those of younger mice in terms of immune response, insulin sensitivity, enzyme activity, and learning. Several experiments were performed in order to test the impact of reduced feeding on mice.

### Experiment 1
The survival rate (the percentage of the mice that survived) was noted over a period of time with different levels of calorie restriction.

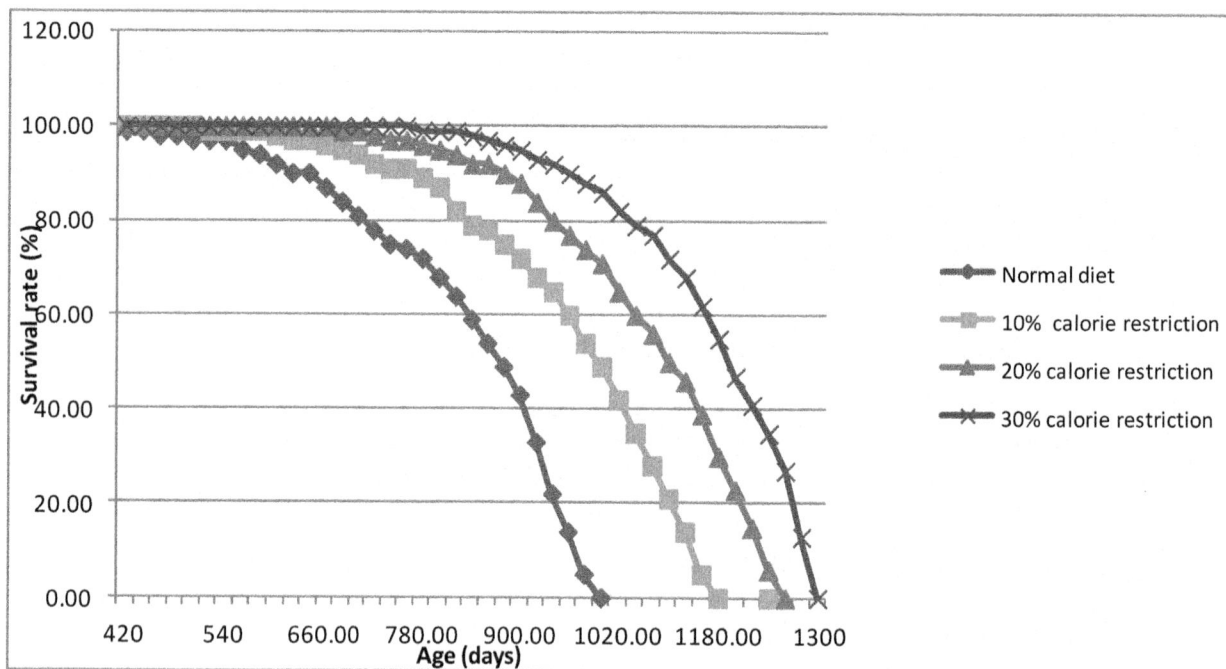

### Experiment 2
In a second experiment, mice with different levels of calorie restriction were monitored for the number of miles run per day on running wheels provided in their cages. The data from the experiment is provided in the table below along with data on the percentage of mice that developed cancerous tumors before they died.

| Calorie restriction | Miles run per day | Tumor incidence |
|---|---|---|
| 0% | 1.0 | 75% |
| 10% | 2.2 | 61% |
| 20% | 3.4 | 46% |
| 30% | 4.5 | 33% |

19. **The maximum number of days a mouse was known to survive with 20% calorie restriction is closest to:**

    A. 800 days
    B. 1000 days
    C. 1200 days
    D. 1400 days

**20. The two experiments together demonstrate that:**

 F. Mice fed fewer calories are healthier and live longer.
 G. Mice fed more calories are healthier and live longer.
 H. Mice fed normal diets are the healthiest.
 J. Mice fed fewer calories live longer but are not healthier.

**21. If a group of mice is put on 90% calorie restriction:**

 A. They can be expected to survive 3 times as long as the mice on 30% calorie restriction.
 B. They can be expected to survive twice as long as the mice on 30% calorie restriction.
 C. They can be expected to survive at least as long as the mice on 30% calorie restriction.
 D. No prediction of their longevity can be made from the given data.

**22. Some critics of these experiments say that the control group (the one given a normal diet) was actually overfed and died earlier than the calorie restricted groups because of diseases caused by obesity. They assert that calorie restriction itself did not increase the life spans of the mice. The best argument against this criticism is to point out that:**

 F. There is no known connection between overfeeding and early death.
 G. When calorie restriction was increased from 10% to 20% and then 30%, lifespan also showed a corresponding increase.
 H. When calorie restriction was increased from 10% to 20% and then 30%, daily miles run also showed a corresponding increase.
 J. Other animals have been shown to live longer with calorie restriction.

**23. A group of mice is put on 15% calorie restriction. The tumor incidence in this group is expected to be approximately:**

 A. 25%
 B. 50%
 C. 75%
 D. 100%

**24. The median number of days that mice on a normal diet survive is approximately:**

 F. 700
 G. 800
 H. 900
 J. 1000

## Qualitative Chemical Analysis

Qualitative chemical analysis is used to identify the presence of a particular ion in a mixture. One method of separating an ion from other ions in a solution is precipitation. A precipitating agent that reacts selectively with one or more of the ions in the solution is added. This produces a solid residue that can be identified by color. The residue can be separated from the solution by mechanical means and the remaining solution can be tested further for the presence of other ions.

The flowchart below outlines the procedure for identifying the ions in a solution that may contain one or more of the anions phosphate, carbonate, sulfate, chloride, and iodide.

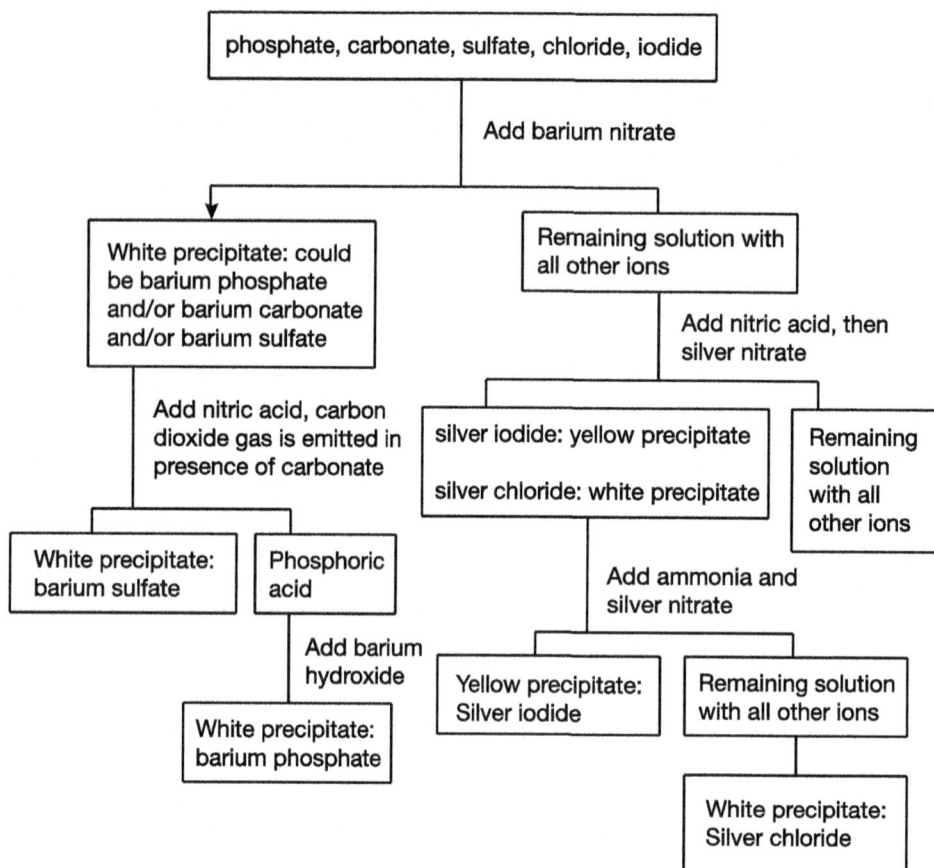

| Formula | Name | Formula | Name |
|---------|------|---------|------|
| $PO_4^{3-}$ | Phosphate ion | $Ba^{2+}$ | Barium ion |
| $CO_3^{2-}$ | Carbonate ion | $Ag^+$ | Silver ion |
| $SO_4^{2-}$ | Sulfate ion | $NH_3$ | Ammonia |
| $Cl^-$ | Chloride ion | $HNO_3$ | Nitric acid |
| $I^-$ | Iodide ion | $H_3PO_4$ | Phosphoric acid |
| $NO_3^-$ | Nitrate ion | $CO_2$ | Carbon dioxide |
| $OH^-$ | Hydroxide ion | $Ba(OH)_2$ | Barium hydroxide |

**25. Barium phosphate is precipitated through the following reaction:**

    A.  $H_3PO_4 + Ba(OH)_2 \rightarrow BaSO_4$
    B.  $H_3PO_4 + Ba_3(PO_4)_2 \rightarrow Ba(OH)_2$
    C.  $HNO_3 + Ba(OH)_2 \rightarrow Ba_3(PO_4)_2$
    D.  $H_3PO_4 + Ba(OH)_2 \rightarrow Ba_3(PO_4)_2$

**26. When barium nitrate is added to a solution containing phosphate, carbonate, sulfate, chloride, or iodide ions, the white precipitate obtained could include any of the following:**

    F.  Barium phosphate, barium carbonate, barium iodide
    G.  Barium phosphate, barium carbonate, barium sulfate
    H.  Barium phosphate, barium chloride, barium sulfate
    J.  Barium iodide, barium carbonate, barium sulfate

**27. In the precipitation reactions used to separate the phosphate, carbonate, sulfate, chloride, or iodide anions, compounds including the following cations are used:**

    A.  $Ba^{2+}$, $Ag^+$
    B.  $Ba^{2+}$, $OH^-$
    C.  $Ba^{2+}$, $Ag^+$, $OH^-$
    D.  $Ba^{2+}$, $Ag^+$, $NO_3^-$, $OH^-$

**28. The purpose of qualitative chemical analysis through precipitation is:**

    F.  Separation of the ions so they can be salvaged from the mix.
    G.  Creating precipitates of different colors.
    H.  Identifying the ions present in the solution.
    J.  Neutralizing the acids.

**29. Which of the following is true?**

    A.  Silver iodide precipitates as a white solid.
    B.  When barium carbonate reacts with nitric acid, carbon dioxide is released.
    C.  Phosphoric acid reacts with barium sulfate to produce barium hydroxide.
    D.  Carbon dioxide is produced when barium sulfate reacts with nitric acid.

## Light Intensity and Transmittance

Astronomical instruments typically measure the intensity of light, not the wavelength. The range of wavelengths over which light intensity is measured is selected using filters. UBVRI filters are broadband filters commonly used to achieve this separation so that the intensity of light can be measured for specific wavelength ranges. These ranges are ultraviolet (U), blue (B), visible (V), red (R), and infrared (I). The percentage of incident light of a particular wavelength that is allowed to pass through a specific filter is known as the transmittance. The transmittance passbands for a typical set of UBVRI filters is plotted below.

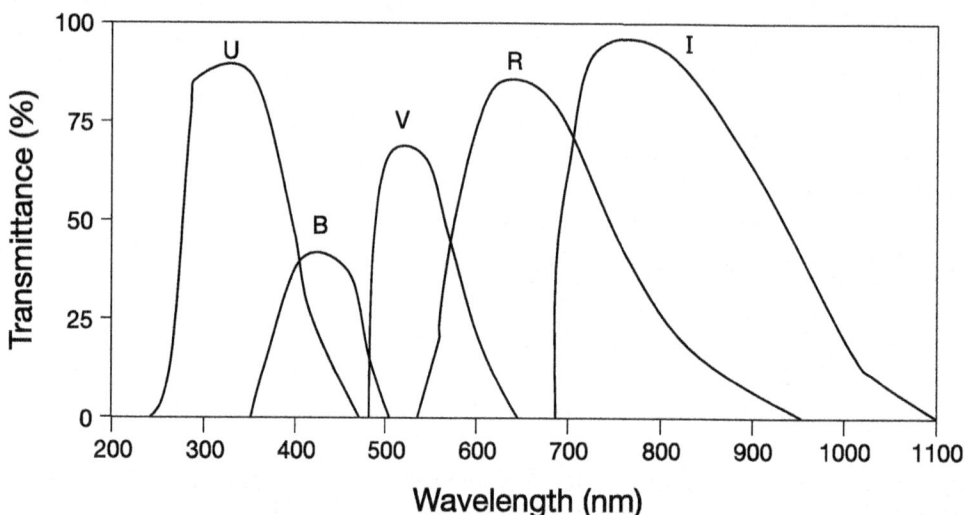

The spectrum of a star is recorded by a spectrograph which is fitted to a telescope and breaks light coming from a star into its component colors, as shown in the graph below. UBVRI filters can be used to focus on specific regions of a stellar spectrum. Note that the wavelength below is given in Angstroms (1 Angstrom = 0.1 nm).

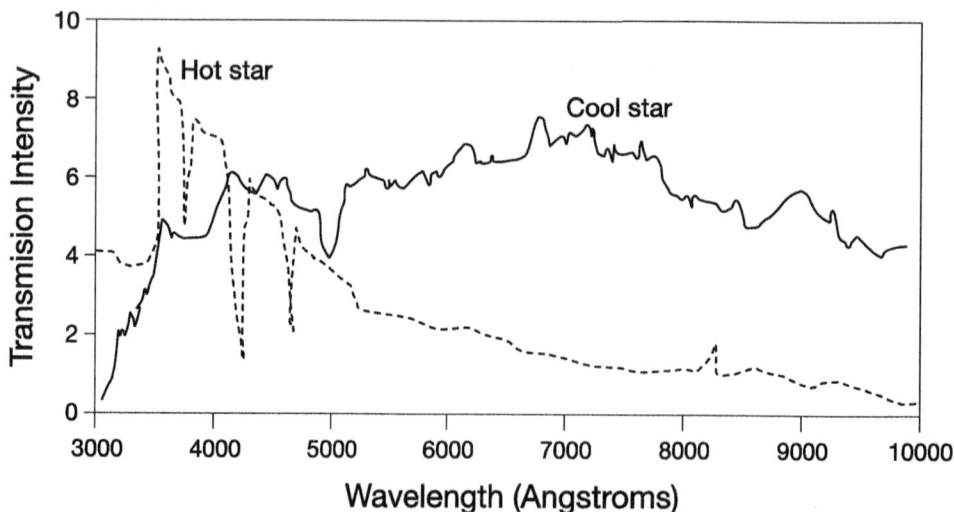

**30. The maximum transmittance of a V filter occurs at a wavelength closest to:**

    F.  350 nm
    G.  450 nm
    H.  550 nm
    J.  650 nm

**31. The stellar spectrum of a hot star differs from the spectrum of a cool star in that:**

    A.  It is confined to the lower wavelengths while the spectrum of a cool star is confined to the higher wavelengths.
    B.  It is shifted towards the lower wavelengths with respect to the spectrum of a cool star.
    C.  Its transmission intensity is generally higher.
    D.  It is shifted towards the higher wavelengths with respect to the spectrum of a cool star.

**32. The full width at half maximum (FWHM) is often used to characterize a broadband filter. This is the wavelength range of the passband at half maximum transmittance. The FWHM for the U filter is approximately:**

    F.  50 nm
    G.  150 nm
    H.  300 nm
    J.  500 nm

**33. An astronomer uses an R filter to study the spectrum of a star. He is most likely studying a:**

    A.  Cool star
    B.  Hot star
    C.  A star that could be hot or cold
    D.  An astronomical object that is not a star

**34. The range of wavelengths allowed to pass through a B filter is approximately:**

    F.  170 nm
    G.  250 nm
    H.  350 nm
    J.  500 nm

## Ecosystem Interactions

In an ecosystem, a community consists of populations of different species of organisms that interact with each other. This interaction can take the form of competition for the same resources, predation of one species over another, or symbiosis in which both species benefit from the interaction. When two species compete with each other, the end result can be the coexistence of both species or the victory of one over the other so that only one species remains. Scientists often carry out controlled experiments in order to understand the nature of the interaction between two or more species in an ecosystem. Two species of salamanders were studied in an area where both are found to coexist naturally.

### Experiment 1
Species A and species B were introduced in the same area and observed for four years. The plot below shows the results of the observation.

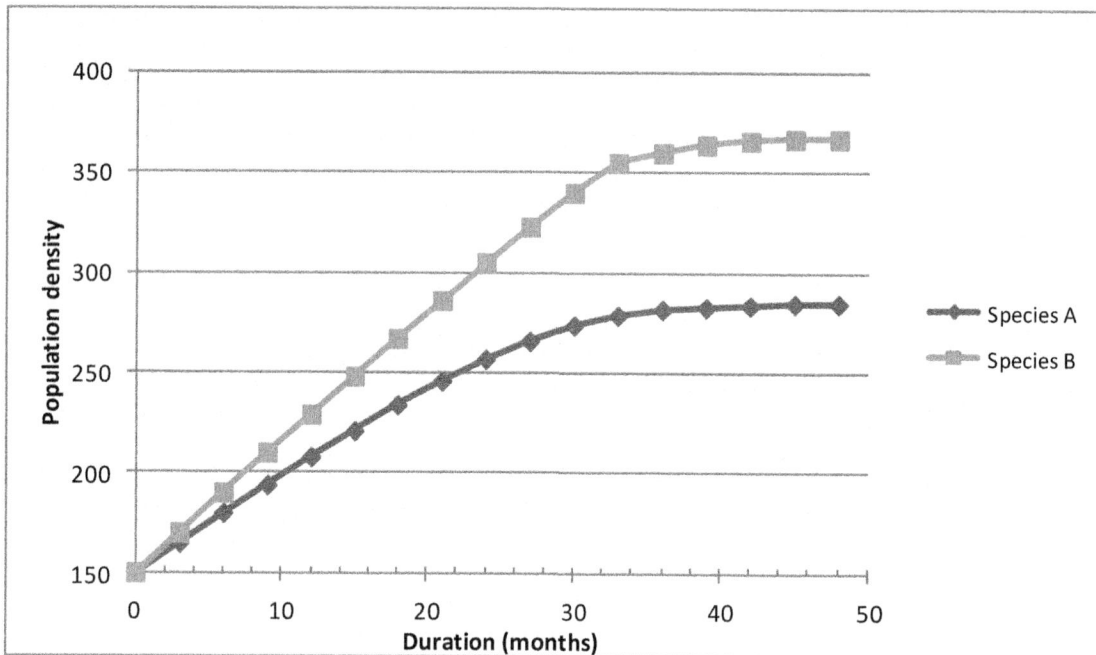

**Experiment 2**

Only species A was introduced in the same region and observed for four years. The plot below shows the results of the observation.

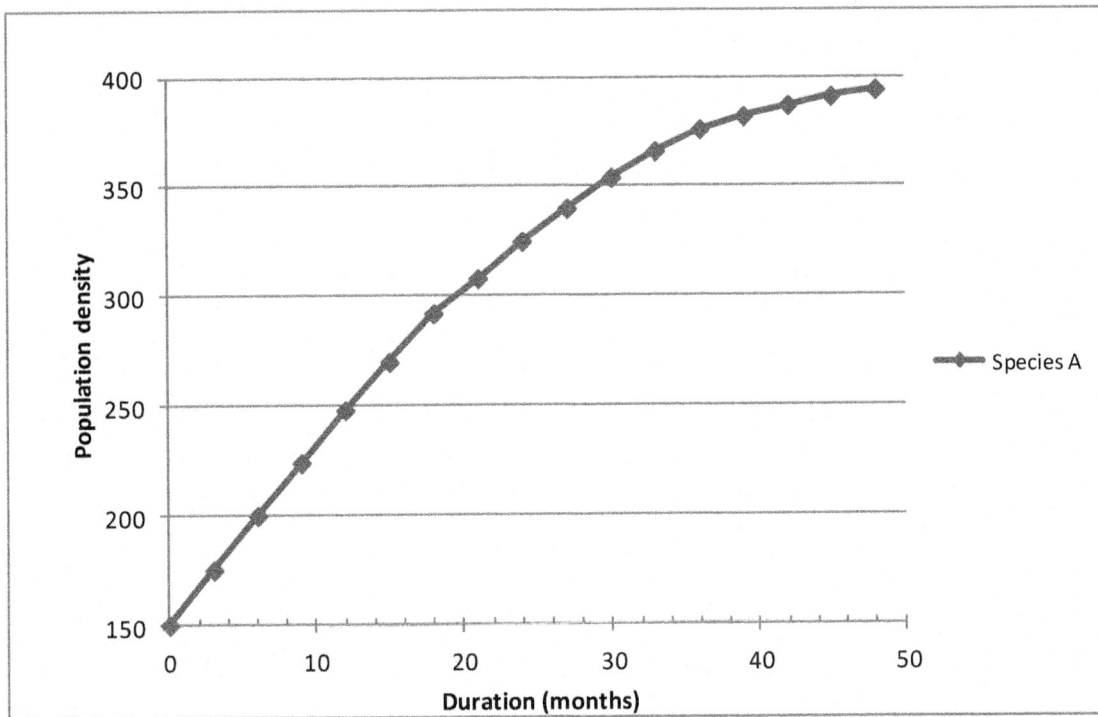

**Experiment 3**

Only species B was introduced in the same region and observed for four years. The plot below shows the results of the observation.

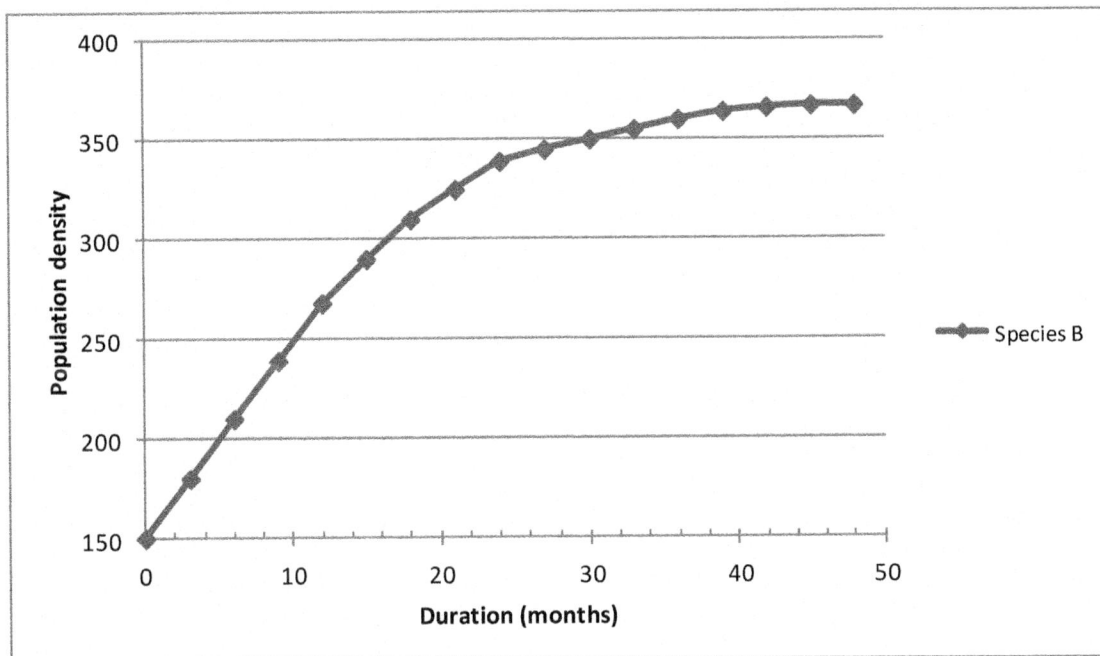

35. **Comparing the results of Experiment 1 and Experiment 2, we see that the net effect of introducing species B into an area populated by species A is to:**

    A. Increase the population of species A.
    B. Reduce the population of species A.
    C. Cause species A to die out.
    D. Leave the population of species A unchanged.

36. **When coexisting with species A, species B reaches a population density of 300 in approximately:**

    F. 15 months
    G. 18 months
    H. 24 months
    J. 30 months

37. **For Experiment 1, the growth in both salamander populations during the first two years can be characterized as:**

    A. Linear
    B. Exponential
    C. Quadratic
    D. Oscillating

38. **When introduced into the habitat on its own, species A most likely levels off at a population density of:**

    F. Close to 300
    G. Close to 350
    H. Close to 200
    J. Close to 400

39. **In the absence of species A, the population of species B:**

    A. Reaches a higher population density after four years.
    B. Grows at the same rate and levels off at the same population density.
    C. Grows faster in the beginning but levels off at the same population density.
    D. Levels off at a lower population density.

40. **The interaction between species A and species B can be characterized as:**

    F. Beneficial to both species.
    G. More harmful to species A.
    H. More harmful to species B.
    J. Beneficial to species B but harmful to species A.

# SCIENCE REASONING PRACTICE TEST 3 ANSWER KEY

| | |
|---|---|
| 1. B | 21. D |
| 2. H | 22. G |
| 3. C | 23. B |
| 4. F | 24. H |
| 5. A | 25. D |
| 6. J | 26. G |
| 7. A | 27. A |
| 8. F | 28. H |
| 9. C | 29. B |
| 10. F | 30. H |
| 11. B | 31. B |
| 12. J | 32. G |
| 13. B | 33. A |
| 14. F | 34. F |
| 15. A | 35. B |
| 16. J | 36. H |
| 17. C | 37. A |
| 18. H | 38. J |
| 19. C | 39. C |
| 20. F | 40. G |

# SCIENCE REASONING PRACTICE TEST 3 RATIONALES

**1. Answer: B. Unmodified fish of the same species.**
The control group used in an experiment is typically a group that is identical to the experimental group in every respect except for the feature being tested. Therefore, the control group in this case is fish of the same species that have not been genetically modified.

**2. Answer: H. The tests did not evaluate wider health and environmental impacts of eating the GM fish.**
According to Expert 2, the tests performed on the GM fish were confined within a range that was too narrow. They only tested whether the fish was safe to eat, not the wider health and environmental consequences of releasing the fish on the market.

**3. Answer: C. The fish will be farmed in land-based facilities and will be 99.5% sterile.**
The environmental concern expressed by opponents of GM fish is that these fish will mate with and destroy wild populations. Expert 1 says that there are containment methods in place to prevent this and the fish will be 99.5% sterile. Choices B and D are incorrect because they refer to the impact on an individual eating GM fish, not the impact of farming these fish on the environment.

**4. Answer: F. Recombinant DNA technology**
The passage states that recombinant DNA technology is the term for the process of inserting a gene from one organism into another.

**5. Answer: A. The GM fish is safe to eat.**
Both experts agree that the fish is safe to eat; however, Expert 2 believes that the wider impact of farming the fish must also be evaluated. Choices B and C are opinions held only by Expert 1. Choice D is an opinion held only by Expert 2.

**6. Answer: J. The combined effect of higher mating advantage with weakness of offspring.**
The Trojan gene effect described by Expert 2 is the combined effect of higher mating advantage with weakness of offspring. This can lead to rapid extinction of a species and is stated by Expert 2 as one concern regarding the intermixing of modified species with unmodified species.

**7. Answer: A. Expert 1**
The new study does not address the objections made by Expert 2; however, it shows that the genetically modified fish is even more beneficial for health than previously thought. This strengthens the case made by Expert 1 for approving the farming of this fish without delay, since it could potentially save the lives of people prone to heart disease.

**8. Answer: F. Cnidaria, algae, and porifera**
Match the symbols shown in the upper limestone layer of diagram 1 with the symbols in the legend at the bottom of the diagram; this shows that this layer contains cnidaria, algae, and porifera.

**9. Answer: C. 1350 ft**
From diagram 1 it is clear that bryozoa are not found in the two upper layers. The paleontologist has to dig at least up to the dolomitic limestone layer which is 1350 ft below the surface.

**10. Answer: F. Highest in limestone**
Diagram 2 shows that the upper and lower limestone layers have calcite content close to 100% through most of their depth. Therefore, limestone has higher calcite content than dolomitic limestone or cherty limestone and A is the correct answer choice.

**11. Answer: B. The lower limestone layer is thicker than the upper limestone layer.**
The upper limestone layer is between the depths of 600 ft and 1350 ft which is a thickness of 750 ft. The lower limestone layer lies between the depths of 4500 ft and 5400 ft which is a thickness of 900 ft;

therefore, B is the correct answer choice. Choice A is incorrect since it's the lower limestone layer that contains bryozoa, not the upper limestone layer. Choice C is incorrect because both layers have high calcite content. Choice D is incorrect because both layers contain algae.

## 12. Answer: J. Cherty limestone layer
Diagram 2 shows the calcite content rising and falling rapidly within the cherty limestone layer as one goes deeper. The other layers also have variations in calcite content but not within such narrow bands.

## 13. Answer: B. 25 - 30%
The middle line in the first graph corresponds to 90 dB. At 20 years of exposure, the graph shows the percent hearing loss to fall between 25 and 30%.

## 14. Answer: F. 80 dB
The second graph shows that, after 30 years exposure to noise, a person in manufacturing has approximately 25% hearing loss. According to the first graph, this level is less than that for 90 dB and 100 dB but greater than that for 80 dB. Therefore, we can conclude that, in manufacturing, a person is regularly exposed to noise between 80 dB and 90 dB. Hence A is the correct answer choice.

## 15. Answer: A. Higher at higher frequencies.
According to the passage, higher threshold intensity corresponds with more hearing loss. The results of Experiment 2 show that higher threshold intensity, and thus hearing loss, is higher at higher frequencies. Choice D is clearly incorrect since the experiment does indeed measure hearing loss by frequency.

## 16. Answer: J. All of the above.
All of the statements in choices A, B, and C are validated by the experimental results. Conclusions B and C arise directly from the results of Experiment 1. Conclusion A is supported by the fact that in both experiments people with no exposure to loud noises still suffered hearing loss, albeit to a lesser degree, as they aged.

## 17. Answer: C. The exposure noise level.
Experiment 2 includes data for a fixed level of noise exposure: 100 dB. Since exposure noise level is the variable that is held constant, it is the control variable.

## 18. Answer: H. 10 times
On the decibel scale, a sound that is at a level 10 dB higher than another is 10 times the intensity of the first one. According to the results of Experiment 2, a person with 40 years of exposure to 100 dB noise has a hearing threshold of 60 dB at 5000 Hz which is 10 times more than the value of 50 dB for a person with 30 years exposure to 100 dB noise.

## 19. Answer: C. 1200 days
According to the graph, the 20% calorie restriction group reaches a zero survival rate at a little more than 1200 days.

## 20. Answer: F. Mice fed fewer calories are healthier and live longer.
The two experiments clearly demonstrate that mice fed fewer calories live longer (approximately 1300 days), develop fewer cancerous tumors (33%), and are able to run longer distances (4.5 miles) than mice on normal diets. Hence A is the correct answer choice.

## 21. Answer: D. No prediction of their longevity can be made from the given data.
90% calorie restriction is far out of the range of the experiments described here which made observations in the range of 0 to 30% calorie restriction. One cannot extrapolate that far based on the given data. Also, from a common sense point of view, mice with 90% calorie restriction would probably die early of starvation, another reason why choices A, B and C cannot be correct.

**22. Answer: G. When calorie restriction was increased from 10% to 20% and then 30%, lifespan also showed a corresponding increase.**

The progressive increase in lifespan with progressive increase in calorie restriction clearly demonstrates that there is a connection between the two. Hence B is the correct answer choice. Choices A and D are incorrect because they are not directly concerned with calorie restriction in mice. Choice C is not as good an argument as choice B because it relates calorie restriction to improved fitness but not directly to lifespan.

**23. Answer: B. 50%**

The chart shows that tumor incidence decreases with increasing calorie restriction. Since tumor incidence is 61% for 10% calorie restriction and 46% for 20% calorie restriction, for 15% calorie restriction tumor incidence can be expected to be somewhere between 46% and 61%.

**24. Answer: H. 900**

The median number of survival days is the number of days corresponding to 50% survival rate (half the mice live longer, half the mice live for a shorter time). From the graph it is clear that the control group on a normal diet reaches 50% survival rate at around 900 days.

**25. Answer: D. $H_3PO_4$ + $Ba(OH)_2$ → $Ba_3(PO_4)_2$**

As shown in the flowchart, phosphoric acid reacts with barium hydroxide to produce barium phosphate. The chemical formulas for these can be found in the table. Notice that choices A and B don't have barium phosphate as end products, so you can eliminate them right away.

**26. Answer: G. Barium phosphate, barium carbonate, barium sulfate**

The first step in the flowchart shows that when barium nitrate is added to a solution containing phosphate, carbonate, sulfate, chloride, or iodide ions, the white precipitate obtained could be barium phosphate and/or barium carbonate and/or barium sulfate.

**27. Answer: A. $Ba^{2+}$, $Ag^+$**

$Ba^{2+}$, $Ag^+$ are the cations used in the reactions listed. Notice that the other answer choices all include anions (ions with negative charge).

**28. Answer: H. Identifying the ions present in the solution.**

According to the passage, qualitative chemical analysis is used to identify the presence of a particular ion in a mixture. Hence C is the correct answer choice.

**29. Answer: B. When barium carbonate reacts with nitric acid, carbon dioxide is released.**

The flowchart states that carbon dioxide gas is emitted in the presence of carbonate when nitric acid is added. Hence B is the correct answer choice.

**30. Answer: H. 550 nm**

Note that the question is asking for the wavelength of maximum transmittance, not for the maximum wavelength at which transmittance occurs. The first graph shows that the peak of the V passband occurs around 550 nm.

**31. Answer: B. It is shifted towards the lower wavelengths with respect to the spectrum of a cool star.**

The stellar spectrums of hot and cool stars are shown in the second diagram. The stellar spectrum of a hot star (dotted line) is shifted towards the lower wavelengths and has higher peaks in that region with respect to the spectrum of a cool star. Choice A is incorrect because the spectrum of the hot star is not entirely confined to the lower wavelengths.

**32. Answer: G. 150 nm**

As shown in the first diagram, the maximum transmittance for the U passband is approximately 90%. At half that value, 45%, the width of the U passband is closest to 150 nm of all the choices given.

### 33. Answer: A. Cool star
According to the first diagram, the transmittance passband of an R filter occurs at a wavelength range of approximately 550 nm to 950 nm. In order to see where this falls on the second diagram, we must convert the nm to Angstroms to give a range of 5500 - 9500 Angstroms. According to the second diagram, most of the spectrum of a hot star is outside the range of the R filter while a large part of the spectrum of a cool star is within the range. It's most likely that the astronomer is studying a cool star.

### 34. Answer: F. 170 nm
According to the first diagram, the B passband stretches from approximately 350 nm to 520 nm which is a range of about 170 nm.

### 35. Answer: B. Reduce the population of species A.
In the absence of species B (Experiment 2), the population density of species A rises to 400 in 4 years. In the presence of species B (Experiment 1), the population density of species A levels off below 300 in 4 years. Therefore, the net effect of introducing species B into an area populated by species A is to reduce the population of species A.

### 36. Answer: H. 24 months
The graph from Experiment 1 shows that species B reaches a population density of 300 at around 24 months.

### 37. Answer: A. Linear
Both the curves in Experiment 1 are approximately linear in the beginning. If the growth was quadratic or exponential, the rise in population would have been much faster and the lines would have curved upwards.

### 38. Answer: J. Close to 400
Looking at the curve from Experiment 2, you can see that population density begins to level off at close to 400.

### 39. Answer: C. Grows faster in the beginning but levels off at the same population density.
Experiment 3 shows the population density of species B, over time, in the absence of species A. As compared to Experiment 1, where the two species co-exist together, the population of species B grows faster in the beginning if it is introduced into the habitat without species A. For instance, at 10 months the population density rises to 250 compared to a little over 200 when species A is present. At the end of four years, however, it levels off at approximately the same population density of about 370.

### 40. Answer: G. More harmful to species A.
The interaction is more harmful for species A because the net population of species A is reduced in the presence of species B. For species B, the population growth rate is reduced in the beginning in the presence of species A, but the net population after a length of time is the same as it would be without species A.

CPSIA information can be obtained
at www.ICGtesting.com
Printed in the USA
BVOW10s1504110817

491837BV00017B/330/P

9 781607 874980